GRANDPA'S

5,001
HANDYMAN SECRETS

BY

DR. MYLES H. BADER

GOT A PROBLEM AROUND THE HOME, YARD OR GARAGE?

IF IT'S BROKEN GRANDPA HAS THE SOLUTION

2

GRANDPA'S
5,001
HANDYMAN
SECRETS

BY

DR. MYLES H. BADER

For more information or to order additional books, visit www.5001secrets.com

Published by:
Allstar Marketing Group
Cole Media Group Inc.

Printed in the United States of America

ILLUSTRATIONS BY: DEBORAH & RANDY PEEK
CLIPART BY COSMI CORPORATION

A WORD ABOUT THE AUTHOR

Dr. Myles H. Bader (Wizard of Food) has been a prolific writer of kitchen reference, household hint and cooking secret books for over 15 years. Dr. Bader is also a recognized leader in the field of preventive care, weight management, nutrition and wellness and has been a guest on over 6,000 radio talk shows and 135 television shows including Oprah, The Discovery Channel, America's Talking, HGTV, QVC, Trinity Broadcasting, Fox & Friends, NBC and Help at Home.

Dr. Bader received his Professional Medical Degree from Loma Linda University and is board certified as a Preventive Care Practitioner. He is experienced in weight control, exercise physiology, stress management, early detection of heart disease, has counseled in all areas of nutrition and has lectured extensively on supplementation and anti-aging for 30 years. He has also established multi-phasic screening prevention programs for numerous safety departments, city governments and executive health programs for over 40 major corporations.

Dr. Bader has authored 17 books including "Cookbook's Companion," "1,001 All-Natural Secrets to a Pest-Free Property" "20,001 Food Secrets, Chefs Secrets & Household Hints," "The Wellness Desk Reference," "1,001 Secret Household Formulas & Money Saving Tips," "10,001 Food Facts," "To Supplement or Not to Supplement," "Grandmother's Kitchen Wisdom" and many more. Dr. Bader's books have formally been marketed by; Barnes & Noble, Amazon, Reader's Digest, Book of the Month Club and Doubleday.

TABLE OF CONTENTS

CHAPTER 1

GRANDMA'S KITCHEN

CABINETS

SQUEAK, SQUEAK
Grandpa fixed the problem of squeaky hinges on grandma's cabinets by using vegetable oil. Best to use a liquid spray oil, however, you can also use a silicon spray. Never use WD-40™ since it contains petroleum distillates that attract dust.

SECRET TO REFINISHING WITHOUT SANDING
Grandpa hated to sand cabinets when grandma wanted them painted or refinished and he never did sand them. He just used a degreaser and painted it on then wiped it off as per the instructions on the bottle. It removed all the grease and grime then he just painted them.

Aerosols hurt the environment

SCRUB-A-DUB-DUB
When the cabinets needed to be cleaned, grandpa was given the chore. He never used abrasive cleaners such as scouring pads or powdered cleansers, he just used liquid dish soap and water and never used aerosols sprays that contain silicones or paste waxes. Also, be careful not to allow oven cleaners to touch the cabinets.

HELP! I'M COMING APART
If you have a loose cabinet hinge you will have to drill out a larger hole and be sure you don't go all the way through the cabinet. Glue in a hardwood peg, usually a ¾" dowel rod. When the glue dries, sand off the top making it flush with the surface of the door then re-drill your hole.

CALL THE CHIROPRACTOR, I NEED AN ADJUSTMENT
If the cabinet doors will not close properly, the door hinge is out of alignment and needs a small adjustment. Usually, one of the screws has loosened and needs to be tightened. If the screw hole is threaded and worn and can't be used, just force a toothpick or a matchstick in the hole and force the screw into it.

I'M GETTING A HEADACHE

If grandma is getting a headache from the cabinet doors banging when they are closed, the bumper pads are probably worn out and need to be replaced. Grandpa just cuts out a small round piece of felt and glues it on.

THINGS ARE NOT ON THE LEVEL

If the cabinet doors are not on the level anymore it is probably the screws that attach the hinge to the frame that is the problem. Just loosen all the screws then realign them and tighten then to fix   the problem.

A STICKY SITUATION

When the cabinet drawers tend to stick it usually means that either the drawer gliders are out of alignment, you have debris in the tracks or they just need to be sprayed with a silicon spray.

Just let me spray it!

GRANDMA MADE A BOO BOO

If you get a small scratch or a small dent in your cabinets, just use some colored putty to fill it in then paint over it.

MY CABINET IS GROWING

Wood cabinets may swell up from moisture. This is usually caused, by putting wet dishes away. It doesn't take very much moisture to cause a problem depending on how the interior wood is protected.

MUSTY ODOR BEGONE

If you have a musty odor in your cabinets, just sprinkle some baking soda around and allow it to remain for 1-2 days.

CABINET DOORS WON'T STAY SHUT

Place a strip of magnetic tape on the inside of the cabinet doors if they won't stay shut.

FIRE HAZARD!

Follow directions for self-cleaning ovens, especially if there are cabinets over them.

CONVECTION OVEN

HOW A CONVECTION OVEN WORKS

The standard oven and convection oven, work very similar to each other.

The notable difference in the convection oven is that it has a fan that increases the distribution of the heat molecules providing heat to all areas more evenly and faster. Because of the fan and the efficiency of the heat circulation, a lower temperature is usually required.

- If you are going to use a convection oven reduce the recommended temperature for a recipe by 25^0-75^0F.
- It is not necessary to pre-heat a convection oven. They heat up very quickly and evenly surround the food with heat.
- When baking in a convection oven lower the temperature by 50^0-75^0F to be safe or the baked goods may burn or over brown.

COUNTERS

HOW CLEAN I AM.........

If you have a laminate counter top you have to careful of how you clean it. Just use a liquid detergent or a very mild abrasive cleaner and use very light touch. If you really have a bad stain use full-strength Pine Sol™.

GRANDPA KNOWS BEST

When it comes to refinishing an old wood countertop, just follow these hints: first sand any bad areas then refinish with three coats of polyurethane for the best results.

Not a food-safe surface

PAINTING OVER FORMICA IS WORK

If you are going to paint over the top of Formica you first have to sand lightly then apply Kilz™ paint and allow it to fully dry. Then three colors of gray, light; medium and dark then marbleize them together. Allow it to dry then apply five coats of polyurethane. Remember this will not be a food-safe surface.

CLEANING THE FANCY STUFF

If you have a Corian® countertop that needs to be cleaned, just use a gentle abrasive powdered bleach on a damp surface. Allow it to remain for 5 minutes before sponging it off then rinse well and dry.

OUCH!

Hot pots, especially iron and aluminum should never be placed on Corian® countertops If the bottom of the pot is wet since it may leave a mark on the surface that will be almost impossible to get off.

I DON'T WANT A SEPARATION

If the counter has separated from the wall it is usually caused by settlement and can be corrected by caulking between the countertop and the wall. Hopefully, there is just a small separation so that the counter does not have to be removed and reset.

GETTING DAMP DOWN HERE

If you have gaps in the calking around the sink it is usually caused by shrinkage and can be repaired by re-caulking or using seam filler.

MY MARBLE IS SCRATCHED

If you have a few small scratches on a cultured marble countertop they can usually be buffed off or polished.

GRANDPA KNOWS BUTCHER BLOCKS

When you install a new butcher, block counter it has to be properly sealed. Grandpa recommends using boiled linseed oil and applying it with a paintbrush. Allow it to dry for 24 hours before applying a second coat then wait another 24 hours. Wipe the second coat off by rubbing with a clean cloth.

CURLING IRON PROBLEM

Grandma left her curling iron on the Formica™ countertop and forgot it was still very hot and left a yellow burn mark. If the burn is not too deep, it can be removed with a scouring cleanser. If it is deep, there is not much you can do about it and just take the curling iron away from grandma.

SHOULD YOU EVEN BUY A FORMICA™ COUNTERTOP?

There are number of disadvantages in buying a Formica™ countertop: abrasive cleaners will scratch and dull the surface, sharp knives will leave scratch marks and hot pots will actually melt the finish. Also, warping can occur if the area is wet for too long a period and the seams are too easily seen depending on the quality, some will even fade in time.

FORMICA™ COUNTER CLEANSER

The following ingredients will be needed:

3	Tablespoons of white vinegar
¾	Teaspoons liquid dish soap
¾	Teaspoon of olive oil
¾	Cup of very warm tap water
1	Spray bottle

Place all the ingredients in a spray bottle and mix thoroughly. Spray the counter and allow it to remain for a few seconds before wiping off with a damp sponge. Rinse the area well to remove all residues.

HIDE THAT BURNED SPOT
If you have a burned spot or bad blemish on your counter, just glue a fancy ceramic tile or small trivet over the spot.

SHOULD YOU BUY A CORIAN® COUNTERTOP?
There are some advantages in having a Corian® countertop since they are fairly stain resistant and easy to clean and most scratches can be repaired. However, if they need repair it must be done by a professional, they may scratch easily and hot pots will melt the surface finish.

WHY GRANDPA LIKES WOOD BLOCK COUNTERTOPS
This is one of grandpa's favorite countertops. He likes "real" wood. It is very durable if cared for and cleans easily. Scratches can be removed by sanding. However, if you allow large amounts of water to remain on them, they may turn black and require sanding and re-sealing, which is expensive. Keep them dry and clean.

CERAMIC TILE COUNTERTOPS
Grandpa hates cleaning the grout and if the grout is not kept clean it will become discolored and mildewed. Tile tends to chip and is not easy to replace. If you break a tile you need to drill holes and remove the tile, clean the area and replace with a new tile.

CERAMIC TILE CLEANER
The following ingredients will be needed:

Don't use chlorine bleach

¾	Cup of white vinegar
1/3	Cup of household ammonia
¾	Cup baking soda
7	Cups of warm tap water
1	Spray bottle

Place all the ingredients in a medium plastic bucket with a well, sealed cover and shake to mix thoroughly. Place the mixture in 2-3 jars, label and save. **Never add chlorine bleach to this mixture.** Use with rubber gloves to protect your delicate hands and spray it on the surface to be cleaned.

FLAT BOARD = FLAT COUNTER

When installing a ceramic tile counter, to be sure that you have a flat surface, use a small perfectly flat board and place it over the tiles and tap gently. This will assure that all the tiles are set firmly and that the counter is level.

SOME OF GRANDPA'S OTHER FAVORITES

Granite is one of the best countertops but it does require proper sealing. It is scratch resistant, hot plates can be placed on it and it is one of the best, looking countertops. Another newcomer is Silestone™ made from quartz, which is harder than granite and does not need to be sealed.

GRANITE CLEANING TIPS

❖ Be sure to blot up stains immediately or they may penetrate the surface
❖ To clean the surface use stone soap available in hardware stores or use mild soap and water.
❖ Always use a soft clean cloth and never an abrasive pad or steel wool.
❖ If you get a stain, try cleaning it with 2 tablespoons of dishwasher soap and water to prepare a thick paste. Place the solution on the stain and cover it with a piece of plastic wrap and allow it to stand overnight.
❖ If the stain is oil-based (grease, milk, etc) make the paste from hydrogen peroxide instead of the dishwasher soap.
❖ Acetone will remove ink stains from granite.
❖ For non-oil stains, try using molding and pure bleach made into a paste; then allow the paste to remain for 30 minutes before rinsing it off.

IS YOUR LAMINATE DULL?

You can brighten a dull laminate counter top by applying a coating of quality car wax. If you buff it off really good, very little of the wax will remain and you will retain the shine. It is safe to place food on the counter afterwards.

SPIT SHINE?

If you would like a quick shine on your countertop, just wipe it down with white vinegar.

CROCK POT

The Crock Pot; was invented in 1971 by Rival. Many consumers still question whether the pot is safe or a breeding ground for bacteria since it advocates all day cooking at a low temperature. The fact is that most slow cookers have settings that range from 170^0F to 280^0F.

Bacteria die at 140^0F, which is below the lowest possible temperature that can be used. However, if the lid is left off it may cause a problem with food not being fully cooked and harboring bacteria that is still alive.

To minimize the risk of food poisoning, do the following:

❖ All foods should be at refrigerator temperature. No frozen or partially thawed foods.
❖ Only cook cut up pieces of meat, not whole roasts or fowl to allow the heat to penetrate fully.
❖ Make sure that the cooker is at least half to two-thirds full or the food will not absorb enough heat to kill any bacteria.
❖ The food must be covered with liquid to generate sufficient steam.
❖ The original lid should always be used and should be tight fitting.

❖ When possible, allow the cooker to cook on the high setting for the first hour then it can be reduced.

❖ Never use the cooker to reheat leftovers. A number of bacteria are usually found on leftovers and it takes high heat to kill them.

❖ Always follow the manufacturers directions for temperature settings.

❖ Never use a crock-pot to re-heat leftovers. The bacterial count will be higher and the food needs time at a higher temperature to kill them.

❖ Vegetables should be placed in crock-pots just before serving depending on their thickness.

❖ All foods should be at refrigerator or room temperature before placing them into a crock-pot.

❖ Never put partially or frozen foods in a crock-pot.

CUTLERY

GENERAL INFORMATION:

One of the most important utensils in a kitchen is your knife. There are a number of different materials used in knife blades, many of which are relatively new and need to be evaluated as to which will suit you best. Make sure the handle is secured with at least three rivets. It should feel comfortable and always avoid plastic grips. When cutting foods the best surface would be a soft wooden cutting board. Hardwoods and plastic boards tend to dull the blade faster and also reduce the life of the knife.

Carbon Steel

This is, by far, the best for taking the sharpest edge and is the preferred knife for the serious chef. However, if the blade is not constantly kept dry it will rust. Acids in foods may also take their toll and turn the blade black, which can be imparted back to foods.

Super-Stainless Steel

This is not one of the better quality blades. Once it dulls and loses its original well-honed sharpness, it is almost impossible to restore to a decent level of sharpness. However, it does resist rust and staining.

Stainless Steel

Has the ability to resist rust and the acid effects from foods. Will take a sharper edge than the super stainless steel, but will dull and does not really take a very sharp edge.

Worth the price!

High-Carbon Stainless Steel

This is the most expensive; of the four types mentioned here and will not rust nor stain. It does not have to be washed and dried continually when in use. Can be sharpened to a sharper edge than either of the other stainless steel knives.

BE NICE TO YOUR KNIVES

When storing a knife: one of the best ways is to keep it in a wooden countertop knife holder that was made for the knife. However, not all wooden holders are quality ones and the holder should not have a hard surface for the blade to lie on. The higher quality holders will have a protective liner that allows the edge of the blade to rest free. When a knife is stored in a drawer with other utensils it will end up with small nicks on the blade and that will eventually ruin a high quality knife.

A SHARP INVESTMENT

When you purchase a knife it is an investment that you need to make. It is a kitchen tool that is indispensable and unless you buy a quality knife, you will not have it very long and will not be very satisfied with the results. Purchase either carbon-steel or high-carbon steel knives. The manufacturer should be a recognized name such as Trident, Wusthof, or Heckles.

The blade and handle should all be one piece and the handle should not be attached to the blade. If the knife has a plastic hilt, it is not recommended.

GRANDPA LOVED HIS GRINDING WHEEL

The old grinding wheel was grandpa's favorite tool and he used to sharpen everything that he could and as often as he could. However, The one method that should never be used on a good kitchen knife is that of allowing a coarse grinding wheel to be used. The blade will only last a few years and will become thinner and thinner. Rotating steel disks are not recommended either. The preferred method is the **"butcher's steel."**

This is just a rough-surfaced, hard metal rod with a protective handle. If the butcher's steel is used frequently it will keep the edge on the knife. If you have a problem keeping the edge it may mean that you are not using the sharpener as frequently as you should and you may have to use a **"whetstone"** to return the edge. The whetstone is made of silicon carbide (carborundum).

GRANDPA'S SHARPENING ANGLES

THE TOOL	THE ANGLE
Axe....................................	45^0
Carving Knife.........................	$15\text{-}20^0$
Draw Knife............................	30^0
Drill Bits............................	$24\text{-}32^0$
Hedge Hammer.......................	$28\text{-}32^0$
Hockey Skates.......................	90^0
Lawnmower Blade..................	30^0
Plane Blade..........................	$25\text{-}30^0$
Pocketknife..........................	$15\text{-}25^0$
Scissors & Shears..................	80^0
Screwdriver..........................	90^0
Sickle & Scythe.....................	30^0
Wood Chisel.........................	$25\text{-}30^0$

DISHWASHER

GENERAL INFORMATION:

Dishwashers have at least one motor that is attached to a pump that forces the water up into sprayer arms. When it is in the drain cycle it pushes the water and debris out of the dishwasher and into the sink that has the garbage disposer.

Larger food particles then wait for the next time you run the dishwasher to be reduced into minute particles that will go down the drain. Most European dishwashers have two motors, one for washing and the other for draining.

The latest dishwashers now have a soil-sensor, which checks the water to see if it is still containing debris from the dishes. If the water is clean, the dishwasher will advance to the next cycle. This is a recommended feature when purchasing a new dishwasher.

SHAKE IT UP

If you want maximum efficiency from your dishwasher, you need to purchase the right detergent. Try shaking the box; if you can't hear the granules rattling around, it would be best not to buy it.

SOMETHING SMELLS FISHY

Kitchen odors are frequently found in the garbage disposal and caused by food from the dishwasher. The best way to eliminate the problem is to run the garbage disposal for a few seconds after you finish washing the dishes.

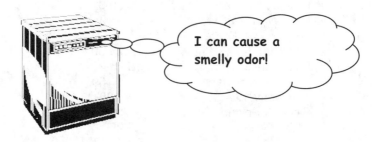

I can cause a smelly odor!

WHOOPS! I'M OVERFILLING

If the dishwasher is overfilling then the float switch has gone bad and stopped functioning and needs to be replaced.

NOT UNDER THE SINK

Best not to store the dishwasher detergent under the sink. It is too warm and moist there and it will cake up too easily. If you are having the problem of caking up, buy a smaller size next time.

GRANDMA'S DISHWASHER IS SICK AND WILL NOT RUN

One of the main reasons that a dishwasher will not run is if water has seeped into the electronics burning out the timer or one of the other six control switches. Call a repairman and don't let grandpa touch the machine!

MY SOAP HAS NOT DISAPPEARED

Grandma is very upset; the soap dispenser in the dishwasher is still full after the dishwasher finished running. When the soap dish or the rinse-aid dispenser does not empty it means that the timer switch has not sent a signal to the bi-metal switch that opens it and needs to be replaced.

IT'S ALIVE! IT WON'T TURN OFF!

The dishwasher did not turn off when the door was opened while it was operating. The door switches may eventually get damaged or get debris in them and not function. This needs a service call to fix, best not to let grandpa near it unless he knows how to change the switch.

HOW DRY I'M NOT..............

If the dishes are drying completely, the drying fan has stopped functioning or is not functioning efficiently to do the job and needs to be replaced. It is usually found in the back right corner. Grandpa can probably handle this job.

THE DISHWASHER IS HAUNTED - FUNNY NOISES

There are funny noises coming from the dishwasher. Sometimes funny noises can be eliminated; by checking to see if a small object or a pit has fallen into the pump assembly. Another job for grandpa!

WHAT A PRETTY RAINBOW, BUT IT'S ON MY GLASSES?

Spotted glasses may be cause by a lack of water flow or from hard water. If the glasses are getting a rainbow hue then it is probably from using too much detergent. This can also be caused by water not being hot enough. Try running the sink faucet until hot water starts running out! Also, opening the dishwasher too soon after it has finished will cause this problem.

YUK! DIRTY DISHES

This is usually cause by obstructed water flow caused by poor loading of the dishes by grandpa.

WEEPING WATER

Grandma opened the dishwasher in the morning and there was water in it and it had not run the night before. If you find water in the dishwasher when there shouldn't be any, this is called **"weeping water"** and is usually caused by a faulty fill valve, which will need to be replaced. Not sure if grandma will let grandpa near the machine this time.

A HEATED SOLUTION

If the dishes are not coming out clean, try running the sink hot water tap until it gets warm before you start the dishwasher. This will help the first cycle to have hotter water. If this doesn't work you need new nozzles.

GRANULES OR GELS

Most dishwasher manufacturers recommend that you use powders or granules and not gels. Gels tend not to perform as well.

APPLIANCES THAT DON'T LIKE EACH OTHER

To extend the lifetime of the dishwasher, never have it next to the refrigerator since both emit heat unless you place an insulation panel between them. Easy job for grandpa!

ARE RUSTY RACKS YOUR PROBLEM?

If your dishwasher racks are getting rusty, purchase a bottle of rack touch up at any appliance parts department. New tine ends are also available. Put grandpa to work, this is an easy one for him.

> ### TESTING YOUR SOAP
> If you are curious to see if the water is hot enough for the dishwasher soap to dissolve properly, just run the sink hot water until it is as hot as it will get then fill a glass and put a tablespoon of the soap in the water. If the soap dissolves before it gets to the bottom of the glass, the water is hot enough.

TANG™ YOU VERY MUCH
If your dishwasher is looking dingy and has deposits on the walls, just add 1 cup of Tang™ to the dishwasher and run it through a cycle. It will clean the interior and refresh the inside.

GETTING MOLDY IN HERE..........HELP!
If you use your dishwasher at least twice a week, you should have no problem with mold from the moisture. Residual water on the bottom will cause mold growth if the dishwasher is not used regularly and should be cleaned. Good job for grandpa!

DISHES GETTING CHILLY, WHAT'S THE PROBLEM?
Some dishwashers put cold water into the dishwasher and the dishwasher must heat the water before it will start. This can take up to 30 minutes in older machines.

NOT TOO HOT OR ELSE
Your water heater should be set at 120^0F for the dishwasher to work at optimum efficiency.

IN-DEPTH CLEANING
For a thorough cleaning, place a bowl with 3 cups of white vinegar on the bottom rack and leave all racks in place. Do not place dishes in the dishwasher. Run the dishwasher through the wash and rinse cycle **ONLY**. Make sure that you ***turn the machine off before it goes into the drying cycle***.

PUT A MUFFLER ON IT
If you want to quiet your dishwasher and have it on a cement floor, just place a piece of indoor-outdoor carpet under it to muffle some of the noise.

BUBBLE, BUBBLE, HERE COMES TROUBLE

If your dishwasher is full of soapsuds and bubbles, you used the wrong detergent or tablet. Place 2 tablespoons of vegetable oil into the soapy, water to break up the suds and sprinkle salt on the suds to disperse them. Placing ice cubes on the suds will also help to alleviate the problem. Keeping grandpa away from the dishwasher may also solve the problem.

Yuk! This tastes terrible!

DISH-O-MATIC

I'VE BEEN ETCHED!

If you place glasses next to each other and they are touching, they may get scratched permanently as well as not being thoroughly washed. Poor loading causes detergent to remain on the dishes.

EXHAUST HOOD (RANGE HOOD)

GENERAL INFORMATION:

Many range exhaust hoods really do not do a good job of eliminating steam, grease, smoke and food odors. Some hoods only re-circulate the air through a filter and return the air to the kitchen.

A range hood has to be vented to the outside to really be effective. Most re-circulating air vents can be converted to one that exhausts outside without too much trouble.

HELP! I'M WORKING TOO HARD

If the motor is getting smelly and hot grandpa will need to clean the fan blades with just soap and water. Dirty fan blades will restrict airflow and may cause the motor to overheat and catch on fire.

DIRTY WORK FOR GRANDPA
If you have a charcoal filter in your range-hood, it can be recharged, by placing it in a 450^0F oven for 30 minutes (after completely cleaning the frame). If there is any grease left on the frame it may catch on fire or smoke up the house. Many activated charcoal filters cannot be cleaned and should be replaced once a year.

BE GENTLE NOW
Light bulbs in vents need to be removed and very gently cleaned with cool water and soap.

GET OUT THE GLOVES FOR GRANDPA
If parts are real greasy use ammonia and water to clean them. Never use abrasive pads or scouring powder on the vent parts. Metal grids need to be soaked once a month in ammonia and water.

FIRE, FIRE! LEAVE THE FAN ALONE!
If a fire starts on the range top, never turn the fan on over the range or you may pull the flames into the hood and into the house attic or ductwork.

THERE IS A GHOST IN MY HOOD
This is caused by the outside wind moving the damper and is a normal sound when it is windy.

FLOORING

GENERAL INFORMATION:
There are several types of kitchen flooring for you to choose from. The following are some of the more popular types:

* ❖ **Earthen Tiles** – These come in two forms, glazed and unglazed. You can even buy handmade ones with custom details. Most of the tiles are made from fine-grained clay and are machine-shaped and pressed. Glazed tiles are very resistant to stains and moisture, however, be sure and treat the grout with a liquid silicone sealer. Colored grout works best. These tiles cost $5 to $25 per square foot with installation costing $3 to $5 per square foot.

  If you are going to install earthen tiles over a deck, be sure and use ¾" concrete backing board nailed over the deck and cement the tile to it. Use only grade 3 for kitchen floors.

* ❖ **Hardwood Floors** – This is normally ¾-inch tongue-and-groove planking. It has a warming affect on a room and will compliment the cabinets and counters. The cost is about $6 to $8 per square foot and can refinished when it becomes worn. Be sure and seal the floor with three coats of urethane. The floor does not do well if water is allowed to remain and will buckle.

* ❖ **Kitchen Carpeting** – This thin, tough carpeting used to be very popular, however, it has not been used very much anymore since it does not handle spills well and doesn't really fit in with today's kitchen styling. It is rubber-backed and does provide a soft, underfoot feel. It is very affordable and does come is stain-resistant.

* ❖ **Linoleum** -Linoleum can be manufactured by using a mixture of resins, small particles of cork or wood fibers) and linseed oil that is adhered to a canvass, burlap or felt backing using high pressure.

  Never use a strong alkali-based cleaner on linoleum since they tend to ruin the linseed oil binder and may cause the floor to develop cracks, thus shortening the usable life of the flooring.

Best to use a mild detergent solution and dry as soon as has been cleaned. A linoleum formula should never be used on a wood or cork floor.

SMALL HOLE REPAIR

If you kept some scraps when the floor was laid, you are in good shape. Just grind up and powder the scraps then mix the dust with a small amount of clear shellac or white glue. Fill the holes and by the next day you will have trouble finding the holes.

❖ **Plastic Laminate Flooring** – This is a wood-grain plastic laminate, which contain silica sand and is harder than countertop laminates or hardwoods. It is bonded to plywood planks or squares. It simulates wood and is a tough floor.

❖ **Pre-finished Veneers** – These are pre-finished tongue-and-groove plywood planks and squares topped with hardwood veneers. Most of these are installed as floating floors. The planks are glued together along the tongue-and-groove joints and then laid over a foam pad. Urethane finished veneers cost about $3 to $6 per square foot installed. The top of the line, however, has a super-hard acrylic-plastic sealant forced deep into the veneer, making it more resistant to scratches and dents.

❖ **Resilient Flooring** – This comes in either vinyl-sheet goods or tiles and is very affordable. The prices range from $6 to $40 per square foot with installation running from $4 to $8 per square foot. There are two types of this flooring: layered and full-depth. The layered has a printed vinyl fused to white, fibrous or foam liner. The second type is inlaid, which has colored composition particles extending the full depth of the flooring.

The recommended is the inlaid since there is no surface layer that can be punctured, snagged or will tear more easily. The price is dependent of the thickness of the wear layer. If you plan to place this type of flooring over existing flooring, it would be best to have a professional do the job.

❖ **Stone Flooring** – These are permanent floors and are marble, slate or granite. They are susceptible to scratching, especially marble. Granite is the most durable and floors run from $12 to $30 per square foot plus installation.

Kitchen Carpeting

SHELF IT!
You can use leftover linoleum to line pantry and cabinet shelves. It will make cleaning the shelves easier.

STICKY PROBLEM
To remove tar, just place some dry ice on the tar and wait for it to harden then scrape it off.

DON'T USE A HAMMER AND CHISEL
The easiest method of removing old flooring is with a heat gun. It will still be a messy job, but it will get done. If you are working to remove tiles, a hair dryer will work just as well.

I'M COMING APART AT THE SEAMS
If the seams of your kitchen carpeting were starting to come apart, it would be best to handle this problem as soon as it appears and before the edges start fraying. There are two ways to correct the problem depending on the location; if the problem is in a high traffic area, pull back the area that has come loose and use carpet glue on the part that has come up. Be careful not to get the glue on the carpet, so don't use too much.

If you use too much and it seeps through when you place a medium weight on the area to hold it down until it dries, you may ruin the carpet. If the problem is at the wall, just use double-sided carpet tape. Grandma better supervise this repair!

FILLER'UP
A gouge can be fixed using almond-colored kitchen and sink

caulking and use a small amount of food coloring to try and match the floor color. It won't remove the gouge, but it won't be very noticeable.

DON'T USE RUBBER BACKING!
Never use a foam or rubber-backed mat or rug on a linoleum floor or it will cause permanent discoloration.

CURLING TILES?
If one of the tiles has started curling on the edges, use a blow dryer on high heat and warm the tile, just enough to soften it. Raise it and place fresh glue down then press it back into place and place a heavy weight on it till it dries. Be sure that there is no glue seeping out or whatever you place on it to hold it in place will be there permanently.

FREEZER CHEST

GENERAL INFORMATION:
All modern day freezers are now automatic defrost freezers that do not need to be turned off and defrosted. When frost builds up in the freezer it automatically melts. The more food you have in the freezer, the more efficient the freezer energy usage. It will take more energy to keep a half empty freezer cold than a full one. The automatic defrost freezers have a timer that turns off the freezer every 6-8 hours and turns on the defrost heater.

Some models also have a timer that can be set to run the defroster at a specific time of the day. The water from the defrosting then goes into a pan under the freezer and is evaporated by either fan blowing warm air over it or by the heat of the compressor.

NOT A NICE PLACE TO BE
If frost is building up in the freezer, the timer is not working sending the signal to the heater motor or the heater motor is not working. One of the two will need replacement. The condenser coils may also be dirty and need cleaning. Grandpa can do the coils but let a repairman do the rest.

OUCH! I GOT FREEZER BURN

Freezer burn is actually dehydration that is caused by the food being exposed to the air in the freezer. Food in supermarket wrapping are not airtight and if frozen for more than a few days the foods need to be re-wrapped in as airtight a wrapping as possible.

HOW COLD IS COLD?

Your freezer should maintain a temperature of 0^0F to 8^0F. If you immediately turn the freezer on and fill it with food it will take about 24 hours to reach this temperature. Best to leave a new freezer on for 24 hours before placing food in it.

IT FEELS LIKE A ROLLER COASTER IN HERE

The temperature of your freezer should never fluctuate more than a few degrees to keep foods at their best. The temperature should be kept at least 0^0F or below for the best results. Thawing and re-freezing is the worst thing you can do to foods. Every time the temperature drops in the freezer, some of those small ice crystals will convert to larger ice crystals and little by little, the dish will be ruined.

TO FILL OR NOT TO FILL

It is best to keep your freezer at least half full to maintain a constant temperature.

FROSTY, THE FREEZER…..

When frost builds up on the walls of a freezer that is not frost-free it needs to be thawed out if it reaches about 1-inch thick.

GETTING COZY IN HERE

If the freezer is not getting cold enough or is not freezing it may be due to a number of different problems. The compressor is not functioning, you may have a refrigerant leak or the timer is not working properly. Need a repairman, not grandpa!

However, if the freezer is running and not freezing properly or developing frost near the top, check the door seal and be sure that the door is sealing properly. In time the seal will need to be replaced. Depending on the climate, the rubber seal will deteriorate and cause abnormal leakage. The magnetic strip may also become loose and not hold the door shut tight. Grandpa can easily handle this problem.

HELP! MY TEXTURE IS CHANGING

When you freeze foods, you are actually freezing the water that is in the food cells. As the water freezes it expands and a number of the cell walls rupture releasing their liquid, which then freezes into ice crystals, thus resulting in the food becoming softer. These changes in texture are more noticeable in fruits and vegetables since they have higher water content than most other foods.

Certain vegetables such as tomatoes, lettuce and celery are so high in water content they literally turn into mush when frozen. When cooked products are frozen, their cell walls are already softened therefore they do not burst as easily. This is especially true when high starch vegetables such as corn, lima beans and peas are included in dishes.

MICROBE ALERT, MICROBE ALERT

Most microorganisms are not destroyed by freezing and may even be present on fruits and vegetables. Blanching does help lower the microorganism count significantly but enough of them do survive and are ready and waiting to destroy the food as soon as it thaws. Inspect all frozen foods, which may have accidentally thawed by leaving the freezer door open or from an electrical failure.

The botulism microorganism does not reproduce at 0^0F.

Cold doesn't bother us microbes!

QUICK, FREEZE ME FASTER

The damage to foods when freezing them can be controlled to some degree by freezing them as fast as possible. When foods are frozen more rapidly, the ice crystals that are formed are smaller and cause less cell wall rupture. If you know you will be freezing a number of items or a food that you really want to keep in good shape, try setting the freezer at the coldest setting a few hours before you place the food in. Some freezer manuals also will advise you which shelves are in the coldest area.

FREEZING FOOD TIPS

- ◆ Foil containers are best for freezing if you are going to go from the freezer to the oven.
- ◆ Only freeze baked goods that are low in moisture. Breads must be wrapped very tightly.
- ◆ Foods that contain spices will not freeze well and retain the flavor of the spice.
- ◆ Vegetables must be blanched before freezing.
- ◆ Frozen fruits do not retain their flavor.
- ◆ Remove fat from meats and they will freeze for a longer period of time.
- ◆ Remove all poultry innards before freezing.
- ◆ Low fat fish freeze better.
- ◆ The higher the fat content of dairy products the better they will freeze.

◆ Cheese will freeze well.
◆ Most sauces freeze well.

PROBLEMS AFTER FREEZING FOODS

Apples ----------------------- Becomes, mushy and may turn dark
Celery ----------------------- Becomes soft and only good for cooking
Cooked egg whites ------------- Turns rubbery
Cooked macaroni and rice -------- Mushy, loss of taste
Cheese in blocks --------------- Tends, to crumble too easily
Cheese, crumbled -------------- Soggy
Cucumbers -------------------- Limp, waterlogged, poor flavor
Custards --------------------- Gets watery
Cream cheese ----------------- Becomes, grainy and crumbly
Cream pies ------------------- Gets watery
Custard fillings --------------- Separates, watery
Egg whites (cooked) ------------ Soft, tough, rubbery
Fried foods ------------------- Loss of crispness, soggy
Gelatin ---------------------- Weeps
Grapes ----------------------- Becomes soft and mushy
Gravy ------------------------ Need to be re-heated if fat separates
Icings made with egg whites ------ Weepy
Jelly on bread ----------------- Tends, to soak into the bread
Lettuce ---------------- Loses shape and very limp
Mayonnaise ------------------- Separates
Meringue --------------------- Toughens
Milk sauces ------------------- Tends to curdle or separate
Onions, raw ------------------- Watery and limp but OK for cooking
Potatoes, Irish --------------- Soggy when frozen in soups or stews
Potatoes, raw ----------------- Texture is lost and they may darken
Radishes --------------------- Texture is poor and they become pithy
Salad greens ------------------ Lose crispness
Sauces with milk or cream -------- May separate
Sour Cream ------------------- Separates, watery
Tomatoes, raw ---------------- Watery and tend to lose their shape

Whole milk ------------------- Separates
Yogurt ----------------------- Separates

GARBAGE DISPOSAL

GENERAL INFORMATION:

The disposer works by using a small motor, which powers a flywheel that throws the garbage into a shredder producing a pulp that will easily flush down the drain. There are two major types of garbage disposal units. They are the batch feed, which is activates by turning a stopper and the continuous feed operated by turning on a wall switch.

CLICK, CLICK???????????

Grandma just tried to use the disposer and it didn't turn on, grandpa has been summoned to the kitchen. If the problem is electrical, try pushing the small red button on the bottom of the disposer. Sometimes a jam will cause the unit not to work at all and it may appear to be an electrical problem, however, removing the jam and pressing the red button usually works.

UNFRIENDLY DISPOSER FOODSTUFFS & ???????

There are a number of foods that will cause a jam and stop the disposer. These include garlic skins, celery strings, cornhusks, potato peelings, tea bag strings, silverware, children's toys, grandpa's false teeth, etc.

AVOIDING A CLOG

Certain peelings will clog most garbage disposals. The best way to avoid a problem when you need to peel potatoes or other vegetables that might be a potential problem is to place a funnel down the garbage disposal to block the debris.

PEEK-A-BOO

If you look down the sink into the unit with a flashlight and see a foreign object use a needle-nosed pliers to remove it.

If the object is jammed into the blade use the "L" shaped metal tool (Allen wrench) found under the sink. Place the small wrench into the hole on the bottom of the disposer and turn it to release a jam before removing the foreign object. The small wrenches are available at any hardware store but <u>should come with</u> your disposer.

THERE'S SOMETHING SWIMMING IN THERE
If the disposal is not draining, try a plunger and be sure it is seated well before trying to push it down a few times. If this does not work you will have to remove the curved trap under the sink and clean it out. Call grandpa to the rescue!

IS YOU'RE FOOD FLYING AROUND THE KITCHEN?
If food is flying out of the disposer you have not place the rubber stopper over the hole. The stopper should have small holes in it to allow water in. If this is not the problem, call Ghostbusters!

COLD SOLUTION
To sharpen the blades of a garbage disposer, just place 3-4 ice cubes into the disposer, and run it for a few seconds. This should be done once a month if the disposer is used regularly. To freshen it, grind lemon peels in it.

A LITTLE BIT WILL DO YA
Never place any type of chemical drain cleaner into a garbage

disposal. If you need to get rid of odors use a small amount of white vinegar.

DEATH BY DRAIN CLEANER
Drain cleaners should never be placed in the side of the sink that has the disposer or it may be damaged.

SEASONING THE DISPOSER
Just pour ¾ cup of table salt in the garbage disposal then run with water as usual. This will clean and freshen up the disposal. However, if you prefer you could pour ¾ cup of baking soda in the drain and flush it with very hot water.

RUN WATER, DURING AND AFTER
Most people are aware that you should run water while running the disposal, however, you should also run the water for 30 seconds after it has finished running to be sure that all the garbage has cleared the pipes.

OUCH, OUCH, THAT'S TOO HOT
Always use cold water when running the garbage disposal.

KEEP ALL YOUR FINGERS
Never place your hand into a garbage disposer. Always use a needle-nosed pliers kept under the sink to remove foreign objects.

HOT WATER DISPENSER

GENERAL INFORMATION:
This unit works with a control valve that is on top of the sink and dispenses hot water. The heating element is under the sink and heats the water to a temperature that is set by the factory.

If the heating element goes bad it is best to replace the entire unit since a service call and repair will usually cost more than a new unit.

TRICKLE, TRICKLE

If you are not getting enough water from the tap then the line is partially clogged and will need to be removed and flushed out. There may also be a leak in the line so check under the sink for water spillage.

COLD TEA IS NOT VERY GOOD

If the water is not getting as hot as you would like, then you will need to read your manual and reset the temperature control, which was set by the factory. If a plumber is installing a new unit, be sure they adjust the temperature control to the desired temperature before they leave. If grandma installed the unit, check to see if she attached it to the cold water line. The temperature of water coming out of a unit should be 190^0F, which is enough to give you a nice burn.

HALF-A-CUP WILL NOT DO

These under the sink units can only supply a few cups of water at a time.

ICE CUBE MAKER

GENERAL INFORMATION:

The ice cube maker is a small appliance that is in the freezer compartment of the refrigerator and continually makes ice cubes. The icemaker works by signaling the water-fill valve to send water to it filling the tray. When the water thermostat signals the water-fill unit that the tray is full it stops sending water. When the ice cubes reach a certain temperature there is a signal sent and the tray empties.

BAD ICE CUBE, BAD ICE CUBE

If your ice cubes have an off taste or smell bad then they have probably picked up refrigerator odors and have been in the icemaker too long. Even if the water is filtered this will still occur.

NO STICK ICE CUBES
If you are making a lot of ice cubes for a party and place them into a bag in the freezer ending up with a big glob of ice there is a solution. Next time just place them into a brown paper bag before putting them into the freezer and they will not stick together.

KICK IT!
If the icemaker won't make ice cubes there a few things you can do: First check and see if it has accidentally been turned off. There is a thin, coat-hanger metal bar on the right side of your icemaker and when the bar is up, the icemaker is off. If the bar is down the icemaker is on. If the bar is up, slowly lower it and the icemaker should work.

A common icemaker problem is freeze-ups. Next time this happens just use the hair dryer to defrost the problem. This problem won't occur if you release a few ice cubes every few days.

CALL THE FILTER CHANGER-GRANDPA
If you start detecting a bad taste it may be from an old worn out filter and should be changed. These filters should be changed every 6 months.

HOW CLEAR I AM...............
Cloudiness in ice cubes; is caused by entrapped air bubbles. If you want clear ice cubes boil the water first and make them in an ice cube tray.

KITCHEN CHAIR

SCRATCH STOPPER
If your kitchen chairs are scratching the floor, just paste some self-adhesive pads on the bottom of the legs.

KITCHEN SINK

Best to buy a new one

NEED A LITTLE REPAIR

If your sinks is scratched and chipped it can be resurfaced for about $300, however it is only guaranteed for about a year. A spray-on epoxy coating can be applied but only holds up well for bathroom sinks and bathtubs since they are not used as much as the kitchen, sink. Buy a new sink! However, most hardware stores have a do-it-yourself kit that works great and can give grandpa something to do.

CAN FALL ASLEEP WAITING

Waiting for hot water at the kitchen sink can waste thousands of gallons of water every year. The solution is the purchase a Chilipepper™ hot water appliance. It is a small pump that speeds up water from the hot water heater to the sink.

DRIP, DRIP, DRIP

Leaky faucets can be expensive when you start to figure that one drip per second over the course of a year will consume about 400 gallons of water. It only takes a few minutes to replace a washer or tighten the faucet insert.

THAT'S TOO TIGHT

It is not necessary to turn faucet handles all the way off, just until the water stops flowing. If you force the faucet all the way as far as you can, you may compress the gasket and eventually make the faucet leak.

OR USE YOU'RE MOUTHWASH

Odors in the sink can usually be eliminated by running very hot water down the drain or placing 2 tablespoons of baking soda in the drain and allow it to remain for a few minutes before running the hot water.

If this fails place 1 cup of white vinegar in the drain and allow it to remain for 20 minutes before flushing with hot water.

STEEL SINK RUST REMOVER

Prepare a thick paste of baking soda and warm water and allow it to remain on the stained area for about 2 hours then buff the entire sink with the paste using a damp, soft cloth. Rinse with cool water.

ALL STOPPED UP AND NOWHERE TO GO

After trying a "plumbers helper" with no success, try the following method. Remove all standing water so that you are able to pour the ingredients into the drain. First pour 1 cup of baking soda, 1 cup of table salt, and ¾ cup of white vinegar into the clogged drain. These will start dissolving any organic matter and grease away immediately. Allow it to stand for 5 minutes then flush 1-2 quarts of boiling water down the drain.

KA-POOSH

If you have ever tried plunging a double sink, it may have been a very unpleasant experience. Next time you try to clear the drain, be sure and have a helper unless you have very long arms. The helper needs to place a rag or stopper into the other drain so that the water will not rush up and out as you plunge. If you have a dishwasher that drains through the disposer use a "C" clamp and two wood blocks to seal the drain hose, which will keep the water from backing into the dishwasher.

MICROWAVE

GENERAL INFORMATION:

The microwave contains a small transmitting antenna similar to one a TV station might use. The microwave oven converts the house current into an extremely high voltage, which feeds the "magnetron." The magnetron converts the current into radio waves, which cause the liquid molecules in the food to vibrate at a fast rate causing friction and generating heat for cooking.

We hate the microwave!

Usually results in short cooking times, which retains the nutrients.

The water content of the vegetables will determine just how well they will cook. Microwave ovens should have a movable turntable so that the food will not have "cold spots." This can result in the food being undercooked. If you wish to brown foods in the microwave, be sure and use a special dish for that purpose. The dish should always be preheated first for the best results. If you don't have a browning dish, try brushing the meat with soy or teriyaki sauce.

A steak will continue cooking after it is removed from the microwave and it is best to slightly undercook them.

Some foods; are not meant to be placed in a microwave such as breads since their internal structure is composed of many air pockets. The structure breaks down easily in the microwave and the bread becomes tough.

WHEN WAS THE MICROWAVE OVEN INVENTED?

In 1946 Dr. Percy Spencer, an engineer at Raytheon Laboratories, was working with a magnetron tube, which produces microwaves. He had a candy bar in his pocket, which he went to eat and found that it had melted and there was no heat source for that to occur. The only thing he could think of that would cause this to occur, was the magnetron tube he was working with. He then tried placing a small amount of popcorn near the tube and the popcorn popped in a few seconds. He then tried focusing the beam through a box at an egg, which exploded on one of his associates much to both of their surprise. The result was the first microwave oven called the Amana Radar Range™ introduced in 1977. The use of the word "radar" was used since the actual beam was invented in England and used as microwave radar to detect Hitler's planes in 1940.

DON'T GET ZAPPED

Microwave doors may become misaligned, especially if you tend to lean on them occasionally. They will leak radiation and should be checked periodically with a small inexpensive detector that can be purchased in any hardware store.

OUCH!

If you microwave a dish with a lid, be sure and aim the lid away from you when you are opening up the container. Escaping steam and spillovers are common causes of injuries.

SAFETY FIRST

If a child accidentally turns on the microwave, damage may occur. To avoid a problem, just keep a cup of water in the microwave when it is not in use.

KA BOOM

Microwave ovens are just as safe as a regular oven. However, make sure you never place a sealed container in a microwave.

MICROWAVE MAGIC?

A microwave oven actually works by emitting high-frequency electromagnetic waves from a tube called a "magnetron."

This type of radiation is scattered throughout the inside of the oven by a "stirrer." The "stirrer" is a fanlike reflector, which causes the waves to penetrate the food, reversing the polarity of the water molecules billions of times per second, causing them to bombard each other and creating friction that heats the food.

NOT A GOOD SIGN

If you hear a hum the magnetron is probably bad or you have a bad high voltage diode. Be nice to grandpa and maybe he will buy you a new one.

IT LOVES ME, IT LOVES ME NOT

If the microwave shuts off periodically, check to see if the fan is running. If the fan is not running when it shuts down there may be a short in the wiring. Another reason may be that the air intake grill is plugged up with dirt. Use a grandpa or old toothbrush to clean the grill.

THE DANGEROUS TEA BAG

Never place a tea bag in the microwave! The metal staple holding it together can ruin a microwave oven.

DO I, OR DON'T I MICROWAVE IT?

Microwave cooking is less expensive than most other methods of cooking, however, it is only desirable for certain types of foods. If you are baking a dish, it will rise higher in a microwave oven, however, meats do not seem to have the desired texture and seem a bit mushy. When it comes to placing something frozen in the microwave, it will take longer to cook since it is difficult to agitate the water molecules when they are frozen.

BAD MICROWAVE, BAD MICROWAVE

If all seems normal and the food is not being cooked it may be a loose high voltage wire, a bad solder joint on the board, magnetron problem or a power relay problem. Best to bring it to a repairman, keep grandpa away from it.

ANOTHER FUNKY PROBLEM

The display counting down and no cooking taking place is usually a bad door switch or a faulty relay.

DON'T BLOW A FUSE

If the microwave goes dead it is usually a faulty door switch that has blown the interior fuse.

TAKE IT FOR A RIDE

If the fan does not run, the microwave needs to be taken in for service since the fan is needed to cool the magnetron.

MUST HAVE BEEN GRANDPA'S FAULT

The fuse will sometimes blow if the sensor sense overcooked burned food. Grandpa can probably fix it by replacing the fuse.

FILL 'ER UP

Used microwave food containers should be saved and used for leftovers; just fill, freeze, and re-heat. It is always wise to check and see if a dish is microwave safe and will not melt. Just place the container next to a ¾ full cup of water and turn the microwave on high for about 1¾-minutes or until the water is boiling. If the dish is hot when you touch it, you will be able to cook with it.

EXPLODING FOODS

Certain foods will explode in a microwave, especially if they have skins that will not allow the water that is expanding to be released. These include eggs, potatoes, squash and any food that has a shell or tight skin.

NEATNESS COUNTS

If you don't clean up the microwave regularly the spills will cook onto the surface. To remove them easily, just place a sponge dipped in water or a small dish with ¾ cup of water in the microwave and cook on high for about 2 minutes then wipe up.

WHY THE GLASS TRAY?

Glass trays are placed in the bottom of all microwave ovens to catch spills and raise the food up off the floor of the unit allowing the microwave energy to hit the bottom of the food.

MIXERS

GRANDPA'S SOLVES MIXER PROBLEMS

MOTOR DOESN'T RUN OR IS SLUGGISH

1. **Food mixture is too thick** — Either use higher speed or thin out mixture. If you keep trying the motor will be damaged.

2. On/off switch dirty — Remove the housing and clean switch as well as all contacts with #400 sandpaper.

MOTOR RUNS BUT BEATERS DO NOT TURN

1. Motor runs but beaters will not turn — Beaters may not be locked into gear shaft.

MIXER MAKING TOO MUCH NOISE

1. Beater hits bowl — The beaters should just clear the bottom of the bowl. If they don't then you need to adjust the height by unplugging the unit and removing it from the stand. Lift up the hinge and turn the screw to raise or lower the hinge.

2. Beaters striking each other — If beaters are damaged or wobbly when they run, they need to be replaced. If the gears are misaligned, unplug the mixer, remove gear cover and realign gears. The base-plate or the gears themselves may be marked to aid in alignment. If there are no markings. Insert the beaters into the gear shafts and use the beater blades as a guide.

OVENS

HELLO IN THERE

If the oven does not come on it may be due to loss of electrical power, clock may not be set to manual, a burned wire connection, bad selector switch, fuse blown, circuit breaker kicked off or a defective thermostat. Grandpa may be able to track this one down.

IT'S GETTING DARK IN HERE

If the oven bake light comes on but the oven is not heating up it may be from a defective bake element, a bad thermostat or a burned wire connector. Usually it is the bake element and will need to be replaced or the oven has a bad thermostat that needs replacement. Depends how handy grandpa is!

OVERNIGHT SENSATION

To make oven cleaning both easy and efficient, all you have to do is sponge on a generous amount of household ammonia and allow it to remain overnight. Let the oven air out the next morning then wipe it clean with a damp sponge.

HOW CLEAN I'M NOT............

If the self-clean feature is not working it may be due to the panel cover for the door glass not being in the right position, the door was not locked, clock improperly set, defective thermostat, the self-clean switch is not closing or a defective clock. Usually it is one of the easier problems and with grandpa's help it should be easily solved.

STOP! YOU'RE KILLING ME

If you have a self-cleaning oven, be careful not to use any type of oven cleaner or the finish will be removed and the oven will no longer be self-cleaning. You can use window cleaner or a mild detergent. Also, if you leave the racks in the oven while it is going through the self-cleaning cycle it will discolor the racks.

HELP! I'M COOKING

If you have ever wondered why you can place your hand into a hot oven and not be burned, the answer is simple, air does not conduct heat well. However, if you leave it in there long enough it will come out medium-well. Water conducts heat more efficiently and will easily burn you.

THE SPEEDY OVEN

If the oven is cooking too fast and at a higher than normal temperature it may mean that the thermometer is not calibrated, has a defective thermostat, the selector switch is bad or the bake/broil switch has gone bad. Time for a repairman to be called!

TIMING IS OFF

Bad clock, defective selector switch, bad wire connection or you don't know how to operate the unit.

SOMETHINGS OUTTA WACK

The oven door is getting too hot, which is usually due to defective door seals, poor insulation or that the door hinges are out of alignment. Another job for grandpa!

RACK 'EM UP

Oven racks and smooth porcelain surfaces can be easily cleaned with a pumice stone in the oven.

LOOKS SPOOKY IN THERE

The red glow in the oven is the "glow-bar," which glows red-hot and when it reaches a specified temperature the gas jets will open. If the igniter is faulty it will not reach the proper temperature and the gas will not be released.

TICK, TOCK, TICK, TOCK

When the range burners work and the oven won't work, it is usually due to the clock being set wrong.

DON'T USE OVEN-CLEANER

Oven cleaners should never be used in self-cleaning ovens.

MY BROILER IS SICK

If you are having problems with the broiler not broiling, the broiler element has burned out and needs replacement. Not too hard a job for grandpa!

IT'S NOT THE 4TH OF JULY

If you ever see sparks coming from the oven, unplug the oven from the wall immediately. After you unplug the unit see if you can tell where the sparks came from so that you can replace the part or call a serviceman.

CLEANING-UP

The majority of aerosol oven cleaners contain sodium hydroxide (lye), which is also found in drain cleaners. When lye is sprayed on burnt fats and carbohydrates it converts them into soap that is easily wiped off with a damp cloth. It would be best to use a number of the newer products that use organic salts and are less dangerous,

REMEMBER TO TURN IT OFF

If you have an oven that is not equipped with a self-cleaning feature then just preheat the oven to 200°F then turn it off. Place a small bowl with ¾ cup of ammonia on the center shelf then close the oven and allow it to stand overnight. The next day, open the oven and allow it to air for 30 minutes in a well, ventilated kitchen then wipe up the mess with a warm, damp paper towel.

BAKED GOODS ARE BURNING

There are a number of reasons that this may happen. You may be using dark utensils, which will absorb too much heat or the utensils are too large for the product. You can also have a blocked exhaust vent.

SOGGY BAKED GOODS, YUCH!

This is usually caused by; the oven not being hot enough or the oven thermostat needs to be reset. The thermostat may have to be recalibrated.

IS UNEVEN COOKING A PROBLEM?

Probably being caused by a defective door gasket or one that is worn and needs to be replaced.

POTS & PANS

GENERAL INFORMATION:

There are a number of materials that are used to manufacture pots and pans, many of which do not really do the job adequately. Remember, the thicker the gauge of the metal, the more uniformly it tends to distribute the heat.

The finish on the metal will also affect the efficiency of the cookware. The names of product lines of a number of cookware companies for 2006 have changed, but the materials have, for the most part, remained the same.

POOR PAN, ONLY HAS A 50:50 CHANCE

There is only a 50:50 chance of saving a non-stick pan that has had an oil fire in it. However, there is one possible solution, try making a paste from baking soda and water and apply it to the pot then allow it to remain overnight. Apply mild pressure the next day and hope for the best.

STORING PAN LIDS

To easily store pan lids, just mount an ordinary towel rack on the back of the cabinet door.

CLEANING NON-STICK POTS

For the most part these plastic coated pots are easy to keep clean, however, they do stain and may over time develop a buildup of grease and oil. If this occurs it will adversely affect the efficiency of the non-stick surface.

To clean the surface, just mix 2 tablespoons of baking soda with ¾ cup of white vinegar in 1 cup of water and clean the pot by placing the ingredients into the pot, place the pot on the range and boil it for about 10 minutes. Wash the pot, then rub vegetable oil on the surface of the plastic coating to re-season it.

I'VE FLIPPED MY LID

If you lose a top knob to a saucepan lid, try placing a screw with the thread side up into the hole then attaching a cork on it.

Poor pot, he has a screw loose!

GET OUT THE HAMMER AND CHISEL

If food gets stuck to a pot, just fill the pan with warm water and place a fabric softener sheet in the water then allow the pan to soak overnight.

GOOD USE FOR MARBLES

If you want to keep the water level up in your double boiler, just p[lace a few marbles in the bottom of the boiler. When the level gets too low they will start to rattle.

YUCKY ALUMINUM POT

If you're aluminum pot is discolored, just fill the pot with water and add 1 tablespoon of cream of tartar and boil for about 20 minutes. Show grandpa how smart you are!

BRASS &COPPER POTS

BRASS AND COPPER POTS FOR EVERYDAY USE

Most brass and copper pots and utensils may have a lacquer coating that should be removed before using the item to hold or cook food in. If the item is just for decorative purposes, than the lacquer coating should not be removed and the item just cleaned with lukewarm water with mild detergent. If the item is to be used with food, than the lacquer must be removed by placing them into a bath of 1 cup of washing soda mixed into 2 gallons of boiling water. After a short time the lacquer will just easily peel off.

Brass and copper will not react with any food and are safe to cook in. Copper is one of the best heat conductors and is preferred by many chefs. Copper pans, however, should only be purchased if they have a liner of tin or stainless steel to be safe, otherwise they may leach metals into the food.

When you cook in glass, remember to reduce the oven temperature by 25^0F.

One of the worst types of cookware is the thin stamped stainless steel pots with a thin copper-coated bottom. The copper coating is approximately 1/50th of an inch in thickness and too thin to distribute the heat efficiently and uniformly.

The *"real"* copper cookware provides excellent heat distribution on the bottom as well as the sides of the pan. The copper, however, needs to be kept clean and if black carbon deposits form to any degree it will affect the heat distribution significantly. These pots are usually lined with tin which must be replaced if it wears out otherwise excess copper may leach into the food causing a health risk. Foods that are high in acid will increase the release of copper. The metal ions in copper will also react with vitamin C and reduce the amount available.

SHINE THAT COPPER

A great cleaner for copper can be made from a paste prepared from white vinegar, salt and all-purpose flour. Another method is to spread catsup on the copper and allow it to remain for 10 minutes before wiping it off.

BRASS AND COPPER CLEANER

The following ingredients are needed:

¾	Fresh lemon or
2	Tablespoons of lemon juice
1	Tablespoon of salt

Place the salt in a shallow dish and dip the exposed end of the lemon in the salt and use to scrub the stained area. Another method is to make a paste of lemon juice and salt and use a cloth dipped in the solution to clean the brass or copper surfaces. If the pot has a green spot, use a solution of ammonia and salt to remove the area that has turned green. Gloves should be worn when using ammonia and always try not to breathe the fumes and work in a well-ventilated area.

ENAMELED COOKWARE

While the enamel does resist corrosion, it is still metal coated with a thin layer of enamel. The coating is produced; by fusing powdered glass into the metal surface, which is in most instances cast iron. The cookware can chip easily if hit against another object and can even shatter if placed from a very hot range into cold water.

GLASS COOKWARE

Rapid temperature changes may cause the glass to crack or break in many brands. Glass has a very low "heat-flow" efficiency rating and when boiling water is poured into the glass cookware, the actual heat that is transferred from the boiling water to the bottom of the cookware will travel slowly back to the top of the pot. Because of this, the bottom of the pot will swell and the top of the pot does not expand creating a structural type of stress and a crack is very possible. Corningware® and Pyrex™ in that order would be the only choices for glass cookware, since both will resist most stresses.

ALUMINUM

The majority of cookware sold in the United States in 2005 was aluminum, which is an excellent heat conductor. Current studies report that there is no risk from using this type of cookware unless you are deep scraping the sides and bottoms of the pots continually, allowing aluminum to be released into the food. Rarely does anyone do this. Excessive intake of aluminum may lead to Alzheimer's disease. Aluminum cookware stains very easily, especially if you are using hard water to cook with. Certain foods, such as potatoes, will also cause the pans to stain easily. If you cook a high-acid content food such as tomatoes, onions, wine or if lemon juice is used in aluminum, it will probably remove some of the stain. If a pan is already stained when the acidic foods are cooked, it may transfer the stain to the food possibly turning your foods a brownish color.

Aluminum pans also tend to warp if they are subjected to rapid temperature changes, especially if they are made of thin gauge aluminum. If they are made of a thick gauge, they will have excellent heat-flow efficiency and will not rust, thus making the thick pan, the best pan for use as cookware. Water and cream of tartar will clean aluminum.

Just fill the pan with water and add 1 tablespoon of cream of tartar then boil for 15 minutes before washing. Lime-soaked pickles should never be made in an aluminum pot even though the instructions state that aluminum is recommended. A chemical reaction takes place, which is not healthy.

ALUMINUM POT, BURNED-ON FOOD REMEDY
The following ingredients will be needed:

1	Tablespoons of baking soda
¾	Cup of warm tap water

Place the warm water over the burnt area; then pour the baking soda on top of the water. Allow the solution to sit for 12 hours before cleaning off.

CAST IRON/CARBON STEEL
A Cast Iron/Carbon Steel pot may only supply a small amount of iron in elemental form to your diet, but not enough to be much use nutritionally. Certain acidic foods such as tomato sauce or citrus fruit may absorb some iron but not enough to supply you with adequate daily supplemental levels. Iron does, however, conduct heat fairly well. These are both non-stainless steel, iron-based metals that have a somewhat porous, jagged, surface. These pots need to be **"seasoned."** To accomplish this, you need to rub the cooking surfaces with canola oil and heat it at 300^0F for about 40-50 minutes in the oven, then allow it to cool to room temperature before using. The oil has the ability to cool and seal the pores and even provide a somewhat nonstick surface. Another factor is that when the oil is in the pores, water cannot enter and possibly cause the formation of rust.

These pots should be washed daily using a mild soap and dried immediately. Never use salt to clean the pot, since this may cause rusting. If a cleaner is needed, be sure it is a mild one. Iron pots tend to release metal ions that react with vitamin C and reduce its potency. Cast iron pots can be cleaned, by just filling the pot with warm water and dropping in 3 denture-cleaning tablets, then allow the pot to sit for 1 hour. This method will not affect the seasoning. To remove rust, just use sand and vegetable oil and rub lightly.

CAST IRON POTS
To clean burned-on food from a cast iron pot, just mix sand and vegetable oil in the pot and scrub with steel wool. Be sure and re-season afterwards.

COOKING TO RE-SEASON

If you need to re-season your cast iron pot, just use it to fry food. The hot oil will do the job. Best to rub the pot lightly with vegetable oil before putting it away after you clean it.

CAST IRON POT CLEANER

Mix the following ingredients together in a small bowl:

| 1 | Teaspoon of ascorbic acid (vitamin C) |
| 2 | Cups of tap water |

To remove rust from cast iron pots, just briskly rub the area with a paste made from the ascorbic acid and water. If the rust spot still persists, try allowing the mixture to remain overnight.

CLAY POTS

Remember to always immerse both the top and the bottom in lukewarm water for at least 15 minutes prior to using.

BRRRRRR, ITS CHILLY IN HERE

Always start to cook in a cold oven and adjust the heat after the cookware is placed into the oven. If sudden changes occur, the cookware may be cracked.

NAUGHTY, NAUGHTY

Never place a clay cooker on top of the range directly on the heat.

GLASS COOKWARE

Best to use a commercial cleaner made specifically for glass cookware. Burned on grease can be removed using ammonia. Never use an abrasive cleaner.

NON-STICK

These include Teflon™ and Silverstone™ and are made of a type of fluorocarbon resin that may be capable of reacting with acidic foods. For 2006 there were a few minor improvements but basically stay with the top brands. If you do chip off a small piece and it gets into the food, don't be concerned it will just pass harmlessly through the body. Never allow any brand of "non-stick" surface pan to heat to a high temperature dry.

The pan may release toxic fumes if heated above 400^0F for more than 20 minutes. This could be a serious problem for small pets and birds. Proper vegetable oil seasoning of most pots will produce a non-stick surface without risk and last for months. These non-stick surfaces are the result of a chemically inert fluorocarbon plastic material being baked on the surface of the cookware or other type of cooking utensil. Silverstone™ is the highest quality of these non-stick items.

The food is actually cooked on jagged peaks that protrude from the bottom, which will not allow food a chance to stick to a smooth surface. The surface is commercially *"seasoned,"* producing the final slick surface. The major contribution of a non-stick surface is that of allowing you to cook without the use of fats, thus reducing the calories of foods that would ordinarily be cooked with fats. The less expensive non-stick cookware usually has a very thin coating and will not last very long with everyday use. With heavy usage and continual cleaning, the coating will eventually wear thin.

TEFLON SURFACE CLEANER

The following ingredients will be needed:

3	Tablespoons of baking soda
3	Lemon slices
1	Cup of hot tap water

Place the baking soda and the lemon slices on the stained area, then add the water to cover. Simmer the pot on low heat until the area appears clean.

STAINLESS STEEL

To be a good heat conductor, they need to have a copper or aluminum bottom. High acid foods cooked in stainless steel may leach out a number of metals into the food, which may include chlorine, iron, and nickel.

I'M ALL STREAKY

If your stainless steel is streaked, just clean with olive oil or club soda.

STAINLESS STEEL POT CLEANER

The following ingredients will be needed:

| 1 | Tablespoon of household ammonia |
| 1 | Pint of cool tap water |

Place the ingredients into a container and mix well, then apply to the stainless steel pot.

MULTI-PLY PANS

The bottoms of these pans usually have three layers. They are constructed with a layer of aluminum between two layers of stainless steel.

NO HOT SPOTS HERE!

Stainless steel does not have the hot spot problem and the heat will be more evenly diffused by the aluminum.

RANGE TOP

GENERAL INFORMATION:

Electric range tops have visible coil burners or may be a *"smooth top"* that has the burners integrated into the glass surface top.

The range tops have a coiled wire beneath the burner area, which conducts electricity heating up the burner or surface area.

LIGHT 'EM UP, IF YOU CAN
If burners don't light chances are that the small holes for the gas to go through are plugged and need to be cleaned out with a very fine piece of wire.

SURE IS DARK IN THERE
If the ovens will not light it may be due to a circuit breaker problem, oven fuse blew if it has any, clock settings; were touched by someone not familiar with the oven or a short in the wiring.

NOT GOOD!
If the burner will not lower and stays on high heat, the switch control is bad and will have to be replaced.

I WORK WHEN I WANT TO
If only one of the burner elements works intermittently you have a worn or bad contact in the receptacle that the element plugs into.

NEVER CLEAN THESE WITH A HARSH CLEANER
The burner top is usually aluminum and should never be cleaned with an oven cleaner. However, with any type of oven cleaner make sure that there is good ventilation or they may burn the lining of your mouth and throat.

THE DIFFERENCE IN RANGE TOPS

TRADITIONAL ELECTRIC COIL
These are inexpensive and work well with all types of cookware. The drip bowls do get soiled easily and it is somewhat difficult to fine-tune the heat.

TRADITIONAL GAS BURNER
These are inexpensive and very easy to control the heat. They also cook fast, however, the drip bowls get dirty easily.

GLASS CERAMIC
These are easy to clean and have good heat control. They will cook more slowly than other types and it is best to use cookware that is heavy and have flat bottoms. Somewhat expensive!

SOLID DISC ELEMENTS

These are easy to cleanup. They are cast-iron elements and need to be polished to look good. Need to use heavy cookware with flat bottoms.

INDUCTION UNIT
Have excellent heat control and are very easy to clean. Need to use magnetic cookware and are very expensive.

SEALED GAS BURNER
Has even distribution of heat and is easy to clean. However, it is more expensive than a standard gas range.

NOT VERY ATTRACTIVE
If you wipe down your walls with a mild solution of white vinegar and water occasionally the walls will not attract grease.

GASPING FOR OXYGEN
One of the best fire extinguishers is baking soda. The oxygen supply is cut off and the flame goes right out. Always keep an open box in the cupboard next to the range.

PUT A LID ON IT
A fire in a pan; can easily be put out by just placing a lid over the fire, thus cutting off the oxygen supply.

WAX ON, WAX OFF, WAX ON, WAX OFF
To make cleaning up easier, just rub the top of the stove with a car wax occasionally and it will stop the grease from sticking to the top.

REFRIGERATOR

GENERAL INFORMATION:

The refrigerator is one of the most complex appliances in the kitchen. There are a number of thermostatic controls, ice and water dispensers, automatic defrosters, compressors, condensers, metering devices, evaporators and lighting. In normal operation very little ever goes wrong with a refrigerator, however, the more electronics we are presently placing in them, the more problems are occurring.

BAD REFRIGERATOR, BAD REFRIGERATOR

When the refrigerator is not automatically defrosting and frost is showing up, the defrost heater, which is located just underneath the cooling coils, behind the back panel has stopped working and probably needs replacement. Will keep grandpa out of trouble for about 1 hour.

GETTING WARM IN HERE

If the refrigerator is not cooling this is one of the more serious problem and you may have to replace either the compressor, the condenser or the capillary tubes may have plugged up and is not allowing the refrigerant to flow. Another solution to the lack of cooling may be that the thermostat has gone bad interrupting the electricity flow to the compressor, which stops the cooling process.

TOP EFFICIENCY

Refrigerators that have a top freezer compartment are more efficient than those that have the freezer on the side. The most efficient size is a 15-20 cubic foot top freezer refrigerator.

HERE A DROP, THERE A DROP

If you have a leaky water dispenser, you will need to replace the water valve. The water pressure may also be too high. Another job for grandpa!

NICE WATERFALL

If water is running down the back of your refrigerator it means that the drain tube is blocked and the water is unable to get to the tray to be evaporated and needs to be cleaned out. You will have to remove the drain tube and blow air into it to clean it out.

IS YOU'RE HAIR STANDING ON END?

If you were shocked when touching the refrigerator there is a bare wire touching somewhere and it needs to be found and fixed. Best to unplug it first!

HATE TO TAKE SIDES

The refrigerator is cold and the freezer is not working or visa versa. If one side is cold and the other is not, it means that one of the temperature gauges is stuck or broken and will need to be replaced. May or may not be a job for grandpa depending on the age of the refrigerator.

STOP RACKS FROM RUSTING

Because of the moisture in a refrigerator, the racks may rust. To prevent this, just coat the racks with floor wax.

FROST-FREE DIRT

Frost-free freezers that don't ice up can still get dirty and collect odors. The easiest way to clean them is to use ¾ cup of isopropyl alcohol in 1 quarts of lukewarm water. The alcohol has the ability to loosen and icy matter and allow you to sponge away the dirt and odors. You won't even have to dry the surface since the alcohol will evaporate very quickly.

COVER UP

To cover a scratch on your refrigerator or freezer, try using the same color enamel paint. This really works great and will last a long time.

CLEAN LIVING

If you have a problem with mildew forming in your refrigerator, just spray the insides with vegetable oil. Spray the freezer after it has been defrosted and next time it will be easier to defrost.

SLICK IDEA

If you have a problem with ice cube trays sticking to the bottom of the shelf, try placing a piece of waxed paper under the tray. Freezing temperatures do not affect waxed paper.

KEEP YOUR FIZZLE IN

The refrigerator is a good place to store many chemicals such as hydrogen peroxide. It will stay active for a longer period of time. Nail polish is another chemical that likes the cold and will go on smoother.

HOW SWEET IT IS!

To eliminate refrigerator odors, just leave ¾ a lemon in the refrigerator. Old coffee grounds in a cup or a few charcoal briquettes works great too. You can also place a few drops of "real" vanilla on a cotton ball and place it into the refrigerator.

LOST LUSTER

Washing and scrubbing the refrigerator will eventually cause the finish to become dull. To liven it up and bring back the shine, just wash the surface with a mild solution of white vinegar and water. Use a cloth to apply the solution for the best results.

CLEAN GASKETS LAST LONGER

Refrigerator door gaskets need to be cleaned regularly with a borax or baking soda solution only. The stronger detergents may cause the gasket to deteriorate faster.

A CLEAN COIL IS A HEALTHY COIL

If you clean the coils underneath or on the back of the refrigerator you will have a substantial energy saving. Purchase an inexpensive **condenser cleaning brush** and be sure to clean the front plate. The backing, which is usually cardboard, is very important to the running of the refrigerator and keeps air being pulled over the hot condenser keeping it cool. If this cover is gone the compressor will eventually burn out.

TESTING THE DOOR FOR LEAKAGE

The door gasket will wear out eventually and cause cold air to leak out.

To test the gasket, place a dollar bill between the door and the gasket and close the door. If you can't remove the bill, the gasket is OK. Another method is to place a 100-watt work light in the refrigerator, close the door, turn off the kitchen light and look for the light around the rubber seal. If you see the light replace the gasket.

I'M GETTING DIZZY

Best not to move a refrigerator on its side unless you really have to. The oil may come out of the compressor and run up the cooling lines.

CAN I PLACE A REFRIGERATOR IN THE GARAGE?

Not a problem unless it is a self-defrosting and the garage temperature drops below 50^0F. When this occurs the oil may become too thick and cause a compressor failure.

IT'S GETTING CROWDED IN HERE!

Best not to pack your refrigerator too full or it will restrict air circulation and give you poor cooling conditions. Freezers, however, can be packed full with no problem.

PRODUCE DRAWER SECRET

If you have a two produce drawer refrigerator, keep one drawer with ¾ -inch of water in the bottom and keep your green, leafy produce in this drawer. It will not hurt the workings of the refrigerator and will keep the greens crispy longer.

UNDER REFRIGERATOR CLEANING

Try using a yardstick with a thin cloth wrapped around it that has been dampened with water and white vinegar. This will work easily under the refrigerator as well as behind it. You may have to move the yardstick around and repeat the process a few times to get the whole area clean.

REFRIGERATOR FRESHENER

The following ingredients will be needed:

1	Teaspoon of baking soda
1	Teaspoon of lemon juice
2	Cups of very hot tap water
1	Spray bottle

Place the hot water into a spray bottle then add the ingredients and mix well.

A light mist sprayed inside the refrigerator next time you clean it out can remain on the walls and shelves. Allow the mixture to dry for a few minutes. This spray freshener can be used anywhere you need a freshener.

SMALL ELECTRICAL APPLIANCES

BLENDER/MIXMASTER

CLEAN ME OR LOSE ME
To keep your blender and mixer working great, be sure and lubricate all moving parts, with a very, light coating of mineral oil (not vegetable oil).

This should be done every 3 months. Before you use a measuring cup to measure a sticky liquid, try spraying the inside with vegetable oil and the liquid will flow more freely.

A CLEAN BLADE IS A HAPPY BLADE
Food tends to get caked in the bottom of the blender around the blades and is difficult to clean off. Just fill the blender halfway with hot water and add 2-3 drops of liquid soap then turn the blender on high for 30 seconds. The face of the blender is also a difficult area to clean, especially around the buttons. A nailbrush does a really good job.

GRANDPA'S TIPS ON BLENDER CARE & USE

❖ Make sure that you clean the blender after you use it. The best method is to fill the container ¾ full with warm, water and a few drops of detergent.

- ❖ Cover it and run it on low speed for about 5 seconds. Clean the base with a sponge but never immerse it.
- ❖ The blade will easily jam on most blenders and special care must be taken to avoid the problem if the machine is used regularly. Every few weeks you need to take the time to disassemble the container unit (jar bottom, sealing ring and the blade) and then wash the parts in warm, soapy water.
- ❖ Never use scouring powder or steel wool pads. The glass jar can be washed in the dishwasher, but not the other parts.
- ❖ Never store food overnight in the glass container.
- ❖ Never insert utensils into the blender while it is running.
- ❖ The container must contain at least 1 cup of liquid before adding any ice cubes to the container.
- ❖ The blades may be very sharp so be careful when the blender is running and when you wash the blades.
- ❖ If the blender is laboring when processing a heavy load, place it on a higher speed.
- ❖ If the blender ever stops while it is blending, turn it off immediately or you may cause damage to the motor.
- ❖ Never place hard frozen cheese in the blender or it may break the blades.

FIXING A JAM-UP

Blade assemblies easily get jammed when you do not use the blender for a period of time. If the unit is disassembled regularly this should not occur. The nut can be unscrewed to disassemble it. If there are tabs around the nut, just bend them out of the way and replace them after you clean the shaft. To free the shaft, gently rap it on a board.

BREAD MACHINE

GOING INTO LABOR

If you hear the motor laboring too much when you are sending something through the machine, allow the machine to rest for 20 seconds before continuing.

HAVING A CRACK-UP

The bread has a crack around the top and sides. The solution is probably that the dough is too dry. Try adding 1-2 tablespoons of liquid. If the machine is programmable, increase the rising time.

I'M TOO CRUSTY

Set the crust control to light or choose the sweet bread setting. You can also remove the bread from the machine 5-10 minutes before the bread cycle ends. Reducing the amount of sugar sometimes helps as well.

A NO, NO

Most bread machines are timed for the use of dry yeast. Compressed fresh yeast should never be used in bread-baking machines.

STOP! YOU'RE KILLING ME

Remember that adding extra salt, fresh garlic, cinnamon or sugar to the dough may slow down or even stop yeast action.

GET A HAMMER & CHISEL

If you have a problem with the paddles sticking to the shaft, apply a small amount of vegetable oil before you add any ingredients to eliminate the problem.

OUCH! I HIT MY HEAD

If the top of your bread is raw, it means that the bread has risen too much and hit the top of the bread machine.

GRANDMA'S SECRETS OF THE BREAD MACHINE

- Use only flour that has not been treated chemically from only hard wheat.
- If you use a delayed cycle, never use fresh eggs and fresh milk. Use powdered eggs and milk.
- Never add any ingredients including hot butter unless it cools or you may kill some or all of the yeast.
- Always check the dough after 5-10 minutes in the first kneading cycle. You may need to add more liquid depending on the weather.
- Dry weather may require additional moister.
- If you are using sweet dough, place the dough in a plastic closed bag in the refrigerator for about 12 hours to allow extra rising time.
- For all heavy flour, such as whole wheat, buckwheat, rye, etc. Use the whole-wheat cycle.
- Any bread that is low in sugar or fat should use a shorter knead time cycle, such as the French bread cycle.
- If the breads are high in fat and sugar or you are using ingredients that burn easily, use the sweet bread cycle
- To prevent soggy crusts, remove the pan and the bread before the cool down cycle starts and allow the bread to cool for 15-20 minutes.
- Most bread machines are timed for the use of dry yeast. Compressed fresh yeast should never be used.
- The flour used should contain at least 12 grams of protein per cup.
- Dry yeast needs to be stored in an airtight container since it absorbs water easily.
- If you replace whole-wheat flour with ¾ cup of gluten flour it will give the bread better texture.

The flour to liquid ratio should be 2¾-3 cups of flour to 1¾ cups of liquid. In the summer (due to higher humidity), however, you will need a little more flour and in the winter use a little less.

- The machine can be opened to check the dough as it is being kneaded, but don't touch the dough.

When using a machine with a delayed cycle, never place fresh ingredients in such as eggs, milk or cheese. Bacteria may have a field day and give everyone food poisoning.

- Always soften butter at room temperature before adding it to the recipe.
- If you use too little yeast, the bread will not rise properly.
- If you use too much yeast, the bread will rise and then collapse.
- Time the completion of the bread to about 1-hour before you will be eating it.
- If the bread is undercooked and somewhat gummy on the inside, the bread did not rise sufficiently

---

The ratio of salt to flour in bread is ¾ teaspoon of table salt for each cup of flour used. Some recipes call for less salt, but it would be best to use the ¾ to 1 ratio.

- The dough should be pliable around the blades. If it's chunky then it is too dry and additional liquid is necessary.
- For a great, nice sweet loaf, just double the amount of yeast; cut back on the salt; use 1/8 teaspoon of vitamin C powder; use the longest cycle on your machine; or remove the dough and form it by hand before baking it in the oven.
- If your bread machine does not have a cooling off cycle, be sure and remove the loaf as soon as it finishes baking.
- High-protein flour will produce high-rising bread.
- Whole grain flours will produce denser, heavier breads.
- If the bread rises, then collapses in the middle, you have used too much liquid.

> **Salt is used in bread for flavor and bread can be made without salt if you're on a salt-free diet. Remember, however, that salt inhibits yeast and the dough will rise quicker if you don't use any salt.**

- In most cases, bread machine dough is better than hand, kneaded dough.
- Use special instant yeast for sourdough or for sweet breads.
- Most bakers who use bread machines prefer instant yeast, either regular instant or instant gold for most all-purpose baking needs.
- If you add raisins or nuts to the machine, it would be wise to add 1-2 teaspoons of additional flour. This helps the dough *"open up"* more easily.
- Never use rapid-rise yeast in a bread machine.
- Normally 1-2 teaspoons of sugar is added to a 1-pound bread.
- Any kind of sugar can be used in bread machines. That includes corn syrup, molasses, honey and all other syrups.

> **The best flour for bread machines is King Arthur's unbleached, all-purpose, high-protein flour.**

- A one-pound bread machine can handle 2-3 cups of flour.
- A 1¾ -pound bread machine can handle 3-4 cups of flour.
- Almost all bread recipes can be made in a bread machine.
- Whole-wheat flour may not be the greatest flour nutritionally as once thought. The additional fiber tends to cause a percentage of the nutrients obtained from the whole wheat to be flushed out of the body.
- Whole wheat is fine for additional fiber and texture.

Lots of bad bacteria here!

CAN OPENER

DE-GUNKER

To clean you're can opener, try running a piece of paper towel through it. This will pick up the grease and some of the gunk.

GRANDPA'S TIPS FOR PROPER USE & CARE

- ❖ Be sure and unplug the power cord before removing parts or when cleaning the opener.
- ❖ Under no circumstances ever immerse the opener in water.
- ❖ Best to clean the cutting wheel (or the blade) and the shaft regularly. Use hot sudsy water and never use a scouring pad on the opener or any other abrasive cleaner. The cutting wheel is very sharp so be careful.
- ❖ Some cans that have a heavy rim may cause the opener to stall. If this happens, just grasp the can and move it counterclockwise to assist with the cutting action. If there is a large dent in the rim, try opening the can at the other end or start the cut just after the dent.
- ❖ Never try to open aerosol cans.
- ❖ Knifes must be clean and completely dry before trying to sharpen them.
- ❖ All can openers are designed with built-in protection from overheating. If you are sharpening a number of knives and the motor stops, you have been overworking the sharpener. It should cool down in about 10-15 minutes and you can resume sharpening.
- ❖ Never sharpen a blade that has a serrated or scalloped edge or it will ruin the knife.
- ❖ Make sure you remove the housing and clean out any metal fillings if you do a lot of sharpening.

COFFEE MAKER

THE STORY OF COFFEE

The coffee tree is believed to have originated in Central Africa where the natives would grind the coffee cherries into a powder and mix it with animal fat, then roll it into small balls, which they would take with them on long journeys or hunting trips. Raw coffee is high in protein (until it is diluted with water) and when combined with the fat provided adequate calories and a stimulant.

The first factual information relating to the actual drinking of the beverage is by the Arabs in the Middle East.

The Arabs protected the coffee bean seed to such a degree that they would not allow it to be exported under the threat of death. However, in 1660 some of the coffee seedlings were smuggled into Holland and then transported to Brazil in 1727 where the climate was more favorable.

The climate and soil conditions were ideal and the coffee trees thrived. Coffee trees need an annual rainfall of over 70 inches of rain with every tree only producing about 2,000 *"coffee cherries"* to make one pound of coffee. The United States consumes 50% of the world's coffee, which amounts to 400 million cups every day. The average coffee drinker drinks 3 cups per day. Eight out of 10 adults drink at least one cup of coffee daily.

Coffee prices have risen dramatically due to major frosts in Brazil, which destroyed 1 billion pounds of coffee, about 10% of the world's coffee supply.

ROASTING THE BEANS

Raw coffee beans must be roasted to change an unappetizing seed into a beverage that is desired by 80% of all adult American. Roasting shrinks the bean about 15% and increases its size by 50% in a process similar to popcorn popping without the full explosion.

The longer a bean is roasted, the darker it becomes. Darker roasts do not necessarily produce a stronger coffee. The following are the steps the bean is subjected to during the roasting process:

1. The roasting process applies heat to the bean in such a manner as to assure that every surface area of the bean receives the same amount of heat. Even heating is important.
2. The heat is applied at the lowest temperature to perform the roasting and for the shortest period possible.

TYPES OF ROASTS

Light City Roast
The bean is not fully matured with a cinnamon color instead of brown. The flavor is somewhat weak.

Standard City Roast
Most popular roasted bean sold in the United States. It may be sold as the American roast or just the brown roast. The beverage that is brewed is somewhat dull and a little on the flat side.

Full City Roast
Popular roast on the East Coast! It is roasted for a slightly longer period than the standard roast, which produces a darker cup of coffee. The coffee bean is a dark brown with no hint of oil on the surface. Most specialty coffee shops on the East Coast will carry this roast.

Brazilian Roast
No relation to Brazilian coffee. The bean has been roasted a bit longer than the full city roast and the coffee has a darker color and a flavor that starts to taste like a very dark roast.

French Roast
The bean has an oily appearance on the surface and the color is a somewhat dark, golden brown. The coffee has a smooth rich flavor and is easily distinguished from the lighter roasts.

French/Italian Roast
Called: Spanish or Cuban roast. The bean is roasted darker than the French roast and this coffee makes excellent espresso.

Italian/Espresso Roast
Darkest roast possible: without carbonization of the bean or roasting it to death. The bean has a shiny, oily surface and looks black.

I'M SPOUTING COLD WATER INSTEAD OF HOT
Current is not passing through the main heating element or something is blocking the flow. If there is no blockage the main heating element will need to be replaced. This is a job for the repair shop not grandpa.

GRANDPA'S PROBLEM SOLVERS FOR DRIP-TYPE

1. **Brewed coffee does not stay warm** – The keep-warm element is not working and either the element or the switch will need to be replaced. If the element has gone bad it is best to just purchase a new coffeemaker.

2. **Coffeemaker is sputtering, leaking or steaming** – It is due to either the rubber tubing that is used to join the heating unit to the reservoir and outlet tube or the water passage is being blocked by a buildup of mineral deposits. Either replace the rubber tubing or clean out the mineral deposits. Loosen the residue with a needle or toothpick then run through brewing cycle with a mixture of half water and half white vinegar. Then twice with clean water.

3. **Coffeemaker is shocking user** - This is caused by; a frayed power cord, an electrically live component grounded to a metal part or leakage current due to faulty insulation. If you think it is leakage current it needs to go to the shop. If bare spots can be seen on the insulation that can be replaced.

4. **Coffeemaker is blowing fuses** – Probably from an electrical overload and the coffeemaker just needs to be on a different outlet. If the problem is in the internal wiring, take the machine in for repair.

TASTE THE DIFFERENCE

Never use soap in a coffee maker. Always clean it with a solution of 50% white vinegar and 50% water. Allow it to run through a complete cycle then refill it with cold water and let it run through another cycle.

ELECTRIC BLANKET

GRANDPA'S TIPS FOR PROPER CARE & USE

❖ When the blanket is turned on, never fold it, lie on it or place anything on it, especially a pooch.

- ❖ Never place the control near the radiator or windowsill since it should have a normal airflow.

- ❖ Never dry clean the blanket, just launder it by hand using lukewarm water and a mild soap (check the label first for washing instructions).
- ❖ Best to set the temperature to high then lower it to the desired temperature.
- ❖ All electric blankets are mothproof and do not need to be stored with mothballs.

FOOD PROCESSOR

ZAP IT WITH SOAP
To keep your food processor clean, try running a small amount of liquid dish soap through it then rinsing thoroughly.

IRON

DON'T GET STEAMED UP OVER STEAM
When your steam iron stops steaming it is probably clogged with mineral deposits. The best way to remove the deposits is to place white vinegar in the water reservoir then place the iron flat on an oven rack and plug it in. Set the steam setting and by the time the steam starts coming out, the mineral deposits will have dissolved.

SEASONING YOUR IRON
If your iron is leaving small black marks on the clothes; sprinkle a small amount of salt on a piece of paper then run the warm iron over the salt to clean the bottom. This will also eliminate starch buildup on the bottom on an iron. Toothpaste will also remove starch.

WHERE OH WHERE HAVE MY LITTLE HOLES GONE

If the holes in your iron are all clogged up with hard water deposits, just mix a solution of 1/3rd cup of white vinegar and 1 tablespoon of baking soda and blend well. Pour the solution into the iron and heat the iron just until it starts steaming. Turn it off and empty it then fill it with warm water to rinse very well. Empty and rinse a few more times. Then run the steam on a piece of old rag to remove any residue.

TOASTER

WHAT HAPPENS WHEN YOU TOAST BREAD?

A French chemist first discovered the browning reaction of toast. He discovered that when bread is heated a chemical process takes place that caramelizes, the surface sugars and proteins turning the surface brown.

The sugar then becomes an indigestible fiber and a percentage of the protein (amino acids) loses their nutritional value. The toast then has more fiber and less protein than a piece of bread that is not toasted.

The protein is actually reduced by about 35%. If you're making your own bread, you can increase the amount of protein by just reducing the amount of regular flour by 2 tablespoons and replacing it with an equal amount of quality soy flour.

HERE YE, HERE YE, TOASTER SHOCKS USER

If you are having a shocking experience with your toaster, the power cord is probably frayed and needs to be replaced. However, if there is a current leakage problem you need to take the toaster to a service center for repair.

MY TOASTER IS BLOWING FUSES

Possible circuit overload and you just need to move the kitchen appliances around to different circuits. However, it may be a bad power cord or even a short circuit inside of the toaster.

GOING DOWN, BUT NO TOAST

Best to see if the power is on or if the cord or plug is broken. If none of the easy fixes work then it is probably the main switch inside the toaster and it needs to go to the toaster shop.

TOASTING BUT COLOR IS NOT RIGHT

The thermostat is broken or out of adjustment. Check and see if color control is set properly or if it has loosened and needs to be tightened. The other reason could be that inside of the shell is stained and needs to be cleaned with bicarbonate of soda (best to unplug it first). You may have a broken heating element and if so it goes to the repair shop.

TOAST IS BURNING UP AND WON'T POP UP, BAD TOASTER!

There are a number of possible problems such as the heating element is broken and you just need to buy a new toaster or the main switch is broken and can be replaced or just the thermostat is broken or out of adjustment.

TOASTER OVEN

YUK! MELTED PLASTIC

When plastic melts on your toaster oven you need to handle the problem immediately. Turn the oven off and allow it to cool then remove the plastic with acetone (nail polish remover). Make sure that the area is well ventilated since the fumes may be hazardous.

TRASH COMPACTOR

GENERAL INFORMATION:

When you place trash into a compactor and close the door and then press the start button, the motor will start and causes a set of reduction gears or operates a belt-pulley system that lowers the ram. The ram exerts high pressure on the trash and flattens it. As soon as the ram reaches its set point, the motor reverses and raises the ram back up to the top.

SQUEEZE HARDER

If the compactor does not work, check the wall socket first then the ground fault interrupter (GFI) and the switches, which include the door, key or micro switches. Try plugging some other appliance into the socket to be sure it is working.

DAMN RAM

If the ram gets stuck or has gone down and won't come back up, there may be a broken drive belt, chain or one of the gears has broken. Easy repair for a sharp grandpa!

Grandma broke it again!

MY DRAWERS ARE STUCK

If the ram partially comes back up and the door opens making a vibrating noise, the garbage is not being rammed down evenly and you have a large object that is not being crushed or broken up.

GET OUT THE CROWBAR

When the drawer is hard to open, it means that there is food or an object stuck and needs cleaning out. If damage has been done then you may have to replace the tracks or rollers.

CLEAN OUT THE ATTIC

You can put any type of garbage into the compactor that you would normally throw into your trashcan in the home.

KILL THOSE BUGS

Use a good bacteria-killing cleaner or a de-greaser to regularly clean the compactor, especially the surface head of the ram. Compactors are breeding grounds for bacteria.

UTENSILS

GREAT, GRATER TIP

Cleaning the grater will never be a problem if you use a small piece of raw potato before trying to wash it out. Sometimes a toothbrush comes in handy too.

WATER PURIFIER

GENERAL INFORMATION:

 There are numerous methods of home water purification systems. If you decide to purchase a system, be sure to investigate the different types and the availability of service for that particular system. A number of units only produce a minimal quantity of pure water, which would not be sufficient for many families while other units do not provide the level of desired filtration. The most common unit for a home is the reverse-osmosis filter system.

This is one of the most popular units sold in the United States and utilizes a duel sediment filter system. The system is effective in removing up to 90% of the minerals and inorganic matter. The system works by forcing water through a thin membrane, which removes the inorganic metals. Most units only produce a few quarts of pure water a day.

PURE AS THE DRIVEN SNOW

One of the best ways to be sure is to purchase a test kit from a hardware store or check with your local water company.

SCIENCE OF WATER TESTING

Grandpa's test will determine if any bacteria are present in your drinking water. Sugar is a food supply for bacteria and they will become very active and feed on the sugar and multiply. Place the sugar in a cup of water and place the cup in a sunny location. If the water becomes milky after about 2-3 days the bacteria are very active.

WHERE'S MY REPLACEMENT, I'VE BEEN OVERWORKED

The cartridge filters should be replaced twice a year for the average home.

NOTE: Never hook a reverse-osmosis unit to an icemaker since it does not generate enough water pressure to operate the water inlet valve properly.

OTHER TYPES OF WATER FILTRATION:

Activated Charcoal Filtration Units

A number of the more popular units filter the water through activated charcoal filters. This method is very efficient in filtering out insecticides, pesticides, chlorine, and organic matter. However, this type of filter is not very effective in filtering out bacteria and un-dissolved metals, such as lead, copper, iron and manganese.

Filters need to be checked regularly and changed or the system will be useless. If you do choose this type of unit, be sure it does not contain silver to neutralize bacteria. Silver is not that effective and a percentage may end up in your drinking water.

Chlorination

Systems that utilize chlorine to kill bacteria usually produce water with a somewhat off-taste and odor to the water. The system must be functioning properly at all times or there is the possibility of the chlorine forming a dangerous element.

Multi-Stage Filtration

These units are one of the most effective and usually recommended above most other units. They utilize a number of filtration methods such as a pre-filter, which will remove iron, rust, dirt particles, and sediments as small as 5 microns. They also have a lead-activated carbon filter, which removes lead and chlorine as well as a carbon block filter to remove chlorine, improve taste, remove odors, and most organic impurities.

Micro-strainers

A good method of filtration, however, it is not able to remove most nitrates and nitrites. It will remove almost all chemicals and bacteria.

Distillation

Distillation is one of the most effective methods of filtration. Water is boiled producing steam, which is then cooled to produce water vapor, which is then trapped. However, certain gasses are not removed through this method. The more efficient distillers utilize activated charcoal filters as an additional organic material remover. Be sure and de-scale your distiller regularly or the efficiency will be greatly reduced.

Aeration

Radon gas is a continuing water contamination problem, especially in the Midwest United States. An aeration filter is the most effective type of filter to resolve this problem. A survey conducted by the Environmental Protection Agency estimated that over 8 million people are at risk from radon contamination.

Ultraviolet Radiation Purifiers

These types of filters are very effective in filtering out bacteria and are normally installed on wells in conjunction with other types of filtration units. This system does require a constant electrical line voltage. It does not remove cyst contamination.

Ozonators

These filters are being used more extensively than ever before and are frequently found on swimming pools built after 1992. They utilize activated oxygen that is capable of purifying and removing bacteria without chlorination. Recommended more for swimming pools rather than drinking water since the system may produce bromate, which may be related to tumors of the kidney.

Carbon Filters

These filters utilize carbon to attract the contaminants, which then adhere to the carbon. They are useful in removing odors, improving the taste of water, and eliminating organic chemical compounds. Their drawback is that they do not remove heavy metals.

Magnetic Water Conditioners

Since all home appliances or equipment that use water builds up scale over a period of time, these conditioners are a must for the homeowner who wishes to protect their investment with a minimum of repairs from water scale damage.

These systems do not affect water purity; however, they condition the water magnetically altering the physical characteristics of water-borne minerals. The mineral will no longer be able to cling to the insides of the water pipes and no scale can be formed.

MISCELLANEOUS KITCHEN TIPS

FILE IT AWAY

If you have a problem with limited space, try using a metal vertical file holder to store your cutting boards and baking sheets. This will keep them in an orderly fashion.

WRAPPING THE REMOTE

Many kitchens have TV's or radios that are operated using a small remote control unit. When working in the kitchen with all sorts of flour and ingredients, it would be best to wrap the control in plastic wrap, which will still allow you to use it while keeping it clean.

RE-USABLE TISSUE BOX

After you use up all the tissues, try using the empty box to hold plastic bags or plastic garbage bags.

2-LITER BAG HOLDER

If you have a little space inside of a cupboard or kitchen pantry, just take a 2-liter soda bottle and cut out the top and bottom, screw it to the wall or inside of the pantry door and fill it with plastic bags then remove them one at a time.

STUFF THOSE BAGS

Use an empty cardboard paper towel holder to hold your plastic supermarket bags and just remove them as needed. This will eliminate the mess.

TIE THEM IN A KNOT

When you throw away dry cleaner plastic bags or supermarket bags, it would be safer to tie a knot in them so that children can't get into them.

UGLY CUTTING BOARD

If your cutting board is stained, just mix 2 teaspoons of household bleach in 2 quarts of water and scrub till it's clean. Allow it to soak for a while if it is really bad. Be sure and rinse several times with very hot water to get rid of all traces of the bleach.

GRAND OPENING

Next time you need to open a stubborn jar, try using a piece of plastic wrap around the top for a better grip. You can also use a pair of rubber gloves or place the jar top down into a dish of hot water to release the vacuum seal.

SERIOUS STICKINESS
To solve the problem of sticky rims from honey or other sticky food, just place a piece of plastic wrap between the lid and the rim before you screw the top back on. Another method is to wipe a small amount of vegetable oil around the rim before you place the lid back on.

BAD FOAM

Using brass or copper utensils in the fryer will react with the oil and create foaming.

THE TRAVELING KNIFE
If you have to bring a knife with you and need to travel a distance, just place the knife inside a roll of paper towels. It will accommodate an 8-10" blade without extending out the other end.

AN EYE-OPENER
Small items such as boxes, jars and extract bottles tend to get lost in the cupboard. If you want to see those items easily, just stack 2X4 pieces of lumber that have been cut to the right length to create different heights in the cupboard or cabinet. This will place the items higher than the others.

KEEPING BRUSHES IN TIP TOP CONDITION

Small brushes used around the kitchen, especially basting brushes are very difficult to get clean. These brushes are usually dipped in oils and sauces and it is almost impossible to remove the stickiness. Just wash the brushes very well in hot liquid soapy water, rinse well and shake dry. Place the brushes with their bristles pointing down into a cup and fill the cup with coarse salt until the bristles are covered.

The salt will draw moisture out of the bristles and keep them dry and in good condition ready for the next use. The salt is easily shaken off.

NO-SKID CUTTING BOARD
Grandma always placed a rubber mat under her cutting board so that it wouldn't slip.

STOP FALLOUT

Small kitchen utensils such as cake testers, pastry tips and other small items tend to fall through the holes in the silverware container. To avoid this problem, just place a small sponge pot scrubber in the bottom of the container.

PROTECTING THE SINK

When you are washing a heavy pot in the sink and you don't have a protective rubber mat, just place some wooden spoons under the pot to protect the sink from scratches or chips.

WARM THOSE DISHES

Serving meals on warm dishes is really the way to go. All you have to do is place the dinner plates in the dishwasher on the dry cycle to heat the plates. This is especially good when serving steak, since as the steak cools it may get somewhat tough.

NAILING DOWN THE SILVERWARE TRAY

Silverware trays are always moving in the drawer and usually end up in back of the drawer. Purchase some florist's clay and place a small piece under all four corners and in the center of the bottom of the tray to keep the tray in its place.

EXTRA COUNTER SPACE

When you a little more extra counter space, just open a large drawer and place a cutting board on top of the drawer.

OIL SPILL!

When you spill oil on the kitchen floor it can be quit a mess to clean up. Next time it happens, just sprinkle a thick layer of flour on the area and wait a few minutes for the flour to absorb the oil. Use a dustpan and broom to clean up the flour then spray the area with a degreaser window cleaner and wipe up the balance with paper towels.

GOOD USE FOR KEY HOLDER

Try placing a small plastic key holder on the inside of a cabinet door or on the cupboard wall to hold your measuring cups and spoons.

SAVING THE COUNTERS

Many countertops cannot handle hot pots being placed on them. To save your countertop and to provide you with more space to place hot pots, try using an inverted baking sheet on the counter as a big trivet.

DRIP, DRIP, MESS, MESS

When you have to pour melted butter, hot oil or any liquid that would ordinarily make a mess from a pan by dripping, just pour off the hot liquid and continue turning the pan through one full rotation over the container you are pouring into and eventually the pan will be right side up again forcing any drippings to end up back in the pan instead of dripping down the sides of the pan.

BURNER PROTECTION

Next time you brown meat or pan fry on the stovetop, try placing inverted aluminum pie plates over the burners to protect them from the splattering grease. The pie tins can easily be cleaned and used.

IN THEIR PLACE

If you need to add ingredients with one hand and use the mixer with the other hand the bowl you are working in may have the tendency to move around. If you want to stabilize the bowl make a circle with a damp kitchen towel and place it under the bowl.

SPLATTER ELIMINATOR

When using a hand-held mixer it tends to make a mess, especially when you are whipping cream. To eliminate the problem, just place a piece of parchment paper over the bowl with an extra inch or so around the bowl and make two holes in the center of the paper. Feed the mixers through the holes and mix away.

REDUCING SPLATTER

When you are frying, try placing a large wire-mesh strainer over the pan to stop the splatter. This is especially handy if you have the different sizes to fit over a variety of pans.

SHARPENING THE VEGETABLE PEELER

You can use a paring knife to sharpen your vegetable peeler. Scrape the backside (not the cutting blade) between the blades of the vegetable peeler to remove the burrs. Then scrape the front side of the vegetable peeler using the back tip of the knife.

EASY DOES IT

A nick on the rim of a glass can be easily removed with an emery board. Don't use a nail file or sandpaper. They are too coarse and will scratch the glass and ruin it.

SOAP WORKS AS WELL

If you are having problems with sticky drawers, try rubbing a candle along the tops of the runners.

BAD SCOURING POWDER, BAD!

Scouring powder will scratch the surface of most appliances. Best to use small amount of baking powder mixed with water.

ODOR EATERS

A number of foods are capable of removing odors. Vanilla extract placed in a bottle top in the refrigerator will remove odors, while dry mustard is commonly used to eliminate onion odors from hands and cutting boards. Other solutions include leaving a small cup of used coffee grounds on 2 shelves.

An excellent method of removing odors from the kitchen is to keep a few washed charcoal briquettes in a shallow dish on top of the refrigerator. Frying a small amount of cinnamon will chase all odors from the home.

STEAL SOME KITTY LITTER

Place a small amount of kitty litter in the bottom of garbage bags or cans to absorb the odors and any spills from breaking the bag. Replace the litter every week.

GETTING IN SHAPE

Butcher blocks will not only harbor bacteria deep down in the cracks but are also difficult to clean. They need to be washed with a mild detergent, then dried thoroughly and covered with a light layer of salt to draw any moisture out that may have gotten into the crevices. The wood can then be treated with a very, light coating of mineral oil. Make sure it is only a light coating since mineral oil may affect the potency of a number of vitamins in fruits and vegetables.

CARING FOR CUTTING BOARDS

One of the best methods of cleaning and caring for a cutting board is to scour them with a solution of lemon and kosher salt then applying mineral oil. Kosher salt is a coarse salt and an excellent abrasive while the citric acid in the lemon will kill some bacteria and the mineral oil will prevent the board from absorbing stains.

TIME SAVER

Keeping a grater clean so that you can continue to work and still grate a number of different foods is an old chef's secret. A chef, will always grate the softest items first, them grate the firmer ones.

NOT A CRACK-UP

A trick used by antique dealers to remove hairline cracks on china plates or cups is to simmer the cup in milk for 45 minutes. Depending on the size of the crack the protein (casein) in the milk will fill in the crack.

NOT A FASHION STATEMENT

A great idea used by professional cooks worldwide is to keep a small plastic baggie handy, in case you have both hands in a food dish or dough and need to answer the telephone.

GLUE REMOVER
The glue on any type of contact paper will easily melt by running a warm iron over it or using a hair dryer on high heat.

OLD CARD TRICK
Save your old plastic playing cards to spread glue with, they work great for many projects and also as a shim.

MEASURING UP
If you want to use the fewest utensils possible, first measure out all the dry ingredients then the wet ingredients. By doing this you can use the measuring spoons or cups for double-duty.

SLIPPERY SUBJECT
When preparing a pan that needs to be greased, try saving your salt-free butter wrappers or use a fresh piece of bread. Remember salt butter wrappers may cause foods to stick.

ONE FOR THE GRIPPER
If your glasses are slick, try placing a wide rubber band on them for so that the children will get a better grip.

HANDLE ME CAREFULLY
Refrigerator handles are a prime source of bacteria lurking and waiting to cause a problem. Best to clean the handle everyday (at least once).

KEEP IT A BIT CHILLY
Check the temperature in the refrigerator at least every other month to be sure that it is holding 40^0F and the freezer is at 0^0F. Best to be safe than sorry!

MOVE OVER, GIVE ME ROOM TO BREATH
Remember for your refrigerator to be efficient the food you store has to have room to breath. Cool air must be able to circulate around the food freely.

CHAPTER 2

BATHROOM

BATHTUBS

HAVING A CRACK-UP

If you are getting cracks in the caulking around the bathtub, the cracks are probably from settling. To fix the problem, remove the cracked old caulking with a putty knife being careful not to damage the porcelain or tile around the tub. Do not use the strip caulking that comes in a roll. This is very difficult to install. Place in new waterproof calking then allow it to dry overnight before using the tub. Best to purchase a bead cleanup tool to help complete the job.

BOY, AM I DISCOLORED!

Most discolorations are from hard water stains. Try covering the bathtub with paper towels that have been soaked in full strength white vinegar. Remove the towels after 2 hours and you will be amazed at the result.

GETTING GLAZED

If you're bathtub needs to be re-glazed it would be best not to purchase a kit from the store, they do not hold up well. Call a professional re-finisher.

THERE'S A FUNGUS AMONG US

To remove mold and mildew from around the tub, grandpa recommends using a solution of one cup of bleach to three cups of water. If this does not work well increase the bleach until it does the job. Wear rubber gloves and rinse the area well before using the bathtub.

KEEP IT ON YOU'RE HEAD!

If you get hair coloring stains on a porcelain tub and on the tile, just use a mild solution of bleach and water and allow it to remain for a while before washing it off.

TOO MUCH MOOD

If you want to get burnt marks from a candle off a cultured marble tub, just sand it off with a fine, then an ultra-fine piece of sandpaper. After sanding use a polishing compound and make sure that the surface is wet while you are sanding.

ARE THE EXPENSIVE BATHTUB CLEANERS REALLY NECESSARY?

Most bathtub cleaners advertise that they contain powerful disinfectants that will kill bacteria as well as cleaning off the soap scum and dirt residues. While they do contain disinfectants, the bacteria killing action only lasts for about 3-4 hours and then the bacteria come right back.

RUST IN THE BATHTUB

Rust stains may appear in metal tubs and can be cleaned with a paste prepared from borax powder and lemon juice. If this fails, try a commercial preparation.

CABINETS

HERE A SPOT, THERE A SPOT

To solve the problem of water spotting on a wood surface in the bathroom, check with you're local hardware store. They have a product that can be applied on the wood surface that will provide a protective shield.

FAUCETS

I'VE BEEN EXPOSED

To stop the damage to metal faucets from exposure to moisture, grandpa paints the bathroom fixtures with a special clear epoxy paint found in most hardware stores.

GO RENT A JACKHAMMER

To remove hard water residue from faucets, you will need to use a non-acid bathroom cleaner, which will not damage the faucets.

SIMPLE SOLUTION

To remove the handles from the faucets, just pop out the decorative insert with a thin screwdriver point.

GRANDPA'S STEP BY STEP METHOD OF CHANGING A SINK FAUCET

- ❖ Turn off the water supply under the sink or at the main water supply to the house.
- ❖ Turn both spigots on to release any water leftover.
- ❖ Remove the water lines running to the faucets using a crescent wrench.
- ❖ Use pliers to remove the two plastic nuts holding the faucets on.
- ❖ Remove the faucets and use a scraper to remove any residue on the sink area.
- ❖ Roll some plumbers putty into a long roll, about the thickness of a pencil. Place the putty on the sink in the shape of the new faucet.
- ❖ Place the new faucet on the putty and press down to seal the faucet to the sink.
- ❖ Replace the plastic nuts under the sink that came with the new faucet.
- ❖ Place the new plastic flexible water lines back on and do not over tighten.
- ❖ Remove any excess putty.
- ❖ Unscrew the aerator and open both spigots before turning the water back on. Any debris will then be released before you put the aerators back on.

DON'T MESS UP THE CHROME
Wrenches have teeth that will damage chrome pipes and scratch them. Before you use them on a chrome pipe, wrap two layers of black plastic electrical tape around the jaws.

FLOOR

BLACK TILE A NO, NO
The secret to getting watermarks and scratches off black tile is to use a marble polish and a non-acid cleaner for the marks.

THE BEST FLOORING
Either tile flooring or Pergo™ flooring.

HAIR DRYER

DOING THE TWIST
You can keep hair dryer cords from twisting up by using ponytail holders on them.

CAN'T BREATHE
If the motor keeps overheating and turning the dryer off, check the exhaust area and clean out the dust that has accumulated blocking the airflow.

MIRROR

MIRROR DEFOGGER
To keep your bathroom mirror from fogging up, place a small amount of shaving cream on the mirror and towel it off.

SHOWER

GENERAL INFORMATION:
Showerheads are one of the major problems with clogging from hard water deposits and using too much water. Most new showerheads only use 2.5 gallons per minute compared to as much as 5 gallons per minute in older heads. Replacing the old head can save as much as $60-$150 on your water bill and energy savings depending whether it is gas or electric. You will save about 1200 gallons per year in the average home.

COUGH, COUGH, I'M ALL CLOGGED UP

If the showerhead is clogged with hard water deposits, you will need to remove the head and soak it in white vinegar overnight. If the holes are clogged badly, you may need to use a strong piece of thin wire and push it through each hole.

CLEANSER FOR SHOWER NOZZLE RESIDUE

The following ingredients will be needed:

1	Cup of white vinegar
1	Teaspoon of lemon juice
1	Cup of very hot water
1	Spray bottle

Place all the ingredients into a small bowl and mix well, then sponge on the showerhead and clean with an old toothbrush.

THE WEEPING SHOWER DOOR

If the shower door tracks are not draining properly, the weep holes may be clogged. Use a pipe cleaner to clean them out.

POLISH THOSE SHOWER DOORS

If the soap and scum buildup is really bad you will have to use full strength white vinegar. After you clean the doors, wipe them down with furniture polish that contains lemon oil. If the film is really heavy, use a steel wool pad soaked in dishwasher liquid and the glass will sparkle.

WHITE CRUD

Soap buildup on shower doors can be eliminated if you squeegee off the door after every shower.

INSECURITY

If you're shower rod becomes loose, you should be able to tighten it by adjusting the tension by turning the ends. If that doesn't work, buy a new rod, it's probably worn out!

A LITTLE DRIP WON'T DO YA

If you're showerhead drips, the head is dirty or defective and needs cleaning or replacement.

A SHARP IDEA
The best way to clean a marble shower if you have a bad area is with a razor blade providing it is wet.

CLEANING FIBERGLASS
Needs to be cleaned regularly with a disinfectant and a white nylon scrub sponge.

BROWN OUT
If you clean the grout and there is still a brown spot or two that cannot be removed, just try using a small amount of correction fluid (white- out).

SINK

WHOOOOOPS

Whenever you work in or around the bathroom sink or really any sink, be sure and place the drain in the closed position. Small parts and tools may fall into the drain and be a pain to retrieve. Grandma has finally learned to close the drain when she puts on a piece of jewelry over the sink, looking into the mirror. Grandpa has had to retrieve two rings, two earrings and four earring backs.

SLOW STREAM, A PROBLEM?
If the water flow from the tap is too slow, it is usually caused by: the aerator at tip of the faucet being clogged. Unscrew the aerator and clean the screen with an old toothbrush then rinse thoroughly.

AIR GOT IN THE LINE
If water is splattering out of the tap, there is probably air in the lines, just open all faucets in the home for five minutes to release the trapped air.

BOY, AM I LOOSE
If you have a water leak under the sink it is usually caused by loose plumbing fittings that just need to be tightened.

NO MORE STAINLESS SINK STAINS
In order to remove spots from a stainless steel sink, all you have to do is rub the spot with automobile rubbing compound. It will also leave a thin layer of wax to spot future spotting.

DON'T BE ABRASIVE
Never clean a stainless steel sink with any type of abrasive cleaner or steel wool. The best thing to use to clean the sink is baking soda. Vinegar will remove water spots.

STEAM ROOMS

GENERAL INFORMATION:
Steam rooms are usually made from tile, acrylic or glass enclosures. The humidity is 100% and the room is filled with steam.

The temperature can get between 98^0-118^0F. A drain is required as well as a gasket around an airtight door system. The steam generator is installed outside and usually very close to the room. After the room has been used, it should be allowed to air out or dried otherwise mold will form very quickly.

The difference between a steam room and a sauna is that a sauna is usually made from wood with wooden benches that are heated to 160^0-190^0F with very low humidity of around 5-15%. You add water to rocks placed in the center of the room to produce a dry invisible steam. No drain is required and the sauna heaters are installed in the room.

SEEING THE LIGHT
Mirrors; can be brightened by rubbing them with a cloth dampened with alcohol. Alcohol will remove a thin film of oil that is left from cleaning agents.

A WASTE OF A COOL ONE
If you wish to "frost" a bathroom window, use a solution of 1 cup of "Lite" beer mixed in 4 tablespoons of Epsom salts; then paint the mixture on the window, it will wash off easily.

TILE COUNTER

GENERAL INFORMATION:
One of the problems with tile is the buildup of soap scum. A small amount of white vinegar or lemon juice on a cloth will solve the problem.

A POOR SETTLEMENT
When grout cracks appear between the tiles it is usually caused by settlement or shrinkage and can only be fixed by removing the old grout and re-grouting.

HERE YE, HERE YE, SOAP STAINS GROUT
Grout stains are usually caused by moisture and soap stains. Could be stopped by wiping down tile after bathing or turning on an exhaust fan.

HOW LOOSE I AM..............
If the soap dish loosens up there is no way to tighten it without removing it and re-installing it. Make sure you calk it well!

TOILET

GENERAL INFORMATION:
Most toilet problems are simple to repair and should be easy for grandpa to tackle. Any replacement parts are available at any hardware store and the parts that may need replacement are easily accessible.

Toilets are made of either porcelain or ceramics and are acid resistant, which is good since most of the commercial toilet cleaners contain either an acid or ingredients that turn into acid when they come into contact with water.

Needless to say if you swallow most commercial toilet cleaners it will most likely lead to your demise in very short order. If you use one of the following formulas and there is still a ring that persists, try using a pumice bar to remove the ring. Just dampen the bar and gently rub the surface to avoid scratching it. A **"00"** piece of sandpaper will also do the trick.

MAKING TOILET BOWL CLEANER
The following ingredients will be needed:

1	**Cup of hydrogen peroxide**
1	**Tablespoon of household ammonia**
2	**Quarts of warm tap water**

Place all the ingredients into a bucket and mix well. You will need about 1 quart of the solution for each toilet. Pour the solution in the toilet and allow it to remain for about 30-40 minutes before you scrub and flush. If this is done weekly, residues and discoloration should not occur. ***Store properly – POISON.***

INEXPENSIVE TOILET BOWL CLEANER
The following ingredients will be needed:

1	**Cup of white vinegar**

Place the vinegar into the toilet and allow it to remain for 8-10 hours then scrub.

BRRRRRRRRRR, I NEED A WRAP
Moisture on the toilet tank is caused from the tank sweating because of the cold water in the tank coming into contact with the cold tank. This causes condensation, which can run on the floor or get on the walls. To solve the problem, just purchase a terrycloth tank cover and it will absorb the moisture. You can also install a mixing valve to warm the water as it enters the tank.

REMOVING THE SEAT OF THE PROBLEM

If you have a problem removing a toilet seat with corroded bolts that has to be replaced you will need to place some penetrating oil on them and allow it to remain overnight or saw the bolts off with a hacksaw. When placing the new bolts on use a small amount of petroleum jelly on the new bolts.

THE TOILETS RUNNING AWAY

The water level in the tank may be too high and the float arm stem may need to be adjusted downward. Lift the cover of the tank and remove it. Pull the float upwards, but do it gently. If the water shuts off then you will have to adjust the float position. This should be attempted before attempting to change or replace the rod. Turn the water supply off and adjust the float position by bending the rod until it is ¾ inch lower. Then turn on the water and flush the tank. Only half the float should be covered by water.

MY TOILET RUNNETH OVER

If the toilet is backing up and overflowing there is probably an obstruction in the line and the toilet needs plunging. Turn off the water at the water valve at the bottom of the toilet to stop the flow of water. Then plunge away and good luck. Hopefully, it's not one of the kid's toys that stuck.

SOUNDS SCARY IN THERE

When the toilet starts to make strange gurgling and dripping sounds, the flapper is probably warped and needs to be replaced.

FILLER-UP

If the toilet bowl will not fill properly there is usually a simple solution. Either the water supply has been turned off or the strap to the flapper may be broken or has come loose.

WATER LEVEL IS NOT ON THE LEVEL

The water level of the toilet seems lower than other toilets I have visited. You probably have a 1.6 toilet that is designed to use less water.

In this type of toilet, the amount of water is determined by the size of the bowl. A low water level; can also be caused by a toilet that is poorly vented or has a clogged vent.

PHEEEEW, SKUNK ALERT
When your toilet starts to smell like a sewer it may be caused by a low water level in the toilet bowl allowing sewer gas from the system to enter. A loose toilet can also release the sewer gas.

WHAT DO THOSE LARGE TOILET CLEANING TABLETS REALLY DO?
The bowl-cleaning tablets that are placed into the toilet tank are not going to clean your toilet; they are only designed to slow down the process of hard-water buildup, which contains imbedded dirt and debris. They contain a strong chlorine bleach compound or quaternary ammonium chloride. Both are strong disinfectants and have good cleaning properties. Some products, however, may be so strong that they will cause scaling of any metal surface in the tank and may cause the toilet to clog up.

THERE ARE GHOSTS IN MY BATHROOM
If the toilet flushes and no one is in the bathroom, this is referred to as "phantom flush" and usually caused by the design of the refill valve. What it is telling you is that your toilet has a leak in the flush valve. The only other cause is if the refill tube is not cut to the proper length.

POP, POP, FIZZ, FIZZ ALKA SELTZER WILL CLEAN TOILETS
Just drop 2-3 Alka-Seltzer™ tablets in your toilet and wait 20 minutes before scrubbing with a toilet brush. Between the citric acid and the bubbles it will work great.

GRANDPA'S METHOD OF REMOVING A TOILET

1. Best to empty the toilet first! Turn off the water supply to the toilet and then flush the toilet and hold down the handle to empty it. Sponge out any water that is left in the tank.
2. Use and adjustable wrench and disconnect the water supply line from the shut-off valves. Keep a towel handy since there may be some water left in the line.
3. Remove the tank, making the toilet bowl lighter to remove and reducing the risk of cracking the toilet or bowl. This is an important step if you are only removing it and then reinstalling it to repair a leak around the base or putting in a new floor.
4. Remove the two bolts at the bottom of the tank that secure it to the bowl. Inside the tank you will need a screwdriver in the head of the bolt and a pair of tongue and groove pliers to hold the nut on the outside of the tank and remove the bolt.
5. Remove the decorative plastic or ceramic caps that are covering the two nuts that are securing the toilet base to the floor.
6. Remove any plumbers putty from around the nuts and base with a plastic scraper or even an old credit card and remove the nuts. If you see any corrosion around or on the nuts, be sure and apply penetrating oil to soften the corrosion. Hopefully, you won't have to cut the bolts off.
7. Rock the toilet back and forth to loosen and break the seal. If you are alone, straddle the toilet and bend your knees when removing the base.
8. Put on the rubber gloves and you will need to keep the sewer fumes from entering the house by placing a big rag with a string tied to it down the hole. The string is to help you remove the rag if it gets too far down the drain.
9. Use a plastic putty knife and remove the wax residue from around the drain opening. If you plan on reinstalling the old toilet, be sure and clean the wax from the flange (underside of toilet) using the plastic scraper.

GRANDPA'S METHOD OF INSTALLING A TOILET

1. First you will need to pack plumber's putty around the old or new bolts to keep them in an upright position. This step will not be necessary if they have a plastic stabilizer.
2. Place the toilet bowl on its side and press a new wax ring on the horn. Only use just enough pressure for the ring to stick.
3. Pull on the string and remove the rag from the drainpipe, lift the toilet bowl and place it into position with the holes fitting on the bolts.
4. After you replace the toilet, rock it back and forth carefully while applying a small amount of downward pressure on the base in order to seal the bowl and the wax ring. Sit on the toilet to seat it solidly.
5. Now you need to install the washers and floor bolt nuts and tighten them by hand. Then you need to gently tighten then with an adjustable wrench, alternating from side to side, tightening the base a little at a time. If you over tighten the bolts it will crack the base.
6. Connect the supply line to the water inlet pipe under the tank. Best to replace the line with a new flexible braided steel line.
7. If the old tank was removed from the old toilet and you are going to reinstall it, be sure and place new rubber washers under the tank bolt heads before you secure the tank to the bowl.
8. Now connect the supply line to the shut-off valve and just hand-tighten. Check for leaks by turning the water on and allow the tank to fill with water then flush a few times. Tighten any connections if necessary.
9. Providing that there are no leaks, run a bead of silicon caulk around the base to keep water from mopping from going under the toilet.

OUCH! YOU'RE SCRATCHING ME

Some toilet brushes have metal rims holding the bristles used to scrub the toilet. Be sure and replace the brush as soon as you start seeing wear on the bristles or the metal will scratch the porcelain and it will be a bear to clean off.

CHAPTER 3

FAMILY/TV ROOM

FISH TANK

Grandpa loves his fish tank and has given some of the answers to questions that he felt might be asked. These answers to the most common questions asked should make it easier to understand your own fish tank.

TAKE THE TEMPERATURE

The average temperature of a tropical aquarium will depend on the type of fish that are placed in the tank. It will also depend on what part of the world the fish come from.

THE STRAIGHT INFORMATION

Substrate is very important in a fish tank especially important! If you are using salt water, use a carbonate substrate designed specifically for salt water.

SCRUB-A-DUB-DUB

A question that I frequently get asked is if you have to give a new fish a bath before adding it into you're fish tank? A bath does not remove any parasites if they are present. It is best to quarantine the fish in a separate tank for a period of time to be sure they are healthy.

IT'S GETTING DARK IN HERE

If you are setting up a new tank, only add one fish and plants to begin the tank cycle. The water should clear up in two weeks. If it doesn't, stop feeding the fish for three days and change 20% of the water.

IS IT SUPPOSED TO BE GREEN

Pea-green algae, is a problem and just reduce the amount of fish food and add live plants. The plants will compete with the algae for nutrients that are in the water.

KEEP A LID ON IT

It is best to always keep a lid on the aquarium so that objects cannot accidentally fall in or the cat can't get to the fish. Some fish are even jumpers and can end up on the floor.

BEWARE OF THE GIANT OSCAR

If fed properly and well Oscar's will grow at about one inch per month until they reach several inches in length. They need at least a 55-gallon tank to do really well.

BROWN-OUT?????

To get rid of brown algae, the tank probably needs more light. If you have a fluorescent bulb it should be changed every 6 months or it will lose its effectiveness.

THERE'S AN ALGAE AMONGST US

Algae; of all types usually grows because of too high a nutrient content in the water. If the problem persists, add some plecos and they will eat the algae. Algae can also grow faster if the tank is placed in direct sunlight for too long a period.

HUMMMMMMMMMMMMM

The aquarium motor should be very quiet and the hum barely noticeable. If the hum starts to get louder than normal, it would be best to have a spare motor handy since it may be ready to go bad.

TANKS MUST BE SEASONED

Never purchase the tank and the fish at the same time. The tank should be set up and allowed to season for a few days before adding any fish. You need to be sure everything is working properly, especially the filters, heater, etc.

THAT'S AN EYE-OPENER

Fish don't close their eyes because they don't have eyelids.

AND AWAY WE GO..........................

It is not necessary to leave a light on in the house if you go away on vacation. If you have a planted tank, the light should be on a timer. If there are no plants the light can remain off as long as you do not have baby fish.

INCHING ALONG!

There is an old saying that if you have a 25-gallon tank, you should keep 25 inches of fish in the tank. However, the one-inch per rule is not a good rule and should not be adhered to. Certain species of fish need more water than others.

GET RID OF CHLORINE

Be sure and always eliminate the chlorine in the water before adding it to the fish tank. Just allow the water to remain at room temperature for 3-4 hours and the chlorine will dissipate into the air. Commercial preparations are available if you don't want to wait.

CAREFUL WHAT YOU ADD

Many fish are killed every year by people placing items into the tank that they think looks pretty. Shells you buy from the dime store or the ones you pick up on the beach may be contaminated with parasites, bacteria or lacquer and kill the fish. Shells from the beach need to be thoroughly cleaned and sterilized before being added to a tank.

CLEANING A FISH TANK

Place some non-iodized salt on a sponge and clean away. Make sure that the salt is not iodized or no more fish and make sure that the fish are out of the tank and the tank is rinsed well.

SAVE THE OLD WATER

Don't throw the old water out when you are changing the water in the fish tank. Use the water to water your houseplants since it is an excellent fertilizer.

FLOORING

HOW ABOUT A RAINBOW
Light color flooring whether wood or vinyl will reflect light and the room will not need as much lighting. A darker surface floor will reflect very little light requiring more lighting.

MAKING A ROOM LOOK LARGER
Furnish the room with lighter color furnishings.

LIGHTING

GRANDPA'S FLOURESCENT LIGHT PROBLEM SOLVER

Tube flickers or partially lights
- Rotate the tube and make sure that it is seated properly in the sockets.
- Replace both the tube and starter if the tube is discolored or if the pins are bent or broken. Starters are only found in older units.
- Replace the ballast if it not more expensive than replacing the entire unit. In many instances the ballast cost as much as the entire unit.

Tube will not light
- Be sure that he wall switch is working properly and repair if needed.
- The tube may not be seated properly and may just need to be rotated a little.
- If the tube is discolored or if any of the pins are bent or broken, it is best to replace the tube and starter to be on the safe side.
- Replace the sockets if they appear to be chipped or if the tube does not seat properly.
- Replace the ballast or the entire fixture depending on the cost.

Loud humming noise and black substance around ballast
- Replace the ballast or the entire fixture depending on the cost.

WHAT IS BALLAST?
Special transformer: that regulates the flow of 120-volt household current to the sockets. The sockets then transfer the power to the metal pins that extend into the tube.

SOMETHING WEIRD GOING ON
If the florescent lights are getting dark on the ends, just reverse the ends to extend their life.

COUGH, COUGH
When fluorescent lights seem to getting darker it usually means that the bulbs have not been cleaned and dusted regularly.

SAVING MOOLAH
New low wattage light bulbs are excellent! They produce high quality light and reduce the heat entering the room. This will make it easier to cool a room in the summer.

FORGET THE GROW LIGHTS
The new fluorescent light bulbs that have become popular in the last 2-3 years will work just as well. They are less expensive to operate and will last about 10,000 hours. These new lights provide the blue end of the light spectrum, which is what the plants desire.

SLIDING GLASS DOORS

LITTLE DAMP IN HERE

Condensation should not be found between window/sliding glass door panes. If you know the manufacturer, they should be contacted since the panes should be sealed for life. There is no way to repair the problem.

TRACK DOWN THE PROBLEM

If the door tracks have become worn and not working well, it would be best to replace the entire door. The tracks are usually an integral part of the door and the cost would be prohibitive to try it.

PUSH HARDER IF YOU DARE

If the doors are too hard to push, first try and adjust the rollers. The adjustments are either on the sides of the door or on the bottom rail of the door. You may have to remove the door and clean the track. Silicone spray may also work.

DAMN LATCH

The mechanism needs an adjustment.

GRANDPA'S HINTS TO KEEP THE SLIDING DOOR SLIDING EASILY

- ❖ Occasionally clean the track. Dirt and debris will build up inside the track and cause a problem. Use your vacuum crevice tool to get inside the groove in the track.
- ❖ The track should also be cleaned using a cup of white vinegar in a bucket of soapy water. Scrub the track well and use a toothbrush to get into the small cracks if necessary.
- ❖ Adjust the roller height, which may get loose and mover over time. The adjusting screw on a wood door is on the inside bottom edge. On aluminum doors you can find it on the inside vertical edge. It should only take a few turns to adjust it.
- ❖ For security, cut a piece of ¾ inch round doweling and place it in the door track when you are away from home.

STEREOS

These are complex pieces of equipment that do need a certain amount of care to keep them working at optimum levels. The equipment is too complicated to repair once it breaks down, however, there are a few prevention tips that will keep them working more efficiently.

- ❖ Be sure and keep the components clean.
- ❖ Oxidation of the electrical contacts on receivers is one of the most common problems. Clean the contacts with a contact cleaner including all jack inputs and speaker terminals.
- ❖ If you are getting a hum from the speakers, make sure that all connections are tight and that the grounding wire is connected to the right terminal. You can also hook the grounding wire to the screw in the plate of an electrical outlet. All components should be plugged into their own outlet.
- ❖ Multiple outlet boxes will sometimes cause a hum if there are too many units plugged into them.
- ❖ If the speaker is not working and the connections are clean and tight then check the speaker wires and possibly replace them. If the run is very long to the speakers, the wires need to be thicker.

TELEVISION SETS

A NO, NO
Be sure and never use an aerosol spray or a liquid cleaner on a TV screen. Be sure and unplug the set when cleaning the screen. Best to use an anti-static dryer sheet.

BAD BIRD!
One of the more frequent problems with reception is from birds landing on a TV antenna and putting it out of line.

WOOD FURNITURE

- **Dark Wood** – Try filling the scratches with shoe polish that matches the lightest shade of the finish. You can also rub a walnut in the direction of the scratch over the scratch.
- **Cherry Wood** – Try using cordovan or any reddish shoe polish that comes close to matching the wood color.
- **Oak Wood** – Use a tan or natural shoe polish or iodine that has been diluted 50% with denatured alcohol.

INSTANT COFFEE SCRATCH REMOVER
If you just prepare a thick paste of instant coffee and water and rub it into small scratches and nicks it will hide them.

OAK FURNITURE REVIVER

The following ingredients will be needed:

¾	Cup of soda ash
1	Quart of warm tap water

Place the ingredients into a small bucket and mix well, then clean the furniture with a soft bristle brush and rinse with cool water. Dry well with a clean, dry, soft-cloth.

PERMANENT MARKER WORKS GREAT
Permanent markers have been used for years to cover small scratches on furniture.

GRANDPA KNOWS HOW TO REMOVE WATER DAMAGE

- Moisten a clean cloth with denatured alcohol or turpentine and try rubbing the spot out lightly.
- Mix a small amount of baking power with water and make a paste. Rub the mixture on the stained area in the direction of the wood grain very lightly.

- If all else fails, try rubbing the area hard with a solution of rottenstone and mineral oil made into a paste. This will remove the stain but leave the area dulled until you polish it.

GRANDPA KNOWS HOW TO FIX CIGARETTE BURN MARKS

- If the burned area is just into the finish it will be easy to clean by just wrapping a small piece of very fine steel wool around your finger and gently rub the area.
- If you notice that the burned area has blisters, just hold a small knife blade at a right angle to the burned area and scrape the area lightly in a side-to-side motion. After the burned area is removed, use a piece of very fine steel wool to rub the area until it is smooth. If there is any finish left, just polish and wax the area.
- If you needed to scrape into the wood and removed the finish, apply thin coats of shellac with a small brush, allowing each coat to dry before adding another coat. Allow the coats to build-up to the level of the finish then dip a piece of very fine steel wool into paste wax and smooth out the area. Blend the damaged area by rubbing the area with matching polish with the grain until the desired effect is achieved.

GRANDPA KNOWS HOW TO REMOVE INK STAINS ON WOOD

- If the wood is not sealed, ink will penetrate deep into the wood and you may never get it out.
- If the finish is protected with wax, blot it up immediately before the ink can penetrate the wood.
- Clean the surface using a damp cloth and never rub the area.
- Try rottenstone or a wood oil as soon as possible if the stain persists.
- Make an oxalic acid solution using 2 tablespoons of the acid to 1 pint of warm water then use an eyedropper and place a few drops on the area. Only allow the solution to remain for a few minutes before rinsing off.

GRANDPA KNOWS HOW TO CLEAN A CLOUDY SURFACE ON WOOD

Grease deposits from cooking or an oily cloth that has been rubbed on the wax finish usually causes this. Use a furniture polish that contains a solvent to clean the area.

DENT REMOVER

Dents in wood furniture can be unsightly and can be removed most of the time by ironing them out. As long as the wood fiber are not cut and just bent, you can set an iron on medium heat and place a damp, cloth over the dent. The heat and moisture will bring the dent out.

GRANDPA KNOWS HOW TO GET RID OF WHITE MARKS ON WOOD

DID YOUR FRIENDS OR FAMILY LEAVE YOU A RING

When a family member or friend places a glass that is damp or has condensation on a waxed, wood surface it may leave a white ring or spots. If the surface is cleaned off within a short period of time, the spot may be easily removed, however, if it is allowed to remain, it will leave a stain that may be more difficult to remove. A mild abrasive made into a paste will usually remove almost any ring or watermark.

The paste can be prepared from any natural oil, which includes olive oil, petroleum jelly, margarine and even butter combined with baking soda or salt. In many instances toothpaste, especially the powdered variety can be used with excellent results. After you remove the stain, be sure and apply a good coating a polish.

GRANDPA'S CAUTIONS WHEN STRIPPING WOOD FURNITURE

♦ Be sure that the product is biodegradable.
♦ Does it have a childproof cap?
♦ Is it flammable?
♦ Will it clean up with soap and water or do you have to use a dangerous solvent?
♦ Do you need special tools?
♦ Do you have adequate ventilation if the vapors are toxic?

♦ Avoid strippers that contain methanol, toluene, methylene chloride, acetone and dibasic esters.

ADDITIONAL PROBLEM SOLVERS

• Sometimes these are a result of a liquid (medicine, alcoholic beverages or perfume) being placed on the wood that contains alcohol. Try a solution made from equal parts of linseed oil, turpentine and vinegar.
• Try a cleaning-polishing wax.
• If all else fails, try rubbing lightly with 0000 steel wool and rub with the grain. If the furniture has a high-gloss finish, do not use steel wool.
• Try using a paste made from powdered pumice or a mixture of rottenstone and linseed oil.
• If you are sure that it was caused by alcohol, try using household ammonia on a damp cloth. Do it quickly then clean with non-sudsy water.

FILLING OAK WOOD CRACKS

The following ingredients will be needed:

> Fine starch flour
> Thick brown shellac

Place the ingredients into a container and mix well, add enough of the brown shellac to the starch to make a paste. After it has been applied and dried, sandpaper the surface and rub with a soft cloth dampened in oil and thin shellac.

THE COPS HATE THIS TRICK

To stop seeing fingerprints on a freshly waxed surface, just rub a small amount of cornstarch into the surface. This will remove any excess wax and keep the surface from showing up any fingerprints or smudges.

FILLING CRACKS IN MAHOGANY

The following ingredients will be needed:

| 4 | Ounces of beeswax |
| 1 | Ounce of red lead |

Yellow ochre

Place the beeswax in a double boiler and melt then add the red lead and enough ochre to produce the desired color. Remove from the heat and allow it to cool, Use the mixture before it hardens and is warm enough to work.

WOOD FURNITURE RENEWAL

The following ingredients will be needed:

1	**Part linseed oil**
1	**Part turpentine**

Place the ingredients into a small bowl and mix well. Using a woolen rag, rub a light coating on the furniture that needs restoring. Immediately dry off with another woolen cloth.

PAN THOSE LEGS
When painting, stripping or staining a table, place the legs in disposable pie pans to catch the drippings.

GRANDPA WISHES HE KNEW HOW TO GET RID OF YELLOW STAINS ON LIGHT WOOD

- Unfortunately as light wood furniture ages direct sunlight may cause areas of yellowing. Nothing can be done except to keep light-colored furniture out of the direct sunlight.

GRANDPA'S TIPS ON CHOOSING A WOOD STAIN

Gel stains

This is the easiest method for beginners to use since it adheres to vertical surfaces and will not run. It will not raise the grain but too many coats will cause darkening. The drawbacks are that it is expensive and difficult to clean up as well as having a limited numbers of colors.

Oil-based stains

This is the traditional stain, however, there are concerns about the effects of the petroleum vapors and the environment. It is best used to touch up or do re-staining. It is permanent and will not fade, doesn't raise the grain but additional coats will darken. It is somewhat difficult to clean up, has an unpleasant odor and is flammable.

One-step stain & finish

This is the fastest method of finishing wood if you are not too fussy about the exact color that is achieved. Used mainly on door and window casings with good uniform results and will not raise grain. The final color is not too deep and will not build up the color.

Penetrating oil stains

These products protect wood as well as stain it and may be called Danish oils or rubbing oils. Good for high traffic areas that have attractive grains. It is easy to apply and doesn't raise the grain. Additional coats will darken and the colors are limited. Somewhat expensive oil!

Water-based stains

They are replacing oil-based stains since they are easier to use and safe for the environment. Used on floors and most other woodwork as well as children's toys. It is easy to clean; safe to use and additional coats will darken. It raises wood grain and will not penetrate too deep but does require a finish coat.

GRANDPA'S TIPS ON CHOOSING CLEAR FINISHES

Danish or tung oil

Can penetrate the wood and harden the grain with moderate resistance to stains, scratches and burns. Very good resistance to water and alcohol! Usually hand-rubbed and will need 2-3 applications to get a deep, rich color. Dries in about 8-12 hours.

Lacquer

Fast drying finish that will produce a smooth finish and is used on the majority of furniture. Best to spray many thin coats and allow the last coat to dry out for 2-3 days before rubbing with fine steel wool. Comes in a wide variety of finishes!

Natural-resin varnish

Will resist scuff marks and is available in many colors as well as clear and used for outdoor applications. Best to apply with a varnish, cheesecloth or artists brush. Should be applied thin and used with the recommended solvent. The finish is from high-gloss to satin to low-gloss. The drying time is 2-3 days and maybe a little more if it humid.

Shellac

Will form a hard finish, however, it is easily dissolved by alcohol and can be easily damaged by water. It is available in either clear or pigmented! Best to use a small brush with a chisel tip and thin with alcohol solvent. Make sure that you protect the top with a coating of paste wax. The finish will come out with a high gloss and if desired can be dulled with steel wool. Drying time is about 2¾ hours and you should allow 3-4 hours between coats.

Oil-based polyurethane

Has good mar-resistant qualities; durable but will yellow over time, however, if used with a fairly dark stain, the yellowing is not that noticeable. Apply with a natural-bristle brush and be sure that it has a chisel point or use a lamb's wool applicator. The finish is from high glossy to dull sheen. It has a drying time of 1-2 hours and make sure that you leave about 12 hours between coats.

Water-based polyurethane

Not as durable as oil-polyurethane, however, it will not yellow, but will need additional coats later on. Apply with brush or use a lamb's wool applicator. The finish is from high-gloss to satin. Allow 3 hours for the first coat to dry and 5-8 hours for the second coat to dry.

DON'T SHAKE ME UP

To reduce and even eliminate bubbles appearing in the varnish or shellac, don't shake the can and be sure and remove any excess varnish from the bristles by gently tapping and not wiping them against the rim of the can.

SMOOTH IT OUT BETWEEN COATS

Always allow varnish or shellac to fully harden then use fine sandpaper or fine steel wool to level the surface between the coats.

This will also help the next coat adhere better. Clean off all dust and any debris before applying the next coat.

VENETIAN BLINDS

GIVE THEM A SHOWER

If you want to clean your blinds with the least amount of effort, just hand them in the shower and let the shower do the work. They will even drip dry there.

CHAPTER 4

AMARA

THE KIDS ROOMS

BEDDING

GENERAL INFORMATION:

Since children tend to play in the dirt, climb trees and play many games that lead to them becoming dirty and carrying dirt and allergens into the home it is important to clean the bedding in a child's room frequently. Grandpa keeps a spare room just for the grandchildren when they sleep over.

BUGS GALORE

Wash the bedding at least once a week in 130°F water. Place a mattress cover on the mattress that will not allow dust mites to get into the bedding. Mite-proof mattress covers are readily available. About 45% (about 44 million homes) of all bedding in the United States contains dust mites.

NIGHTY NIGHT

For babies the crib mattress should be firm and should be tight-fitting. Make sure that the bedding cannot be dislodged. For older children, always purchase a new mattress that has good support. Never purchase a used mattress under any circumstances.

CARPETING

GENERAL INFORMATION:

The carpeting is capable of holding many allergens as well as the bedding and should be washed and vacuumed regularly. The carpet is also housing a number of biological pollutants that may be coming from the chemicals used in the manufacture of the carpet.

DESIGNING SPACE FOR CHILDREN

GENERAL INFORMATION:

INFANTS & TODDLERS

- ❖ Need safe spaces that can be explored.
- ❖ Must have sturdy furniture.
- ❖ Toys that keep their interest for prolonged period.
- ❖ Constant supervision.
- ❖ Toys that is safe for their age group.

PRESCHOOLERS

- ❖ Need adequate open space to play in.
- ❖ Furnishings should be sized for the child and their environment.
- ❖ Toys or learning equipment must relate to their age group.
- ❖ Should be responsible for their room and space.
- ❖ Have a safe area for them to explore and to promote their independence.

ELEMENTARY AGE CHILDREN

- ❖ Area to study and complete projects.
- ❖ Board to display their artwork and special school projects.
- ❖ Safe storage for collections.
- ❖ Area for special pets.
- ❖ A degree of privacy.

TEENAGERS

- ❖ Privacy.
- ❖ Area where they can be with friends.
- ❖ Computer desk and bookshelves.
- ❖ Ability to organize their own space and belongings.

ELECTRICAL SAFETY

GENERAL INFORMATION:
All electrical outlets in young children's rooms should be covered with a plate that utilizes the screws in the original plate to secure the plate. Cords to lamps need to be secured to the outlet with a special device found in hardware stores for that purpose.

DO NOT USE PUSH-IN PLASTIC SOCKET COVERS!

FIRE SAFETY RULES

GENERAL INFORMATION:
The importance of teaching kids fire safety and what to be aware of around the home or what to do in a fire emergency is very important. Fires in the home, while not common occurrences; do cause thousands of injuries and death to children every year.

Children are at risk from fire dangers and are not aware of them and what to do when various problems arise. Different rooms and times of the day relate to a variety of dangers. In a school setting many of the factors relating to fire safety are not taken seriously enough because of the number of students in the class and distractions. Most fires occur between midnight and 6AM.

- ❖ Don't allow children to play in the kitchen when parents are cooking since hot water can be spilled, a range top may be hot or an oven may have a hot door.
- ❖ Kids should only cook when an adult is present.
- ❖ Never allow children to wear long sleeves when cooking.
- ❖ If food catches fire in a pot, don't move it, just cover it and turn off element.
- ❖ Always sleep with bedroom door closed so that heat and smoke won't hamper your escape.
- ❖ If there is smoke stay close to the floor and crawl to window or exit.
- ❖ Never hide so that firefighters can find you.
- ❖ Have an escape ladder in your room if bedroom is on

second floor.
- ❖ Practice home escape plan.
- ❖ Never leave a child alone in a room where there is a candle burning or a lit fireplace.
- ❖ Know what the smoke alarm sounds like with a test.

STEAMING THE NAP UP

Indentations from furniture can be raised back to its original level by using a steam iron. Hold the iron just above the indentation (don't touch the carpet) and allow the steam to penetrate the area. The carpet nap should rise back up again. If this doesn't work, place an ice cube on the area overnight.

FURNITURE

A GOOD SEPARATION
The slats and spindles in a baby's crib should be spaced no more that 2 3/8th apart. Be sure that there are no slats missing or the baby will escape. Also, there should be no more than 1" between the edge of the mattress and the crib wall.

BUNK'EM-UP
Bunk beds are not recommended for children under the age of 6.

LOCATION, LOCATION, LOCATION
A child's bed can be placed anywhere in the room as long as it is not near the window. Children have broken windows with their feet by accident more often than most people realize.

That's one thing we have over cats!

HERE KITTY KITTY
Pets tend to leave a number of potential allergens around the room. These include hair, dead skin, saliva, urine or fecal drops, dander and even pollens from outside. Cats are actually more high risk than dogs when it comes to dander, hair and allergens.

DANGER LURKS IN A LOCKED TOYBOX

The toy chest should never be the type that locks when closed. There should not be any type of a catch on the chest. However, the chest needs to have a safety hinge installed so that it does not close on the child's fingers.

LOOK OUT BELOW

Make sure that the dresser you purchase has drawer stops so that the drawer does not come out easily and fall on the child.

PETS IN THE BEDROOM

GENERAL INFORMATION:

Pets are capable of causing allergic reactions in susceptible children or adults. If your child suffers from allergies or symptoms that may be related to airborne allergens then your family pet may be the problem. Many pets sleep or interact for many hours in your child's bedroom. The proteins from animal droppings are capable of sensitizing children and may cause an allergic reaction or an asthmatic attack. If you think that a pet is the problem verify it with your family physician with allergy tests.

GRANDMA'S PET RULES

1. Leave the pet outside if possible and play with them there and change clothing before going in the house.
2. Wash the pet regularly, however, this only provides a temporary solution. Pets can be bathed once a week.
3. If the problem was identified as being related to the pet and the pet is now living outside, be sure and thoroughly clean the home including the walls, steaming the carpet and upholstered furniture and removing any bedding and dishes the animal used.
4. Wash any clothing that had contact with the pet.
5. If all else fails, find the pet a good home.
6. Remove all of the pet's toys from the house.
7. Wash all children's stuffed animals.
8. Keep pets away from any fabric-covered furniture.
9. If you suspect that the pet is causing allergies, make the bedroom a "pet-free" zone.

ROCK-A-BYE-PET

Pet is sleeping on the bed. Many people like their pets sleeping with them on the bed. When the weather is cold, they like having the warmth of a pet alongside them. Best to have a washable cover on the area that the pet sleeps on to catch the dirt, dander and hair.

SAFETY & TOYS

GENERAL INFORMATION:

Every year hundreds of children are injured or killed by toys! Parents must realize that there are dangers in allowing certain age children to play with certain toys. Supervision is necessary even with toys for some older children. While manufacturers try to produce products that are safe, it is almost impossible to produce a product that will be 100% safe for all children. Unfortunately, when a problem is found after manufacture it is sometimes too late to pull the product from shelves until after the children have been injured.

YOU BETTER BEWARE, YOU BETTER CARE............

Problems relate to choking on small parts, strangulation, loud noises that affect hearing, toxic materials in toys, and even projectiles. The law requires labeling of choking hazards in toys for small children. Be sure and look for the label.

Nobody's here, I guess I'll eat the toys!

GRANDPA'S TOY RULES

❖ Supervise children when you give them any toy with a cord or piece of elastic attached to it. Yo-yos can be dangerous depending on the age group using the toy. Strangulation and injuries to eyes, face and neck have been reported using yo-yo water balls.

❖ Try not to purchase toys that create too much noise. About 15% of children between the ages of 6-17 are presently showing signs of hearing losses.

❖ Be aware that some plastic mouthing toys may contain harmful chemicals from a group of chemicals called "phthalates." Craft clays and play cosmetics may pose a problem.

❖ If buying on the Internet, be sure that the warning labels are displayed on the web site. Almost 75% of toy sellers do not show the label. Check with www.recalls.com

❖ Hand-me-down toys may not be in good condition and pose a risk factor.

❖ Never give a small ball with a diameter less than 1.75 inches to a child under 3 years of age. Look for the choking hazard label.

- ❖ Balloons at a party can be a potential choking hazard.
- ❖ Toys in vending machines may not display a warning label.
- ❖ Projectile toys are rated to be amongst the most dangerous on the market.
- ❖ Do not allow a child to reach a crib mobile.

AND AWAY WE GO…………….
Injuries occur frequently from scooters. Be sure and purchase safety gear for scooter, bike and skates.

FREEZE THE LITTLE BUGGERS
To keep stuffed animals free from dust mites place the stuffed animal in a large plastic bag and place the bag into the freezer for 24 hours once a month.

CHOKE TEST

Use a cardboard toilet paper roll and place the toy into the tube. If it goes into the tube it is too small for children under 3 or older children if they place objects in their mouth frequently.

STORAGE

GOING DOWN UNDER
Try and use the space under the child's bed for storage. The easiest way is to use drawers that are made to go under the bed with special rollers.

NO CLUTTER HERE
There an easy storage method so that a child's room does not look cluttered all the time. Just use plastic lidded storage boxes, which can be stacked and make great storage containers.

UP, UP, AND AWAY
There are many items that can be hung from the ceiling or special shelves that hang from the ceiling can be easily installed.

WINDOW COVERINGS

GENERAL INFORMATION:

Pull cords from window coverings have become a concern in relation to children strangling. Almost 200 deaths have been reported from children strangling on pull cords. Most deaths have been in children under the age of five.

THE HANGING CORD

Deaths are caused by cribs being placed to close to the cords. Young children who are left alone in rooms with hanging cords or climbing on furniture to look out windows.

GRANDPA'S SUGGESTIONS FOR A SAFE ROOM

- ❖ If you have horizontal blinds you need to cut the cord above the tassel, remove the equalizer buckle and add a separate tassel and the end of each cord. You could also cut the cord above the equalizer buckle then add a breakaway tassel, which will come undone if a child becomes entangled in the loop.
- ❖ If you have pleated or cellular shades leave the cord near the head rail in place. Cut the cord just above the tassel and add an additional tassel at the end of each cord. If the shades expose a loop cord when raised, be sure and keep the cord above a level that a child can reach.
- ❖ If you have vertical blinds, a continuous loop system or drapery cords you will need to install a cord tie-down device. It should be permanently attached and you should have the tie-down attached to floor. Wall or window jamb.
- ❖ If cords can be affixed so that they are never in the reach of children some of the above measures are not necessary.

CHAPTER 5

GRANDPA LOVES PETS

BATHING

GENERAL INFORMATION:

It is best to brush your pet before giving them a bath to get all the tangles out and any debris that is caught in their fur. Also be sure and avoid getting water in pet's ears since they could easily get an infection.

WHOOOOOPS

If your dog keeps slipping in the bathtub, be sure and place a rubber mat in the bathtub for the pet to stand on. Only use that mat for the pet.

HAIR WE GO AGAIN

To keep dog hair from clogging up the drain, cut a piece from an old screen and place it over the drain. You can also use a tea strainer if it is a small drain opening.

BIRD FEEDERS & HOUSES

CLEANING PLASTIC TUBE BIRD FEEDERS

Use a long-handled bottlebrush, hot water and a small amount of liquid detergent. Be sure and allow it to dry thoroughly after it has been rinsed. Never use bleach or any harsh chemical or the slightest residue could make the birds sick or kill them.

DOES THE COLOR OF THE FEEDER MAKE A DIFFERENCE

The color of a bird feeder will not make a difference as to which bird will feed from it. However, you will have better luck attracting birds with a feeder that is a neutral color.

GRANDPA'S SECRETS TO ATTRACTING BIRDS

BARN SWALLOW

These birds like an area where there is available water and mud and you must provide straw for their nests. They like a 6"X6" shelve for their nesting support and it needs to be 8-12 feet above the ground. They like eaves and well-protected areas.

BLUEBIRD

These birds like a birdbath that is high enough off the ground so that cats can't get to it. They prefer mulberry, holly, blueberry, wild cherry and Virginia creeper plants to munch on. They are fussy about their birdhouses and they would prefer a 5"X5"X8" birdhouse with 1¾" entry holes about 6 inches above the floor. If you place the nest 5 feet off the ground it will discourage the sparrows; who prefer nest that are higher up.

CHICKADEE

They prefer a diet of peanut butter, suet, sunflower seeds and some breadcrumbs. Their birdhouse should be 4"X4"X8" with the holes 1 1/8th inches and should be 6 inches above the floor. The house needs to be 8-15 feet high.

I'm helping grandpa

KESTREL

Wild birdseed is their favorite, a good mix will do. Their birdhouse should be 8"X8"X12" with a 3 inch hole that is 9-12 inches above the floor. It should be at least 10 feet above the ground but not more than 30 feet.

KINGLET

Prefers to eat suet, wild birdseed, cracked nuts and raw peanuts. Likes to nest in conifers preferably near the northern gardens.

Grandpa loves birds!

MOCKINGBIRD (from the hill)

These birds are fussy and insist on a nice birdbath and attractive surroundings. They prefer to eat crab apples, cherry, blueberries, grapes and blackberries. However, they won't turn down a meal of dogwood, pasture rose, red cedar, elderberry, mulberry, manzanita and Virginia creeper. Mockingbirds like a nice birdbath!

OWL (old hooty)

Prefers to nest in large shade trees, oak trees or conifers. If they find a dead tree with a hollow hole they will reside there before almost any other location. They are night hunters and eat rodents and prefer a grassy area to hunt in.

OWL (barn)

They are fussy and require that you build them a nesting box 10"X18"X16" that has a 6 inch opening and about 4 inches from the floor. They dine on rodents and small animals and like an open field or pasture nearby.

OWL (saw-whet)

You will need to build a nesting box that is 6"X6"X10" that has a 2¾" entry hole that is 8 inches above the floor. The house needs to be securely fastened 15-20 feet above the ground.

I do give a hoot about a nice home

OWL (screecher)

Their home must be 8"X8"X14" and have a 3 inch hole. The house must be about 12-30 feet off the ground and must be in a secluded area since they like their privacy.

PHOEBE

These birds require a nesting platform that is about 6-8 inches square and 8-12 feet off the ground. They would prefer to be under an eave or in any protected area.

PURPLE MARTIN

These are apartment dwellers but don't put the apartment house up until the Martin's arrive or the starlings will move in. You will need 15-20 small apartments measuring 6"X6"X6" with the entry hole about 2¾ inches and 1 inch from the floor. The birdhouse should be 15-20 feet off the ground. They eat wild birdseed and insects with a worm or two for dessert.

TITMOUSE

This bird will do anything for a doughnut but also loves to eat suet, nuts, sunflower seeds, peanut butter and breadcrumbs. The bird likes to be around elderberry, wild strawberry, pine, beech, mulberry and pine. The birdhouse needs to be 4"X4"X8" and have a 1¾ inch entry hole about 6 inches off the floor. The house ideally needs to be 8-15 feet off the ground.

WARBLER

Prefers nice landscaping and pleasant surroundings (fussy bird). They will go crazy for mulberry and especially raspberries but also like wild rose, barberry, hedge, privet, grapevines, current, elder, which provide additional nesting sites.

WREN

The birdhouse must be 4"X4"X6" with 1 inch holes for entry and the holes should be about 4 inches off the floor. The birdhouse should be 8-10 feet high.

GRANDPA BUILDS A BIRDHOUSE

Build a house & the birds will come

- Don't bother with a perch since they are rarely used.
- Drill some ventilation holes just under the roofline and a few in the floor for drainage.
- The house should blend in with the scenery and not be frilly.
- The inside should be rough and even if bark is showing it is best.

- Use screws not nails to insure the stability and quality.
- Hollowing out a small log works great as a birdhouse.
- The roof must be waterproof.
- The dimensions should be for the bird for which you are building it.
- Never use screw eyes to hang the house up since they will loosen in time.
- Hinge the bottom so that it will be easy to clean. The house needs to be cleaned after the birds leave.
- You can be creative as long as the house does not look out-of-place in its surroundings.
- If you are not handy, buy one in your garden shop.

PROBLEM BIRDS

If birds are a problem it is best to identify which bird is really causing the problem. Only three birds are really bad pests that will damage a garden enough to warrant going after them. They are crows, starlings, woodpeckers and blackbirds. However, damage that looks like birds are doing it may be from raccoons or other animals.

BUZZ AROUND, BUZZ AROUND

If you want to keep all birds away from your garden and plants, try using a piece of commercial buzzing or humming tape. This tape is stretched across an area near the garden and will make noise when the wind blows to scare away the birds.

ORDER A CAT SCARECROW

Make a cutout of a cat and decorate it to look like the real thing. If birds are a problem this works great.

THE OLD "MOVEABLE HEAD" HOOTY OWL

This really works better than almost any other means of keeping all birds away. Make sure that you purchase an owl with a movable head. When the wind blows the head moves around the body.

DOG HOUSES

GENERAL INFORMATION:
To keep fleas out of the doghouse, try sprinkling salt in all the cracks and around the corners. Also, by placing fresh pine needles under the blanket or mat should solve the problem. A piece of foam rubber under the bedding will deter fleas as well as a few drops of lavender oil in the bedding.

GRANDPA BUILDS A DOGHOUSE

Items Needed:

Hammer
Nails (roofing & misc.)
Shingle utility knife
Pressure-treated lumber

Quality plywood
Shingles
Circular saw
Tape measure & pencil

 Measure the dog and determine what size doghouse they will need. Do not make the house too big or it will be difficult for the dog to retain body heat in cold weather.

- Start by making a square base frame using four 2X6 boards that are nailed together at the ends. Be sure and use quality materials for this project.
- Next cut a piece of ¾-inch plywood that will fit over the frame. Be sure that it is flush with the frame's edges.
- Use a quality exterior paint and paint the plywood base before going any further.
- To complete the floor you will need to nail the plywood to the frame along every side. Be sure it is sturdy!
- The wall can be framed with 2X4 studs that need to be cut to the proper size for the house then dry-fit the frames.

I hope he measures me right this time

- Once you are satisfied that you have the correct size, nail the walls together. Don't forget to add center studs for the side and rear walls for added support. When placing the stud on the rear wall, the stud should be about 2-inches off center giving you easy access when securing the roof strut.
- Measure and cut ¾-inch plywood for the outside frames and make sure that the edges are flush.
- Now dry-fit the finished walls then nail them into place through the bottom of the wall frame. If you toenail each corner it will provide increased stability.
- Be sure that the entrance is large enough for the dog to enter easily, but not too big or it will allow too much cold air to enter.
- When attaching the roof you will need to cut struts, ridge boards and rafters from 2X4 boards. The height of the roof struts will depend on the desired roof pitch and the size of the dog. The most common pitch is 45^0, which means that the ends of all rafters must be cut at a 45^0 angle as well.
- Next, you will need to center the front roof strut on the top edge of the wall frame and nail it into place from the underside of the frame. If you toenail the strut it will provide additional reinforcement.
- Center the rear roof strut on the top of the back wall frame then carefully nail it into place.
- Cut the top ridge board to the length of the doghouse including the amount you desired for the overhang.
- Position the ridge board on the struts then nail it into place then cut three rafters for each side to the desired length. Be sure that the ends of the rafters are mitered to the angle that is determined by the pitch of the roof.
- Use the corner of the doghouse to mark notches on the rafters where they will meet the top of the wall frames so that they will fit snuggly over the top of each wall.
- Be sure and hold the rafters making them even with the ridge boards and then determine the angle before cutting the boards and nailing them into place.
- Attach the bottom of every rafter to the wall where the notch meets the wall frame.
- Next cut four 2X4 boards. You will need two for each side

that will fit horizontally between the rafters then nail them into place.

♦ These boards will eliminate the gap between the overhang and the sidewalls.

♦ The fascia board will be cut from ¾-inch plywood and will match the overhang on the sides of the doghouse. Nail the fascia boards to the bottom ends of the rafters.

♦ The overhang rafters should be cut from pressure-treated wood then painted providing some protection from the weather. The overhang rafters should now be nailed to the ends of the ridge board and side fascia.

♦ Use quality ¾-inch plywood to cover the roof.

♦ The front and back of the roof openings need to be filled in with triangular plywood sheets cut exactly to fit the space.

♦ The shingles should now be attached to the roof. It would be best to use 12 inch gray sheet shingles. These will absorb less heat than darker shingles and keep the doghouse cooler in the summer months. Always start from the bottom and work up when installing shingles.

♦ To do the job efficiently, mark a horizontal chalk line 11 inches from the bottom of the roof edge. The shingles are 12 inches in length and it is best if they hang over by about 1 inch on the sides.

♦ Now mark a vertical chalk line 35 inches from the front edge of the roof since the shingle sheets are 36 inches giving you a hang over of 1 inch on the front.

♦ The next line is a vertical line that is drawn 29 inches back from the front edge. If you have two vertical lines it will help to establish two "starting points" for the shingle sheets and create offset rows: the odd numbered rows will begin at the 35 inch mark and the even numbered rows will begin at the 29 inch mark.

♦ The row on the bottom should be two shingles thick. Be sure and turn the first layer upside down. This will place the darker portion of the shingle sheet hanging over the edge and the second layer needs to be positioned right side up to match all subsequent rows.

- When all the shingles are nailed down in place, use a knife with a single-edge razor blade and trim the sides even with the edges of the plywood roof.
- To cover the exposed ridge board, you will need to cut shingle sheets into single shingles then place them sideways over the top making sure that they overlap. The single shingles should be tapered on the back end so that the black area doesn't peek out from under the shingles on top.

Hope he finishes it before winter

EXOTICS

TURN UP THE THERMOSTAT
Cold-blooded pets such as lizards and snakes need more than one heat source? To keep cold-blooded pets healthy, you should have two different heat sources.

BIRD FEATHERS
Birds do lose their feathers and will re-grow their feathers once a year.

FOOD DISHES

GENERAL INFORMATION:
Many of the pet's health problems are directly related to the cleanliness of their environment. If food and water dishes are not kept clean it could affect your pet's health.

SET UP A SCHEDULE

Pets should always be fed from their own dishes to avoid competition for food.

COME BACK HERE

Pet dishes tend to move easily on the floor when the pet is eating. To stop the problem, just place a rubber mat under the dishes.

ANTS ARE EATING THE PET FOOD

Place the food dish in a pan of water or sprinkle some crushed bay leaves around the bowl. The water works the best, since some pets will eat anything!

PET DOOR

GRANDPA'S HINTS FOR INSTALLING A DOGGIE DOOR

- ❖ Before getting started, be sure and measure to determine the proper size door for your pet. The opening should be just a little wider than the widest part of your pet. The height should be 2 inches above the pet's shoulders.
- ❖ Buy a pet-door kit from PetCo™. Use a level to position the template and tape the template to the door.
- ❖ Use a hammer and nail to mark the door at the crosshairs on the template. These will be the 4 corners of the frame and will hold the screws.
- ❖ Remove the template and use a straightedge and draw a cut line between each of the corner marks. Drill through each corner with a ¾" drill bit.
- ❖ Cut along the lines with a jigsaw fitted with a woodcutting blade. For metal doors, use special cutting blade.
- ❖ Drill pilot holes through the door at the points that were marked for the frame screws.
- ❖ Set the door in place and attach the interior and exterior frames with screws.

PROTECTING YOUR FURNITURE

TIMBBBBBER
If you have a dog that likes the taste of you're furniture legs, paint the legs with oil of cloves. This will not hurt the furniture legs and will stop dogs and kids from chewing.

AH CHIHUAHUA
To stop cats from chewing on you're furniture legs, just place a small amount of crushed red pepper into a glass of water and allow it to stand overnight. Sprinkle a very small amount on the areas you are having a problem with. Best to place the liquid underneath any upholstered area so that it won't stain. It will be just as effective.

RABBITS

You can try and keep me out!

PUT UP A BARRIER
A very effective method of keeping rabbits away from your vegetable garden is to build a cylindrical barrier enclosure. It should be about 3 feet high around all trees and plants and use ¾ inch hardware cloth then bury the bottom of the enclosure 3 inches below the ground.

Make sure there is 1-2 feet between the barrier and the plants. You can also build a 3-foot high fence of chicken wire since rabbits are not good climbers.

SCRATCHING POSTS

GENERAL INFORMATION:
Cats rarely scratch furniture or use a scratching post to sharpen their claws.

They scratch mainly for communication letting other cats or people know where they are and want attention. When they are outside they leave the marks to tell other cats that this is their territory.

I'm tired of being ignored!

THE BORED CAT
Cats normally scratch for attention; be sure and purchase a number of scratching posts and place them in areas that the cat frequents or scratches. Scratching posts are easy to make with a few pieces of wood and an old piece of carpeting.

Don't try and force a cat to use the post, just play with their favorite toys around or over the post.

GRANDPA BUILDS A CAT SCRATCHING POST

Items Needed:
Cedar Post about 30 inches high and 4 inches in diameter
50 feet of non-oiled 3/8-inch sisal rope
4-inch plywood for base about 16X16 inches in diameter
Wood glue
Stain or paint and brush
Tools & circular saw
Gloves & mask

- ❖ Make sure that the wood used is dry.
- ❖ Wear gloves when you wrap the rope around the post. Nail the rope to the top of the post then use wood glue to attach the rope. Be sure that there are no spaces, so wrap the rope tight. Nail the rope to the bottom after you glue it down.
- ❖ Make sure you sand down any rough areas.
- ❖ The base must be very heavy so that the post will not tip over easily.
- ❖ Make sure you use at least 4 nails when attaching the post to the base.
- ❖ You may have to show the cat how to use the post a few times.

CAT REPAIR KIT NEEDED

To protect an area that the cat has already damaged, cover the area with plastic making it less appealing. Place a scratching post next to the area or place some oil of clove on the wood.

SNAKES

SNAKE-PROOF FENCE

Best to use a very heavy galvanized screen about 36 inches wide and use ¾ inch mesh. You will need to bury the lower edges 2-3 inches in the ground and then slant it outward from the bottom to the top at a 30-degree angle. Your supporting stakes should be inside the fence and the gates must be tightly fitted. This is an expensive method if you have a large yard. Best to just fence in your children's play area.

WATER

GENERAL INFORMATION:

Pets should not be allowed to drink stale or dirty water. Pet's water needs to be changed everyday. If you feel that the tap water is not safe for you to drink then don't give it to your pet. Buying a gallon jug of water just for your pet is inexpensive.

> **All driveway deicing chemicals; are toxic to your pet's feet. Driveway salt will also burn their feet and if they lick their feet it may make them ill.**

CHAPTER 6

LIVING ROOM

CARPETING

GENERAL INFORMATION:

Carpeting can provide luxury, fashion and will insulate the flooring in most climates. Choosing just the right carpet for your needs can be a chore. Carpeting is also not recommended if you have allergies to dust, mold and pollens since they tend to be very difficult to remove even with regular cleaning.

CARPET MAGIC

If your carpet has an indentation, you can remove it by laying a damp towel over the depressed area and pressing down with a warm iron. The depression should be gone by the time the towel dries fully.

I HATE BAREFOOT, GET OFF ME!

Your skin releases natural oils and walking on carpeting in bare feet can leave traces of those oils in the carpet. These oils have the tendency to attract dust. Best to wear socks or slippers.

PATCH-EM-UP

GRANDPA HAS THE ANSWER TO REAPIR CARPETING

- ❖ If the carpet only has a small burn area or other small damage, use a small pair of manicuring scissors and cut away the damaged fibers. Be sure and feather out the side areas when you are working so that the area is not too noticeable.
- ❖ When you patch the area, make sure that you use a pattern. Pick something that will cover the damaged area, possibly a small block of wood. Using a very sharp utility knife to cut around the block then remove the damaged area.

SHARPENING TIP FOR UTILITY KNIFE

To easily sharpen a utility knife, just run the blade across a smooth concrete block about 10 times should do the trick. This will put a sharp edge on the blade.

❖ Using that pattern: cut a perfect piece from a piece of scrap carpeting. If you don't have a piece, look for a piece in a closet you can cut from or under a piece of furniture that will never be moved.

❖ Place the patch to the floor with a piece of double-sided carpet tape and cut it to fill the hole. Peel the backing off the tape and put into place. Be sure and match the pattern if possible. Press it firmly into place.

JUST A SHAMPOO, NO HAIRCUT

When grandma wants the carpet shampooed, grandpa heads for the supermarket and rents a big carpet cleaner. These heavy, duty machines will prevent the soaking of the carpet and reduce the possibility of shrinkage IF used as instructed. However, steam cleaning is still the preferred method.

TYPES OF CARPET WASHING

1. **Steam Cleaning** – This method: is recommended by all major carpet manufacturers, since it is done without the use of harsh brushes. The hot water is shot into the carpet to loosen the dirt and grime and then vacuumed out.

2. **Shampooing** – Commonly, used by the do-it-yourselfers since the equipment is easily rented at most supermarkets or home stores. It has rotary brushes, which work the shampoo into the carpet and can be vacuumed out when it is dry. The problem is that the vacuum used may not be powerful enough to get all, the residue out of the carpet leaving the carpet dull and lifeless.

3. **Dry Cleaning** – This method uses a powerful granule or liquid solvent that is sprayed on then mechanically brushed into the carpet. It is then vacuumed out, however, it is not good at getting out a bad stain as well as being hard on the carpet fibers.

TOILET BRUSH YOUR CARPET

The corners of a carpeted room are the hardest places to clean and usually get permanently dirty if not cared for. The vacuum can't reach these areas but all you have to do is to purchase an extra toilet bowl brush and use it in the corners.

LEG PROTECTOR

When you are washing the carpet, be sure and protect the wooden furniture legs from the chemicals and water. Just place small plastic bags over the legs and tape them. This will also make it easier to just move the furniture out of the way and return it immediately without hurting the carpet or the furniture.

STEEL WOOL TO THE RESCUE

If you have a surface burn on the carpet that is not too deep, just use a piece of steel wool to lightly scrub the burned area from the fibers.

CANDLE WAX REMOVER

Scrape off as much of the wax as you can using a dull knife blade. Cover the area with paper towel and then iron the spot using the synthetic setting. The paper towel will show through the wax, remove it and repeat until all the wax is out of the carpet.

EENIE MEENIE MINEE MOE

Most people are not familiar with the types of carpet materials and padding, which is best for their needs, however grandpa is an expert in the field.

There are four basics to carpeting that need to be considered

> **Fiber** – This in the carpet material itself. Single carpet fibers are spun together to make two, three or four-ply yarn, which is then attached to a woven backing.
> **Pile** – The height of the fiber.
> **Density** – This is the amount of fiber tufts per square inch. Carpet weight and quality will refer to ounces per square inch.

The more ounces per square inch the better the carpet.

Texture – This refers to the way the fibers are looped, whether twisted or cut to provide texture.

Types of carpet fibers:

Wool – This offers a deep, rich look and has excellent resilience and durability. It is naturally stain resistant but requires a high level of maintenance.

Nylon – The most common carpet material and has the strongest fibers. Excellent for high traffic areas and is the most durable of the synthetics. It is one of the easiest carpets to clean and is soil and mildew resistant.

Olefin – Produced originally for outdoor carpeting and basements since it resists mildew, water damage and static.

Polyester – Is very wear-resistant but not as good as nylon. Tends to shred easier than most carpets but is resistant to moisture and mildew.

Acrylic – Closer to wool than any other synthetic and mainly used for commercial offices. It is soil and mildew resistant and less likely to fade from direct sunlight.

Be sure and foot-test the padding under a piece of your carpet before choosing the padding. Remember thick padding may not be the best for your location.

BE TENDER NOW!
Carpet needs to be vacuumed regularly. Dirt in carpet acts like a piece of sandpaper.

OUT, OUT AND AWAY
Stains will set permanently if they are not removed quickly in many carpets.

GETTING A LITTLE DINGY OVER HERE
Brown areas; are usually caused by over-wetting that leaches vegetable dyes from the jute backing and produces a wick effect to the surface. The carpet must be professionally acid rinsed or topically sprayed with a solution of a souring agent.

TRAFFIC LANE AHEAD
These are dark traffic lane areas, which receive the highest amount of foot traffic. The damage is in the form of scratches and abrasions to the fibers, matting, flaring, or tip compression (cut pile). There is no way to repair the problem without replacing the area. If shoes are removed before coming in the home, these areas rarely show up.

GET OUT THE PAINTBRUSH
If you're carpet is losing its brightness. It may be caused by a poor quality, cleaning compound that was used on the carpet. Once this problem occurs, there is no way to reverse it.

SPRINKLE, SPRINKLE
If you want to sharpen up your carpet colors, try sprinkling a small amount of salt around. The salt provides a mild abrasive cleaning action that won't hurt the fibers.

AVOIDING A SHOCKING EXPERIENCE
To eliminate getting shocked when walking across the carpet, just leave a vase with water in every carpeted room.

THROW RUG SECRET
If you want to keep your throw rugs looking great all the time, just place them into the dryer between washings on a **NO-HEAT** setting.

DON'T HAVE TO NAIL THEM DOWN

To keep throw rugs in place, just use double-sided tape under the corners of the undersurface. It can't hurt the floor and works great.

VERY UPLIFTING

An easy method of raising the nap of a carpet after a piece of furniture has matted it down is to place an ice cube on the matted down area overnight.

DECORATIVE METAL

GENERAL INFORMATION:

A large number of furnishings now have decorative detains that are made from metal. These include substances such as ivory, brass, chromium, leather, marble, iron, etc.

GRANDPA KNOWS THE SECRETS TO CLEANING DIFFERENT STUFF

Aluminum

Wash with hot, soapy water and rinse well. Never use abrasives or cleansing powders. Strong soaps and detergents will cause pitting.

Brass, Copper, Bronze Fittings

Many fitting contain a lacquered coating to protect them from corrosion. They can only be cleaned with warm, soapy water and never polished or cleaned with an abrasive cleaner. Antique brass can be cleaned with a solution of boiled linseed oil.

Chrome Fittings

Only wipe with a soft damp cloth: since abrasives will wear off the plating material.

Gesso

This is a hard, plaster material that is molded to resemble carved wood or used in picture frames. Vacuuming is the best method. If an area really needs cleaning, try using a small piece of sliced lemon and gently rubbing the area then rinsing the area immediately with a solution of one tablespoon of baking soda mixed in one pint of warm water.

Ivory

Ivory tends to yellow when it is stored without a light source. Piano keys should never be closed up. Clean only with a mild soap and water solution and dry immediately.

Heavily Tarnished Leaded Pewter

Prepare a paste made from fine whiting and boiled linseed oil. Dip a small piece of 0000 steel wool into the paste and rub lightly on the pewter in one direction. This may not remove all the tarnish, but should make it look better.

Slate

Clean with a small amount of boiled linseed oil on a clean cloth then rub briskly.

DRAPERIES

TEMPERATURE CONTROL

Draperies can be utilized to help control the temperature in the house. When the weather is cool outside, you should open the drapes to allow sunlight to enter. Draw the drapes at night to keep the heat in. Be sure that the drapes do not block the heat vents.

NEED A PERMANENT ECLIPSE

Sunlight can have a negative effect on draperies. Constant exposure will damage the strength of the fibers. Best to line the draperies with a high quality lining to protect them.

POOR DRAPERIES

Household chemicals will harm draperies; especially fumes from chimneys, auto exhaust and cooking, which may combine with oxygen and cause deterioration of the fabrics.

TURN ON THE DE-HUMIDIFIER

The level of humidity in the air in the home will cause draperies to shrink or stretch.

DRIP, DRIP CAN CAUSE A PROBLEM

Window condensation marks on draperies are almost impossible to remove and should be avoided if possible.

DUSTING

TICKLE, TICKLE

Feather dusters tend to scatter dust rather than picking it up and holding it.

SPECIAL CARE NEEDED

When dusting silk plants and flowers, the best method is to use damp cloth then use a commercial silk cleaner. The cleaner is available at craft or floral shops.

DUSTING ODDS & ENDS

Knick-knacks are easier to place in the sink and wash instead of trying to dust them. Best to vacuum the tops of the books. Dusting is not very efficient no matter what you use.

I SMELL PRETTY………..

You can deodorize while dusting if you are using a duster, just try spraying the end with your favorite deodorizer.

TO DUST MOP OR ?

Dust mops are only effective if you vacuum the floor first. Never depend on the dust mop to do a complete job. Same with a sock, you have to vacuum the floor first. However, grandma used an old sock on her hand and then threw it into the washing machine with the other clothes, but only to do furniture.

GRANDPA METHOD OF CLEANING BOOKS

❖ Books get dirty and need to be cleaned. Always start at the top of the bookshelf and work down so that any dust will move to the lower books.

- When vacuuming dust covers, be sure and place a piece of cheesecloth over the end of the vacuum cleaner hose so that the suction will not remove any loose pieces of paper.
- If you have any smudges or spots, you should be able to erase them with a soft eraser called a "pink pearl." These can be obtained at any artists supply store or stationary store.
- If you have a large smudge, you will have to use "Opaline" from an artists supply store.

GONNA NEED STILTS

To reach those hard to reach locations, use a long artists brush and place furniture polish on the tips.

LESS IS BETTER

To reduce the amount of dust in the house, have your ductwork and air filter cleaned regularly.

A LITTLE OF THIS & A LITTLE OF THAT

You can make your own dusting oil by mixing three parts of light mineral oil mixed with one part of corn oil then add one drop of lemon or clove oil.

MONEY SAVER

Don't bother buying fancy dust, cloths that are treated to attract dust when all you have to do is to dip a piece of cheesecloth in a mixture of 2 cups of water and ¾ cup of lemon oil. Allow the cheesecloth to air dry and it will do just as good as the expensive ones.

GLASS-TOP TABLES

NO LINT MY LADY

After you clean a glass-top table, be sure and add a capful of fabric softener to a bucket of warm water then rinse the tabletop with the mixture. This will keep them lint-free and sparkling clean.

HARDWOOD FLOORING

GENERAL INFORMATION:

All hardwood flooring needs some type of protective coating to protect the surface of the wood. There are a number of chemical protectors that can be used depending on the wood floor you have in your home. Most are either oil-based varnishes or polyurethane.

PROTECTION A MUST

If you are going to try and place a protective coating on your wood floor you need to know what type of coating to put on. If possible bring a piece of the hardwood flooring to the store when purchasing the protective coating. Best describe the type of wood and the age of the wood and the coating presently on the wood to get the best protective coating. Also be sure and find out about the correct application method for the chemical chosen.

HOW DRY I AM..........

Make sure that you apply the proper number of coats or allowing a coat to dry fully before applying the next coat. Also, be sure and purchase the correct brushes, applicators and chemicals to do the job right.

GRANDPA RECOMMENDS THE MOST POPULAR FLOOR PROTECTORS

Oil-Based Varnishes:

This will provide a very tough and durable sealant and is capable of lasting the life of the floor if applied properly. It is expensive and does require additional coats and adequate drying time between coats.

Protect it or lose it!

Some older floors may not be usable for as long as 1-2 months and may need 3-4 coats. Commonly used on doors that may get wet.

Polyurethane:

This coating can be applied in two days and will provide a very hard water-based finish. The floor can be walked upon in about a week. Needs two coats to be really durable.

BLACK HEEL MARKS

To remove black rubber marks on wood floors, try using lemon juice or 0000 steel wool very lightly with the solvent-based wax you would ordinarily use.

? DARK SPOTS

If you see dark spots from alkaline substances, just apply vinegar to the area and allow it to remain for 4 minutes before removing with a damp cloth.

SCRATCHES & WORN SPOTS

Apply a small amount of wax with very fine steel wool. Make sure you apply the wax in the direction of the wood grain. Rub until the colors blend in.

SPECIAL CARE NEEDED

Clean hardwood floors weekly with just a damp mop. However, they should also be cleaned once a month using 2 ounces of white vinegar in a bucket of cool tap water. Just mop the wood and towel dry immediately. This should improve the luster of the floor.

MARBLE TOP FURNITURE & FLOORS

MY TOP ISN'T SHINY ANYMORE

If your marble top has lost some luster it may be caused by dust. Try wetting thee marble well then wash it with a mild detergent and use a soft brush. Never use an abrasive cleanser on marble. There is also a marble cleaner and polish that is available at most hardware stores.

You can also wet the marble surface and sprinkle the surface with a marble-polishing powder. Rub it in and then polish with a clean cloth. Putty powder (tin oxide) is recommended.

I'M NOT A CAR
A light coat of wax will protect the surface, but is not really necessary. Never wax white marble or it may turn yellow. A warm water bath with a mild detergent is only recommended twice a year. Make sure you wipe completely dry.

SEAL-EM-UP
Marble tops are very porous and should be sealed. If you spill a liquid on a marble surface it will need to be wiped up immediately or it may stain. If it does stain it will need a special treatment to repair the surface. The treatment may involve using a chemical and a buffer.

GRANDPA'S MARBLE RESTORATION TIPS

- ❖ Prepare a poultice of 6% hydrogen peroxide mixed with just enough flour to make it into a paste. You will need about 1 pound of the paste for every square foot of surface.
- ❖ Place the mixture on the surface of the marble and use a wooden spatula to spread it over the surface. Be sure that the thickness is about ¾ inches and that the mixture extends past the dirty area.
- ❖ Tape plastic over the area and allow it to remain for 48 hours then dampen the area and remove it with a wooden spatula.
- ❖ Rinse, the area with clean cool water then blot it off and let it dry.

GRANDPA'S MARBLE ENTRY HALL TIPS

MARBLE, THE TOUGHEST OF THE TOUGH, BUT BE GENTLE!
Marble is one of the toughest floor surfaces is basically naturally, compressed, crystallized limestone, that can range from somewhat porous to very compact. It can be polished to a high

shine and will remain that way with very little care almost forever.

The following solutions will clean and keep the marble shining with a minimum of effort. Strong detergents and abrasives should never be used on marble since they will dull the shine and may cause deterioration of the marble.

GREAT MARBLE CLEANING FORMULA
Mix together the following ingredients in a small bucket to make a paste:

> **6% hydrogen peroxide**
> **White all-purpose flour**

The thick paste mixture needs to be placed on the complete marble floor area; not just a soiled spot or the balance of the marble will not have the same clean color. Place enough of the mixture to heavily coat the floor and place plastic sheeting over the mixture, taping down all around the edges. Allow the mixture to sit on the marble for 36 hours, then carefully remove it with a plastic spatula and rinse the marble thoroughly with cool water.

REMOVING OIL STAINS FROM MARBLE
The following ingredients will be needed:

9 ¾	Ounces of cereal flour
13 ¾	Ounces of hydrochloric acid (use with care)
4	Ounces of chloride of lime
2	Teaspoons of turpentine

Wear gloves and a mask. Place all the ingredients into a glass or porcelain container and blend into a paste. Smear the paste on the stains and allow it to remain for 6-8 hours. Remove the paste with a brush or piece of soft leather. Polish the area after the stain has been removed. This formulation will remove grease from marble very easily.

A NON-RESILIENT FLOOR NEEDS TLC
This category of flooring includes ceramic tile, concrete, brick, and all types of stone flooring material.

Best to just clean stone and brick surfaces with a solution of vinegar and water (1 cup of vinegar to 1 gallon of water) whereas concrete needs to be cleaned with an all-purpose detergent or concrete cleaner. If tile is in bad shape and needs cleaning to remove ground in dirt and residues, the following formula will be needed otherwise just use a mild soap solution.

SPANISH TILE CLEANER & CONDITIONER
The following ingredients will be needed:

2 1/3	Cups of oleic acid
1	Tablespoon of triethanolamine (from drug store)
3	Cups of cool tap water

Place the ingredients into a double boiler and just heat; do not allow boiling. Remove from heat and beat with an electric mixer until the mixture becomes milky. Apply the mixture to the tile floors with a sponge and allow it to dry for 8-10 hours before rubbing off with a dry bath towel.

SILVERWARE

SLOWING DOWN TARNISH
If you place a small piece of chalk in a silver chest it will absorb moisture and slow tarnishing. Calcium carbonate (chalk) absorbs moisture very slowly from the air. If you break the chalk up and expose the rough surface it will be more efficient.

RUST PREVENTION
If you place a few mothballs, a piece of chalk, or a piece of charcoal in your toolbox you will never have any rust on the tools. If you don't use certain tools very often and they get rusty, just clean them with steel wool and then coat them with a thin coating of petroleum jelly.

SERIOUS TARNISH
If silver is too badly tarnished and silver polish won't remove it, you will have to try another method. If the following method does not work it would be best to have the silver re-plated.

Try sprinkling the silver with salt then rub it with a sponge that has been lightly dampened with white vinegar. The reaction should remove the tough tarnish without a problem.

DARK STAINS ON STAINLESS

The high mineral content of hard water and certain detergents or foods with a high salt content may cause stainless steel flatware to develop dark areas. To remove these dark spots, just use stainless polish. Remove the cleaner immediately to avoid damaging the flatware.

It will ruin the silver

DISHWASHER ALERT

Keep your good sterling silverware out of the dishwasher since many of the detergents use chemicals that may harm the surface of the silverware.

UPHOLSTERED FURNITURE

LEATHER

LEATHER LOCATION, LEATHER LOCATION

Make sure that you maintain at least two feet between the furniture and any heat source. Radiators, vents and fireplaces will cause the leather to dry out and crack. Direct sunlight will cause leather to fade over time.

YOU SPILLED OIL ON MY LEATHER

This is a serious problem since oil will eat the leather. Blot up as much of the oil before it has a chance to seep into the leather and keep dabbing it until all the oil is gone. The small amount that escapes should not be a problem and will seep into the leather.

HOW CLEAN I FEEL

There are only certain chemicals or cleaning solutions that can be used on leather. Use a mild solution of Ivory Liquid Soap on a clean wet sponge. Wash and rinse immediately and dry thoroughly. This should be done monthly.

Never use saddle soap, oils, abrasive cleaners, furniture polish, soaps, varnish or ammonia-based products. When cleaning leather, check for the direction of the grain (if its real leather) and clean in that direction.

LEATHER REVIVAL
If you want to revive the beauty of leather try beating two egg whites lightly, then applying the mixture to the leather with a soft sponge. Allow it to remain on for 3-5 minutes before cleaning off with a soft cloth, just dampened with clear warm water. Dry immediately and buff off any residues.

FABRIC

BAD STAIN, BAD STAIN
Stains on upholstered fabrics are difficult to remove. Mix ¾ teaspoon of a mild liquid detergent in a quart of warm water then beat with a hand mixer. Clean the area using only the suds and work on one small area at a time. Overlap areas to avoid spotting. Rinse with clean damp cloth and dry with a fan or hair dryer.

EL STINKO!
If the fabric gets an odor grandpa will just sprinkle baking soda on the area and allow it to remain for 3-4 hours before vacuuming it off.

WOOD FURNITURE

RETURN IT TO THE STORE
If you a table with one leg shorter than the other and the table wobbles just build up the short leg with layers of plastic wood. If you get it too tall, just sand it down to the right height.

A BAD JOINT (on a chair)
If a joint has become loose on a chair it may cause the piece of furniture to eventually fail. If possible, try and insert some glue (you don't need a lot) into the space and clamp it to hold it together. If possible, scrape out any old glue and clean as best as possible before applying the new glue.

PAIN IN THE GROOVE

To remove old paint from the grooves in turned wood, just use a string that has been saturated with a paint remover solvent. Try working the string back and forth until the paint loosens.

GETTING MESSY ON HERE

To remove the dried paint from a surface that has a varnish finish and has been waxed, just use a hair dryer on low heat and move it back and forth for a few seconds until it loosens up. Peel it off gently with a dull knife.

NEED SUNGLASSES

Direct sunlight will dry the wood out and may cause the color to bleach out.

HUMIDITY IS GETTING HIGH

Very moist air will damage the wood furniture.

GET THAT YUCKY STUFF OFF ME

To remove candle wax or chewing gum from wood furniture, just hold an ice cube over the wax or gum for a few seconds until it hardens. Remove with fingernails or a dull knife trying not to go into the surface.

DON'T BRING ME TO A BODY SHOP

A small dent or depression in wood can be repaired and raised back to their original level. Place several layers of clean damp fabric over the dent. Touch the fabric with a warm steam iron, which should cause the wood fibers to swell up and go back into place. It should go back to the same level as the area around it. If the wood fibers have been split, this will not work.

FILLER UP

If you need to repair a hole in a piece of wood, try adding a small amount of instant coffee to the spackling or a thick paste made from a laundry starch and warm, water.

A SALAD SOLUTION

If you run out of wood oil, try using mayonnaise. A very, light coating rubbed into the wood will help protect the finish. It should be rubbed in well and be sure not to leave a residue. Leftover tea is a beverage that can be used on wood furniture and also to clean varnished furniture.

CHAPTER 7

GARAGE

CARS

REMOVING TAR
The easiest and least expensive method is to use some sodium bicarbonate on a damp cloth. However, you can also use kerosene or a special tar remover from an auto supply store.

FROZEN LOX
If your car locks become frozen in the winter, just use a hairdryer on them for a few seconds.

BABY, IT'S COLD OUTSIDE...............
If you have trouble starting your car on cold mornings, the problem usually has nothing to do with the battery but with the oil. Freezing temperature tend to turn your oil into a thick syrup making your battery work harder to turn the engine over. Manufacturers make higher amp batteries that may help alleviate this problem or you may want to consider a heated blanket to keep the motor oil from becoming a semi-solid.

GIVE EM A SHOT
If your windshield wipers are smearing the windows, try wiping them with rubbing alcohol.

REFLECT ON THIS
Place reflector tape on anything that may be in your way at night in the garage if you do not have good lighting.

PAINT REMOVER
Paint can be removed from a car finish by using Benzol™.

MORE MILES, LESS GALLONS
Add 4 ounces of Benzol™ to every 10 gallons of gas.

AUTO RESUSCITATION
To revive a dead battery, just dissolve 1-ounce of Epsom salts in warm water and add it to each cell.

AN EASY SOLUTION

If you want to keep your windshield free from frost, just mix up a solution of 1-part white vinegar to 3 parts of water and apply to windshield. You can also just cut an onion in half and rub the fleshy area on the windshield.

I USED TO BE SHINY

To remove rust from a chrome surface, just rub the area with a piece of aluminum foil.

GETTING BACK ON SOLID GROUND

If you get stuck in snow or mud, try using your car floor mat or a blanket kept in the trunk for traction.

HOW DOES ANTIFREEZE WORK

Antifreeze is composed mainly of propylene alcohol which when added to water lowers the freezing point and also increases the boiling point. Therefore water can't freeze at 32^0 F. and it will not boil at 212^0 F. The coolant is circulated through the engine by the water pump and the engine heat is transferred to the coolant, which returns to the radiator. The radiator is cooled by the outside air, which cools the antifreeze preventing boil-over.

WHAT IS THE DIFFERENCE BETWEEN A CAR POLISH AND A WAX?

A car polish is only meant to enhance and restore the luster to a wax coating. They remove dirt and debris trapped in the wax and restore, a smooth finish to the surface. The polish will not provide any protection; it will just keep the wax clean.

LET THERE BE LIGHT

Used milk containers can be filled with old candle wax and kept in the car for emergencies. Place a long candle in the center for the wick. It will burn for hours.

RUB-A-DUB-DUB

To prevent the rubber around your car doors from freezing, try rubbing the rubber moldings with vegetable oil.

BE GENTLE
Steel wool pads make an excellent white wall cleaner. Best to use as fine a steel wool pad as you can find.

TO THE SEAT OF THE PROBLEM
If you place a sheet of fabric softener under your car seat it will keep your car smelling fresh. Cleaning it out will help too.

BIGGER IS BETTER, WHEN IT COMES TO TIRES
Next time you buy tires, consider replacing the old tires with a larger tire. Check your manual and put on the largest tire that is acceptable on your car. Larger tires will last longer, the engine will operate slower at any given highway speed, it will increase mileage and even reduce engine wear. Most cars come with undersized tires since they cost less.

BUG SLIDE
Oven Guard or spraying vegetable oil on a clean car bumper before a trip will make it easy to remove the bugs when you return.

REMOVE CIGARETTE ASHTRAY SMELL
To really clean and deodorize car ashtrays, use baking soda and leave some in there after you clean it. It will keep the smell from getting into the car upholstery in most cars.

OIL AND WATER DON'T MIX
Oil is easily contaminated from moisture. To get rid of the water in your crankcase, you need to drive the car at least 7 miles in a warm climate and at least 10 miles in a cold climate each time you use the car.

If you don't, the engine does not get hot enough to evaporate the water. Most people don't drive that far so be sure and change your oil every 3,000 miles at the most.

YOUR BRAKE OIL NEEDS A BRAKE

Because of the newer disc-brake systems on today's cars, you should change the brake oil every 2 years to be on the safe side. Brake fluid has an affinity for moisture, which may corrode the brake parts.

ALUMINUM CHROME CLEANER

Try using a piece of aluminum foil to shine the chrome on your car. Just turn the shiny side out, dampen the chrome and polish the chrome with the aluminum foil.

DRIVEWAYS

CONCRETE

HAVING A CRACK-UP

Driveways will sometimes develop cracks in the concrete. This is usually due to shrinkage or settling. Most cracks can be sealed with a concrete sealant.

I CAN SEE A RAINBOW..............

Sometimes a white/gray or rainbow discoloration may occur on a newly paved driveway, however, it will usually disappear over time.

DON'T NEED AN ARTIST

You need to use the right paint for the job if you are going to paint concrete. Never use a latex paint since it will react with the rubber car and bicycle tires, even lawnmower tires. The latex will end up peeling. Use alkyd floor enamel, which are more moisture-resistant, will hold up better, but are more slippery when wet. To clean the floor use TSP and water.

HERE KITTY, KITTY

If you have a driveway that has oil residue that is hard to remove, just cover the area with sand or cat litter and allow it to remain for 2-3 days before sweeping it off.

RUB-A-DUB-DUB

To remove grease and rust stains from a concrete floor, just sprinkle dry TSP on a wet or oily surface and allow it to remain for at least 30 minutes before washing off. You can also mix 1 part of sodium citrate in 6 parts of water and add enough Fuller's Earth to prepare a thick paste. Spread the paste on the area that needs cleaning and allow it to remain for 5-7 days before scraping it off. Keep adding new paste if it dries out.

PRE-PAINTING PREP

Before painting a concrete slab, the surface must be sealed. If you are just pouring the slab you will have to wait 3 weeks before applying a sealant with a brush. Allow 1 day for it to dry and the lime to work its way out. Vacuum up the white powder then use a stiff brush and water to clean the concrete before paining it.

WATERPROOF YOUR CONCRETE

The following ingredients will be need:

1¾	Pound of ammonium sterate (from pharmacy)
1	Gallons of hot tap water

Place the ingredients in a large pain and mix thoroughly. Apply immediately to concrete walks, driveways or cement walls.

CLEANER FOR CONCRETE
The following ingredients will be needed:

3	**Pounds of metasilicate**
1	**Gallon of hot tap water**

Place the ingredients in a bucket and mix well. Use a broom to scrub when applying. For stubborn areas, allow the mixture to sit for 15-20 minutes before scrubbing. Sometimes a more concentrated solution may be needed in bad areas.

ASPHALT

GENERAL INFORMATION:
Materials that will be needed include emulsified liquids, plastic fillers and solid cold patches. If there are impressions left by car tires, this is an indication of a poor construction job. Buckling or cracking in cold weather are signs of poor drainage. Both these conditions will require a new driveway and cannot be repaired.

BLACKTOP CRACKS
It would be best to fill any crack as soon as you spot it to keep water from getting under the slab. If the cracks are ¾" or wider, they should be filled with cold patch. If the crack is narrow, fill it with crack filler. Make sure you clean out any small pieces of material before you patch. Clean off any dust with a power washer or garden hose.

WHERE'S MY CAR?
If you are going to repair a chuckhole, make sure that you remove any loose material and dig out the dirt down to a solid base. Make sure the edges are solid and remove any dust from around the edges. Place fluid cold patch in the hole and work in with a trowel to be sure there are no air pockets.

Compact the area to within 1-inch from the top and allow to set for a short period time before adding the balance of the patch material to just above the surface. After 12 hours, place a board on top and drive your car over the top a few times. Seal coat the entire driveway.

Good preparation is really needed if you want the job to come out right and last for a while. The following are the steps you need to follow:

- ❖ Sweep the driveway well to remove any loose stones and debris and be sure to trim back any weeds or grass that has crept over the edges.
- ❖ If you have oil or gas stains they should be treated with a driveway degreaser and sealed with a spot sealer. If this is not done, they will bleed through the asphalt.
- ❖ Use a driveway applicator brush and apply a driveway cleaner working it in good. Allow it to dry before filling in any holes or cracks.
- ❖ Fill small cracks or holes with a flexible crack filler. Anything more than ¾ inch in diameter will need blacktop patch applied with a trowel.
- ❖ Pour out a small amount of sealer at a time and spread evenly with the squeegee side of the driveway applicator. Only work a four-foot area at a time.

GRANDPA'S SAFETY TIPS

- ❖ Make sure that the material you are using does not come into contact with your skin.
- ❖ Try not to breathe in the fumes for too long a period without wearing a mask.
- ❖ Wear gloves and old shoes you can discard when you're done.
- ❖ Wear eye protection when chipping away the old asphalt.

GARAGE ROLL-UP DOORS

GRANDPA'S ROLL-UP MAINTENANCE TIPS

Sluggish Operation

Make sure the rollers are lubricated as well as the hinges and pulleys. This maintenance should be done about twice a year. Never oil or grease the tracks, however, they should wiped down and sprayed with a silicon spray or penetrating lubricant.

Rollers do not operate smoothly

Make sure that the rollers are not damaged; if they are replace them. If they are clogged with grease and grit, they should be removed and cleaned in a solvent solution, such as mineral spirits then reinstalled. If you see that the rollers are OK then check the alignment of the tracks with a level. Adjust the brackets until the vertical parts of the tracks are plumb. If you find any bent tracks they will need to be replaced. Best to tighten all screws on loose hinges.

The cable is frayed

Make sure that the door is locked open when replacing cables. Be sure that the cables are of equal length or the door will not move smoothly.

Door is opening too fast

While the door is raised, loosen the tension by repositioning the hook ends of each cable, making them closer to the springs on the cable anchors.

Door is getting hard to open

While the door is raised, just tighten the tension by repositioning the hook ends of each cable closer to the springs on the cable anchors. The tension needs to be equalized on the springs and make sure that the tracks are not too far apart.

The door lock is sticking

Try lubricating the latch mechanism with powdered graphite. Check the fit of the lock bars into the slots on the strike plate. Adjust the brackets up or down until they will support the lock bar in the correct position.

WINTERIZE THE BOTTOM OF THE GARAGE DOOR

Use some spray-on antifreeze and lubricate the rubber weather stripping on the bottom of the door. This will stop snow and ice from forming on it.

WHOOPS, IT WENT THROUGH THE WALL

The torsion springs are very dangerous and should only be adjusted by a garage door professional and NOT grandpa.

KEEP CROOKS OUT OF THE HOUSE

When you go away for an extended period, be sure and reinforce the overhead door with a long shackle padlock. Place the padlock through the door track, just above one of the door rollers to prevent entry.

GARAGE DOOR OPENERS

PREVENTION A MUST

Regular servicing is needed for garage doors. The springs should be lightly lubricated. The chain should be greased and you should make sure that you check for loose screws.

THE MOST COMMON PROBLEM

The most common problem results from dirty tracks.

STRANGE NOISES

If you hear grinding and scraping noises, the problem is with the gears in the motor or the sliding mechanism is going bad.

SPRINGING INTO ACTION

The springs can be very dangerous if they break and need to be secured with safety cables, which can easily be purchased in any hardware store.

GRANDPA'S SAFETY TEST FOR GRAGE DOOR OPENERS

- ◆ To test for the downward force of the door, place a piece of 2X4 on the garage floor in the center of the doorway and trigger the door to close. When the door comes into contact with the 2X4, it should strain slightly and then open. If you see that the pressure is too great or too slight, you can make the proper adjustment.
- ◆ There are 2 screws on the front of most units that control the down force of the door. Unplug the power unit and adjust the down force screws.
- ◆ To test the door then stand in the center outside the door and place your hands so that the door will hit them. See how much force is exerted that stops the door and reverses it. Think of a child under the door and how much pressure should be allowed before the door reverses.
- ◆ If you have safety reversing sensors, they should be checked to be sure they would stop and reverse the door if the beam of light is broken.

GARAGE FLOORS

GRANDPA'S HINTS FOR PREPARING A GARAGE DOOR FOR PAINTING

- ❖ To prepare a garage floor for painting you will need to clean it thoroughly.
- ❖ Use a stiff broom to sweep it first then remove any oil spills with cat litter.
- ❖ Wash the floor with a concentrated garage floor cleaner using a stiff brush.
- ❖ If any stains remain you will need to clean them off with muriatic acid wearing a respirator approved for chemicals.

- ❖ Wear gloves, eye protection and old clothes and shoes.

- ❖ Rinse well and clean twice. Purchase paint that resists flaking from hot tires.

HOT WATER HEATER

GENERAL INFORMATION:
If you go on vacation, be sure and turn the hot water heater to its lowest setting to save energy.

DRAIN ME, DRAIN ME
The hot water heater may need to be drained depending on the type of water in your area. If you are in an area that has high mineral content water, the hot water heater should be drained according to the instruction booklet that came with the heater. If you can't find the booklet, try and drain the heater about every 2-3 months until the water runs clear.

IS YOUR HEATER HOT?
If you feel the heater and it feels warm, you are losing heat and should purchase an insulated blanket. This will help retain the heat and save you about $15-$20 a year.

BRRRRRRRRRRRRRR
If the water is not hot enough it is usually one of two problems. Either the thermocoupler or the thermostat is bad.

BUY QUALITY
The recommended water heater is the Rheem™ brand found in plumbing supply houses. Be sure that the heater you choose has the same wattage and holds the same amount of water as the one you are replacing. Also, be sure and purchase a new relief valve, which should be replaced every time you replace the heater.

PERMIT ME?
Check with the local building department since some areas of the country do require a permit when you change the water heater.

WHERE'S MY HEAT?

If the water heater will not light up or stay lit, it is probably a bad gas valve or thermocouple or both.

DRIP, DRIP, DRIP

When the heater leaks from both the top and bottom or from the temperature control, the glass liner is probably cracked and it is best to drain it as soon as possible and buy a new one.

PLEASE, PRESS MY BUTTONS

Having to continually press the reset button means that the heating element housings are corroded and allowing water to drip on the element and cause a short. It would be cheaper to just replace the element instead of buying a new heater unless it is an old one.

POP, POP, POP

If the electric heater keeps popping the overload reset button, it is probably the element, which should be replaced or if you have hard water, you can wait until it builds up enough to stop the leak. Best to replace the element.

WHERE'S MY HOT WATER?

If the water is not heating enough, the problem is usually due to a bad heating element or thermostat.

DIRTY THERMOSTAT CONTACTS

It is not unusual for the contacts in the thermostat to become dirty and cause a problem. This is an easy fix and all you have to do is run a new dollar bill or other clean sheet of thin, stiff paper between them to clean off any dirt that may have accumulated.

THERE'S A GHOST IN MY WATER HEATER

The strange rumbling noise when the water is heating up is probably heavy sediment moving about in the tank. The only way to solve the problem is with a new water heater.

THE SECRET ANODE ROD

Inside almost every water heater there is a magnesium bar called an "anode rod." This metal rod protects the water heater tank from rust by corroding before the tank does. However, when the rod disintegrates and rusts away, the tank will start rusting. You can double the life of your water heater if you replace the rod before it has a chance to dissolve completely. The rod should be replaced about every 4 years depending on the quality of the water.

GRANDPA KNOWS HOW TO REPLACE THE ANODE ROD

❖ First you will need to shut off the cold water supply line to the heater then you need to turn off the gas supply and the circuit breaker.

❖ Next attach a garden hose to the drain cock and slowly drain off several gallons of water.

❖ To remove the old rod you will need to loosen the hexagonal fitting located on top of the heater with a long-handled ratchet wrench.

❖ Lift out the rod and before installing the new rod, wrap its threads with Teflon tape so that it will seal better.

❖ Insert the new rod back into the heater and tighten the fitting.

❖ Bendable rods are available if there is not the room to put in a straight, solid rod.

I'M NOT RECOVERING WELL

You probably have a bad, heating element that is slowing down the recovery time and needs replacement. Call a plumber!

ENERGY DRAINER

Heating water for taking a bath, washing the dishes and clothes, preparing food and general housecleaning uses about 20% of all the energy used in the average home. Your water heater should be turned to 120^0F instead of the average 140^0F that the heater is set at in most homes. However, if you have a real old model dishwasher it may require the 140^0F water so that the detergent will work properly.

A LITTLE HERE, A LITTLE THERE, WATER EVERYWHERE

Water on the floor around the hot water heater usually means that the tank is rusting away and you need a new hot water heater. If you only see water occasionally then it is probably the thermostat or pressure release valve that has gone bad.

STORAGE SPACE

GENERAL INFORMATION:

Garages can be a storage nightmare, especially if you have a small garage and no storage shed. Some garages do have a storage area above the car parking in an attic, which is helpful, however, many garages do not have an easily accessible one.

GRANDPA SOLVES STORAGE SPACE PROBLEMS

Developing storage space in a minimal space area that can accommodate items that cannot be stored in the house. Allowing the cars to still be parked in the garage.

1. Install a collapsible ladder or a bunk-bed style ladder with a hook in the overhead storage area to make the area more easily accessible. Place floorboards on top of the studs to create storage space without disturbing the insulation.
2. Utilize the back wall and build cabinets that overhang the front of the car allowing the front to go underneath the cabinets.
3. Make a workbench with collapsible legs so that it can be placed in the down position when not being used.
4. Utilize a grid and modular storage system that is configured to hold all garden tools and ladders.
5. Utilize bicycle flush wall mounts to keep bikes out of the way.
6. Use ropes and pulley systems to store larger light items (canoe, etc.) next to the ceiling.

7. Electrical cords should be stored in cardboard tubes from roll of paper towels. Then label them as to which appliance they go to.

STORING CHEMICALS

HOME PROTECTION A MUST
If you store chemicals in the garage and there is a door that opens from the house to the garage. The door from the house to the garage should be fire-rated and should withstand fire for 20 minutes.

SAFE STORAGE
Chemicals that are sold in their original containers are safe to store in the garage as long as there is no damage to the containers. Make sure that they are in a cool, dry location.

KA-BOOM
Gasoline containers should only be filled 95% full. Place the cap on securely. Store the containers out of direct sunlight and be sure that the temperature is below 80^{0}F. Use a fuel stabilizer like Sta-Bil™ or Pri-G™.

MISCELLANEOUS

This one's a winner

DE-KNOTER UPPER
To stop cords from separating when you are working in the garage, just tie a knot with the two cords you are using then plug then two cords together. The strain will only be on the knot not the electrical connection.

TRY, SODIUM PHOSPHATE
TSP will remove grease stains from concrete after you scrape off the excess.

TRY IT, YOU WILL BECOME A BELIEVER
If you want to remove glue residue on almost any surface, try using vegetable oil on a rag. Residue; from sticky labels are also a breeze to remove. The vegetable oil tends to neutralize the glues

bonds.

PREVENT WOOD FROM SPLINTERING

Driving nails into wood that splits easily is a problem that can easily be solved. Just barely blunt the tip of the nail with your hammer. The flattened out tip is less likely to split the wood. You can also try placing the nail into a block of soap before nailing it.

A GIRL'S BEST FRIEND

All diamonds and gold jewelry; can easily be cleaned by mixing a solution of 50/50 white vinegar and warm water. Dip a soft toothbrush into the solution and brush gently. Opals, emeralds, and pearls are too delicate for this type of treatment. Costume jewelry should only be cleaned with a weak solution of baking soda and water to avoid damaging the glue bonds.

Diamonds
- Diamonds can be chipped and should never be worn when doing rough jobs.
- Chlorine bleach will discolor the setting.
- Have the prongs holding the stone checked annually.
- When storing your jewelry, make sure they don't touch each other.
- Diamonds will scratch other pieces of jewelry very easily.
- Clean your diamonds regularly with a milk detergent and warm water.

Colored Gemstones
- Never expose the gemstones to salt water or harsh chemical solutions.
- Check with your jeweler for cleaning methods for colored stones.
- Emeralds need special care, check with your jeweler.
- Hairspray will dull gemstones.
- Wipe gemstones with a soft cloth after each wearing.

10-24 Karat Gold Jewelry
- Gold scratches easily, keep pieces away from other jewelry.
- Do not bathe or shower using soaps and shampoos.
- Use a soft bristle brush.
- Grease is easily removed with rubbing alcohol.
- Try not to get makeup and powders on the gold.

Silver
- Store silver in a cool, dry location.
- Only rub silver with a soft cloth. Paper towel and tissues will scratch it.
- Never wear silver into a swimming pool that is chlorinated.

Pearls
- Put on pearls after applying cosmetics, perfume and hair spray.
- Quality pearls should be re-strung annually with knots between each pearl if worn regularly.
- Store pearls in a chamois bag or wrap in tissue to store.
- Never use harsh chemical to clean pearls.
- Special pearl formulas or mild soap and warm water can be used to clean them.

MAKING JEWELRY CLEANER
The following ingredients will be needed:

1	Tablespoon of household ammonia
1	Tablespoon of washing soda (from supermarket)
1	Tablespoon of liquid dishwashing detergent
3	Cups of very warm tap water

Place all the ingredients in a medium bowl and mix thoroughly. The solution should be stored in a sealed, glass jar. When you want to clean your jewelry, just soak the pieces in the solution for 5-7 minutes and brush with a soft-bristled toothbrush. Rinse the jewelry in warm water and dry well.

CAUTION: Do not place pearls or emeralds in this solution and never add chlorine bleach to these chemicals. Keep out of the reach of children.

SILVER JEWELRY CLEANER
The following ingredients will be needed:

¾	Cup of white vinegar
2	Tablespoons of baking soda

Place the ingredients in a small bowl and mix well. Place the jewelry in the bowl and allow it to stand for 2 hours before rinsing with cold water and drying with a soft dry cloth.

DE-KNOTTING A CHAIN
If you get a knot in a chain, just place a drop of vegetable oil on the knot and work it out with a straight pin.

JEWELRY POLISH
The following ingredients will be needed:

2	Tablespoons of ferric oxide
2	Tablespoons of calcium carbonate
	Cool tap water

Place the ingredients into a small bowl and mix well using just enough water to produce paste. Rub on the jewelry with a soft cloth
and the buff with another clean soft cloth.

A POPPER OUTER
Tough nut and bolts are easy to remove after you pour some cola or other carbonated water on them and allow them to sit for about 20 minutes. The mild: acidic action of either citric or phosphoric acid will usually do the job.

CLOGGED SPRAY CAN NOZZLE
If you turn a spray can upside down after you use it and spray until it comes out clear, it will not clog up. If it does clog up, just soak the nozzle in paint thinner for a few minutes. You can also try

placing the nozzle on a can of WD-40 to clear the nozzle very quickly.

NEUTRALIZE ME
The acid around a battery post can easily be cleaned with a thick solution of baking soda and water. Allow it to soak for 10-15 minutes before washing it off. Baking soda is a mild base and will neutralize the weak acid.

DON'T HAVE A SCREW LOOSE?
Trying to remove a screw can be a difficult task and may take a lot of patience. Grandpa has a few suggestions that may make the task easier.

❖ If you heat-up the tip of your screwdriver you may be able to loosen a stubborn screw.

❖ If the slot is filled with garbage, you must clean it out before you try and remove it.

❖ Be sure that the blade of the screwdriver fits the slot.

❖ Place the screwdriver into the slot and tap it gently since the vibration may loosen the screw.

POWER STEERING FOR A SCREWDRIVER
Slit an old tennis ball and place it over the handle of a screwdriver to give you extra turning power.

❖ If you only get the screw partially out, try squirting a little penetrating oil on the part you can see and then screwing it back in before trying to remove it again.

REMEMBER, LONGER SCREWDRIVERS WILL HAVE MORE LEVERAGE

SUPER HAND CLEANSER
The following ingredients will be needed:

4	Quarts of cold tap water
1	Box borax soap chips or powder
1	Box of Lux™
1	Pint of corn meal

Place all the ingredients together in a medium bucket and mix thoroughly into a paste. Place the paste into jars with lids and label as a super hand cleaner.

MASKING TAPE DRIED OUT?
Masking tape should be stored in an empty coffee can with a lid to stop it from drying out.

BEGONE STINKY HANDS
Often when you pump gasoline, you get gas or the smell of gasoline on your hands. After pumping gas, just use some baking soda on your hands to remove the smell then wipe them clean with a piece of damp paper towel or keep a box of damp handy-wipes in the car.

CIGARETTE FIRE
Keep a box of baking soda in the glove box for a small fire emergency. Just sprinkle it on to put out the fire.

REVIVING A DULL RAZOR BLADE
You can bring a dull razor blade back to life and make it sharp again by sharpening it on the striking edge of a matchbook cover.

CHAPTER 8

GARDEN SHED

CARING FOR GARDEN TOOLS

YUMMY, MOTOR OIL & SAND

If you want to keep your garden tools clean and always ready to use, try mixing ¾ quart of motor oil in a 5 gallon bucket of sand. Leave enough room to place some tools in and stick your shovel, small rakes and garden tools in the sand. It will clean and condition them.

NASTY, RUSTY

When your garden tools get rusty, just sand off the rust with medium sandpaper and place the tools in the bucket of sand and oil. Make you sure you move them in and out a few times to clean them off. Rust can also be cleaned off using white vinegar. Just soak the metal end of the tools for a few days or until the rust disappears.

BE SHARP!

Always have a whetstone or a file handy to sharpen the blades on your garden tools, as they need it.

WINTER STORAGE

To keep your garden tools in great shape and ready for the spring, just store them all winter with end in the bucket of sand and oil.

DARN SOCK?

Use an old sock that you would not darn to clean your yard tools. Just place some WD-40™ on the sock and clean them after removing any debris that has accumulated on them.

IT'S A STICKY WICKET

When the joints of your garden shears become sticky, just clean them with rubbing alcohol then spray them with WD-40™.

GARDENING HAND TOOLS

SHARPENING HEDGE TRIMMERS

Secure the hedge trimmers in a D-vise with the cutting edge up and the bevel toward you.

Work the Dremel (#932) at the angle of the trimmer edge's bevel (don't alter the original bevel). Always start the pass at the edge and move left to right.

A file can also be used to sharpen the blade by moving the file away from and diagonally across the sharp edge (maintain the factory bevel). Then you need to decrease the angle slightly and hone just the last 1/16th of the blade with a sharpening stone.

SHARPENING A WEED CUTTER
First disassemble the weed cutter and screw the blade to a wood block and be sure that the blade overhangs one side. Place the block in a vise and use a double-cut flat file. Push the file toward and diagonally across the sharp edge and be sure and maintain a factory bevel (45^0-60^0). Reverse the blade and repeat.

SHARPENING A PRUNER
Maintain a sharp cutting edge with a medium-grit sharpening stone. Be sure and wet the stone with water or lubricate it with honing oil, depending on the type of stone you are using.

SHARPENING DIGGING TOOLS
The majority of digging tools are not sold sharpened. You will need to sharpen them with a coarse file working to a 45^0 bevel.

SHARPENING A GARDEN SAW
Place the saw in a vise and use a triangular file to sharpen the blade. Sharpen each side of every bow saw tooth to a 45^0-60^0 bevel of any saw that cuts in both directions.

BAD CORROSION
Since garden tools get wet, they must be protected against corrosion. Be sure and clean the tools after every use with a wire brush and wipe down the metal with light oil.

REPAIR A WOOD HANDLE
When the wooden handle becomes rough, try smoothing it out with medium-grade grit emery cloth.

Sandpaper will work but tends to tear too easily. Wipe the handle down with a heavy coat of boiled linseed oil and dry well.

REPAIRING YOUR HEAD
When a tool head becomes loose, the best way to repair it is to mix equal amounts of 2-part epoxy resin and a hardener on a piece of scrap wood. Coat the end of the tool that goes back into the ferule and drive the end back in with a block of wood and a hammer.

REPLACING A WOODEN HANDLE
Lock the tool in a vise and remove the broken handle by drilling ¾-inch holes in the end and cracking it apart. Slip the new head over the new handle and hit the butt end of the handle down hard on a wooden block to draw the head tight. Then drive a small hammer wedge to expand the wood, which will secure the head.

POWER MOWERS

WALK-A-BOUT MOWERS
There are three categories of these mowers: Side discharge, rear discharge and mulching mowers. Best to have two blades and always keep one sharpened.

I prefer the mulching type

Side-Discharge Mower – The discharge chute is located on the right side of the mower. Best for smaller lawns and can be purchased as an electric or gas-powered mower.

Rear-Discharge Mower – The grass clippings are thrown out the back into a catcher. Many models have a door that can be opened or closed if a bag is not used.

Mulching Mower – Cuts the grass into very fine particles that can be absorbed back into the turf. The clippings can then provide moisture and nutrients back to the lawn.

PUT, PUT, SPUT, SPUT

The motor will start but will shut off after a few seconds. Best to remove the tank and engine covers to expose the carburetor and governor linkage. Clean everything well with a stiff brush. Remove the air cleaner and carburetor and dismantle the carburetor. Wash all the parts with a spray can of carburetor cleaner and replace the air filter element. Oil the governor and throttle linkage and wash out the tank with clean gas. Change the oil and replace the spark plug.

VERY DISENGAGING

If the cutting deck will not disengage, the "A" spring or lever may be gone or bent and needs replacement.

REPLACING A STRETCHED BELT

Cut the belt off and take it to your dealer for an exact size replacement. When you are there be sure and get a threading diagram and procedure.

GETTING MIXED UP

Be sure and prepare the right mixture of oil and gas. Check you're instruction book. Many new 4-cycle engines do not require oil to be mixed with the gas. If you have an older 2-cylcle engine, the mixture is 16 to 0ne or ¾ pint of oil per gallon of gasoline. Some books recommend 32 to one, but 16 to one seems to work better.

SPUTTER, SPUTTER

If your power mower is losing power, just remove the air filter and see if the power comes back. If it does, wash the sponge filter in gasoline and replace or remove the tank and upper cover and check the governor spring. The spring should be opening the throttle wide under spring tension when the engine is shut down. This spring is probably the problem. Other problems that cause this are a dirty carburetor or a partially plugged gas line.

WHOOOOPS

If the lawnmower keeps stalling be sure that you have changed the oil twice a season and replaced the filter and spark plug. The engine compartment may be plugged up with old grass or dirt.

Remove the spark plug and add a small amount of starting fluid then replace the spark plug and start the engine.

HELP! I'M HALF CHOKING
The carburetor needs to be disassembled and cleaned thoroughly.

OIL, OIL, EVERYWHERE
If you have oil going into the filter and oil is coming out of the exhaust it would be best to purchase a new motor.

BAD COIL, BAD COIL
If the motor runs fine and then decides to stop and not restart until it cools down, you probably have a bad coil in the electrical circuit or clogged cooling air passages. First try removing the engine cowl and clean the cooling fans, degrease the engine, replace the air filter and spark plugs, then change the oil.

EASY DOES IT!
Remember to always mow across a slope if you are using a walk-behind mower. This will keep you safe from a slip or fall and never attempt mowing on a steep hill with this type of mower.

If you are using a riding mower on a hillside or slope, be sure and mow up and down instead of across the hill to prevent the mower from tipping.

POWER YARD EQUIPMENT

CHAIN SAWS

IS BIGGER BETTER?
For around the home use it is best to purchase one with a 12-14-inch bar. The bar is the portion of the saw that the chain attaches to. These are usually lightweight and easy to use.

SAW WEAR, THE LATEST STYLE
You should wear certain protective clothing when using a chain saw. Invest in a pair of cut-retardant chaps.

The fabric is made to jam the chainsaw blade if it comes into contact with the fabric. An eye, face and ear guard is also recommended.

HEAVE HO
Always carry a chain saw with the blade to the rear and be sure that the scabbard is on.

CALL 911
The most serious injuries occur from "kickback." This happens when the chain bar kicks back in the direction of the operator. This may occur when the saw hits an object such as a nail or screw in a piece of wood.

CHIPPER/SHREDDER

MULCH, MULCH, MULCH
Whether you need to purchase a chipper/shredder depends on your yard. These machines will turn leaves, garden refuse and tree trimmings into raw material for a compost pile or provide mulch for your garden. The size of the unit will depend on your needs. It is really two machines in one. The chipper will turn tree limbs and branches into small chips and the shredder converts plants and leaves into usable material for a compost pile.

FRESH CHIP ALERT
Best not to place fresh wood chips on the garden soil. They tend to rob the soil of nitrogen and should be composted for a year before using them.

I'M ALL CLOGGED, MUST BE SPRING
Shredders tend to clog easily and this is the nature of this piece of equipment. Be sure and purchase one with a shredding chamber that is easily accessible.

If the shredder has a discharge screen it will be more likely to clog than one without a screen. However, it is recommended that the shredder have a screen, which will improve the quality of the shredded material by being pushed through the screen first. It will just need regular cleaning.

SHREDDER SAFETY
Be sure that children and pets are kept away from the machine. Never wear loose-fitting clothing. Wear gloves, ear protection and safety goggles. When filling the shredder chute, always use the plunger to push material into the unit. Always disconnect the spark plug if the unit becomes jammed and wait for all parts to stop before clearing the jam.

GARDEN TILLER

AVOIDING WARPING
Always idle your tiller on a level surface for 1-2 minutes before you shut it down. If the engine cools evenly it will reduce the chance of warping and allow oil to lubricate all parts.

OIL CHANGING TIME
Change the oil shortly after you use the tiller while the oil is still warm and any dirt or residues are still in suspension. Residues will settle out after the engine cools down.

STORE THAT TILLER
When you store the tiller, make sure you close the fuel shutoff valve all the way to stop gas from seeping into the engine or leak on the floor.

DO I NEED A ROTOTILLER
This is the most efficient method of turning the soil, weeding and aerating. When aerating the soil, oxygen is put back into the soil causing an increase of microbial activity, which feeds on organic matter and speeds up decomposition.

HOW OFTEN DO I TILL'ER
Usually, once a year: anymore and you may damage the soil. Never till the soil if the soil is wet.

WHAT TYPE OF TILLER IS BEST
Front-tine tillers are very hard to handle because of lack of weight over the tines. They may bounce around and you are forced to walk behind the tiller compacting the soil as you go.

Rear-tine tillers are recommended since the engine is in front of the tines, the machine is more stable and you can walk to the side and not compact the soil.

IS THERE A LOOSE NUT AROUND HERE
Make sure you always check the tiller for loose nuts and bolts every time you store it.

A CLEAN TILLER IS A HEALTHY TILLER
Cleaning any residue when putting the tiller away will increase the life of the tiller and reduce the chances of overheating the gear housing and shaft.

HEDGE TRIMMERS

GENERAL INFORMATION:
These are sold as gasoline powered, electric or rechargeable battery-powered tools. The new designs are lighter and reduce vibration with special holes in the units. The newer machines will stop in ¾ second when the trigger is released for safer operation.

LAWN VACUUMS

GENERAL INFORMATION:
Most have a large capacity bag on walk-behind machines and can clear leaves and twigs from large areas quickly. Most bags have a 6-bushel capacity and some models can easily be converted into a blower. Engine size varies from 5hp to 8hp and it is best to get one with a hose attachment for hard-to-reach places.

LEAF BLOWERS

GENERAL INFORMATION:
Leaf blowers are a very noisy method of clearing large areas. Best to check on the ordinances in your area before purchasing one. Local laws sometimes only permit their use during certain hours of the day. However, some cities ban them altogether.

LOG SPLITTERS

GENERAL INFORMATION:
These are hydraulic-powered rams that drive wooden logs against a solid steel wedge to make firewood. Be sure and purchase one with a forward ram control that must be engaged before the log splitter will operate. Make sure it also has a jack stand to keep the log splitter level while it is in operation.

SNOW THROWERS

WHAT HORSEPOWER IS BEST
There are several sizes of snow throwers and it depends on the area that you need to clear. The smaller ones are only 3hp and will do a short walkway, patio or steps. The medium ones are 5hp to 8hp and can handle snow up to 12". If you live in an area that gets a lot of snow you will need one with 8hp to 12hp engine. These are great for long driveways and small retain parking areas.

There are single-stage throwers that are powered by 2-cycle or 4-cycle engines and use a single auger to clear a 24" path of snow and throw it 5-55 feet away. The double-stage throwers use a large front auger and a secondary impeller to throw even farther.

STRING EDGER/TRIMMER

TO PURCHASE A GAS OR ELECTRIC TRIMMER
Electric edger/trimmers do not really have the power to do a good job. Gas trimmer do a much better job and have the power. String trimmers are not really recommended since they are very noisy and tend to spew out a large amount of pollutants. If you do purchase a string trimmer, purchase one that has a 4-cycle engine rather than a 2-cycle engine since the 4-cycle uses just gas and not a gas and oil combination.

PROTECT THYSELF

Recommended to wear long pants and closed-toe shoes. Also, protective goggles, earplugs and a dust mask. If you have anti-vibration gloves, it would be best to wear them. Injuries occur from the constant vibration to the hands and wrists.

RIGHT OR LEFT?

All trimmers are designed for right-handed people with the hot part of the engine and muffler are away from the body.

CHAPTER 9

HOME OFFICE

COMPUTER

CAMCORDER CONFUSION SOLVED
In order to connect a camcorder video output to your computer you will need to purchase a special USB to video or S-video adapter.

NEED A USB PORT?
To add a USB port to a MAC or PC you need to install a USB controller card to your MAC or PC. Make sure you know what you are doing or call a professional to put it in.

HERE A CORD, THERE A CORD
Be sure and save all your old telephone cords to wrap around all those unsightly wires on the back of the computer or stereo system keeping them organized and looking tidier.

CALL RESCUE
If your computer dies first make sure that it is turned on and that a circuit breaker has not tripped. Be sure that there is no disk in any of the slots when you first turn it on.

MY COMPUTER CAN'T READ?
If your computer won't read files from a floppy disc the disk has been mishandled and some of the files may be corrupted. Very common: when children are present or someone using the computer who is not familiar enough with it. You lost the files, but have a professional check and see if they are on the hard drive before you panic.

TWO PRINTERS ARE BETTER THAN ONE
If you want to hook up two printers to your computer you will need to purchase a switchbox and cables to connect it to the printer.

SHARING PRINTERS
To share two printers with two computers, you need to purchase an auto switchbox, two normal printer cables and two DB25 male to DB25 male cables.

BETTER INTRODUCE THEM

When your computer fails to recognize your mouse, just hold the mouse in front of the screen and introduce them properly or check the connection in the rear of the hard drive (more than likely to be the problem).

COPIERS

DAMN JAM

Non-Machine Causes

The majority of all paper jams; are caused by using the wrong paper. If you are getting jams frequently, try switching to a higher quality paper and you will see the difference. Purchasing the cheapest paper is a mistake. Humidity can also cause paper jams and be checked by looking at the paper. If the paper has small bumps or appears uneven it is probably high humidity.

Machine Caused Jams

Dirty or worn rollers or separator belt damaged. Timing switches are malfunctioning. Clutches may not be working right. When clearing a jam, avoid tearing the paper at all costs.

IS QUALITY A PROBLEM?

Light or Dark Copies

Due to improper exposure adjustment or poor quality paper! Adjust the light/dark setting and replace present paper with better quality. Also light copies may be caused by low toner concentration and you may need toner.

CAN'T SEE MY COPY
Blank Copies
You may have a broken or missing corona wire or faulty corona block contacts. Need to call service tech for repair.

AWFULLY DARK DOWN HERE
Black Copies
May be caused by a blown exposure lamp, faulty exposure lamp thermo fuse, contaminated lamp contacts or a light path/optics obstruction. The lamp or fuse can be replaced and the lamp contacts can be cleaned. If there is an obstruction in the optics path it needs to be cleared.

THERE ARE STRANGE LINES EVERYWHERE
Vertical Line Problem
Usually caused by a scratched drum, faulty drum or scratched upper fuse roller. This problem needs the attention of a service tech.

Horizontal Line Problem
Usually caused by scratched upper fuse roller or scratched drum. Best to call service teach.

I'M SEEING WHITE & BLACK SPOTS
White Spots
The drum may have a pinhole or you have a bad photoreceptor. Replace the bad item or call service tech.
Black Spots
This is usually the result of a dirty copy board glass or pin-holed drum. Cleaning the glass usually resolves this problem. The other possible problems may be a contaminated drum cleaning roller or contaminated toner.

BAD COPY, BAD COPY
Print Smearing or Coming Off
This is usually caused by depleted fuser oil and oil needs to be added.

ELECTRICAL

GENERAL INFORMATION:
When you set up a home office, be sure to purchase a high quality surge protector. One of the easiest ways to damage office equipment is a power surge. It is also best to keep cords from touching each other with a spiral plastic wrap.

FAX MACHINES

CLEAR OUT THAT JAM
The following steps will help you to clear a paper jam:
 * First unplug the machine
 * Open the cover and remove the thermal paper roll
 * Hold down the start and stop keys at the same time and then plug the machine back in.
 * Release the two keys and the display should read *"OUT OF PAPER"*
 * Open the cover and replace the thermal paper roll then close the cover
 * The display should return to the date and time

NOT RECEIVING, BUT SENDING OK
Set the fax machine to *AUTO* reception.

WHERE OH WHERE HAS MY LITTLE FAX GONE
If your fax machine will not receive an incoming fax when it is connected to your answering machine, make sure that the phone line of the fax machine is plugged into the *TEL LINE* of the fax machine. The phone line that comes from the answering machine should be plugged into the *TEL SET* position of the fax machine.

TELEPHONES

WHERE IS MY RINGI-DINGI
If your phone won't ring, first, be sure that the ringer volume is up and that the set is plugged in.

Also be sure that the receiver is not off the hook, even the slightest.

I'M SUPPOSED TO HAVE A DIAL TONE
When there is no dial tone, make sure that the phone is plugged properly. Try replacing the phone cord with another phone cord. Try another phone in the same jack to eliminate the possibility of the phone being bad.

HUMMMMMMMMMMMMMM
If you encounter a strange hum on the line, it is usually caused by one of the dialing buttons sticking down. Just drag your finger across the buttons to release it.

WHY STATIC?
Static on the line is usually a problem with too many phones on the same line. It can also be moisture in the jack or a faulty cord. To check if there are too many lines, just unplug all the lines in the home and then plug back in the one that you were getting static on. If no static keep plugging phones in one at a time until you get static. Try another phone on the static jack phone to see if it is a phone problem and then switch cords around.

WIRES THROUGH WALLS
If you want to easily feed a phone wire through a wall horizontally, just pick a straw big enough to hold the wires and allow them to slide easily through. Drill the hole through the wall and make it slightly larger than the diameter of the straw. Place the straw in the hole and thread the wires through it. Best to remove the straw before adding the plug.

PHONE KEYS GETTING STICKY
Just remove the housing and blow away any accumulated dust that is between the keys with a can of compressed air and eliminate any remaining gunk with a foam swab that has been dipped in denatured alcohol.

CHAPTER 10

EXTERIOR OF THE HOME

BRICKS

HUFFING & PUFFING, NOTHING HAPPENING
If you are going to buy a brick house, it will cost a little more than other construction material, however, it makes up for the additional expense by reducing the cost of maintenance.

BRICK MAINTENANCE
Brick needs no maintenance and should easily be cleaned with a stiff brush and soapy water.

ENERGY EFFICIENCY
Brick has the ability to store heat and slowly release it. It keeps the house warmer in winter and cooler in summer.

SAVING MONEY WITH BRICK
A brick home reduce my home insurance costs; you should receive a lower insurance rate.

WELL PAINT MY BRICK!
New brick should be allowed to cure for 1 month before painting. It should not be cleaned or treated with acid solutions. Alkali-resistant paints should be used and a zinc chloride solution may need to be applied to the brick to neutralize the surface.

HELP! I'M BEING DISLODGED
Vines will grow on bricks and do damage. The runners will get into the cracks and dislodge the bricks.

PREMATURE AGING
If you want to make interior brickwork look older, brush on boiled linseed oil. Allow it to remain for 2-3 hours then scrub off the excess oil with a rag. Dispose of the oily rags carefully.

Egg Splatter

Dissolve oxalic acid crystals in tap water and be sure and follow the manufacturers instruction. Use a non-metallic container and use a brush on the surface.

Efflorescence

Best to try just water and a brush first then wait a few days to see if it comes back. If you decide that you need something stronger, scrub the wall with a solution of 1 part muriatic acid to 15 parts of cool water. Be sure and rinse well with water when through.

Hardened paint

First, scrape off as much as you can with a putty knife then scrub with a metal-bristled brush using cold water. If you have trouble removing the stain, it would be best to try using a commercial paint remover. Be sure and test the bricks in an inconspicuous location to be sure that it will not stain or discolor the brick.

Graffiti

The best method is to use a spray-paint remover and follow the directions to the letter.

Iron rust

First try scrubbing the area with household bleach at full strength and allow it to stand for about 15 minutes before rinsing it off. If you are not successful then try using a solution of 1 pound of oxalic acid in 1 gallon of water. Allow it to remain on for about 15 minutes before rinsing very well. Be sure and try a small area that is out of the way first in case it does damage to the brick.

Iron Stains

Brush a solution of oxalic acid crystals; dissolved in tap water and follow the manufacturers instructions for use. It will need to be applied directly on the stain.

Ivy

First, cut all the vines away from the surface (never pull them off). Allow remaining stems dry up before scrubbing them off with a very stiff brush and regular household cleaner.

Mortar smears

Use a stronger muriatic solution of 1 part of acid to 10 parts of cool water to clean dark-colored brick and 1 part acid to 15 parts cool water to clean light-colored bricks.

Mildew

Try using 1 part household bleach to 3 parts cool water and add some TSP to the bucket. Allow it to stand for about 15 minutes before rinsing off.

Oil

Just apply a paste of mineral spirits and sawdust to the area. Allow it to remain for 10 minutes before wiping off.

Paint Stains

Best to remove new paint with a solution of trisodium phosphate (TSP) and water. Just follow manufacturers instructions for the use of TSP. Old paint can usually be scrubbed off with a brush or sandblasting as a last resort.

Smoke Stain

Start by scrubbing the surface with a household cleaner that contains bleach or you can use a mixture of ammonia and water (wear rubber gloves). Be sure and never mix chemicals such as products containing ammonia and bleach.

DOORBELL

TRY EASY FIX FIRST

The first thing to check if the doorbell is not working would be the circuit breaker, which may have tripped. This is an easy fix since you just turn it back on! If the doorbell is on a garage circuit, then check the GFI if you have one in the garage and press the red button.

ZAPPPPPPPPPP

Check and see if the doorbell button is getting power. Remove the screws from the cover and gently pull the button away from the wall. Be sure that all the connections are tight then dust off all the contacts with a paintbrush. Try testing the button again. If that does not work, remove the wires from the terminal screws and carefully hold the insulated part of the wires and touch the exposed ends together. If the bell rings, replace the button.

BUTTON, BUTTON, WHOOSE GOT THE BUTTON?

This is easy because all you have to do is buy a new button and attach the wires from the wall to the new terminal screws. Be sure they are secure and that should solve the problem.

GUTTERS

WATER, WATER, EVERYWHERE........

If there is excess water around my foundation causing leaking into the basement, the gutter termination next to the home probably needs a water diverter. One should be placed under each downspout.

GUARD MY GUTTERS

Gutter guards serve an excellent purpose by keeping clutter out of the gutters. If you do install them yourself, be sure and tuck them under the roof shingles. Always overlap the guards by ¾" when you are placing them in position.

JUST DUCKY

If you have a problem with leaky gutters, just line the leaky areas with duct tape to solve the problem.

GUTTERS VS SHINGLES

Should gutters be placed up close to the last row of shingles? No, they should be placed low enough on the fascia so that snow and ice coming off the roof would slide by harmlessly. Make sure that the gutters have enough clearance if you live in a snow and ice area of the country.

BE FIRM WITH YOUR GUTTERS
If you need to clean your gutters, try using an old fan belt. It has excellent flexibility, and is firm enough to do the job without scrapping the paint off.

GUTTER CUTTING SECRET
If you need to cut a gutter, be sure and place a piece of 2X4 into the gutter up to the point you will be cutting to avoid the gutter from deforming. It will also give you better support and make it easier to cut.

PIPES

BABY IT'S COLD OUTSIDE
Be sure and purchase some pipe wraps to keep your pipes from freezing in the winter. The best are the foam wraps or cover them with straw in an emergency if you live on a farm. If you leave the water dribbling out, the pipes won't freeze if you are really worried. If the pipe does freeze, thaw it at the tap end not the middle or you may burst the pipe. Hair dryer works great!

ROOF

DRIP, DRIP
If you have a water leak and you can't find the source, it is probably from rain blowing in through the vents. May have to place partial covers on them.

ASPHALT SHINGLE REPAIR
Before attempting to start the repair, be sure and locate shingles of the same type, color and size. Lift the tab above the shingle that has been damaged and pry out the nails of the damaged one. Snip off the top corners of the replacement shingle and don't tear the roofing felt. Nail on the new shingles, placing the nails under the shingle

above. After you drive in the nails, daub the nail heads with roofing cement.

AGING ASPHALT SHINGLES BEFORE USING

If you would like the new shingles to look like the old ones so that there is a better match, just wipe the new shingles with mineral spirits then rinse them well. This will eliminate some of the granules and will allow more of the asphalt to show through. This actually simulates the effects of the sun and rain on the roof.

? FELT PAPER

If you are wondering when you should use felt paper, it is recommended for asphalt and fiberglass, but not for cedar shingles.

LAYER ON LAYER

You can place one layer of shingles over another layer, however it is not recommended. Best to remove the old material and replace it with the new shingles.

IT'S A BIT CHILLY OUTSIDE

Best to shingle in the fall or spring. In the winter the tabs do not seal completely until the temperature reaches 50^0F. If it too hot the shingles will soften too much and walking on them can damage them.

SAFETY FIRST

If you need to get a closer look at your roof or second story, try using a pair of binoculars instead of a ladder.

ASPHALT NAILING

When nailing an asphalt shingle during a repair, be sure and nail by hammering against a pry bar placed on the nail head.

HELP! I SPLIT MY SHINGLE

To repair a wood shingle, close the gap between the two pieces and nail them to the roof deck then seal the crack and nail heads with roofing cement.

AGING WOOD SHINGLES BEFORE USING

When you add new wood shingles to repair an area, they probably will not match the color of the old shingles. If you would like a closer match grandpa has the method to give them the weathered appearance: just spray the new shingles with a solution of 1-pound of baking soda dissolved in 1-gallon of water then place them in direct sunlight for about 5 hours.

SIDING

GENERAL INFORMATION:

The most common sidings are aluminum and vinyl. The recommended new vinyl siding should be .042 gauge or higher. These are just about maintenance-free and can be easily cleaned with a brush and a hosing off. If you have a problem, try using a small amount of detergent to loosen stubborn dirt. A small amount of chlorine bleach added to a bucket of water and detergent will also handle a mildew problem. Be sure to wash the area you have cleaned before the soap dries.

WHAT'S BEST?

Vinyl siding is by far the best. You have the beauty of wood siding and don't have to paint, scrape or stain. It is durable and will not be damaged easily.

PROTECT THE SIDING FROM WASPS

If you have vinyl siding on your home, never spray a wasp or hornets nest with a poison spray. The sprays contain petroleum-based products, which may react with the chemical components of the vinyl and will permanently discolor it. If you have already stained the vinyl siding, it is possible to lighten the discoloration by dampening a white cloth with mineral spirits then dabbing it on the stain. Rinse well after you clean it.

THERE IS A DIFFERENCE

The following are the different styles of siding:

- ❖ **Beaded** – This a decorative variation of the traditional styling. It features a half-round molding-like effect cut into the bottom of the panel, which will create shadows and dimension. Frequently used on Southern colonial and classic Victorian houses.

- ❖ **Blends** – This is a style of siding produced to resemble natural wood. It features a slightly weathered, stained-wood finish.

- ❖ **Dutchlap** – The face of the siding is beveled, which adds dimension. The unique bevel cut of its edges recreates a style used extensively by the early American settlers.

- ❖ **Scalloped** – This is siding with a rounded bottom edge and has overlapping rows. The scallops tend to create a decorative style reminiscent of Victorian or Cape Code homes.

- ❖ **Shakes** – This siding has a square-edge design with a rich cedar texture that looks like hand-cut cedar shingles. They can be used on the entire home or maybe used as a decorative accent, which would add New England flair to the home.

- ❖ **Traditional** – A style in which each plank will appear to overlap the plank that is underneath to create the look of real wood siding.

Too big a job for me!

SOMETHING MISSING HERE

If you have missing or damaged parts, the majority of the time, minor replacements should be easy and inexpensive. However, if a large section were damaged, it would be best to get an installer to replace the section. A professional should be able to replace the area with matching materials and match the color.

I'M GOING BAD

The caulking is normally placed around the windows, doors and seams in the siding, which seals and waterproofs the gaps in the homes exterior. However, the caulking can dry out or crack over time and ultimately undermine the integrity of the siding. Replace the caulking with new siding after removing all traces of the old caulking and cleaning area well.

THERE'S A FUNGUS AMONG US

Dry rot on wood siding is a problem! Basically, dry rot is a fungus that will cause wood to crumble. Sometimes this type of problem is hard to detect since it is not easily noticeable. When noticed, the only thing you can do is to replace the siding. Remove mildew with tri-sodium-phosphate (TSP).

HERE A CHIP, THERE A CHIP

If your siding has chips it can be painted; however siding is prone to warping and cracking, which may cause chipping and peeling. If re-painting does not work, you may have to replace the siding with one of a more suitable color.

I'M CRACKING UP

This is a result of the siding expanding and retracting with weather changes and is usually only associated with vinyl siding. Warm weather will cause the siding to expand and cooler weather will cause it to retract. If panels become damaged, just replace them.

NOW I'M BUCKLING

If your vinyl siding has warped and buckled after being repainted, you have a problem. This can happen if the siding was painted with a darker color than the original color since darker colors tend to absorb more heat from the sun. The

TERMITES

Grandpa used my food for the termites again, boo hoo

DOWN WITH THE QUEEN

Termites; are really not a bad insect. They are the best wood recycler around and will turn a dead log into food for many other insects. Unfortunately, they are not fussy where they find wood and your home is a handy source of food. The queen is the key to the termite "swarm." One method of killing the queen is to mix up a batch of queen delicacy food. This is a small amount of grape jelly, some canned cat food and a teaspoon of boric acid. The workers will not eat a treat of this magnitude, but bring it back to the queen as a treat.

WOOD TRIM

MAINTAIN IT OR LOSE IT!

Maintaining the wood trim on any house is usually the most costly part of a paint job. If the wood trim is not maintained well it will deteriorate, warp and rot away. It takes extensive sanding and painting to keep the trim up. It is recommended that you replace the trim with a vinyl or aluminum siding trim to eliminate any leaking and rotting problems found in wood.

CHAPTER 11

THE GROUNDS

FOUNDATIONS

IT'S A LITTLE DAMP AROUND HERE
Wetness around the foundation is usually caused by the settlement around the home. You will need to fill settled areas.

MY HOUSE IS GETTING OVERWEIGHT
Excess weight in the house can affect the foundation. Placing items like a baby grand piano and a large safe in the same area will eventually affect the foundation. Be sure and don't water too much in these areas and make sure that rain drainage is efficient.

LAWNS

GENERAL INFORMATION:
Remember grass for the most part is a cool weather plant and grows better in cooler climates. If you are going to seed a lawn, remember to seed a lawn in the early spring for the best results. To reduce the possibility of diseases attacking your lawn, use a mixture of grasses since diseases attack different varieties. Eventually a turf disease will reach an area of grass that is resistant to the disease and terminates it.

WATERING INFO
If your lawn is watered in the early morning hours less water will evaporate due to wind and sun. If you must water at a different time then try and water about 2 hours before sunset to give the lawn a chance to dry and reduce the risk of fungal disease.

If you live in an area of the country that has frequent high humidity, it would be best not to water late at night. Watering just after the sun goes down is ideal in these areas.

CRAZY PATTERN
It is best to occasionally altering the mowing pattern. Best not to go in the same direction every time you mow. However, altering the direction every time you mow is not the best idea either.

ARE YOU ON THE LEVEL?

A lawn bed should be as smooth and flat as possible allowing for a slight pitch to accommodate drainage. A grade that is from 6-10 inches in about 100 feet is not too much. Once the roots have reached their saturation level the water should run off easily and not be allowed to form standing puddles.

PHEEEEW

Before starting a new lawn it is always recommended to work a phosphate fertilizer into the soil. This is an important nutrient to have in the soil, especially for a new lawn. Phosphates do not move into the soil well after the lawn has been planted.

TIMING IS EVERYTHING

The best time to plant a new lawn is in the fall, allowing at least 6 weeks of temperature around 50^0-70^0F. This is the preferred time and temperature to guarantee success with a newly planted lawn.

OUCH!

If the tips of the grass blades are turning tan or are frayed, the cause maybe dull mower blades. Be sure that your mower blades are sharpened regularly.

SOD GAPS?

Usually caused by insufficient watering. Fill in the gaps and water better.

HELP! I'M TURNING YELLOW

If your grass is turning yellow or does not maintain a nice green appearance, it is usually caused by lack of fertilizer or infestation. May need to have a professional evaluate. If your shrubs are turning yellow, it is a lack of adequate fertilizer or using the wrong fertilizer.

GETTING THIN DOWN HERE

If the lawn is thinning out after mowing several times, it is probably caused by thatch buildup. Lawn needs aeration and de-thatching.

BIGGGG MISTAKE

One of the more common mistakes people make is to drag a hose across the newly planted area. Make sure that you have a hose that is long enough to do the job.

NOT THE BEST RETAINER

Peat moss is commonly used to cover seeds, however, it does not retain water well. If you do use peat moss, be sure and wet it down and saturate it really well. One successful method is to pre-soak the moss before you apply it to the area. Keep mulch dark with adequate moisture.

STOP! YOU'RE KILLING ME

If the grass is wet or frozen it should not be mowed. A frozen lawn should not even be walked on.

IT'S NOT IN FASHION

When working a newly seeded area, be sure and wear shoes that are flat-soled, tennis sneakers or go barefooted. Never wear shoes with heels since they tend to dig in and leave an indentation that is difficult to remove easily.

Can't wear high heels in the garden

FAUX GRASS

Dichondra is not really a grass, but a broad-leafed plant. It is more popular in the warmer southwest climates and needs a lot of watering.

If it gets below 25^0F it may die out and need to be re-seeded as soon as the weather warms up. Grows best in light-sandy loam so that water can penetrate easily.

GRANDPA'S MOWING TIPS TO THE WISE

- When mowing try and mow the grass at about 3 inches high. High mowing keeps the weeds from getting sunlight.
- Only mow as often as the growth requires mowing.
- Never cut more than 1/3 of the length of the grass blade or you will slow down the food production capabilities of the blade.
- Make sure you continue mowing into the fall and until the grass stops growing. In the fall maintain a grass height of 2-3 inches.

SPROUTING TIMES FOR LAWN GRASSES

	DAYS
Bentgrass	7-12
Chewing's fescue	10-20
Common ryegrass	7-14
Creeping red fescue	10-20
Kentucky bluegrass	20-28
Merion Kentucky bluegrass	20-28
Perennial ryegrass	7-14

MOWING LIKE THE PROS

SHARP BLADES – Dull blades tend to pull and make ragged cuts, which may lead to lawn disease problems.

REGULAR MOWING – At least once a week is recommended during the height of the growing season.

MOWING DIRECTION – It is impossible to get a clean cut if you cut your lawn in the same direction every week.

MOWING DURING DROUGHT – Best not to mow your lawn during a drought period because the lawn is in a stress situation.

WET GRASS – Mowing wet grass tends to leave wet grass residue, which can damage a healthy lawn.

DRY CLIPPINGS – Clippings should be raked up within 48 hours of mowing. The lawn disease, thatch is the result of leaving clippings on the lawn for too long a period of time.

IF YOU ARE GOING TO REPLACE YOUR MOWER BLADES, BE SURE AND REMOVE THE SPARK PLUG BEFORE REMOVING AND REPLACING THE BLADES.

COOL SEASON GRASS

Bent Grass
- **ASTORIA** - Has fine leaves and is a dull green color, is not very vigorous and tends to get summer diseases easily. It does not like deep shade and prefers full sun.
- **HIGHLAND** - Has upright leaves and is grayish-green in color. Likes full-sun or part-shade.
- **PENNCROSS** – Has flat, narrow leaves and is bluish-green in color. Prefers sun or part shade. Should be mowed at about ¾-inch.
- **SEASIDE** – Has flat, narrow leaves and bluish-green runners. Very susceptible to summer diseases and should be mowed ¾-inch.

Fine Fescues
- **CREEPING RED** – A fine-textured, dense turf that mixes well with bluegrass. Works good in shady areas and should be cut 1¾ to 2-inches.
- **ILLAHEE** – Has a very fine texture and is bright green. Very susceptible to summer diseases and tends to grow in clumps. Should be cut 1¾ to 2-inches.
- **RAINIER** – This is a very delicate, soft grass with a deep green color. Prefers shady locations.
- **CHEWING** – A delicate grass that is soft and gray-green in color. Does well if moisture and food are in short supply. Tends to yellow in winter.

Blue Grass
- **KENTUCKY** – A very dense sod with dark green leaves. The best all-around lawn for the cool-season grass areas! Growth is slow in summer and it tends to grow faster in cool seasons. Does not do well in shade and prefers full sun.

- **MERION KENTUCKY** – A denser grass than the traditional Kentucky bluegrass. The dark blue color is more resistant to drought conditions, but has a tendency to be susceptible to rust and should be mowed ¾ to 1-inch.
- **NEWPORT** – Has the same texture as Merion Kentucky, however, it less susceptible to rust. Should be cut no lower than 1¾-inches.

Rye Grass
Does not produce a really tight, knitting grass. Used as a temporary ground cover in the Southwest.
- **CLOVER** - Has the ability to make its own nitrogen, which means that the grass will require fewer feedings. Grows in a dark green color and is very lush.

St. Augustine Grass
Very wide blade, rugged tough grass. Does not need a lot of feeding nor watering to survive. Requires a power mower and turns brown in winter months.

LEAF RAKING

GENERAL INFORMATION:
To maximize the effectiveness of your raking in the fall, there is more to just raking up the leaves and pine needles. There is thatch, which is a layer of dead turf grass tissue between the green vegetation and the surface of the soil. This layer should be removed in order to maintain a healthy lawn. You will need to rake deep enough to remove the thatch as well as the fallen leaves and pine needles.

LIGHTING

HIDING THE LIGHTING
It is always best to conceal the garden lighting. Use either a glare guard or hide the fixture behind or in a bush, branch, wall, rock or large shrub. You should not see where the outside lighting originates.

TOO LITTLE, NOT TOO MUCH

Too much garden lighting takes away from the garden plants and the effect you planted your garden for. Use bulkhead luminaries for security or if you are lighting a commercial area.

BUY QUALITY

When purchasing lighting fixtures and equipment for outdoor use, it is always best to purchase the highest quality you can afford. Outside fixtures do not have a long life unless they are of a good quality. It will also give you more options and a better look.

TOO BRIGHT

When you are going to light a deck, be aware of where people will be sitting to avoid glare. You never want to position the lights so that there will be glare.

BUG MAGNET

Remember, lighting will attract bugs, so be sure and place the lighting well away from where people may be sitting. Never locate the lights so that they never shine directly on an entertainment area.

PESTICIDES

There are hundreds of pesticides available on the market and most work very well. The following are some of the more common ones. If you have a pest problem in your garden it is always best to bring a sample of the problem to a gardening professional and get advise as to the specific pesticide and its safe use. ***Most of the following are poisons, however, it is recommended to use all-natural substances as much as possible.*** www.pestfreeproperty.com

ALCOHOL
Use 70% isopropyl alcohol (rubbing alcohol) to control a number of common pests. Works good on scale infestations, but be sure and test an area before spraying. Best to dilute 1-2 cups of alcohol in 1 quart of water.

ALL-PURPOSE INSECT SPRAY
Grind up 1 whole garlic bulb, 1 small white onion and add 1 teaspoon of cayenne pepper and place the mixture in 1 quart of water. Allow the mixture to stand for 1 hour then strain through a piece of cheesecloth and add 1 tablespoon of liquid dish soap and mix well. Spray on plants and be sure and spray the underneath side of the leaves.

AMMONIA
Mix 1 part ammonia with 7 parts tap water and spray the leaves. Try the mixture on a few leaves to see if any damage will occur first. This spray works well on aphids, fleas, beetles, scales, thrips and whiteflies.

BAKING SODA
When used in a spray bottle, baking soda has fungicidal properties. It will protect the plants as well as eliminate a number of pesky critters. Dissolve 1 teaspoon of baking soda in 1 quart of warm tap water, then add 1 teaspoon of liquid dish soap. When sprayed on this solution will last a long time and keep its effectiveness.

BLEACH
Bleach is excellent for disinfecting garden tools. Bleach should always be used in its diluted form since it is very toxic. Best to use 9 parts cool tap water to 1 part bleach.

BORIC ACID
One of the best baits to control ants is with boric acid. Works great when combined with grape jelly to attract them.

CAYENNE DUST
This hot pepper herb can be used as a dust to repel onion maggots, ants and aphids. It will also discourage most animals from damaging your plants.

CITRUS OILS

Citrus oils obtained from the peels of citrus fruits have chemical properties that tend to kill or discourage certain insects. The active ingredient "limonene" will be on the label of certain products.

Some of the insects that are susceptible to the effects of limonene are the leaf-eating caterpillar, potato beetle, fire ants, aphids, mites, flies and wasps. One of the best commercial products that contain citrus oil is Aphid-Mite™.

DIATOMACEOUS EARTH (DE)

This abrasive dust has been used for years to kill common pests. It is composed of fossilized silica shells of specific algae. The sharp needle-like projections in DE penetrate the insect outer shell and kill it by dehydrating it. A light dusting of DE is very effective in controlling aphids, caterpillars, leaf-hoppers, snails, slugs and thrips. Best to wear a dust mask when using DE. One of the problems with DE is that it will cause irritation to all animals and will kill the beneficial insects as well.

FUNGICIDE

Two of the most common are copper and sulfur, which are deadly poisons. They will eliminate the growth of fungal spores. Best to follow the directions of a gardening professional before using any products that contain these fungicides.

GARLIC OIL

When sprayed on plants will kill a number of common insect pests, however, it may also kill a number of beneficial insects. If you use garlic oil with soap added to the spray it eliminates even more of the beneficial insects. Garlic has also been known to damage certain foliages so you might want to test a small area before general spraying.

LIME

Has been used for hundreds of years to control a number of insects. If you do use lime, you must wear a mask to avoid inhaling the dust. Needs to be re-applied after every rain to be effective.

MINERAL OIL

For the best results using mineral oil it should be added to garlic oil or a soap mixture. The oil actually traps the insects, coats their bodies and suffocates them. Has been used for many years on ears of corn to eliminate the problem of corn earworms. Just apply 1-2 drops of mineral oil to the tip of each ear of corn after the silks have wilted to solve the problem.

NICOTINE

Nicotine is extracted from tobacco and is very poisonous. Depending on the concentration used it can kill most soft-bodied insects. If mixed with soapy water it is even more effective. It is used to kill aphids, mealy bugs, scales, fungus gnats and spider mites. Be sure and wear gloves when handling nicotine since it can enter the body through the skin. It is also very harmful to all animals.

SALT

One of the best uses for rock salt (NaCl) has been in the growing of asparagus plants. However, table salt that is iodized is not recommended. Rock salt produced from calcium chloride is not recommended only from sodium chloride (NaCl). Rock salt may be sold as pickling salt. If used, apply about 2 pounds of rock salt per 100 square feet of your asparagus bed.

SOAP SPRAYS

This is an oldie but goody. Simmer a pot of water with shavings of Fels Naptha™ soap. After it has simmered for about 20-30 minutes remove the pot and strain the solution. Allow the mixture to cool before using in a sprayer. Best used on aphids, chiggers, whiteflies, earwigs, mites, scales and flies. Always spray the solution on a few leaves to be sure it is safe for the plants. Doesn't do any good to kill the bugs if you end up killing the plant as well.

STARCH SPRAY

This is another old remedy for a variety of garden pests. A number of starches have been effective over the years such as potato starch dextrin and even all-purpose flour. Just mix 2-3 tablespoons of potato starch or flour in 1 quart of water and to make it more effective, add 2-3 drops of liquid dish soap. Mix well and spray covering the leaves on all sides. The all-purpose flour has been used as a dust and gets very sticky when it becomes damp, trapping the insects.

SULFUR

Sulfur is a very effective protective fungicide and is used both on plants and trees. Best to wear protective clothing when applying sulfur. The problem with sulfur is that it may kill the beneficial insects as well as the pests and fungus. Use a sprayer with all plastic parts since sulfur may corrode metal. Instructions for its use can be obtained through your local gardening supply store.

APHIDS BEGONE

The following ingredients will be needed:

1	Small white onion
2	Medium cloves of garlic
2	Cup of cold tap water
1	Spray bottle

Place the ingredients in a blender and mix on high for a few seconds until thoroughly blended. Strain the mixture through a piece of cheesecloth and pour the remaining liquid into a spray bottle. Spray the solution on a "fine mist" setting on rose bushes. Both the tops and bottoms of the leaves must be sprayed.

NOTE: A piece of aluminum foil placed around the base of rose bushes and tomato plants will keep the aphids from climbing the plants.

ANT POISON FOR GARDENS

The following ingredients will be needed:

2	Tablespoon of calcium sulfide
1	Quart of cool tap water
1	Egg white

Place all the ingredients into a container and mix well. Place small amounts in areas where you have an ant problem. **Keep out of reach of children and pets.**

ALKALI-FREE GENERAL INSECT ELIMINATOR

The following ingredients will be needed:

1	Ounce of diglycol oleate
25	Ounces of pyrethrum extract

Place the ingredients into a medium container and mix thoroughly, then spray as needed to eliminate most insects. If the solution becomes too thick, water may be added to dilute it.

HOUSEPLANT BUG KILLER

The following ingredients will be needed:

¾	Cup of isopropyl alcohol (from drug store)
¾	Cup of insecticidal liquid hand soap
1	Cups of cool tap water

Place the ingredients in a small bucket and mix well, then place into a spray bottle and spray the bugs. Care should be taken not to spray too much on the plant leaves, especially ferns or leaves with hair-like projections. Never spray on food bearing plants in or out of doors.

I'm scared of spiders

KILLING THE DREADED SPIDER MITE

The following ingredients will be needed:

¾	Cup buttermilk
4	Cups of whole, wheat flour
2	Gallons of cold tap water
1	Spray bottle

Place the ingredients in a large bucket and mix thoroughly. Place a portion of the liquid in a spray bottle and spray their living areas or anywhere the problem may exist. This formula will suffocate any species of mite.

ARE MEALYBUGS ON YOUR PLANTS?

The following ingredients will be needed:

1	Bottle rubbing alcohol
	Cotton swabs

Wash the insect cluster on the plant with the alcohol on a cotton swab. Wash the area with insecticide soap and isolate the infected plant if possible.

ELECTROCUTE SLUGS
The following ingredients will be needed:

1	Roll of copper wire
	Wire cutter

Place a circle of copper wire around the base on the plant and the slug will electrocute itself. The minerals in the slug's body reacts with copper and causes enough current to kill them.

I hate hot peppers!

NATURAL INSECT REPELLANT
The following ingredients will be needed:

3	Hot, jalapeno peppers
3	Clove of fresh garlic
¾	Teaspoon of any liquid soap
3	Cups of cold tap water
1	Spray bottle

Place the garlic and peppers in a blender and puree. Pour the puree into a spray bottle and add the liquid soap and water; shake and allow it to stand overnight. Strain the solution through a piece of cheesecloth and return the liquid to the spray bottle to be sprayed on tops and bottoms of leaves. Test the spray on a few leaves and allow it to sit for 2-3 hours before you spray all the plants. This solution can be used on all plants.

SPICY AND SMELLY BUG SPRAY
The following ingredients will be needed:

1	Tablespoon of red pepper
1	Small yellow onion
10	Cloves of garlic (not 10 bulbs)
¾	Teaspoon of liquid mild hand soap (not detergent)
1	Quart of warm tap water

Place the garlic cloves and the onion in a blender and puree, then place in a container and add the red pepper and water. Mix well and allow it to steep for about 6 hours. Strain the mixture through a piece of cheesecloth, then add the soap and mix well. This will get rid of most bugs and should be sprayed on the tops and bottoms of leaves of plants that have a bug problem.

PROTECT TREES FROM BUGS
The following ingredients will be needed:

1	Pound of canola oil
1 ¾	Pounds of rosin
4	Ounces of beeswax

Place the ingredients into a double boiler and heat until all the ingredients are melted together and mixed. Remove from the heat and allow the solution to cool somewhat then use a paintbrush to spread the solution around the tree in a 4-inch wide band from the bottom of the tree. Use care since some of these ingredients are flammable.

CONTROLLING WHITE BARK WORMS
The following ingredients will be needed:

2	Ounces of granulated glue
1	Pound of table salt
2	Ounces of arsenate of lead powder (poison)
4	Pounds of quicklime (poison)
2	Ounces of nicotine sulfate (40%) (poison)
2	Medium containers
1	Large container

Place 1 pint of cool tap water into one of the containers, then add the glue and dissolve fully. Place 2 quarts of cool tap water into the second container and dissolve the salt then mix the two solutions together. Add the arsenate of lead and the nicotine sulfate and mix well. Place the quicklime into the large container and add sufficient cool tap water to prepare a creamy paste, then add this solution to the other solution and add additional water to prepare a heavy whitewash.

Remove the soil from around the base of the tree and paint the solution on the bark to a height of about 18 inches above the ground. Replace the topsoil after the solution has had sufficient time to dry. Additional applications are sometimes needed every 2 weeks usually in May and June when the worms are active.

CATERPILLAR ELIMINATOR
The following ingredients will be needed:

8	Ounces of pyrethrum
¾	Pint of summer oil
12 ¾	Gallons of cool tap water

Place all the ingredients into a large basin and mix well. Place into a spray bottle and spray your trees when they have their leaves.

GENERAL GARDEN FORMULAS

ALL-AROUND PLANT PROTECTOR
The following ingredients will be needed:

1	Tablespoon of corn oil
1	Tablespoon of liquid hand soap
1 ¾	Tablespoons of baking soda (fresh)
1	Tablespoon of white vinegar
1	Gallon of cool tap water

Place the vinegar, baking soda and 1 cup of water in a medium bowl and mix well. Slowly add the white vinegar and mix. Pour the solution into a hand pump sprayer and add the balance of the water. Spray the tops and underneath sides of the leaves once per month for the best results. Will reduce the risk of disease and keep a number of pests away.

PLANTERS

THE BEST WAY TO GET POTTED
Ceramic planter pots will collect more heat than wooden pots, however, they also subject the plant's roots to greater temperature changes. Wood creates a more stable environment and results in better plant growth and more flowering.

Clay pots should be soaked in water for 3 hours before using them when repotting plants. If you don't, the new pot will absorb water when you water your new plants.

PLANTS & TREES

GENERAL INFORMATION:

Many plants and trees prefer to be planted in the spring before their leaves begin to open. These include birch, holly, dogwood, magnolia and maple. Trees and plants will also stand a better chance of withstanding the transplanting. Most plants produce their food in the early part of the day. Plants have difficulty producing food, as the day gets hotter, especially in the afternoon sun.

GET THE GOOD STUFF

An excellent potting soil is one part of vermiculite, two parts of peat moss and one part of perlite. These are required to give the soil body and to aid in water retention and drainage. Perennials need a different type of potting soil composed of two parts of common topsoil, one part peat moss and one-part sand.

TO WATER OR NOT TO WATER

Watering should never be done at high noon since plants tend to perspire at around this time. The process is called "transpiring."

Plants must do this to regulate their temperature from the sun, humidity and wind. If you do water at this time, the majority of the water will be wasted through evaporation.

If you poke your index finger into the soil around a plant, the soil should be completely dry before watering. If the soil is the slightest bit moist, the plant does not need water.

FALL TREE WATERING

Trees are damaged in the winter when they are unable to acquire water. If you water your trees in the fall, it will minimize damage. Water in the late summer and fall when the leaves fall off the trees. Water even if there is snowfall anticipated.

BOG & POND GARDENING

A bog garden is basically a marshy area with plants that will survive in a year-round moist climate. It is not necessarily a pond. A pond is usually made using a ready-made shell or plastic liner. In a bog it is essential that the soil is kept very moist all through the year. The best is one that will be low-lying and collects surface drainage.

It doesn't take very much water to keep a bog garden moist, and just a trickle will do. Ideally: to make a bog just dig out about 2 feet of the topsoil. Place this aside and place about 5 inches of smooth rocks on the bottom. Prepare a mixture of half peat and half loam and fill the hole to the top, keeping it level with the surrounding area. Two feet is the maximum depth for a successful bog garden.

GRANDPA'S BOG & POND TIPS:

SKIP THE RUBBER DUCKY

Just place the pool liner on the bottom of a new pond instead of rocks then puncture it to allow for drainage. This can be used for a bog garden as well.

DRIP, DRIP, DRIP

If you have a natural flow of water, no problem! If not, you will have to provide a small artificial trickle, which must be just enough to keep the bog garden well saturated.

CALL FOR THE WATER BOY

To allow a bog garden to suffer from drought will probably kill all the plants in a short period of time. Bogs are not recommended for the southwestern United States.

CAN'T FIND AN ISLAND WHEN I NEED ONE

Be sure that your bog garden has a shallow end to allow any small amphibians to enter and leave without drowning and getting trapped.

WATCH YOU'RE FINGERS
Carnivorous plants do very well in a bog garden especially when planted in sphagnum moss. The ones that do best are:

Sundews   *Venus Flytrap*   *Pitcher Plants*

GROW A CORSAGE
Orchids do well in most bog gardens. The most desirable ones are the white or orange fringed, grass pink, rose pogonia and the pink lady slipper. Best to purchase the orchids from a nursery.

GET OUT THE WHIP!
Some bog plants tend to do too well and need to be controlled. These include cranberry plants, rosemary, bog laurel, bog bean, horsetails and cotton grass. Be firm with these and don't let them get out of hand.

GETTING POTTED IS OK!
Deep-water aquatic plants can be planted in plastic pots with soil as long as you place small rocks or gravel around the top of the soil. Metal pots may disintegrate and rust. The gravel will stop any fish from bothering the soil. The best soil will be rotted turf. Don't use soil rich in organic matter such as manure.

THE PICK OF THE LITTER

Most landscape or gardening businesses will have a selection of plants that will do well in a bog garden and provide you with planting and feeding tips for the plants you choose. Color of the plants, planting location and height selection is important.

The following are some of the more common plants for a bog garden

Lysichitum (yellow skunk cabbage)	Flag iris versicolor
Osmunda	Hosta
Astilbe	Primula

Many plants are edible and have been very successful in bog gardens for centuries. The following are a few of the more common varieties:

WATERCRESS will grow very nicely in areas were the water is about 2 inches deep. The seeds can be used as a mustard substitute. Watercress; should be started by seed or a cutting, which will take root easily.

BROOKWEED prefers shallow water and very wet soil. Only the young leaves can be eaten either cooked or raw.

CREEPING DOGWOOD will grow better on the outer edges of the bog, but does not do well if the soil is too chalky. The fruit is edible.

CAPE PONDWEED grows well in bogs when the water is between 6 inches and 2 feet. Prefers a highly fertilized soil and the tubers are edible as well as the flowering spikes. The tubers are often substituted for spinach.

YELLOW WATER LILY prefers water of 1-2 feet in depth and full sun. The roots and stalks can be eaten either cooked or raw. The flowers can be used to make a tea.

WHITE WATER LILY prefers the deepest area of the bog garden and likes the sun and a rich soil diet. The seeds may be roasted and used as you would coffee.

ARROW HEAD likes water levels of about 1-2 feet in depth. The tuber can be cooked and mashed and is a very popular starch in China.

WATER CHESTNUT likes water 1-2 feet deep. The seeds can be consumed raw, dried or cooked. When dried the seeds can be powdered and used as a flour.

SMALL CRANBERRY does best grown in an acidic soil. The fruit is edible and a tea can be prepared from the leaves.

BULBS

Bulbs are actually storage tanks for nutrients. They are normally planted in the early spring, but certain varieties can be planted at various times of the year depending on when you want the flowers to bloom.

HELP! I'M DROWNING
The biggest problem that ruins bulbs and bulb plants is over-watering. If the water is left standing around the plant, the bulb will be worthless for the next season.

GET OUT THE RULER
Bulbs should never be placed on the bottom of a pot. Always plant them about 2 inches deep for the best results.

THIS IS FUN! I'M GETTING POTTED
Planting bulbs in a small pot, then burying the pot is a favorite method of growing flowers from bulbs and makes it easier to remove the bulbs for the next season. When storing the pots be sure that the soil is very dry or the bulbs will rot during the winter storage.

A LITTLE BIT WILL DO YA
After you dig a hole to plant the bulbs in, be sure and add a handful of a fertilizer that contains about 9% phosphorus, 9% nitrogen and about 6% potassium. If the bulbs are not removed just add some fertilizer to the topsoil every year.

STUPID IS, WHAT STUPID DOES
Be careful not to plant bulbs upside down. The narrow end goes up, which should not have any sign of roots. However sometimes the roots do not show.

THIS IS EMBARASSING
Bulbs should be stored in a brown paper bag that has been filled with peat. This will control the level of moisture during the winter months.

OUCH, OUCH
To grow the largest flowers from a begonia plant, just pinch off the smaller buds on either side of the larger one.

BEGONE, BEGONIA
Begonias will start to go dormant usually in August and should not be fertilized or you will interfere with their dormancy period. They need to have time to store up food for the next season.

ALWAYS KEEP ME CONTAINED
Dahlias tend to do better if planted in a container. Add mulch around the bulb to keep the moisture contained, especially if the weather is very hot.

YOU'LL BE GLAD YOU DID
Gladiolas are excellent for flower arrangements. Make sure when they are cut, so that at least half the flowers have not opened yet, since they will open shortly.

I'M STARVING, GET ME SOME FAST FOOD
Daffodils must be left alone and the yellow leaves must be allowed to remain until they equal about 1/3 of the leaves on the plant. If they are removed too soon you will remove too much of the food supply and the plants will not have stored enough energy.

DINK-A-LING
Spanish bluebells should always be planted in the shade. They require no special care and will do just fine on their own.

A "COOL" TULIP IS THE BEST TULIP
Tulips can be grown in every color except blue. They like full sun if you live in a northern climate. Late fall or early December is the best time to plant tulips. If the ground warms up before they are ready, they will not do well.

GRANDMA'S HERB GARDEN

Grandma loved to cook with fresh herbs and grew her own. Most of the herbs were grown in pots and old containers on the porch where they would get good sun. Remember, herbs release their best flavors and aroma when bruised. When the weather gets too cold, remember to bring in the herb plants. The following are her favorites:

Thyme, marjoram & parsley
These herbs only grow a few inches high, so make sure they are placed where the larger herb plants don't overshadow them. Usually best around the edges of the area.

Rosemary & bay leaves
These herbs tend to grow best when planted in clay pots. They will easily grow the year round and provide plenty of fresh herbs.

Tarragon, coriander, dill
These herb plants will grow to about 2 feet high and may be a little difficult to bring inside. Probably best to grow them in the garden and away from the shorter plants.

Mint
This plant will take over the whole area if you let it. Best to just plant it in a pot and keep trimming it.

DON'T LET ME FLOWER

If you want to get the best flavor from your herbs, you need to cut them before they flower. Their oils will be at their peak and they should be cut at mid-morning on a sunny day. Fresh herbs can be frozen, but allow them to fully thaw before using them.

SEEDS & SEEDLINGS

GENERAL INFORMATION:

When planting seeds, it is always best to follow the instructions to the letter. There are many variables when planting seeds and not all seeds should be planted in the same manner. Before you plant seeds, soak them in warm tap water for about 30 hours to soften the seed coat. This will cause the seed to sprout faster. The preferred method is to place the seeds into an insulated bottle, such as a thermos to keep the water warm for a prolonged period of time.

If you are starting seedlings indoors, make sure that the water you give them is at room temperature. Cold tap water may slow the growth of seedlings since it tends to chill the roots.

I'LL HAVE MINE STRAIGHT

Very hard seeds may need to be soaked in a container of strong tea for about 8-10 hours before planting. The tannic acid in the tea will soften the seed covering allowing for faster sprouting.

NOT TOO HOT OR YOU'LL KILL ME

Bean will sprouts faster if you warm them by placing them near a 75 watt bulb, which will provide just enough heat to help them sprout. Place the beans in a large jar and wrap the jar in a towel allowing one end to remain open for ventilation.

I'M CRUSHED

Beet seeds will be easier to germinate if you spread the seeds on a piece of wax paper and roll them lightly with a rolling pin. By slightly crushing the outer husk it allows the seeds to germinate faster.

STERILIZATION IS RECOMMENDED

It is recommended that when you start seeds it is done in a sterilized soil mixture, however, you can use a mixture of sphagnum moss, perlite and vermiculite. The seedling should be transplanted as soon as the first leaves appear since there are no nutrients in the mixture.

I'M CRUSHED

A mistake many people make when planting seeds is planting the seeds too deep with a heavy layer of soil. Most people use a trowel or their hands to cover the seeds resulting in too heavy a layer.

Try using a soft bristle paintbrush to brush the soil over the seeds and they will germinate faster.

BEST IDEA YET

One of the best seeds holders is half an orange or grapefruit that has been eaten. These make excellent containers to start seeds. Just fill them with soil and plant the seed; then place the holder in the ground when the seeds germinate. The holder will rot away leaving nutrients in the ground around the seed.

A HEATING PAD WILL WORK AS WELL

For fast germination, try placing your seed trays on top of your water heater. There will be just enough heat to speed up germination without harming the seeds.

BAG 'EM DANO

Seeds in flats tend to dry out very quickly. To avoid the problem, just place the seed flat into a plastic bag and check it at regular intervals to be sure that there is not too much moisture in the bag, which may cause mold or disease.

KEEP 'EM DRY

Most vegetable seeds will last for 3-5 years if stored properly. Place them into well-sealed jar with ¾ cup of flour or non-fat dry milk to absorb any excess moisture that might still creep in. Pre-packaged silica works well in the jars.

I'M VERY FRAGILE
When watering newly planted seeds and seedlings, be sure and water gently so that you will not damage or uproot them.

SEED DUSTING
If you are planting seeds that are as fine as dust, just broadcast them over a smooth-surfaced bed and then press them gently into the soil with a float. They should not be covered with mulch.

DON'T HURT MY ROOTS
Transplanting seedlings from a seed flat to a larger flat is called "pricking out." This step is very important in assisting the small seedling to better develop their root and leaf system before being plants in the garden. As soon as the seedling has two sets of leaves they should be pricked out. Make sure when you remove the seedling you do not injure the delicate roots.

NO DIRECT SUNLIGHT, PLEASE!
When setting out newly transplanted seedlings the best weather would be cloudy or overcast days. When that is not possible then the late afternoon would suffice. It is best not to place newly transplanted seedlings into the direct sunlight until they have a few hours to recover from the transplanting shock.

A LITTLE DRINK WILL DO ME
When you prepare a hole for a transplanted seedling, be sure and place water in the bottom of the hole, especially if the soil is very dry.

GETTING A LITTLE CRAMPED IN HERE
If a seedling has yellow leaves at the bottom, it may indicate that the seedling has been in too small a pot for too long a period.

I NEED A ROOT-CONTROL PROGRAM
Be sure when purchasing seedlings that the roots are not coming out the pot in all directions. This indicates a root-bound plant and that is not a healthy sign.

CALL THE PLANT DOCTOR
Seedlings should not show signs of browning or wilting. If

browning is evident it has probably been caused by over-watering, or a plant disease.

BUSTING OUT ALL OVER
There are flowers that when cut regularly they will produce more flowers. These include roses, antirrhinum, cosmos, verbena, viola, nicotiana and heliotrope.

GET ME SOME SHADES
Some plants prefer shade and will grow better if not in direct sunlight. These include begonias, some varieties of viola and coleus.

Seedlings need to be pinched in their early growth stages to assure that they will have more than one stem. If the seedling is not pinched properly it will not bush out.

HOUSE PLANTS

GENERAL INFORMATION:
Over-watering is the cause of most plant failures. Leaves will wilt, turn yellow and drop off. It is easier to revive a plant that has had too little water than to try and save a plant that has been killed from over-watering. Crushed eggshells should be added to the soil of indoor plants to provide better drainage and some needed trace minerals.

Use an old clean, cotton glove and dip into room temperature water then clean both sides of the leaves.

Small pieces of foam used in the packaging industry works better than pebbles in the bottom of flowerpots. They don't add excess weight to the pots and tend to retain some of the water more efficiently.

I WONDER WHERE THE YELLOW WENT

Stale milk will do a great job of cleaning plant leaves. The protein "casein" has a mild cleansing effect on the plant cell walls.

I'M WILTING AWAY, POOR ME

Wilting is usually the result of improper watering. However, if sudden wilting occurs, check the roots, pot or soil to locate the problem. Some of the more common cause are lack of water, too much water, root rot, excess fertilize or a salt buildup.

Check the cause by just pressing your finger up to the first knuckle, into the soil. If the soil feels dry to this to this depth, best to water the plant. If the soil feels wet, you probably have too much water in the root area. The roots may be rotting and not capable of absorbing water. Plants that have been over-watered need to be repotted into fresh soil.

I'M LOSING MY BEAUTIFUL LEAVES

Sudden loss of leaves is usually caused by rapid temperature changes. However, it can also be caused by prolonged hot or cold drafts, dry air, and exposure to gasoline or furnace fumes or by just a change in location from a sunny to a darker location.

WHY ARE MY LEAVES TURNING YELLOW?

Yellowing leaves may indicate a nutrient deficiency, usually from lack of iron or nitrogen. Try giving the plant a nitrogen fertilizer and if that does not work after a few days then try giving the plant a chelated iron product. However, the problem may also be due to excessive moisture or root rot. If you remove the root ball, the root tips should be white or cream-colored. If the roots are rotted, they will appear a brown-black color and will appear slimy. If they are severely rotted, they will be hollowed out and easily broken between your thumb and forefinger.

WHY ARE MY LEAVES GETTING POLKA-DOTTED?

This is probably a spider mite infestation and if you remove a leaf and shake it over a piece of white paper, you may see little specks moving around.

I SMELL GAS EVEN IF YOU DON'T

Plants are very sensitive to gasses and will show symptoms before the gas concentration is at a detectable level for humans.

MY LEAVES ARE STARTING TO BLUSH

Bronzing or abnormally reddening of the leaves may indicate damage by too cold a temperature or a deficiency of phosphorus or potassium. Best to check the recommended temperature range for the plant. If you think that the problem is from a nutrient deficiency then it is best to repot the plant then add a complete fertilizer.

THESE BROWN TIPS DO NOT LOOK VERY NICE

If your plant is developing brown on the tips of the leaves it is usually caused by exposure to hot dry air, improper watering, insect feeding, salt accumulations or some object is rubbing against the leaves. Chlorinated water may also cause the problem.

I'M GETTING UGLY

There are a number of leaf problems such as leaf thickening, curling, leaf and flower drop that are usually also accompanied by leaf yellowing and browning. These may be due to gas fumes or pesticides, which are toxic to the plant.

SOILED AGAIN
Garden soil that is contaminated with agricultural chemicals and then used for potting soil on house, plants can result in chemical injury to the plants.

SHOWER WITH YOUR PLANTS
If you really like your houseplants then take them into the bathroom when you take your shower. They love the heat and humidity!

LOOKS LIKE SNOW
White substances on the soil surface may indicate two things. If the white area is crusty or crystalline in nature, it's probably an accumulation of salts. This crusty layer on the soil can be removed and replaced with fresh soil when the plant is potted in a different container.

BEHOLD! A MOLD
If there is a white or light yellow mold-like growth on the soil, it may indicate the presence of saprophytic soil fungus. This is a fungus that lives on dead and decaying matter and will not harm the plant but may very well indicate a non-sterile potting mixture or an over-watered plant.

BROWN SCABS, YUK!
If you see light brown corky scabs on the underneath side of leaves along the stems, it usually means you have over-watered the plant. This condition is called "oedema" and more careful watering and good drainage will solve the problem.

FLOWER, LIFE EXTENDER
The following ingredients will be needed:

3	Tablespoons of granulated sugar
2	Tablespoons of white vinegar
1	Quart of warm tap water

Place the ingredients in a small bowl and mix well, then pour the solution into the flower vase. The stems of the flowers should be in at least 3 inches of the solution.

MAKING NUTRIENTS MORE AVAILABLE

When your houseplants start looking a little peaked and pale, they are probably undernourished and need a booster. If you're using hard water to water them, the nutrients are harder to remove for the plant. A small amount of vinegar added to the water will make the minerals and nutrients more available and will produce a healthier, better-looking plant.

FERTILIZER FOR FLOWERING HOUSE PLANTS

The following ingredients will be needed:

3	**Parts bone meal**
3	**Parts cottonseed meal**
3	**Parts wood ashes**

Place all the ingredients into a large mixing bowl and blend thoroughly. All ingredients can be found at a nursery. Mix the fertilizer into the soil with a plastic fork. A six-inch pot will require about 1 teaspoon every 5-7 weeks to remain in super health.

PEPPER-UPPER FOR HOUSE PLANTS

The following ingredients will be needed:

1	**Tablespoon apple cider vinegar (5% acidity)**
1	**Gallon of cool tap water**

Place the ingredients into a medium bucket and mix well and add 2 teaspoons to your water whenever you water. This supplementation will make additional minerals more available to your houseplants.

OUTDOOR PLANTS

GENERAL INFORMATION:

Many outdoor plants are called "annuals." Annuals are plants that flower, set their seeds and die off. They have a short lifespan and most of their energy goes into producing flowers instead of a hearty root system. They usually grow very quickly and produce a flower the first year they are planted.

Biennials are plants that take about 2 years to grow and produce flowers. Many of the annuals and biennials will self sow and keep producing flowers. Perennials are just plants that always continue to self sow and have a different lifespan.

Never work soil that is too wet or you will damage the soil. When you can squeeze a handful of soil and it crumbles then it is OK to work or till. Never walk back and forth on wet or very damp soil. This will damage the soil by compressing it too much. By compacting the soil you can damage the root system of the plants.

The day before you plan on planting any plants, be sure and turn the soil over well. Be sure to also water the soil to allow it to settle.

I'M SMALL FOR MY AGE
If you plant a few very rusty nails around your African violets, the blossoms will be larger. The plants like a little iron in their diet

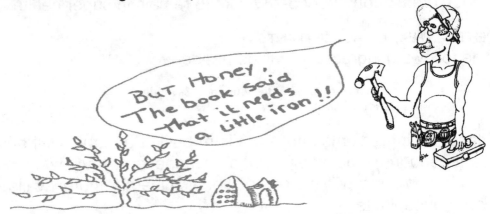

ISOLATION IS A MUST
When you add a new plant to an existing bed of plants, be sure and place the new plant in isolation for 2-3 weeks before you plant it. Be sure and inspect the plant every 3-4 days to be sure that there are no insects or areas of disease forming before planting it. Even new plants from nurseries can pose a problem.

WHAT A SHOCKER
New plants that have been grown in a greenhouse environment often go into "greenhouse shock." The healthy leaves wilt, there is a tendency to over-water and the plant dies.

To avoid greenhouse shock, try placing a plastic bag over the plant for 1-2 weeks and gradually open the bag over the 1-2 week period, just a little each day. The plant will acclimate to the different humidity of its new surroundings.

GREEN METAL TIES CUTTING INTO YOUR PLANTS?
Old pantyhose can be cut into narrow strips and used to tie up plants. This works better than green metal or plastic ties. The pantyhose expand as the plant grows.

DON'T LET THIS SLIP BY
Save your banana, peels and eggshells to be used for plant fertilizer. Banana peels are an excellent source of potassium and phosphorus and eggshells contain a number of minerals especially calcium. Crush the egg shells into a fine powder and slice the banana peels into as small a pieces as possible, then just mix them together and place a small amount around the base of the plants or mix a small amount in with potting soil when you are transplanting.

A SAFER PLANT DRINK
Most of the tap water in the United States contains chlorine. The chlorine is not going to kill the plant but might make it ill. If you allow tap water to remain at room temperature for 24 hours the chlorine will dissipate into the air and the water will be safer for the plants. Cold water also has a tendency to shock plants and room temperature water is best.

BAG 'EM
If you can't plant cuttings immediately, the best way to store them is to place them into a plastic bag and save them in the vegetable drawer in the refrigerator. Spray a small amount of room temperature water into the bag and seal well. The cuttings should last and still be in good shape for up to 5-7 days.

SUNLIGHT TO THE RESCUE
Potting mixes should be sterilized to kill bacteria and weed seeds. One of the simplest ways to do this is to place the potting mix or compost soil mixture in a clean wheelbarrow.

Only place a 2-3 inch layer and cover the layer with plastic bags and leave it in full sunlight for about 8 hours. The mixture should be turned 3 times during this period.

HOLY MIX
To make it easy to start plants and seeds, just purchase a bag of planting mix or peat and poke holes in the top while the bag is lying on its side. Plant small starter plants or seeds in the holes and punch holes in the bottom for drainage. When the seeds or plants are ready to be planted, just plant the entire bag as is.

YOUNG ONES ARE BEST
Best to purchase young, small shrubs. They are much easier to grow and will actually grow more rapidly than larger ones, which will be more expensive as well.

GET OUT THE MAGNIFYING GLASS
Be sure and check the roots of any plant you are purchasing to be sure that the root system is adequate and not in a stunted condition for that size plant.

GRANDMA'S ROSEBUSH SECRETS

Next time you plant rosebush slips, try inserting the slip into the center of a white potato. The rose slips will take root faster. The old-fashioned clothespins work great to hold onto rosebushes while you are trimming them. When planting roses, be sure and add some chopped banana skins to the hole. Banana skins will improve the texture of the soil as well as help the soil to retain moisture.

Before planting roses, be sure and place them into a bucket of water for 1 hour or more so that you will be able to untangle the root ball before planting. The hole that you prepare for the root ball should be about twice the size of the root ball for the best results. If you are going to plant roses in a heavy soil, make sure that you do not add any type of organic matter that tends to retain water.

Organic matter tends to draw water out of the moist soil and create a very wet area around the roots. This may cause damage to the root system

A CHILLING FACT
Many plants, trees and shrubs have certain chilling requirements. Many trees and plants need a number of hours below 45^{0}F before their buds may be ready to break dormancy. If the buds do not open in time they will drop off before blossoming. Fruit trees are especially susceptible to this problem in California.

OUTDOOR WIRING

PROTECTION
When burying an electric wire or cable, be sure and place a pressure-treated or redwood piece of board on top of the wire to protect it from accidental digging.

ORGANIC FERTILIZERS

There are two schools of thought regarding organic fertilizers versus inorganic fertilizers. Most organic farmers do claim that their produce tastes better, however, most will admit that the produce tends to lose a certain amount of eye appeal. Chemically, plants cannot discern between a nutrient coming from an organic source or one coming from a chemically prepared concoction. The following is general information regarding organic fertilizers, which do provide well-balanced nutrients needed by the plants.

ANIMAL MANURE (dried)
Not the best source of nutrients but does contain a good level of trace minerals. Should be mixed with peat for the best results. The nitrogen, phosphorus and potassium content are about 1% for each.

ANIMAL MANURE (liquid)
Most contain the major nutrients but not in high amounts. It is high in trace minerals. The nitrogen, phosphorus and potassium content are about 1% each.

FISH MEAL

Normally sold as semi-organic since certain nutrients are usually added. Contains about 9% nitrogen and 2-3% phosphorus. Best if potash has been added on the label.

BONE MEAL

This is one of the more popular fertilizers and has the ability to activate root growth better than most. If you purchase bone meal the label must state that it is "steamed." Raw bone meal may carry anthrax virus, however, it is safe if steamed. Best to wear gloves and a quality mask when using bone meal as an extra precaution. Contains about 3-4& nitrogen and 22% phosphorus.

DRIED BLOOD

One of the fastest acting nitrogen fertilizers; used when a farmer feels that the plants need a "nitrogen boost." Best not to use dried blood if you expect frost or are in a rainy period. Tends to wash into the soil too easily.

Mid-summer is the latest this fertilizer is usually recommended. The nitrogen content is about 12-14% and the phosphorus content is less than 1%.

GENERAL ALL-PURPOSE

Should be composed of animal manure, seaweed, minerals and plant residues. This combination supplies the best all around nutrition for your plants. The nitrogen and phosphorus content will vary but should be in very adequate supply.

HOOF & HORN

These are very good sources of slow-release nitrogen fertilizer components. The horns and hoofs are high-heat processed to $140^{0}F$ before they are packaged making them safe to use. Needs to be broken down by soil bacteria and should be applied at least 2 weeks before it is needed.

Best used in the spring on cruciferous plants. The nitrogen content is about 12-13% and the phosphorus content is about 2%.

POTASH (rock)

Excellent source of potassium: which is missing from most fertilizers. Has poor solubility so it will remain on the soil and not be absorbed when it rains that easily. This allows the plants to use the fertilizer as needed.

SEAWEED (liquid)

Contains excellent source of nitrogen, phosphorus and potash. High in trace minerals and contains natural growth hormones. Good potassium level of about 3%.

SEAWEED (meal)

One of the best substitutes for general all-purpose fertilizer! Tends to be well balanced and has a slower release of nutrients. High in trace minerals and has an excellent combination of nutrients. Higher priced than most general all-purpose fertilizers. Best applied when the soil is warm. Has nitrogen content of 3% and is high in potassium and low in phosphorus.

WOOD ASH

Excellent source of potassium and phosphorus when limbs and small trigs are shredded; burned and composted into ash. The level of the minerals depends on the materials burned.

PLANTING IN POTS

GENERAL INFORMATION:

If the planting pot will remain outside year round, the pot should not be made out of terracotta or clay, especially if you live an area that freezes.

Many pots are porous and may drink up a lot of the water you are providing for your plants. Be aware that these plants may need more frequent watering. Clay or cement pots are guilty of high water consumption.

Wooden planters and boxes are ideal for planters. Be sure, however, that the wood has been pressure treated, if so they will be a better quality and last longer. Plant holders made from wire lined with sphagnum moss are excellent planters and do not require special watering methods.

Best to spray these and not just pour water in. The moss does not absorb the water very fast. The moss will also take water from the plant and you need to be sure that the moss is good and damp.

GRANDPA'S POTTING TIPS

BAD SOIL, BAD SOIL
Be sure and use potting mix instead of regular soil when planting in a plant container. The soil from the garden does not drain well and if brought indoors, the warmth may cause different diseases to get a start.

PLASTIC BETTER THAN CERAMIC
If you have plants in clay or ceramic pots, they will need more frequent watering since the pots are porous and causes water to evaporate more quickly. Plastic pots tend to work better, especially if you are using the pot as a hanging pot.

SCIENCE EXPERIMENT
Make your own potting soil for potted plants by using one part perlite, one part peat moss and one part vermiculite. Always add a fertilizer to a potting soil. Sterilized organic compost is ideal as an additive to potting mix.

FOAMING AT THE BOTTOM
A layer of small pebbles or rocks should be placed in the bottom of the pot to allow for drainage and to keep the potting mix in the pot. To avoid making a large pot too heavy, try using Styrofoam peanuts in the bottom.

NEED MY SPACE TO DRAIN
Never purchase a pot if it doesn't have a drainage hole in the bottom. When you place a plate under the hole, be sure that the plate does not touch the hole and cover it. There should be a small distance between the hole and the plate.

A COLD SOLUTION
Perennials should be planted in deep pots for the best results. The root systems need all the room they can get. This will also help them make it through the winter months.

MY ROOTS ARE DROWNING

Water in a drip pan cannot be left in the pan or it may damage the root system of the plant. One-inch of water, left for a week can permanently damage the roots. Potted plants should be checked at least 3-4 times a week.

I'M STILL HUNGRY

When feeding potted plants, it is always better to underfeed than to overfeed them. Use either a water-soluble fertilizer (one that dissolves in water) or a quality dry fertilizer. Watering washes away the fertilizer so if you can find a time-release fertilizer it would be the best way to go. Wait at least two to three weeks before feeding a newly planted potted plant.

KEEP THE DOG AWAY

Potted plants should be brought in the house in the fall before the first freeze to keep them safe. If possible place them in a warm, sunny location, especially the annuals and herbs.

IT'S MOVING DAY

If plants in pots are not doing well in the location you chose for them, don't be afraid to move them around and try different sites.

SOIL PREPARATION

There are only 5 main soil types: these include silt, limestone, clay, sand and peat. They all contain a unique blend of minerals and nutrients. The proportions of these essential elements will vary, however, even in a small area.

Managing these various soil types will determine when you cultivate the area as well as the type of plants that will grow there successfully.

SILT

When silt is wet, it tends to pack down turning it into a cold, heavy and badly drained soil, very similar to clay in consistency. Manure tends to help improve the consistency.

SAND

Has the tendency to warm up fast in the spring, which makes it easier to cultivate earlier than most other soils.

CLAY

Very heavy and cold and when compacted it becomes hard. Will not drain easily and is very difficult to work when wet. Usually a very fertile soil that is high in nutrients.

PEAT

Always a dark color and has a high degree of organic matter and nutrients. Must have some type of drainage and usually needs liming.

LIMESTONE

Limestone is a dry soil with a pale color usually with many small stones. Loses nutrients very quickly. Not good for deep-rooted plants.

WALKWAYS

KNOW ITS PLACE

To keep flagstone in place, use these suggestions: While most flagstone walkways are put down using only sand, they tend to move around. To secure them better, fill the joints with 1 part of dry Portland cement and 5 parts of sand (normally used to fill the joints). Pack the mixture in and sprinkle it with water.

WALKWAY MATERIAL

Use bricks that are weatherproof. These bricks have been baked longer and have a hard surface that won't absorb water. Hard bricks are usually a little smaller than standard bricks. Soft bricks will not last too long since they will absorb water.

WATERING

GENERAL INFORMATION:

When talking to a gardening professional, there is one comment regarding watering that I will always remember. When you water, **WATER THOROUGHLY AND INFREQUENTLY.**

Over-watering is one of the biggest problems most plants and gardens face. If you want a good deep healthy root system, then you need to water deep. Roots will develop deep if there is adequate water, good soil and nutrients to feed on.

Many people tend to water just enough to cover the ground. Watering needs to be adequate and allowed to percolate deep enough to do some good. Some plants are capable of developing root systems from 2-10 feet, which requires that the water sit on top of the ground and gradually enter the soil. Grapes and tomato plants can have 10-foot deep root systems if watered properly.

A 100 square foot garden will require 125 gallons of water to soak down 2 feet. If there is a loam layer then 190 gallons are required and if you have clay soil you will need 330 gallons to water the same area.

I NEED AIR!

Depending on how dry the soil is you are watering, the water runoff may be significant. If you have heavy soil, the penetration will be very slow and you can lose 50% of the water. One of the ways to overcome the problem is to aerate the soil by spiking.

GYPSUM TO THE RESCUE
Adding gypsum to the soil can help with water penetration. You can add as much as 10 pounds per 100 square feet of garden area.

GLUB, GLUB
Over-watering can fill the interspaces around the plant roots and actually cut off the plants oxygen supply. If the respiration of the plant is reduced or cut off it will affect the growth of the plant and can even kill the plant. When too much watering is done and the soil becomes low in oxygen, certain bacteria and fungus can become active and damage or kill the plant.

The days between watering, is dependent on the depth of the root system. Your gardening shop should have a chart telling you the root depth of your plants. The following is a chart on how many days to allow between watering:

	Sandy	Loam	Clay
Shallow-rooted	4-6	7-10	10-12
Medium-rooted	7-10	10-12	15-20
Deep-rooted	15-20	20-28	30+

WATERING TREES
The most effective method of watering trees is to dig a small basin around the tree to hold water and allow it to seep into the ground at its own pace. Some plants will also do better using this basin method of water retention. Make sure that you do not scrape away the plants surface soil to make the basin. Basins around full-grown trees should be at least 9-12 inches deep.

One of the best methods of slow watering to achieve the best penetration is to use a soil soaking hose. This hose has small holes and only allows a small amount of water to be released.

FURROW WATERING
Scooping out the soil between rows and leaving a furrow for the water is an excellent method of watering. Your furrows should be wide and narrow for the best results. Make the furrows before the plant roots develop or you may damage the plant.

A.M. ONLY

One of the best methods of watering is with an overhead sprinkler system. It will spray water evenly over an area. A fine mist spray is recommended, which allows for gradual water penetration.

If you use this method, make sure you only water in the morning so that the leaves are dry before nighttime.

DON'T PLANT MORE WEEDS

When you hoe to eliminate perky weeds, be sure and never hoe more than 2 inches deep. Hoeing deep may force weed seeds to germinate, surface hoeing is recommended.

WEED KILLERS

A GOOD HOME FOR BUGS

Many weeds seem to attract bugs that may be harmful to your flowers and plants. Weeds; such as Queen-Anne's-lace is a favorite of many beneficial bugs. Clover and lamb's quarter tend to be the favorite meal for rabbits. A few weeds will never hurt the garden. If you do need to kill them off, try using a more natural chemical approach instead of the commercial weed killers that tend to foul the ground water.

WEED KILLER

The following ingredients will be needed:

1	Quart of warm tap water
1	Ounce of baby shampoo
1	Ounce of white vinegar
¾	Shot of gin
1	Spray bottle

Place all the ingredients in a small bucket and mix well. Spray the weeds with a stream not a fine spray. The solution will adhere to the weed and dry them out. The gin helps to kill them and alleviate their suffering.

DANDELION KILLER
The following ingredients will be needed:

1	**Pound of iron sulfate**
1	**Gallon of cool tap water**

Place the water in a small basin and dissolve the iron sulfate. Place the solution in a sprayer and spray on the area where the dandelion problem exists. This solution should cover an area of about 400 square feet. If you notice that a slight burning of the grass has taken place, don't be concerned, the grass will return in 2-3 days as before. A second application may be needed if the dandelions are especially strong.

FENCES

INNER OR OUTER?
Posts, normally go on the inside area that is being enclosed. Some codes state that you must face the better looking side toward the neighbor or street. If you want to keep a dog, place the posts on the outside to be sure that the fence will be as strong as it can be.

TO MIX OR NOT TO MIX
If you don't know whether to just dump pre-mix concrete in a 4X4 pressure-treated fence post hole or if you have to mix it first, it is best to mix the concrete with water before pouring it into the post hole. If you do decide to place the concrete in before mixing, the area next to the pole may not get wet enough to cure properly.

VINYL FENCE COST
There are many grades of vinyl fencing! The fence sections are about $133 each, a line post costs $20 and the caps cost $2.50 each. This will vary depending on the quality since

WOOD GATE INFO
The best wood gate is one that has a welded steel frame with wood pickets attached to the frame. They will not sag like most wooden gates.

REMOVING FENCE POSTS

In most cases re-using fence posts does not work well. If the post is not in cement, just moving it from side to side should loosen it.

If it is cement, you will need a chain and pulley system or machine to easily get them out. Digging them out is quite a job, but can be done.

> Better put it in cement

It is also not recommended to use the same posthole if you can avoid it. If you are not using the same hole, just cut the posts off just below ground level and leave them there.

PLACEMENT MATTERS

It is best to place a hummingbird feeder away from other feeders for the best results.

BE NICE TO FINCHES

Finches like tubular-style feeders filled with Nyjer seed and sunflower chips.

GOING UP

A feeder should be placed about six feet off the ground on a pole with a baffle to keep the squirrels off.

PICNIC TABLES

DON'T TREAD ON THEM

Linoleum or floor tiles are excellent for covering the tops of picnic tables. A piece of linoleum can also be used instead of contact paper on kitchen shelves. It will last longer and is easier to keep clean.

SPRINKLER SYSTEMS

SHUT-OFF THE DRIP

If water is dripping from the outside shut-off valve, check for a loosened packing nut. The solution is to open the valve all the way then tighten nut.

Spray heads

These can be either pop-up that come out of the ground or they can have a stationary head.

The spray head is usually used in small areas where there is turf, shrubs or flowerbeds. The heads are designed to spray in all different directions. The most common patterns are full, half and quarter circles. They can also spray rectangular and square patterns and put out a lot of water in a very short amount of time.

Rotor Heads

These are available in two styles: stream: which are divided by a gear or impact. They are best used in large areas and can apply the water more uniformly than spray heads. They can spray in full or partial circle patterns with some brands adjustable to many different angles. Since they have a slower output compared to the spray heads, they are used on all soil types and with less cycling.

Drip System

Very popular system for irrigating non-turf areas and usually consists of a tube or hose with spaced holes or emitters along it. The emitters can be spaced at fixed distances so that they can cover uniform, closed spaced plant beds, or randomly to just water certain plants. If installed properly, drip systems can save time and money since it applies the water directly to the specific areas.

GET OUT THE MAGNIFYING GLASS

Be sure and turn on your sprinkler system during the day at least once a month and check the heads to be sure that none have a clog. If you notice a brown area then check the system immediately for a problem.

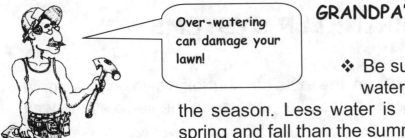

Over-watering can damage your lawn!

GRANDPA'S TIMER TIPS

❖ Be sure and adjust your watering schedule to the season. Less water is needed during the spring and fall than the summer.

❖ The best time to water as recommended by most landscapers is between the hours of 6PM and 10AM. Never water during the hot times of the day or you will lose too much water to evaporation.

❖ Never water after a rainstorm to help conserve water.

❖ Program your timer to work with the type of soil you are watering. Clay soils and certain areas that have a mild or steep slope usually cannot absorb the water fast enough to prevent a large percentage of the water from running off. Program the timer for shorter, more frequent runs with at least an hour between the runs to allow the water to seep in.

❖ Make sure that the battery is fresh in your timer and keep a copy of the schedule handy in case a power outage happens and you have to re-program the timer.

CHAPTER 12

ATTIC

ATTIC FANS

GENERAL INFORMATION:
In the winter be sure and cover the attic fan with a plastic bag covered in fiberglass insulation to keep the cold air out of the attic.

THE LOWER, THE BETTER
It will reduce energy costs by exhausting super-heated air trapped in the attic and replacing it with cooler air from the outside. The fan can reduce the temperature in the attic by as much as 55^0F. An attic fan can lower utility bills by as much as 25%.

The roof will last longer!

FAN TO THE RESCUE
An attic fan can have a positive effect on the life of your roof. Hot air trapped in an attic can cause heat damage to roof sheathing, felt and composition shingles. Many shingle manufactures will not honor warrantees unless an attic fan is installed.

FAN CREATES MORE COMFORT
By lowering the attic temperature, the heat is prevented from getting into the living areas.

GOOD PLACEMENT, A MUST
The fan should be placed as close to and above the roof peak as possible. If two or more fans are installed, be sure that they are at the same height.

It will be important to choose the right size fan for the job. Multiply the square footage of the living area by 3. This number should be less than the CFM fan rating at high speed. One air change per minute is what you are looking for.

INSULATION

The "R" value is a measure of how a material resists the passage of heat. The higher the value, the more effective the material will be.

GRANDPA'S INSULATION TIPS

Mild Climates
R-11 Used in floors and walls
R-19 Used in ceilings below ventilated attics

Moderate Climates
R-19 Used in walls and floors
R-30 Used in ceilings below ventilated attics

Cold Climates
R-19 Used in walls and under floors
R-38 to R-49 Used in ceilings below
ventilated attics

PROTECTION, A MUST!
Be sure and always wear protective goggles, dust mask or respirator and gloves as well as long sleeves and long pants. For added protection wear a hat, tuck your sleeves into your gloves and be sure and tuck your pant legs into your socks.

DANGER IS LURKING EVERYWHERE
Moving around your attic can be dangerous so watch out for overhead rafters and be sure and only walk on ceiling joists. If there is room, it is best to lay a plywood panel across the ceiling joists to walk or kneel on.

THE RIGHT ANGLE MAKES A DIFFERENCE
When you add batts or blankets; be sure and install them at right angles to the first layer.

AIR LEAK, GET A CORK

Best to avoid disturbing the existing insulation, especially if it is loose fill. Moving it may create gaps where air can leak through.

NEED MY SPACE

Never place insulation over recessed lighting fixtures, ceiling fans or ventilation fans. When using loose-fill insulation, use sheet metal to create a barrier around the openings. Be sure and also keep insulation at least 3-inches away from chimneys and gas flue pipes.

I NEED BREATHING SPACE

Be sure and allow for adequate ventilation. Never cover an attic vent and leave about 1-inch of airflow between the insulation and the roof. However, don't forget to insulate and weather-strip the attic opening.

HOW MUCH IS TOO MUCH?

If you live in the Midwest, you will need to insulate at R-38. However, check your local building codes for the appropriate "R" value in your area.

WHAT INSULATION IS BEST?

The easiest to use is batt insulation and always use unfaced batt since the paper or foil vapor retarder will trap water vapor causing a mold problem. It should also be installed perpendicular to the attic floor joists, which will reduce heat loss through the joists. You can also use loose fiberglass or cellulose.

SCRATCH, SCRATCH

If you are going to use fiberglass insulation, be sure and purchase the "no-itch" products. They are worth the extra money, are much easier to handle and safer to work with.

Put a cork in it!

SHOULD THE ATTIC FLOOR BE INSULATED?

The attic floor can be insulated if you are not using the floor for a living space.

FLOORING

PLYWOOD FLOORING AND INSULATION

How should the plywood floor be placed if we have blown-in insulation? Move the insulation aside and don't place the plywood on top of any insulation that is on the joists. Place the plywood on top of the joists.

AVOID SPLITTING UP

To stop plywood from splitting when you are cutting it, try applying a strip of masking tape at the point where you will begin sawing.

CHAPTER 13

BASEMENT

FLOORS

PEEL ME A FLOOR
Painted cement basement floor are notorious for peeling after they are only a few months old. To avoid the floor-peeling problem, just place white vinegar into a bucket and paint the floor with the vinegar first. After the vinegar dries, apply the coat of floor paint.

FUEL STORAGE

TANKS-A-LOT
The oil heat tank lines; should be checked by fuel company delivery personnel at least once a year. Usually before you put in the oil for the winter.

SECURITY OF ABOVE GROUND TANKS
They should be 100% level, on a secure cement slab and preferably anchored to the slab. The tank must definitely be anchored if you are not in a flood zone.

COPPER LINE INFO
If the tank has copper lines that run from the tank to the furnace, be sure that there is no direct contact between the line and any concrete in walls or floors. The chemicals in concrete tend to react with copper and may cause excessive corrosion of the line.

FILL-ER-UP
Be sure and install a vent alarm, which will tell the delivery person when the tank is full.

MOISTURE HAZARDS

DIY, NOT A GOOD IDEA
When it comes to waterproofing your basement, don't try it unless it's a minor problem. Call a professional.

BASEMENT WALLS
The best method of testing a basement wall for moisture or

condensation; is to tape a 1-foot square piece of aluminum foil to the wall with duct tape and after two days, inspect the foil. If the foil side that was facing the wall feels moist, you probably have a water seepage problem. Best to use a good masonry sealer and waterproof the walls.

BASEMENT SWIMMING POOL
The most common cause of water in a basement when it rains is from either a poor grade around the property that does not allow water to drain away from the house or poor gutters that do not drain at least 10 feet from the house.

LEAKAGE MAY BE A PROBLEM
A small amount of leakage may not cause a foundation problem, however, it may become a problem over time. You should have the drainage checked around your home and consider waterproofing the basement. If the hydrostatic pressure gets too great it may cause foundation problems and even cause a wall to collapse. A water leakage problem will affect the value of your home.

WATERPROOFING IS WORTH IT
If your home has been professionally graded and drain tiles installed and you still have leaks, it may depend on the water table in your area. Consult a waterproofing professional to assist with this problem. Waterproofing will increase a homes value.

ARE YOUR PIPES PRESPIRING?

If you have exposed cold water pipes in the basement, they can drip and create puddles. This will probably be worse in the summertime when the pipes collect water from the air and form condensation. The pipes need to be wrapped with an insulating material that is waterproof. The material can be found in any hardware store and grandpa can easily do the installation.

GRANDPA'S BASEMENT MOISTURE SEALING TRICKS

◆ The first step is to wire brush the surface of the cement wall to remove any loose or broken mortar or other extraneous material that has adhered to the wall. Old paint needs to be removed using the wire brush or sandblasting.

◆ Look for any multi-colored stains, which will affect a good bond between the cement wall and the waterproofing material. If there are any of these stains they will have to be cleaned with muriatic acid. Make sure when using an acid you wear protective gloves, clothing and a mask.

◆ Any cracks or holes should be patched with fast-drying hydraulic cement that sets even if it is wet. This can be purchased from a paint dealer.

◆ Be sure and seal the joint between the floor and the wall first. In most instances this area is the first area to shrink and pull away from the wall. If there is even the slightest space, water will enter. Fill the areas with a sealer such as Drylok Fast Plug™.

◆ The first coat of waterproofing should be applied with a brush so that it can be worked into the pores of the cement wall.

- ◆ Additional coats can be put on with a masonry roller. Be sure that you have good ventilation when working with these products so leave a window open if possible.
- ◆ One gallon of waterproofing should cover about 75-100 square feet.
- ◆ Best not to spread the waterproofing on the floor since these products will not take the abuse of walking on them. These products are made for walls. Be sure and spread it on thick, however, a second coat may be necessary if the seepage is bad, especially if the seepage continues for several days.

SUPPORT POSTS

HIDING THE POSTS

Posts can be disguised by just covering the post with slatted oak pole wraps that can be purchased in most hardware stores or home centers. They look good and are easy to install using construction adhesive.

CHAPTER 14

THE PATIO

BARBECUES

DIFFERENT TYPES TO CHOOSE FROM

Briquette Barbecue – These can only be used outdoors and takes about one hour to heat up. The temperature is impossible to control, but some chefs say that it does enhance the flavor of some foods.

Gas Barbecue – Very fast and the temperature can be controlled. Produced for outdoor use only. They may be banned in apartment and condo developments.

Wood-Burning Barbecue – These will heat rapidly and can only be used outdoors. Depending on the type of wood used, it may impart some excellent flavors to meats.

Electric Barbecue – Takes more time to heat up and cooks   more slowly. However, it can be used indoors as well as outdoors.

WHAT BTU LEVEL?

This relates to cooking heat intensity. The BTU (British Thermal Units) of a barbecue should be 35,000 BTU if you are only cooking for two people and 40,000 BTU for a family unit.

SHAPE MATTERS

The burners should be in the shape of an H, an 8, butterfly or serpentine. These will do a better job of spreading the heat evenly than a burner in the form of a horizontal bar.

BARBECUE SURFACES

Barbecue surfaces range form 273 to 611 square inches. Select a barbecue with a surface that will be adequate for the number of people you will be serving on a regular basis.

CERAMIC OR LAVA ROCK, THAT IS THE QUESTION

These briquettes serve an important purpose in the barbecue. They prevent grease from falling down directly onto the burners and absorb some of the smoke. The ceramic briquettes hold and distribute heat more efficiently but need to be replaced every three years. Lava rock must be replaced every year.

WHICH COOKING GRATE IS BEST?

Cast iron and stainless steel will conserve heat longer, however, they are a little more expensive than the porcelain ones. The porcelain is easier to clean.

TURN OVER A NEW BRIQUETTE

If you want to freshen up briquettes that have grease on them, just turn them over and use the fresh side.

DECKING

WOOD DECKING

GETTING LOOSE ON DECK

Wood has the tendency to expand when it gets wet and shrinks when it dries out. The deck will get elastic and tends to move more when you walk on it. The nails and screws get loose and the problem must be fixed immediately.

SWAYING BEAMS & POSTS

Beams and posts will lose their stiffness over the years and become more, elastic and bouncy. To repair this problem, just install cross braces between the posts and beams. Cut 4 X 4's or 6 X 6's (the longer, the better) with 45^0 angles on each end. Use 6-inch or longer lag bolts and secure the ends to the posts and beams.

LOOSE GUARDRAILS, POSTS & PICKETS

You will need to install lag bolts and washers to firm up the guardrail posts and pickets. Drill holes then install one or more lag bolts to hold the pickets and posts in place to the deck rim.

BOUNCY, BOUNCY, DECK SURFACE

You will need to add blocking between joists to reduce the bounciness. This will unify the joists so that when weight is applied to one joist it is partly distributed to those on either side. Never install blocking directly under gaps between the deck boards since this may cause areas that will hold water.

ARE YOUR STAIRS GETTING LOOSE?

You will have to temporarily remove the stairs and add solid stringers to the two outside stringers. You may also have to add 2 X 4's to both sides of the middle stringer, which will increase the strength.

BAD JOIST HANGERS

The joists may shrink so that the bottoms can no longer rest on existing hangers. To repair the problem you will need to install wedges and drive them into the gap until they are good and snug. If your deck is constructed without joist hangers, you will need to install them using 16d galvanized nails and secure them to the ledger strips and beams. For the joists you need to use galvanized stubby nails.

IS YOU'RE WOOD CHANGING COLOR?

You will need to apply a wood conditioner then pressure-wash the wood to remove the old coatings. Prepare the clean surface by allowing the deck to dry before sanding and repairing any flaws. Be sure and use an oil base, naturally pigmented, penetrating finish for natural wood surfaces that will protect the deck from rain and sun. However, be sure it will still show the grain of the wood.

SCRUB-A-DUB-DUB

If you want to clean your wood decking, just use a mixture of 2-cups of baking soda in 1-gallon of water. It will give the deck a weathered look, but be sure to test an area first to be sure that it won't affect the finish or affect the present stain.

FURNITURE

ALUMINUM

GIVE 'EM A WAX JOB
To keep aluminum lawn furniture in tip-top condition and looking great, just coat the aluminum with auto paste wax at the beginning of every season.

CANE, WICKER & RATTAN

GENERAL INFORMATION:
Reed furniture may need to be protected from too much moisture. It can withstand a certain amount of moisture, however, it is always best to protect it with a plastic bag if possible. When cleaning cane furniture use as little water as possible.

IT'S STARTING TO SAG AND GET LIMP
If the furniture has become wet and is limp, loose and sags, just allow it to dry and it will tighten up and retain its original shape and size. If it is dry and there is a separation, just wet it well and allow it to dry in the sunlight. If you have a cane-bottomed chair that has loosened, try applying very hot water to the underside and allowing the chair to stand in direct sunlight until it dries.

CLEANING WICKER
To clean wicker, you will need a toothbrush or other type of stiff bristle brush. Use vegetable-based oil soap like Murphy's Oil Soap to clean the furniture. Always tip the furniture when using any liquid to clean it so that the excess liquid will fall off. Another method is to use an old paintbrush and spray it with furniture polish to get into those hard-to-reach areas.

CANE PRESERVATION
Apply two coats of equal parts white shellac and denatured alcohol. The shellac will soak into the cane and preserve it. Then

brush on a coat of clear varnish to keep the cane clean and tight. Coat the underneath side as well or it will absorb moisture and stretch out of shape.

DISCOLORED WICKER, YUCH

To lighten the wicker, use a paintbrush to apply a solution of ¾ cup of household bleach mixed into 1 quart of water. Be sure and wear rubber gloves. You can also use ¾ cup borax mixed into 1 quart of water. If you want a finish then spray the wicker with clear satin urethane varnish or lacquer after it is fully dry.

VINYL FURNITURE

WARM THAT VINYL

After you remove the vinyl strapping, how can you get it taught again when re-weaving it? Use a hair dryer to warm the vinyl that you are working with and it will cool and be taught.

BUYING VINYL STRAPPING

If you can't find a location to purchase vinyl strapping, try the following Internet site. www.umbrellasusa.com.

RUB-A-DUB-VINYL

Cleaning vinyl straps can be a problem. If regular liquid soap and water will not do the job, start adding a small amount of liquid bleach to the water. Try using about 20% bleach to 80% soapy water to start and then keep adding more bleach until it does the job. If a 50/50 bleach/soap solution does not clean them then replace them.

POOL VINYL

Vinyl will only last 2-3 years when used near a pool. Chlorine, bleach, the sun and solvents will damage the finish and eventually lead to failure of the vinyl. If the vinyl is subjected to suntan lotions the pores will clog and the vinyl will not last very long.

WATER BEWARE
Avoid using unfiltered water from wells or ground water to clean vinyl. Unfiltered water will cause staining of outdoor furniture due to the high sulfur content of the water. This is especially true in Florida.

LIFE EXTENSION
Placing a towel that has been draped on the vinyl furniture will extend the life of the vinyl.

POWER WASHING
Power washing using plain filtered water is one of the best methods of cleaning vinyl furniture.

WROUGHT IRON FURNITURE

A DAB HERE AND A DAB THERE
This is very difficult furniture to paint and it is much easier to use a sponge and just dab it on.

CHAPTER 15

SPAS & HOT TUBS

CHEMICALS

GENERAL INFORMATION:
Chemicals are used in swimming pools, hot tubs and spas to control the growth of algae and bacteria. The chemicals that are available on the market are safe when used as directed and most contain chlorine. The most common is calcium hypochlorite and is used every few days. If the chemical is used in sunlight, a large percentage of the active hypochlorite is lost to the air as chlorine gas.

The buildup of chlorine gas is only of concern if you have an indoor pool. Since most chemicals are strong oxidizers and corrosives, they are toxic is ingested. Never drink pool water or you may become sick or develop a skin rash.

HOT TUBS

WOODEN TUB WAS EMPTY FOR A YEAR AND NOW LEAKS
Never allow wooden tubs to dry out, the staves shrink. The wood may reabsorb water after a while. If not get a leak sealer from a spa shop.

YUCH, CLOUDY TUB WATER
The water may be out of balance, you may have a clogged filter or the sanitizer level is low. Adjust pH and change water if over 90 days old. Have children shower before using spa.

I'M NOT BALANCED
If the water turns milky white from small bubbles when jets are running then the water is out of balance. Adjust pH level or possibly just replace filter.

FOAMING AT THE MOUTH
Usually caused by high contamination or soap residue.

I'M GETTING IRRITATED
If you are getting a skin irritation, rash or burning eyes, the problem is probably too much chlorine and the water is out of

balance. Open spa cover and allow spa to aerate for 10-15 minutes before using it.

RING AROUND THE TUB............
Maybe from body oils or cosmetics and filter are too old to handle the contaminants.

WHAT'S THAT GREEN STUFF?
You may have hot tub algae forming. The sanitizer level is too low and there may also be contaminants in the water. Need to add an ozonator and shock the hot tub.

IS THE WATER TURNING BROWN, BLACK OR GREEN?
This is usually due to excessive mineral content. Metal parts in tub may be eroding. Filter needs to be run more.

BAD ODOR IN THERE!
The sanitizer level may be low. You may have mold forming or have contaminants in the water.

I'VE GOT SCALES ON MY SURFACE
Caused by high mineral content in water. Use a surface stain remover.

WHY IS MY HEATER SO NOISY
The heating element is rarely at fault. The element may need to be re-aligned to reduce the vibration or tying down the noisy part with a clip or piece of wire.

UH OH, pH GETTING TOO LOW
Low pH results in the water becoming too acidic. This problem can cause erosion of parts and ruin the spa.

NOT GETTING HOT ENOUGH
In 80% of all cases, you will need to replace the filter. If that doesn't fix it, it would be best to call a professional.

I NEED MY THERMAL BLANKIE
Great investment to keep the heat in the tub if the tub is outside! They also work great for indoor tubs.

GRANDPA'S KIDS POOL SAFETY

GENERAL INFORMATION:

The following are safety tips and recommendations to protect children around swimming pools:

- ❖ Children older than 4 should learn to swim from a qualified instructor.
- ❖ Never allow children to swim alone. They may accidentally hit their head.
- ❖ Don't allow horseplay since it is too easy to get injured.
- ❖ Be careful about diving and the depth of the water.
- ❖ Never allow your child to rely on an air mattress, inner tube or inflatable toys as a life preserver.
- ❖ Keep a safety ring with a rope beside the pool.
- ❖ Keep a phone around the pool.
- ❖ Children should always wear a life preserver even if an adult is present if they are unable to swim.
- ❖ Never allow anyone to swim during a lightening storm.
- ❖ Someone in the home should know CPR.

SPAS

WHAT CHEMICALS ARE NEEDED TO CLEAN?

Use a special cleaner designed for spas and hot tubs. Do not use common household cleaners since they may affect the pH of the water. Cleaners should not contain abrasives or cause water foaming.

CLEANING THE FILTER CARTRIDGE

This really depends on the bather load; however, it is recommended to clean it every other week using fresh water from a garden hose to dislodge hair and any foreign matter.

HOW CAN I GET RID OF A SCRATCH

The only product that will do this is Novus™ Scratch remover.

PLASTIC FITTING ARE GETTING BLACK STAINS

Metals in hard water will cause this problem. They can be removed with a spa stain and scale remover.

TREAT ME TENDER

Best to treat the wood with a good quality water repellant sealer. The wood will resist cracking better.

LIGHTS OUT

If the bulb goes out in the ozonator it can be replaced. It should not be a problem obtaining a new one from a spa or pool supply store.

I THINK WE HAVE A LEAK

The leak is usually from the pump seal. If you can't find the leak, try adding some food dye to the water and watch for the leak.

PUMP IS JUST HUMMING AND NOT PUMPING

You probably have a jammed or broken impeller or the bearings have seized up. If the motor shaft can be rotated by hand then it may just be a dirty pump switch, defective starter capacitor, burnt motor winding or electrical problem with the motor.

MOTOR RUNNING BUT NO HEAT

Usually caused by a clogged filter, which will restrict water flow and affect the heat. Try and run the spa with the filter out, if that solves the problem, just replace the filter.

WHERE'S MY HEAT?
Check the filter first then the heater indicator light and make sure it is glowing. If not there is no power to the heater. You may have a bad switch or a stuck thermostat.

NOW IT'S OVERHEATING, I CAN'T WIN!
This may be caused: by a stuck thermostat or a stuck relay switch.

MY JETS HAVE LOST THEIR POWER
Usually caused by a worn out filter cartridge.

CHAPTER 16

SWIMMING POOLS

SWIMMING POOLS

GENERAL INFORMATION:
The majority of pool water problems are the result of the following: No free available chlorine, poor water circulation, poor maintenance, poor fresh water replacement or poor water circulation.

MY STEPS ARE CRACKING UP
Go to your local boat store and purchase fiberglass paint and gel-repair kit. The small cracks will cause the fiberglass resin to be damaged by pool water. The gel coat does need to be fixed.

SOLAR BUBBLES????
If you have air bubbles in your pool after installing a solar heater, the pump is probably undersized. Solar systems require a larger pump than is normally on a pool.

BUGS ARE EATING MY POOL
Whoever installed the above ground pool did not use sufficient non-petroleum based pesticide and herbicide treatment on the ground before the pool was completed.

THINGS ARE SURE GETTING DULL AROUND HERE
If the white metal side topping on your above ground pool is getting dull, It is probably starting to oxidize and needs a coating of aluminum polish and to be waxed. Check for these products at an RV store.

GLUB, GLUB
If your pool light fixture has water in it you need to replace the lens

gasket. This was probably not done when the bulb was replaced.

THE BEST FILTER
Diatomaceous earth filters are the best. Cartridges are easier, however, they are not as efficient.

GRANDPA SOVES POOL CLEANER PROBLEMS

SUCTION SIDE CLEANER

MOVING AS SLOW AS A SNAIL
First, check the pump basket to see if there is any debris in it then be sure that the filter is clean and water is flowing properly. Also, check the throat of the cleaner for any toys or other obstructions. The hose may have a break or split, which would cause the problem.

ONLY DOING HALF THE JOB
Check the length of the hose or the cleaner may be following the flow pattern of the pool. Be sure that the fittings are positioned so that the water flows somewhat downward. If fittings can't be adjusted then there are fittings that will fit over the existing fitting.

PRESSURE SIDE CLEANERS

CHECK THE BAG REGULARLY
This type of cleaner has very few problems. The only problem that may occur is that the filter bag gets full and was not emptied. The unit will keep working but will not suck up any more debris until you empty the bag.

ROBOT CLEANERS

IT'S NOT MOVING ANYMORE?
Be sure that the indicator light is glowing on the transformer, if not the transformer may not be turned on or the 3-volt fuse has blown. Be aware that the indicator light may still glow even if the fuse has blown. Check the electrical outlet to be sure that it is working. Make sure that the pulley

belt is not broken or worn out.

If the belt is OK then the motor may have shorted out and needs to be replaced.

MOVING BUT NOT PICKING UP DEBRIS

When you lift the unit up near the surface of the water it should gush water, if not the pump motor may be bad. Be sure that the impeller does not have any debris wrapped around it, if not make sure it is turning freely. If the unit is having trouble climbing the wall, this is another indication that the pump motor is bad.

YUCH! MURKY & CLOUDY WATER

The cause for cloudy and murky water are: algae, the hardness level may be too high, the filter is not working properly, too frequent backwashing, plugged filter, precipitating calcium compounds, wrong pH, the total alkalinity is wrong or there are dissolved solids in the pool.

GRANDPA IS AN ALGAE EXPERT

Algae spores are in the air and are always entering your pool. They are brought in by the wind, rain and may even be in your equipment or on a bathing suit. If the conditions are just right, the algae bloom can show up almost overnight. The conditions that algae, prefers is out of balance water, warm temperatures, sunlight, the presence of nitrates and even carbon dioxide. The usual cause is poor water circulation, lack of adequate filtration or sanitation problems. Algae can clog the filter and reduce filtration significantly.

There are 21,000 known varieties of algae. The most common varieties found in pools are the green, yellow, black and pink. Prevention is your best method of avoiding algae and proper chemical balance and sanitizer residuals is the key. There are a number of specialty chemicals that you need to be aware of.

Types Of Common Pool Algae

Green Algae
Common variety and may show up after a hazy condition in the water exists. If not treated immediately will turn into a green slime. It is usually caused by poor filtration or lack of adequate sanitation. It can be free-floating or clinging to the walls.

Yellow Algae
This may also be called mustard algae and is a wall clinger and usually on the shady, side of the pool. It forms a sheet and is very difficult to get rid of. Re-infection throughout the entire season is common. Takes a lot of chemicals to kill it.

Black Algae
This is one of the worst forms of algae and it is usually with you almost forever. It will appear as black or blue/green spots and their roots will extend into the plaster or tile grout. It can be brought into the pool in a bathing suit from someone who was at the ocean recently.

Pink Algae
It is really a form of bacteria that will appear as streaks in corners and crevices. It is a slow spreader and easily dealt with.

Algae-fighting Chemicals

Chitin
Chitin will help to bind up and remove a wide variety of impurities found in the water, allowing a sanitizer to work more efficiently to kill contaminants. It also has the ability to help the filtration system worm more efficiently. It may be sold under the name "Sea Clear."

Copper-Based

Copper has proven effective as both a mineral that will stop algae from forming as well as killing the algae. It can be purchased in a non-foaming strength of 3-10% and is effective on all forms of algae. The only problem with its use is that it mat stain white plaster surfaces.

Polymers

These are complicated chemicals that will either stop the growth of algae or kill them depending on the strength used. The percentage of strength runs from 3-60% and they do not cause foaming.

Potassium Tetraborate

If this chemical is added to the water in the proper amount it prevents the algae from converting carbon dioxide into the fuel it needs to grow. May be sold as "Protein Supreme."

Quaternary Ammonium Compounds

This is a low-grade algaecide; called "Quats." They are an effective algaestat and used as a preventive instead of a cure. If you see Quat 10 it means that there is 10% active ingredient.

Silver-Based

Works to prevent bacteria from reproducing and very effective in killing pink algae. It is non-foaming, but may cause black stains on white plaster. If you are going to use it ask for a sequestering agent to add to it.

Death to Algae!

- ❖ First, balance the water and make sure that the pH is where it should be.
- ❖ Check the filter system and clean it if necessary.
- ❖ Adjust the valves for maximum circulation and allow the pool to run 24 hours a day until it is clear.
- ❖ Turn on the automatic cleaners to stir everything up.
- ❖ If you have suspended green algae you will have to shock the pool. Add as much hypochlorite as it will take to turn the pool a cloudy, bluish/gray color.
- ❖ Brush the walls and floors toward the main drain.

❖ Backwash the filter as needed.

❖ If you cannot see the bottom of the pool and it has debris and leaves in it, it would be best to drain the pool and acid wash it before re-filling.

❖ If the problem is ongoing, it is best to drain the pool and acid, wash it.

STOP! YOU'RE EATING MY CHLORINE

Algae: actually creates a demand for chlorine and will consume chlorine that should be handling the problem.

It's probably your fault!

COUGH, COUGH, I'M ALL CLOGGED UP

If your pool filter is clogged, it may just be due to poor pool maintenance, chlorine level is too low or the pool is being heated to high temperatures too often and not chlorinated enough to handle it. A clogged filter; can also be caused by algae, calcification, hair, suntan lotion, improper pH or improper total alkalinity. Clean the filter and adjust the pH and alkalinity levels.

FOAMING SOAP BUBBLES

Usually cause by too high a concentration of algaecide or there is organic debris in the water. Adjust the pH, total alkalinity and free chlorine residue to proper levels. You may have to super-chlorinate and discard some water.

WATER IS TURNING COLORS

Usually cause by organic debris in pool, such as leaves, etc. Can also be caused by algae. Clean pool well and super-chlorinate.

SCALING, STAINING & REDUCED CHLORINE EFFICIENCY

Usually caused by not enough fresh water being added to pool. You may have to change the water if adjusting pH and chlorine levels do not work.

REPLACE ME, I'M GETTING OLD

Pool motors only last about 8 years before they need to be replaced or rebuilt. The motor will probably start screeching to let you know when there is a problem that needs attention.

GRANDPA SOLVES POOL HEATER PROBLEMS

The pilot will not light

The cause may be due to low pressure, poor air supply or poor ventilation. Be sure that the gas is turned on and that there is gas in the tank. Make sure that there was no water runoff from the roof or the sprinkler system and that the pilot light tubing is not clogged or has a hole in it.

The heater will not reach the right temperature

Check the thermostat first to make sure that it is set at the right temperature, however, if the heat loss is greater than the heater output, the heater may be too small for the job or you may just not have enough of a gas supply. The heater will also respond to the outside temperature and if it is too low that may be the cause of the problem. Solar covers help to slow the heat loss and you may need one.

Every heater also has a high limit switch preventing it from overheating. If the switch is bad it could shut off the heater, however, if the exhaust is blocked, that may be the cause for the overheating.

Heater keeps going on and off before reaching desired temperature

This may be caused by poor water flow due to a dirty filter, closed valve, external bypass needing adjustment, you reversed the water connections or the pressure switch is out of adjustment. Occasionally, the thermostat will get out of adjustment or may need to be replaced.

Strange clicking noises and sparking coming from the heater

Best to call a service man and shut the heater down until they come.

The heater is leaking water

Sanitizer damage may have occurred due to leaking of chemicals into the heat exchanger. The damage could also be caused by a winter freeze if the leaking started after the spring thaw. Other causes could be a faulty gasket or loose connection going to the pressure switch.

Heater is only leaking when the burner is lit

If you are heating very cold water, the problem could be from condensation, a missing or damaged bypass or excessive water that is flowing through the heater from a pump that is oversized. Also, check the heat exchanger for sooting and be sure that the internal bypass is functioning properly. If all else fails, try installing an external pool heater bypass.

The exhaust is dark or the heater top has blackened

Possibly low gas pressure or a poor air supply and venting. Best to call a serviceman.

Excessive heat has caused damage to the heater

Possibly due to low gas pressure, down drafting, poor air supply or inadequate venting. You may have to install a high wind stack or the unit may have been installed too close to a vertical wall or in a windy area. You must have proper clearance all around a heater.

Rust going into the pool

Usually cause by an imbalance of sanitizers or chemicals. Best to re-balance chemicals or replace any damaged components. Be sure that all chemical feeders are installed properly and you may need to place a check valve in to prevent backflow.

It whistles while it works

Probably caused by low gas pressure in the burners. Best to contact a serviceman.

LOCATING A HISSSSSSSSSSSSS

A good trick when trying to locate an air leak is to shut off the motor when it is under full pumping head pressure and look for water spray-back out of a void where the water was entering. You better be quick to locate the spray-back.

GRANDPA SOLVES POOL PUMP PROBLEMS

Leaking pump

The most common problem is that the threaded fitting carrying water out of the pump shrinks and allows the water to drip and eventually spray.

Replace with a high temp fitting. Water can also leak from a worn out mechanical seal. The seal is located between the wet end and the dry end (motor) of the pump.

There's air in my pump basket

The pump needs to operate without any air in the basket. Check the water level in the pool first and check to see if the pump basket lid is on tight and the "O" ring is lubricated.

The pump is not being very efficient

Possibly caused by the skimmer basket being filled with debris. Be sure that the pump basket is clean and is positioned properly. The pump basket can also have a crack in it and need replacement.

The motor is cycling on and off

When the motor runs for a short period of time then turns off and then on again later, it is probably overheating. If the motor is old it will have to be replaced. If the motor is relatively new then the problem may be in the electrical lines and there are connections that need to be corrected.

Motor making strange noises

If the noise sounds like screeching it is probably either the front or rear bearings and they will need to be replaced by removing the motor and bringing it to a repair shop. Another problem if it sounds more like a grinding noise may be that the motor is being starved for lack of water. Open more valves or find the cause of the obstruction blocking the water flow.

Motor is humming but not starting

The impeller may be clogged with debris and needs to be cleaned out. If it doesn't turn freely you will have to remove the motor from the pump and clean out the impeller.

CHAPTER 17

GENERAL PROBLEM AREAS

AIR CONDITIONERS

CENTRAL AIR CONDITIONING

GET OUT THE BUCKETS
If the roof unit is leaking water into the house, the drain line is probably plugged up causing a backup and should be cleaned out as soon as possible.

Attic fans are a must!

INSULATE THOSE DUCT
The ducts in the attic should be insulated.

IT'S COOL UP HERE
If the upstairs is too cool, place a gable fan in the attic and be sure the attic is well insulated. You can also try closing the bedroom doors.

WHERE'S THE AIR?
If the airflow stops after the unit turns on and will not start up again unless the unit is turned off for hours, the refrigerant level is probably low. I would try adding refrigerant before going further to see if that solves the problem.

WHY CAN'T I RUN?
This problem may be that the thermostat is set incorrectly or there is no power to the unit. You need to be sure that the room temperature is above the thermostat setting. Be sure and check the fuses and breakers.

NOT COOL ENOUGH!
If there is not enough cold air coming out to reduce the temperature to the set point, the blower motor may be going bad or the unit is low on refrigerant. If the refrigerant is too low, you will have to call a professional to fill it. You also need to check for a clogged filter.

NEW COMPRESSOR, BUT AIR NOT COOL ENOUGH
Since the problem is not the compressor, it is probably the blower

motor or the refrigerant level is low. They may have installed the compressor wrong as well.

KICK IT!
The fan on the outside unit only turns when I hit the top of the unit. The fan probably needs oil. Do not use WD-40. If that does not fix the problem, it may be the run capacitor, which is only about $10.00.

ON & OFF, ON & OFF
If the system is cycling too often it may indicate that you have an airflow problem or a defective thermostat. Best to check the condensing unit's airflow then check the blower and the filter as well as the thermostat.

WINDOW AIR CONDITIONERS

GENERAL INFORMATION:
Window air conditioners work similar to your refrigerator. They have a system that cools the air as it enters the unit allowing the air to condense on the cold coils and allows water to drip into the tray at the bottom. The warm air that is in the room is then drawn over the evaporation coil, which then collects the heat. The heat is then conducted into a refrigerant gas, which is then circulated to the condensation coils on the back of the unit and dissipates back to the outside.

WHERE'S THE AIR?
If you are not getting adequate airflow, the filter is probably dirty. The filter should be cleaned at least twice a month for maximum efficiency. Wash the filter in lukewarm water then gently shake off the excess water.

CAN'T HEAR A THING?
If the air conditioner will not operate it is normally that the plug has gone bad, the outlet has a short or the fuse or circuit breaker has blown.

OILY WATER IN DRIP PAN
If your air conditioner is not cooling properly and you see oily water in the drip pan, it indicates that you have a freon leak. Best

to call a serviceman.

TOO WARM IN HERE

If you do not feel cold enough air coming out there it may be that the temperature setting is incorrect, the air filter may be clogged with dust or the air flow from the outside is obstructed. If you cannot find the problem, turn off the air conditioner and bring it to a repair center.

HUMMMMMMS, BUT NO AIR?

The fan motor has seized up and you will have to replace it.

WATER FROM THE FRONT

If there is water coming out the front, the drain system is plugged and the unit needs to go in for a complete servicing.

OILING, BUT WHERE?

Some fan motors have oil plugs, which should be removed and a few drops of oil placed into the hole.

FINDING THE RIGHT SIZE UNIT

ROOM SIZE/SQ.FT	CAPACITY UNIT/BTU PER HOUR
150 to 250	6,000
250 to 325	7,000
325 to 375	8,000
375 to 425	9,000
425 to 475	10,000
475 to 575	12,000
575 to 725	14,000

If the room gets direct sunlight increase the capacity by 10%. If the room is well shaded decrease the capacity by 10%. Kitchens will need a higher capacity unit depending on the size of the kitchen.

ARTWORK

CIGARETTE SMOKE KILLS PAINTINGS
Airborne pollution, which includes smog and cigarette smoke contain harmful substances that will damage fine artwork.

NO WATER, PLEASE!
Some paintings cannot be cleaned with water, such as watercolors, tempera and acrylic pastels. These should just be gently dusted.

I'M CRACKING UP
Professional conservators recommend that you check fine oil paintings regularly for hairline cracks and have them repaired by a professional. If the paint is in good condition, just brush it gently with a small flat brush no more than 2-3 inches wide to remove dust. Go from top to bottom with very light short, downward strokes.

SWAB THAT GRIME
Surface grime can be safely cleaned off oil paintings using a cotton swab slightly dampened with distilled water. Do not soak the cotton and try it on an area that will not show. If there are any cracks, even hairline ones, **DO NOT USE WATER.** Change the swabs frequently.

I'M NOT TICKLISH
Never use a feather duster or cloth to clean a painting. The threads or feathers may get caught in any surface that is lifted or an area that has a small crack will catch the treads. If there is dust in hard to clean areas, use a small empty soft plastic bottle and blow air on the area.

CEILING FANS

GENERAL INFORMATION:
Ceiling fans are an excellent addition to any home in all parts of the country. They will make a room warmer in winter with better air circulation

and assist an air conditioner to keep the home cooler with less energy expenditure in the summer.

In the winter, reverse the fan and place it on low to draw warm air up to the ceiling and force it back down to the floor.

CERAMIC TILE

GRANDPA'S SECRETS ON SELECTING THE RIGHT TILE
When selecting tile you should know the right tile for the job to get the best results. Water can cause cracks in tile since they can absorb water and can cause damage beneath the surface. Buying ceramic tiles that have bee kiln-dried for longer periods at high temperatures will absorb less moisture. However, they are more expensive, which is why it is best to choose the right tiles for the specific job.

Non-vitreous
Best used for decorative purposes indoors and in dry locations. May be used around a fireplace or in a dining room but not in the kitchen.

Semi-vitreous
Best used indoors in dry and occasionally moist locations. This will include a kitchen wall or in a serving area.

Vitreous
Good multi-purpose tile that can be sued indoors or outdoors either in a wet or dry location. Can even be used on a bathroom floor, walls or patio floor.

Impervious
This is a more expensive tile that is normally used in hospitals and restaurants or other commercial buildings. The tile can be thoroughly cleaned and will not absorb moisture.

IT'S GETTING GLAZZZZY
The glaze on tile is placed on as a protective coating that is colored and fired into the surface of the tile. The glazes may be

glossy, matte or have a textured surface. Glazing will keep moisture from entering the surface, but the bottom, which has not been glazed, will still absorb moisture.

TILING OVER EXISTING TILE

Tiling can be done over existing tile if the surface is flat and sound. However, you will need to rub down the existing glazed surface with silicon carbide paper so that it will accept the new tile.

USING PENCIL TO CUT TILE

All you have to do to do a straight cut is to score the tile to be cut and place the scored area over a pencil and gently press both sides at once.

GRANDPA'S TIPS ON CHOOSING THIN-SET MORTARS

Water-mixed mortar

This is also referred to as dry-set mortar and is a blend of Portland cement, sand and some additives. It needs to be mixed with water.

Latex/Acrylic-mixed mortar

Similar to water-mixed mortar, however, it has either latex or acrylic added to it. These additives will improve adhesion and also reduce moisture absorption. They can be premixed with the mortar in dry form or added as liquid by the mixer. Best for wet or dry installations!

Epoxy mortar

This is a mixture of cement, sand, liquid resins and a hardener. It is expensive, however, it is excellent when used with any setting materials. Especially good: when used on a substrate that is not compatible with other adhesives.

Medium-bed mortar

This adhesive will stay stronger than standard thin-set mortar when applied in layers of more than ¾-inch. Best used with tiles that do not have uniform backs, which would include handmade tiles.

GRANDPA KNOWS HIS GROUT

All grout is, is a mortar that is used to fill the joints between the tiles. It helps to prevent moisture from seeping into the joints and stiffens the installation. In most cases, just add liquid and mix to a pasty consistency. However, stores are now selling grout-calking guns, which work very well.

Plain grout

May be referred to as un-sanded grout and is a mixture of Portland cement and special additives. Normally, used for grout joints of $1/16^{th}$ of an inch or less. Commonly used for absorptive tile and marble.

Sanded grout

Similar to plain grout but with sand added to it. Usually used for grout joints more than $1/16^{th}$ of an inch.

Epoxy grout

Contains epoxy resin and hardeners and is normally used when chemical and stain resistance is necessary or when high temperatures are expected.

Colored grout

Sold in pre-mixed packaging and in a large assortment of colors, which makes it easy to match any color tile. It is capable of filling any type of grout joint. If you prefer the look of cement, natural colored grout can be used.

Mortar
Similar grout to the sanded grout, however, it is normally used for joints between brick pavers, slate or other types of masonry material.

Pre-mixed grout
These are container-mixed grouts and are ready to use from the container. Not a big variety of colors and are somewhat costly. Best for small jobs!

CLEANING

GRANDPA'S CLEANING SOLUTIONS

Car odors
If you place a few charcoal briquettes under your car seat they will absorb odors.

Carpet Matted down
Place an ice cube on the area that is matted down from the furniture leg and allow it to remain overnight.

Carpet Stains
Remove a carpet stain immediately! Use baby wipes and you will be amazed that they will remove almost any type of stain by just blotting the stain out after any excess liquid is removed with paper towel.

Coffee Grinder
It is best to clean out your coffee grinder once a month if you use it at least 4-5 times a week. Just run 1 cup of rice through the grinder to clean it out.

Copper Polish
Just rub a lot of catsup on the copper bottom and allow it to sit for 6 minute then rinse it off with very hot water to bring back the like new shine.

Crayon on Walls
Just spray with WD-40® and wipe off with a clean cloth. If there is still a residue, just wipe with a damp sponge. A hair dryer will also work to melt the wax then wipe clean.

Decals

Transparent decals may be easily removed using a solution of lukewarm water and ¾ cup of white vinegar. Place the solution on a sponge and dampen the area thoroughly for a few minutes. If this doesn't work saturate the decal and allow it to stand for 15 minutes then try again with very hot water.

Flower Vase

To clean the insides of a flower vase or wine bottle, just use a solution of 2 tablespoons of salt, some raw rice and 1 cup of white vinegar. Shake vigorously for a minute or so.

Ink Stains

Place rubbing alcohol on the stain and it should make it disappear. If you get ink on the walls, just use bleach on it.

Kitty Litter

To keep the cat litter fresh smelling, just mix some baby powder in the litter.

Permanent Marker

Dab a sponge in rubbing alcohol and dab lightly on the stained area (do not rub). Don't over do any one area.

Pet Urine

After you blot it up and clean the area with hot soapy water and rinse it well, try cleaning the area with 1/3 cup white vinegar in 2/3 cups water. Dab the vinegar solution on then rinse well.

Shower Doors

One of the best cleaners is Resolve® to get rid of the soap scum residue.

GREASE CUTTER FOR SERIOUS CLEANING

The following ingredients will be needed:

¾	Cup of white vinegar
1	Tablespoon of liquid dish soap
¾	Cup washing soda
1	Gallons of very warm tap water

Place all the ingredients into a bucket and mix well until sudsy. Mop the area with the solution. Not recommended for waxed floors may make the wax gunky.

PORCELAIN SINK STAIN REMOVER

The following ingredients will be needed:

1	Teaspoon of liquid detergent
¾	Cup of liquid chlorine bleach
¾	Cup of white vinegar

Place a closure over the drain; then place 2-3 inches of warm water in the sink. Place all the ingredients into the sink, mix well and allow the mixture to remain for about 8-10 hours. Rinse with hot water.

DEHUMIDIFIER

GENERAL INFORMATION:

Dehumidifiers remove moisture from the air and protect the home from excess damage from the moisture. They will help prevent mildew, rusting of items, swelling of floors, drawers and doors. It does this by passing moist air over a cold coil. The moisture condenses out of the air onto the coil and drains the moisture into a bucket that must be emptied.

DEHUMDIFIER DOESN'T LIKE COLD ROOMS

The room temperature has dropped to 65^0F or below making the room too cold for the dehumidifier to work efficiently.

DEHUMIDIFIER IS ICING UP

If the unit is icing up you will need to move it to a warmer location or increase the temperature of the room. The room is getting too cool and forming ice on the coils. Other reasons may be that the condenser fins have clogged up with dust or the unit is too close to a wall or draperies.

IT'S STOPPED WORKING

If the dehumidifier does not work it is usually due to an electrical problem such as a fuse blown or bad cord or the water bucket if full and needs to be emptied.

I STILL HAVE A LOT OF MOISTURE?

Not removing moisture: can be caused by a slow fan or a fan motor that is not working. If the coils are too dirty this can also cause the problem.

IS THERE A MOUSE IN DA HOUSE - IT'S A BIT NOISY IN THERE

 Squealing noises; are usually caused by a bad fan motor that will need to be replaced. However, the sound can also be caused; by screws, trim or exterior panels rattling or vibrating.

The other common problem is that the rubber; in the mounts have hardened over time.

CLICK, CLICK, NO WATER

The clicking noise is caused by the compressor trying to start but cannot. The problem is either a bad start relay or a bad compressor.

GETTING EXPENSIVE

Your electric bill will be higher when running a dehumidifier. It is almost equal to running a window air conditioner.

IT'S RUNNING AWAY

The unit should not run all the time unless you are finding the water reservoir filled frequently. This just means that there is a lot of humidity. If it is running all the time and the reservoir is not filling there is a mechanical problem that needs to be repaired.

RUN, RUN, RUN, I'M GETTING TIRED

Dehumidifiers usually do not need to run all year long. In northern climates they only need to run during the hot months. In southern climates if you run an air conditioner you probably don't need to run the dehumidifier at all. If you have a damp cellar or basement, you may have to run one all year round in that location.

DOORS

ARE YOU GETTING IN A BIND?

If you are having a problem with a door binding, just place a chalk line down the door then close the door and open it. Wherever there is a smear in the line is where the binding is taking place. Now you will know where to plane.

MY INTERIOR DOOR IS STICKING

- ❖ This is normal due to humidity causing door, jamb expansion. It can also be caused by settlement or swelling from moisture. You will need to adjust striker, hinges or jambs.
- ❖ Check the hinge screws on the door and the hinge screws on the jamb. They may be loose and just need to be tightened.

- ❖ If they are loose, the door will sag and rub against the frame. Open the door as far as it will go and tighten the screws.
- ❖ If the holes have become enlarged, just pack the holes with wooden toothpicks that have been dipped in glue. Make sure that the glue has set completely before attempting to place the screw back in.
- ❖ If one of the hinges need to be adjusted, just cut a piece of sturdy cardboard the same size as the hinge and place it behind the hinge before you replace the screws. It may be either the top hinge or the bottom hinge. If one thickness does not work, use two thicknesses.

DOOR WON'T STAY CLOSED
The striker plate is out of adjustment.

REMOVING A STUBBORN HINGE PIN
If you have a problem removing a stubborn hinge pin, just insert a nail into the hole from the bottom of the barrel. Tap the nail with a hammer, forcing the pin out of the hinge.

SQEAKY HINGES
Use a silicone spray, you have metal rubbing.
REMOVING A HINGED DOOR EASILY
Try removing every screw except the top one in the top hinge. You can then control the door as you remove the last screw.

BAD LATCHING ON ENTRY DOOR
Weather stripping needs to be replaced or adjusted.

OFF WITH THE DOOR HANDLE
To remove a door handle on an interior door, just look closely at the shank of the interior door handle and you will see a tiny slot or hole. Push a small screwdriver head or nail set tip into the hole and when you tug on the knob it will come right off.

I'M BECOMING DULL AND LUSTERLESS
Door has not been cleaned often enough. Apply a small amount of varnish.

HELP! MY PANEL HAS CRACKED
Caused by expansion or excess humidity. Putty the crack and seal the panel by either re-painting or applying a clear coat of varnish.

EXTERIOR DOOR IS LETTING AIR & WATER IN
The threshold is out of adjustment or the sweep needs to be adjusted or replaced.

WOOD DOOR TRICKS
Wood entry doors are not as popular as they used to be. They are subject to shrinkage and swelling with changes in weather. Because of this, wood doors only carry a 10-year warrantee. However, if they have cracks in them, just purchase some plastic wood and coloring stain to match the door, patch and sand lightly.

DID SOMEONE STEEL MY ENTRY DOOR
They are sturdy and resistant to shrinking, swelling, warping or splitting. They have a core of foam insulation making them very energy efficient. They also carry a 25-year warrantee.

IS A FIBERGLASS DOOR PRACTICAL?
These are now manufactured with a "porous fiberglass" and can be stained with wood gel stain. They look like a wood door and are more expensive than steel doors but will last the lifetime of the home.

DOOR, STOP!
A solid brass stop or a flexible spring base stop can be mounted

onto the door or on the wall and is just screwed in. A doorstop can be placed into position by removing your hinge pin and inserting the stop.

REMOVING THE OLD DOORKNOB
Remove the trim carefully by either unscrewing the plate or placing a screwdriver gently under the plate and lifting it up. There are two long screws holding the doorknob.

Remove the screws one at a time. The two parts of the knob can now be pulled out. You will then notice two screws; remove them and the bolt. The strike plate can be replaced if you wish.

GRANDPA'S DOORKNOB TIPS

- ❖ New bolts and strike plates may feel loose sometimes and can be fixed by using screws that are little longer than the original ones.
- ❖ When removing the parts, place them in order on the floor so that you will remember how they go back.

GRANDPA SOLVES BI-FOLD DOOR PROBLEMS

- ❖ If you don't know how to remove the door, just lift it up out of the bottom pivot and swing it away from the bottom bracket. Then pull the top pivot out of the bracket.
- ❖ When the door has been removed you can easily loosen the adjusting screw and then slide the bracket into the desired position. If the doors do not meet then move the top and bottom brackets toward the center. If the doors are pressing together too hard and won't close at all, just move the brackets away from the center. If the door is uneven and looks like it is sagging toward the center, only move the top bracket just slightly away from the center position.
- ❖ All bi-fold doors have a liner down the inside that helps hold them closed and normal wear and tear may bend them. If this happens, gently bend the liner back into shape with a pair of pliers.

PEEK-A-BOO, I CAN'T SEE YOU!

If you have a solid door and need to install a viewer, grandpa has the method to follow:

- ❖ First, determine how high you want the door viewer to be and mark off the height in the center of the door on both sides.
- ❖ Next you will need to drill a hole straight through the door. Make sure you use the right size drill bit or you will have a BIG problem.
- ❖ Roll up a piece of sandpaper that is small enough to fit through the hole and pull it back and forth several times to smooth it out.
- ❖ Insert the door viewer then screw both sides into each other.

STOP THAT WARP, STOP THAT WARP

Warping can be a serious problem! To prevent warping, which happens as wood expands and contracts; just use the same type of sealant (polyurethane or lacquer) on all six sides of the door. Be sure and seal the inside and outside faces as well as the top and bottom, left and right edges. If this is not done the door will swell and eventually warp.

DOOR LOCKS

SUPER GLUE TO THE RESCUE

If you broke off your key in the lock, just place some super glue on the broken part, wait a few minutes and pull it out.

PENCIL ERASER TO THE RESCUE

If you lose the cap to the glue, just use a rubber pencil eraser. When you store the glue; be sure and store it upside down from a binder clip.

REPLACING A DOOR LOCK

The following are the steps necessary when replacing a door lock:

TROUBLE FINDING THE LOCK AT NIGHT

If you have a problem finding the lock at night, just place a few drops of luminous paint around the keyhole to make it easier.

Latch-plate
It may be necessary to deepen the latch-plate mortise to enable the faceplate to sit flush with the door. Use a wood chisel and deepen the mortise area just a little.

Template
The new template should enable you to determine whether the hole on the face of the door is the right size (diameter) to accept the replacement lock. If you need to enlarge the hole, use a wood rasp.

Strike-plate
The existing strike-plate can be allowed to remain in place; however, you will want to replace the screws with ones that are 3-inches long. Check the hole and be sure it is deep enough to accept the new latch-bolt. It has to be in the proper position to depress the plunger on the deadlocking latch.

If you do change the strike-plate assembly, you will find additional hardware available, which is stronger and more resistant for this purpose.

If needed, you can reduce the gap between the door and the frame by just placing a cardboard shim behind the strike-plate. Be sure and use 3-inch screws.

CROOKS LOVE KEYPAD ENTRY SYSTEMS
The keypad entry system has gained in popularity over the last few years and crooks are having fun checking them out and finding them easy to open. The keypad tends to give many clues to the crook to figure out the code. Best to clean the keypad regularly to remove the fingerprints and smudges making it easy to decipher the code.

HELP! MY KEY HAS STOPPED TURNING AROUND
The following are solutions to the problem of a key not turning in the lock, even though it is the right key:

❖ Try using penetrating oil in the lock, but if you don't have any use spray vegetable oil both in the lock and on the key. Turn it back and forth several times to lubricate all the moving parts as best as you can.

❖ Pencils are made of graphite and they can be used to rub on the end of the key. After it builds up a little insert it and try moving it around.

❖ If it does work, move it around several times to lubricate all the insides. Be sure and use a "soft" pencil.

❖ If you don't have a pencil, try using talcum powder, which has a similar effect as the graphite. You can also get a small plastic bottle and spray the talcum powder into the lock.

❖ If you live in a cold climate and your lock is frozen, just heat the end of the key with a match or the cigarette lighter and try it again. The heat from the key should melt the ice and loosen it. A hair dryer will also do the job.

DRINKING WATER

GENERAL INFORMATION:

Most drinking water in the United States is safe to drink and is tested regularly. However, more and more pollutants are being released into our water supplies and the safety may be more difficult to obtain in some areas. If you trust the drinking water in your area than drink it! If not best to have a filter system on your home or drink bottles water to be on the safe side.

If you have a well on your property and that is the source of your water it should be checked regularly, especially if you have children since they are more susceptible to waterborne diseases than adults. Remember children's immune systems are not as strong as adults, therefore the quality of the water is even more important.

MY PIPES ARE KILLING ME

If the pipes that carry water in your home are too old they may be releasing harmful contaminants since some older homes still have lead pipes. When cooking use only cold water since hot water tends to have more contaminants from the pipes.

WATER PURIFICATION METHODS

There are numerous methods of home water purification systems. If you decide to purchase a system, be sure to investigate the different types and the availability of service for that particular system.

A number of units only produce a minimal quantity of pure water, which would not be sufficient for many families while other units do not provide the level of desired filtration.

Activated Charcoal Filtration Units

A number of the more popular units filter the water through activated charcoal filters. This method is very efficient in filtering out insecticides, pesticides, chlorine, and organic matter. However, this type of filter is not very effective in filtering out bacteria and un-dissolved metals, such as lead, copper, iron and manganese.

Filters need to be checked regularly and changed or the system will be useless. If you do choose this type of unit, be sure it does not contain silver to neutralize bacteria. Silver is not that effective and a percentage may end up in your drinking water.

Chlorination

Systems that utilize chlorine to kill bacteria usually produce water with a somewhat off-taste and odor to the water. The system must be functioning properly at all times or there is the possibility of the chlorine forming a dangerous element.

Multi-Stage Filtration

These units are one of the most effective and usually recommended above most other units. They utilize a number of filtration methods such as a pre-filter, which will remove iron, rust, dirt particles, and sediments as small as 5 microns.

They also have a lead-activated carbon filter, which removes lead and chlorine as well as a carbon block filter to remove chlorine, improve taste, remove odors, and most organic impurities.

Micro-strainers

A good method of filtration, however, it is not able to remove most nitrates and nitrites. It will remove almost all chemicals and bacteria.

Reverse Osmosis

This is one of the most popular units sold in the United States and utilizes a duel sediment filter system. The system is effective in removing up to 90% of the minerals and inorganic matter. The system works by forcing water through a thin membrane, which removes the inorganic metals.

Most units only store 5 gallons of water or less. This system only produces 20% drinking water and discards 80% as waste. Commercial systems are used to remove salt from seawater producing drinking water.

Distillation

Distillation is one of the most effective methods of filtration. Water is boiled producing steam, which is then cooled to produce water vapor, which is then trapped. However, certain gasses are not removed through this method. The more efficient distillers utilize activated charcoal filters as an additional organic material remover. Be sure and de-scale your distiller regularly or the efficiency will be greatly reduced.

Aeration

Radon gas is a continuing water contamination problem, especially in the Midwest United States. An aeration filter is the most effective type of filter to resolve this problem. A survey conducted by the Environmental Protection Agency estimated that over 8 million people are at risk from radon contamination.

Ultraviolet Radiation Purifiers

These types of filters are very effective in filtering out bacteria and are normally installed on wells in conjunction with other types of filtration units. This system does require a constant electrical line voltage. It does not remove cyst contamination.

Ozonators

These filters are being used more extensively than ever before and are frequently found on swimming pools built after 1992. They utilize activated oxygen that is capable of purifying and removing bacteria without chlorination. Recommended more for swimming pools rather than drinking water since the system may produce bromate, which may be related to tumors of the kidney.

Carbon Filters

These filters utilize carbon to attract the contaminants, which then adhere to the carbon. They are useful in removing odors, improving the taste of water, and eliminating organic chemical compounds. Their drawback is that they do not remove heavy metals.

Magnetic Water Conditioners

Since all home appliances or equipment that use water builds up scale over a period of time, these conditioners are a must for the homeowner who wishes to protect their investment with a minimum of repairs from water scale damage. These systems do not affect water purity; however, they condition the water magnetically altering the physical characteristics of water-borne minerals. The mineral will no longer be able to cling to the insides of the water pipes and no scale can be formed.

COMMON CONTAMINANTS IN TAP WATER

Copper

Usually more of a problem in older homes: stemming from the metal leaching out of the pipes.

Fluoride

Water companies add fluoride to reduce the incidence of tooth decay. While fluoride does reduce the incidence of cavities, it is also a very toxic chemical and must be carefully controlled.

Chlorine

Sometimes added as a disinfectant. People who frequently swim in pools that are chlorinated have reported arthritis and immune system disorders.

Lead
Leached out into tap water from older pipes.

Chlorocarbons
If chlorine is present it may react with organic compounds producing a harmful contaminant.

Organic Molecules
Includes hydrocarbons, gasoline, and cleaning solvents.

PVC's
Plastic materials: from water pipes.

Radon
Naturally occurring contaminant!

Minerals
Sodium content of some water may be too high.

Pesticides/Fertilizers
Filter through the ground and end up in our water supplies.

Microorganisms
Include fungi, bacteria, and parasites.

Nitrates
Residues from fertilizers!

Drugs
Residues from prescription pharmaceuticals

GRANDPA'S WATER TIPS

RISK OF DYING FROM PESTICIDES IN WATER SUPPLIES
The risk of getting cancer from drinking pesticide, contaminated water is about 1 in one million if you drink 8-10 glasses per day. The chances of getting cancer from smoking cigarettes (1 pack per day) are about 80,000 in 1 million.

YOUR TAP WATER MAY BE DRUGGED
Reports are surfacing that show drug residues in tap water, surface water and groundwater. These residues are from antibiotics, chemotherapy agents, numerous pharmaceuticals, tranquilizers, hormones, etc. They are excreted by humans and domestic animals and may be spread by flushing toilets, manure fertilizers and most types of sewage. German scientists have

identified 30-60 drugs in typical water samples.

GIVE IT TO THE PLANTS
Tap water should always be allowed to run for 2-3 minutes first thing in the morning in case contaminants have seeped in during the night.

YOU NEED TO GET THE LEAD OUT
Over 5 million private wells in the United States may be exposing millions of people to high levels of lead. A warning has been issued by the Environmental Protection Agency that certain types of submersible pumps may leach lead into the water. The problem pumps have fitting made from brass that contains copper and zinc and 2-7% lead.

It is possible to drink water with 51 times the allowable limits of lead in water prescribed by the EPA. Pumps should be made from stainless steel or plastic to eliminate the risk. For more information call the EPA's

---

Safe Drinking Water Hotline (800) 426-4791

ELECTRICAL

When it comes to any electrical problem, we recommend that a qualified electrician be called in all instances. The following information is to assist you in identifying the problem only.

BAD OUTLET
If one or more outlets on the same circuit breaker, is not working, you have an open line somewhere, which can be dangerous and possibly start a fire. If you have recently done any work on the line, check your work.

BAD SMALL APPLIANCE
If one outlet is not working after plugging in a small appliance, but the rest do on the same circuit, this is probably a GFI (ground frequency interrupter) that has tripped and should be checked first.

Know the location of all GFI's in the home. If the problem is not a tripped GFI or a circuit breaker, it is probably a loose wire in one of the outlets or wall switches. If you push the red button it may fix the problem.

THAT WAS SURE BRIGHT

If the lights get bright for a few seconds after turning on a small appliance you may have a neutral wire in your panel box that is loose. This is dangerous and needs to be fixed immediately. When you call a serviceman, mention that you have a "loose neutral" and he will be there very quickly.

SMALL APPLIANCES ARE TRIPPING GFI

If this only happens at night it means it is a low voltage problem and one of the wires coming into the house has a partial connection that has become loose.

HELP! EVERYTHING HAS GONE OFF

Reset the main breaker. Call the power company.

RECESSED LIGHTS KEEP TURNING ON & OFF

The light fixture is overheating. You may be using too high a wattage bulb.

WIRE COLOR & FUNCTION

Bare Copper
Used as a grounding wire.

Black
Be careful, this is a hot wire carrying current at full voltage.

Green
Used as a grounding wire

Red
Be careful, this is a hot wire carrying current at full voltage.

White
This normally a neutral wire that carries current at zero voltage

White & Black
Be careful, this is a hot wire carrying current at full voltage.

> Know your wire colors!

GRANDPA'S ELECTRICAL SAFETY TIPS

❖ Make a plan of attack for every project. Know what you are going to do before you do it.
❖ Did you turn off the power?
❖ Be sure you look at the unit and how it was originally installed. Make a sketch if you have to. Grandpa uses an instant camera to take a picture before starting and always keeps the original instruction books.
❖ Be sure and have a few small holders to place the tiny parts in.
❖ Save all the screws and small parts that you replaced for possibly future use.
❖ Make sure that you use the exact replacement parts unless you are upgrading the unit.
❖ Be sure that all electrical parts have the Underwriters Laboratory (UL) stamp of approval.

NOT A SHOCKING EXPERIENCE

To remove a broken light bulb, turn off the electricity; then try placing ¾ a raw potato or ¾ a small apple into the broken base and screwing out or just use needle-nosed pliers.

REPLACE BULB WITH DUCT TAPE

Place duct tape on your fingers; when you want to replace a light bulb to give you a good grip. Be sure to put the tape on sticky-side out.

BE CAREFUL EXTENDING

Extension cords have caused thousands of fires and are a hazard when not used properly. If you have to use one be sure that it is rated and is thick enough to carry the load. If the cord is rated for 15-amps you can't use it on a 30-amp appliance. If it gets hot it may start to burns and hopefully the circuit breaker or fuse will blow first.

FIREPLACE/CHIMNEY

SMOKE GETS IN YOUR EYES........................

To reduce fireplace smoking, try placing a brick under each leg of the grate. Make sure that you have opened the flue damper. Close the forced air heating vents near the fireplace. Check the roof for obstacles in the chimney.

FORGET THE ALUMINUM FLASHING

Aluminum is commonly used as flashing and extended around the chimney. However, it would be best to remove the aluminum if there is any brick near the chimney and use either copper or galvanized steel flashing. Lime from mortar will cause the aluminum to corrode.

A LITTLE SQUIRT WILL DO YA

When you are cleaning the ashes out from the grate, use a spray bottle on a fine spray to keep the ashes down before you sweep them out. This will keep the ashes from flying around the room.

PUT A LID ON IT

It is a good idea to place a chimney cap on top of your chimney to keep the squirrels, bats and birds out of the house. It will also shed rainwater, but make sure it is not one that will impede the airflow.

CONTROL THAT BURN

Controlled burns to clean out chimneys are done, however, they are not recommended since they do pose a risk.

STEAMING OUT A FIRE

If you have a small chimney fire, just throw about 2 cups of water on the hot coals to create steam, which will rise and put out the fire.

FIRE WILL NOT STAY LIT

The wood is probably wet or unseasoned. The firewood used to start the fire may be too large.

FIREPLACE LOG STARTER
The following ingredients will be needed:

5	Pounds of sawdust (clean)
1	Quart old auto oil

Place the ingredients in a safe container and mix well, then allow at least an hour for complete absorption. Sprinkle a small amount around the smaller logs or twigs and then light.

SNIFF, SNIFF
A smoke, smell in the house; is probably caused by dirty flue or leftover ashes that were not cleaned out. May need a chimney cap installed.

TOO MUCH SOOT ON INSIDE OF FLUE
Caused by burning poor quality wood or items that are not wood.

FINISH GETTING DULL ON FIREPLACE
Needs to be re-pained with a heat-resistant paint.

COLORED FLAME FROM LOGS
The following ingredients will be needed:

¾	Pint of methanol (denatured alcohol)
¾	Teaspoon strontium nitrate (red flame)
¾	Teaspoon barium nitrate (green flame)
¾	Teaspoon table salt (yellow flame)
¾	Teaspoon copper sulfate (blue flame)
¾	Teaspoon copper sulfide (purple flame)

Place the methanol into a spray bottle and add one of the above chemicals to the solution and mix. Spray the logs to be used and allow them to dry before lighting the fire.

CAUTION: Never spray the logs while the fire is lit. Methanol is also poisonous.

ASHES TO ASHES
Remember to save the old ashes from a fireplace, dry them and use them as a fertilizer in the spring to increase the pH (alkalinity) of the soil.

THE CURE FOR A DISCOLORED FIREPLACE

If your bricks are getting discolored; by smoke and soot, just clean it off with a spray-on oven cleaner.

CHIMNEY CLEANING TIP

One method of keeping your chimney clean is to place ¾ cup of salt on burning logs. The salt will place a lot of the soot in the chimney into the air leaving the chimney.

THE EQUIVALENT OF ONE CORD OF WOOD
The pile would equal 4X4X8 feet
You could make 7.5 million toothpicks
The usable wood totals 500 board feet
The wood would make 30 adult rocking chairs
The paper would make 450,000 personal checks
You could make 6 kitchen tables and their 4 chairs
You could print 245 copies of the Sunday Los Angeles Times

GRANDPA KNOWS FIREWOOD

Beech
Very tough to split and slow to dry out, however, it will burn good and provide plenty of heat.

Elm
This wood is best if cut in the dead of winter and dried for at least 2 years. Very hard to split and is not one of the better woods to burn.

Hornbeam
This may be called ironwood and burns hot and will last longer than any other wood. Very hard to find and only harvest dead trees.

Oak
One of the best firewood but needs to be seasoned. Tends to spit and sizzle if kept too long under cover.

Red Maple
Easy to cut, dry and split, however, it doesn't burn as hot as other wood.

Sugar Maple
Dries slowly and splits hard, but it burns hot and lasts a long time.

White Birch
This wood burns fast and not very hot. It is good for a quick fire and to keep slow burning wood going. Best to use as a fire starter if you strip off the bark.

HEATING

COLD AIR COMING IN MY DRYER VENT
The dryer vent needs to be calked all around the exterior opening.

CLOSE THOSE REGISTERS
Since hot air rises, it would be best to close some of the registers upstairs.

DIFFERENT TEMPERATURES IN DIFFERENT ROOMS
There may be an obstacle in the register or you may have to close off some vents.

RATTLING REGISTERS
Cause by loose louvers. If not call professional service.

LOW AIR FLOW FROM REGISTERS
This is usually a dirty filter problem. Replace or vacuum.

Good way to save money!

STOPPING WINDOW LEAKS
Window leaks can now be stopped using an expandable foam spray that will seal the area around the windows. This will only cost about $15.00 to do the entire house and will probably save you $60.00 every year.

HUMIDIFIER

GENERAL INFORMATION:
Humidifiers usually work when there is a furnace running and the home needs some moisture placed into the air. The humidifier works by allowing water to flow either into a reservoir that has a pad mounted to a cylinder that turns or the water goes through a screen or wick then into a drain.

A fan then blows air across the damp area and the water evaporates into the air. The warmer the air, the more evaporation takes place and most humidifiers are placed near a furnace. The colder the weather, the more humidity you will probably need since colder air is usually drier air.

The humidifier has the following components:

Water
This comes from a small valve that is attached to the household's water supply.

Pad or screen
If there is a pad, it will be mounted to a cylinder and there will be a small motor rotating through a small reservoir of water. If there is a mesh or screen, the water will flow through a trough located at the top of the screen in order to distribute the water evenly across it.

Fan
Usually the furnace blower fan that will blow air across a damp medium and cause the evaporation of the water.

Valve
This may also be a float, which allows the water to flow either into a reservoir or across the pad or screen then into a drain.

Humidistat
This will determine the amount of moisture the air needs and will turn on the humidifier when needed with the furnace blower.

BACTERIA IN WATER RESERVOIRS
Bacteria will grow in standing water and you should add a bactericidal solution at the beginning of the winter season.

CLEANING A WATER RESERVOIR
See the owner's manual since it has to be disassembled to do the cleaning. Minerals will build-up in the reservoir.

BEST TYPE TO PURCHASE
The most efficient are the type that is attached to your furnace and works when the furnace blower is on.

PREVENT LIME DEPOSITS
To prevent lime deposits from building up in your humidifier, just drop a copper scouring pad into the water container.

LOTTA RACKET IN THERE
The drum or belt drive mechanism may be clogged with residue and can be cleaned with a solution of 50:50 white vinegar and water. The fan motor bearings may also be dry and in need of lubrication.

INDOOR AIR QUALITY

GENERAL INFORMATION:
Indoor air can be more, unhealthy than the air you breathe outside! It can actually be harmful to your family's health.

The basement; especially can contain the most polluted air in the home since it is next to the ground. It is susceptible to a radioactive gas called "radon," which is a known carcinogen and a risk factor for cancer.

Moisture tends to be more of a problem in basements leading to mold and mildew problems and can cause an allergic reaction in many individuals. Condensation may form on walls and the basement is a source of sewage leaks. Carbon monoxide may also be a problem from heaters, furnaces or poorly vented dryers.

SIDE STREAM CIGARETTE SMOKE
Try not to smoke in the home since this is a source of many pollutants that can get into the furniture and carpets.

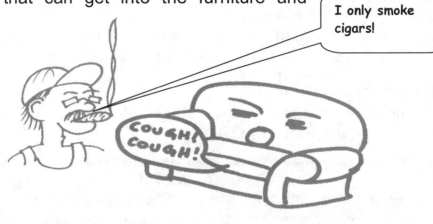

FOOD SPILLS = INSECTS
Remove food spills immediately.

HOUSEHOLD & PEST CONTROL CHEMICALS
Keep windows open whenever possible or run fans to circulate the air.

DRY CLEANING & CARPET CHEMICALS
If installing new carpeting, have the store unroll the carpet and allow it to air out for at least one day before laying it in the house.

PETS BRING IN ALLERGENS
Be sure the pets are clean.

BASEMENT MOLD, HARMFUL GASSES, MOISTURE
Have your basement tested for radon gasses. Be sure and ventilate the basement. Clean all areas with a quality bactericide product. Be sure that all furnaces are tested for leaks and sealed. Be sure that all vents from the furnace and gas-dryers are free of debris and cleaned of any mold at least twice each year. Purchase a carbon monoxide detector for the basement.

BASEMENT ROOMS A PROBLEM

Seal up any possible areas that could allow moisture to enter reducing the possibility of mold growth and other allergens to survive. If the humidity is high in the home don't have a lot of houseplants around the home. Be sure and wipe down walls in showers with a squeegee. Clean-up mold: using 10 cups water to 1-cup bleach. Improve air circulation with air-conditioners or other ventilation. Never use a charcoal grill inside the home.

GRANDPA'S CARBON MONOXIDE POISONING SYMPTOMS

Headache..........Nausea..........Vomiting..........Dizziness..........Confusion..................Tiredness..........Breathing Problems..........Sleepiness.........Chest Tightness....

HAZARDOUS CLEANING PRODUCTS

GENERAL INFORMATION:

Homes are loaded with potentially dangerous products to both adults and children! These may include cleaning chemicals, bleach, rat poison, mercury thermometers, mothballs, lighter fluid, drain cleaners, shoe polish and insect sprays. In 2006 almost 20,400 children were treated for overexposure to chlorine bleach in the home alone. Disposing of unsafe chemicals has caused hundreds of children to be hospitalized.

GRANDPA'S STORING AND PRODUCT LABEL TIPS

Products are not used the right way. Children are exposed to unsafe products. Many products can burn your skin even if they do not come into contact with the skin. Products are not stored properly or disposed of safely. Not reading the label and adhering to the warnings.

1. Read all labels completely before using any product that has a warning label on it.
2. Be sure and adequate ventilation when using any chemical product.

3. Wear protective gear if stated on the product label unless you fall into the Superman category.
4. Never mix any two products together especially bleach and ammonia, you are not a scientist and it will produce a poisonous gas.
5. Be sure and affix the top securely when closing a product.
6. Keep all chemicals away from the reach of children.
7. Purchase "Syrup of Ipecac" and have it handy it handy to make a child or adult throw-up. This should only be used if advised to do so by the Poison Control Center.
8. Try and use natural products and solutions to a cleaning or bug problem.
9. Keep batteries and gasoline away from direct sunlight.
10. Bring dangerous wastes to a recycle center.
11. Purchase products in childproof containers.

POISON CONTROL CENTER (800) 222-1222

LEVEL

MAKING A LONGER LEVEL
If you need a longer level, just place the level on a straight board and attach it with electrical tape. Do not use duct tape since it may lump up.

PLUMBING

BOY! DO I SWEAT
Sweating pipes can be fixed by placing foam pipe insulation around the pipes. This will keep the humid air from condensing on the pipes.

MY COPPER PIPE HAS A LITTLE LEAK
You will need a piece of firm, but flexible rubber and a hose clamp. Place the rubber around the area that is leaking and put the clamp on it and screw it tightly shut.

PLUG IT WITH BREAD
To stop a pipe from dripping water when you need to solder it, just plug the pipe with bread. The bread: will be easily dissolved by the water after you turn it back on.

TOILET BLOCKS & DRAINS HAVE A BAD ODOR
This problem may be caused by the vent stack through the roof being blocked causing the traps to be suctioned of water every time you flush the toilet. Chances are that if you hear a gurgling noise that is definitely the problem. Just run a snake through it and unplug it.

DRAINS ARE NOT FREE-FLOWING & STINK
To keep drains free flowing and to have a better odor, just place ¾ cup of baking soda in the drain and slowly add ¾ cup of white vinegar. This works well for smaller drains. For larger drains double the amount.

NOW I CAN FISH IN THE TOILET
The worms are coming in through a break in a pipe and the break needs to be found and repaired as soon as possible or this will cause more serious problems.

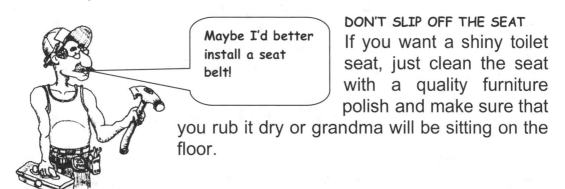

Maybe I'd better install a seat belt!

DON'T SLIP OFF THE SEAT
If you want a shiny toilet seat, just clean the seat with a quality furniture polish and make sure that you rub it dry or grandma will be sitting on the floor.

BROWN-OUT
Brown stains can be unsightly in the toilet bowl. The best way to remove them is with household bleach. Just pour 2 cups of bleach into the toilet bowl and swish it around then close the lid and allow it to remain for about 1 hour.

You should be able to just flush and the brown stain will be gone. *Be sure not to mix the bleach with any other type of toilet cleaner or you may end up with toxic fumes.*

PROPANE TANKS

TESTING A PROPANE TANK
To check and see if your propane tank is getting low on gas, purchase a stick-on gauge at any refill location and activate the gauge by pouring hot water on it. The gauge will change colors and tell you how full it is. Orange is empty and yellow is full.

ROOF PROBLEMS

THE WICKER DRIPPER
If you have a small leak in the roof and the water is flowing down a rafter, this can cause serious water damage to the attic joists. You can divert the water temporarily using a "rag wick" until you can fix the leak. Just tack a long piece of cloth or an old sheet in a strip along the rafter in the water's path and place a bucket under it. The strip of cloth will redirect the water into the bucket.

ARTIFICIAL CATCH BASIN
If there are leaks spread over a large area, just staple a plastic sheet to the walls and use it as a catch basin. Be sure and turn up the sides to create a shallow bowl that will hold the water. Be sure and mop up the water at frequent intervals.

SCREENS

SCREEN WEAVER
Get a long needle and try weaving the screen back together. Once you have everything back in its place, be sure and paint both sides with a clear coat of nail polish then allow it to dry. If you don't have nail polish, try using rubber cement or even airplane glue.

NOW HOW DO I SWAT FLIES?

In grandpa's early days screening material was made from horsehair and it wasn't until the 1920's when galvanized screening material was introduced to the public. Steel wire has the tendency to rust and eventually aluminum was used. Screening today is produced from either aluminum or vinyl-coated fiberglass (the more popular).

OUCH! There must be a better way to make a

The vinyl-coated fiberglass is the most popular screening material and won't corrode, rust or stain; however, it will stretch and tear more easily than aluminum. If you get a tear or hole in a screen door or window, the bugs will invade your home. There are a few easy methods of repairing these holes and grandpa knows just how to do it.

BIGGGG HOLE

If the hole is too large to weave back together, you will have to patch it or buy a new screen. To patch it, just cut another piece of screen about ¾ inch longer than the hole. Be sure and unravel a few strands on each side then bend the wires and insert the patch over the hole. Use the long needle to weave the wires back into place.

THERE'S A LITTLE HOLE IN THE SCREEN

The small hole can be fixed either by using a number of layers of clear nail polish or use waterproof glue. If the screens are plastic, you will need to use acetone-type glue.

STONE TILE

Marble

This is a natural stone composed of crystals that can be found in different colors and patterns. Used in many famous buildings worldwide and known for its durability and beauty. It must be sealed and can easily be scratched and stained by most liquids.

Granite

Has a tough, glossy appearance with colors ranging from light to dark and patterns will vary with graining. It is harder than marble and will resist scratching better, even resists acids. Can withstand freeze/thaw cycles. Be sure and get the hardest quality granite since some are softer than others.

Silestone™

Produced from quartz and is superior to granite for use on kitchen countertops. Will not scratch or stain and does not have to be sealed like marble or granite.

Slate

Rough-textured tile that is produced from quarried stone. Can be purchased in slabs or tiles, which are about 12-inches square.

Comes in two types: gauged slate, which is ground smooth on the bottom, while ungauged is rough on both sides. Very reasonably priced but somewhat brittle and does not have much of a range of colors. The darker slate has a tendency to fade in direct sunlight. May be somewhat difficult to work with.

STORAGE PROBLEMS

GENERAL INFORMATION:
There are many places in a home that could increase storage capacity without any major construction. Most homes have enough storage space, however, people are not aware of how easy it is to better utilize the space.

GRANDPA'S STORAGE SOLUTIONS

Most people feel that increasing storage space is too expensive and their home may need structural changes. Finding the locations for more storage space is grandpa's specialty.

❖ Extend upper cabinets to the ceiling. This usable space that is left unused or filled with soffits. These areas can easily be accessed with the use of a step stool and you can store items that are rarely used.

❖ Closets that are not in full use can be converted to provide shelves or a bookcase by adding the space to a room behind the closet.

CEILING MIRROR

If you store things on the top shelf of a closet making them hard to see and then forget what is up there, just glue a mirror square on the ceiling above the shelf.

❖ Access lost cabinet space that is at the back of the shelves by installing pullout shelves or lazy Susan's.

❖ Low closet doors make access to storage areas on top of closets. Install ceiling height doors.

SHELF FACTS

Never use particleboard for shelving, always hardwood or softwood and purchased in plywood 4X8 sheets.

NO. 2 PINE BOARDS

Very easy to work with and will be easy to paint. Be sure and seal all knots before painting. Be careful of warped boards so handpick straight ones with the fewest knots.

CLEAR PINE

Same as No. 2 but with no knots and is more expensive.

HARDWOOD BOARDS

These look great when stained or with a clear finish. The birch and maple can also be painted. Hardwood is harder to work with than the softwood.

BIRCH PLYWOOD

Fairly easy to work with and can be painted or coated with a clear finish. It is hard to stain and any raw edges need to be covered with molding.

OAK PLYWOOD

Very easy to work with and is easy to stain. However, it is more difficult to paint and will need molding on the exposed edges.

FIR PLYWOOD

Very easy to work with and grade AB can be painted or stained.

Stay away from the lower grade CD, which will not accept a finish.

VINYL FLOORS

YELLOW HERE, YELLOW THERE ?????????

This is usually caused by moisture or the floor has a rubber-backed mat. Rubber-backed mats and many padded area rugs should not be used in an area that may have a moisture problem. Many of these mats and rugs have a petroleum-base and the stain will never come out.

GRANDPA'S TIPS ON LAYING A SELF-ADHESIVE VINYL FLOOR

Follow the directions!

Step One:
Be sure and remove all the rooms' shoe molding, if any exists including the toilet if you are working in the bathroom.

Step Two:
Snap a chalk line from the center point to the center point of opposite walls. At the point where the lines intersect will be the center of the room. Using a carpenter's square: be sure that the two chalk lines are at a 90^0 angle where they meet. If not, adjust!

Step Three:
Place the tiles without removing the backing in a dry run along the chalk line. Make sure that you have at least ¾ of a tile going around the perimeter of the room. If this is not the case, you may have to change where the chalk lines intersect.

Step Four:
Start installing the tiles at the point where the chalk lines intersect. Peel off the backing from the first tile and set it, making sure that is aligns with the chalk line. Press it down firmly!

Step Five:
The tile should be laid in one quadrant at a time, follow the chalk line and keep butting the tiles edge to edge.

Step Six:
When you come to the perimeter of the room, be sure and cut

those last tiles to make them fit.

Measure the tile that you have to cut by placing two full tiles on top of the last full tile: then you will need to slide the top tile over so that it is about ¾ inches away from the wall. Use the top tile as a straight edge and draw a pencil line on the tile sandwiched in between.

Step Seven:
Now use a utility knife and straightedge to score the tile along the pencil mark and then just snap the tile in two. Peel the adhesive back and fit the trimmed tile into place. Be sure that the factory, finished edge goes next to the adjoining tile leaving the trimmed side next to the wall.

Step Eight:
After all the tiles are in place, roll the floor with a rented tile roller or use a rolling pin.

Step Nine:
Re-install the shoe molding or if it in a bathroom, it would be best to re-calk the areas around the toilet and tub.

REPAIRING A GOUGE
Gouges and dents in a vinyl floor can easily be repaired. Just shred a scrap of the vinyl with a food grater and watch your fingers then add a small amount of clear acrylic glue to the shreds and make a paste. Work the paste into the gouge or dent until its flush with the surface.

NAIL POLISH ACCIDENT
If you spill nail polish on the floor, don't use nail polish remover or you may cause even more damage. Use a scouring pad or fine steel wool and be gentle.

FOOD STAINS BEGONE
To remove coffee or fruit juice stains from a vinyl floor, just mix 1-part of glycerin in 3-parts of tap water. Soak a kitchen towel in the mixture and place it over the stain overnight. Wash the area thoroughly in the morning. You can also use household bleach, which works great on food stains.

HEATING PAD TO THE RESCUE

If you need to remove vinyl tiles, just use a heating pad to loosen the glue. Set the pad on high and place it on a tile for about 15 minutes. A hair dryer can also do the job.

WALLS

GRANDPA'S WALLBOARD REPAIR

A large hole can be repaired; by using a scrap piece of wallboard and placing a backup plate behind it. The following is a step-by-step method of completing the repair:

- ❖ First, using a sharp utility knife or small saw, make the hole into an even square.
- ❖ Use a piece of wallboard that is cut to about two inches larger than the hole, but barely narrow enough to fit through the hole. Drill a hole in the center of the back plate just large enough to place your finger in.
- ❖ Place glue around the overlapping area and carefully place the back plate through the hole and force it gently next to the hole until the glue catches. Remove your finger and allow the glue to dry fully before going any further.
- ❖ Cut a piece of wallboard about $1/8^{th}$ of an inch small than the hole and glue it to the back plate even with the rest of the wall.

- ❖ Next fill the area around the patch with joint compound, allow it to dry then sand and match the texture of the balance of the wall.

HOW FIRM I AM............

If you dip screws into water before you drive them into a plaster wall, the damp plaster will set up around them and hold them firmly in place.

MY STUCCO HAS A CRACK

This is caused by expansion or contraction. Repair by caulking or re-painting. If you don't fix the crack insects will end up moving in and the neighborhood woodpecker will have a meal and make the crack larger.

REDUCE SANDING TIME & TROUBLE

When you are going to fill a hole or repair a dent in drywall, just reduce the sanding time by rubbing the dried joint with a damp sponge. The texture you create will help blend the patched area into the rest of the wall.

WATER PIPES

KNOCK, KNOCK, WHO'S THERE?

If the problem is banging, you will need to locate the pipe that is not fastened down and fasten it securely.

The hammering; can be fixed by draining the water out of the pipes and adding some air. An air cushion chamber can be installed in the line to solve the problem.

CURING FROZEN PIPES

If the pipe has not burst already and you need to find the location of the frozen clog, just swab along the suspect pipe with a damp cloth until frost forms on the area as you pass over it.

INSULATE ME

Be sure and clean the pipes well. If you choose foil or fiberglass, be sure and wrap it around the pipes with a ¾" overlap before taping it closed. If you use fiberglass, wear the proper protection and wrap them in plastic after the fiberglass is installed to keep them from dripping condensation.

WINDOWS

GENERAL INFORMATION:

Quality windows can increase the value of a home and save money on energy costs especially if the home has older windows. There are many indications that will influence the purchase of new windows such as the condition of the present window frames, poor insulation, single pane without storm stutters. There are also different window finishes for different locations throughout the house.

KNOWLEDGE IS PRICELESS

When replacing windows, lack of knowledge is common regarding the different window types, poor evaluation of your present window frames or purchasing inexpensive windows that will not really do the job, however you can work within a budget and get good quality windows.

Choose a well-known company to evaluate and install new windows and remove the old ones. Learn about the four major types of frames: vinyl, aluminum, wood and fiberglass composite (new one). Choose energy efficient windows:

Low "E"
This window eliminates the majority of UV light that can damage furniture, paint and other objects. You still get the light but not the harmful rays.

Double-Pane
These windows have a gas between the panes that is pressure sealed. The gas acts as an insulator between the outside temperature and the inside temperature.

WINDOWS ARE FOGGING UP

These are probably double-paned windows and the seal is shot. There is no way to fix it and the windows need to be replaced.

Can't see outside

ALUMINUM WINDOWS BIND
This may be caused by a broken window balancer, which needs to be replaced. Or the tension adjusted.

REMOVE GLASS SCRATCHES WITH TOOTHPASTE
Shallow scratches; can easily be removed by dabbing them with a small amount of toothpaste and then vigorously rubbing the area. The "extra-whitening" brands will work better sine they are a little more abrasive.

KEEPS SHUTTING, WON'T STAY OPEN
The balancer is probably weak and needs to be replaced. If the balancer seems OK then try and adjust the tension.

TENSION ROD IS JAMMED
The tension rod is jammed. Call a repair company.

HELP! MY WINDOW IS STUCK
To release a stuck window: take a sharp blade (large X-acto knife or spackling blade) and go around the edge of the frame. You could also take a two-by-four and lay it flat against the frame and tap lightly with a hammer.

GETTING ON THE RIGHT TRACK
Windows will slide more easily if you rub a bar of soap across the track occasionally.

THE CASE OF THE RATTLING WINDOW
Almost all old windows tend to rattle and grandpa has the answer, just glue ordinary "corn pads" to the frames and they will quiet down immediately.

ON A CLEAR DAY
To prevent windows from steaming up, rub then with equal amounts of glycerin and methyl alcohol. This combination will neutralize the buildup of minor condensation.

FIXING A HOLEY WINDOW

If you have a few very tiny holes in a windowpane, you don't have to replace the window. Just place a small amount of clear finger nail polish in the hole.

MY WINDOW HAS MOISTURE ON IT

Usually the humidistat is set too high. Moisture accumulates on windows when they are cold and you have taken a long hot shower or are boiling water. Turning on a ventilation fan should help the problem.

STREAKER

If the sun is shining on your windows, try not to wash them until they are in the shade. When they dry too fast they tend to show streaks.

GRANDPA'S METHOD OF REPLACING A BROKEN WINDOW

1. Make sure you are working on a horizontal surface and remove all the broken glass pieces from the frame. Best to wear safety glasses and leather gloves. Place a piece of newspaper over the window and tap it with a rubber mallet to loosen all pieces of glass.
2. You will need to remove all the old putty using a heat gun on medium or possibly a hair dryer on the high setting. Use a putty knife or small chisel to scrape away all traces of the old putty.

CLEANING A PUTTY KNIFE

Cut a slit down the side of a 2-pound coffee can and place the dirty putty knife into the slit then pull it out and it will come clean and leave the residue in the can.

---

3. Remove all the old metal glazing points. There are usually 2 or more on each side of the frame. Be sure to find all of them.

4. Dip the end of a sponge in boiled linseed oil and then wipe around all four sides of the frame. The oil will prevent the glazing putty from drying out too fast.
5. Place a small rope of putty on the back-bed to keep the glass from rattling.
6. Position the new piece of glass in the frame and gently push it into the back-bed putty. Reposition the glazing points using the putty knife then place a small amount of putty around all sides of the glass. Smooth it out with the putty knife and scrape away any excess.

WINDOW SILLS

RAIN & SUN HAVE DAMAGED THE SILLS
Sills need to be cared for and kept painted and caulked as needed to last the life of the house. When you build a new home ask to have pressure-treated sills and they will last forever.

WOOD FLOORS

WOOD FLOORS, A TOUCH OF THE OLDEN DAYS
The combination of wooden flooring and carpeting is becoming more common in the last 5 years and lends a bit of the olden days to your home. The care and cleaning of these floors, however, take more time since they must be cared for as if they were a fine piece of furniture. Wood floors are more expensive than most carpeting and should be vacuumed regularly or the dirt and grime will scratch the surface and the floor will need re-finishing after very few years.

If your floor has been sealed with a varnish or shellac, never clean them with a water-based product or even clear water.

A turpentine product is recommended, in fact, most wood floors will be damaged if water is used since the water tends to raise the grain and permanently dull the wood. The only exception to the rule is if the floor has been water-sealed.

If the wood has been oiled, it would be best to just clean the floor with a mild solution of dish soap and just damp mop it to remove the suds and any scum leftover.

GENERAL CLEANER FOR WOOD FLOORS
The following ingredients will be needed:

2 ¾	Cups of mineral oil
¾	Cups of oleic acid (from drug store)
2	Tablespoons of household ammonia (toxic)
5	Tablespoons of turpentine (toxic)
2	Quarts of cool tap water

Place the mineral oil and oleic acid in a container and mix well, then add the ammonia and turpentine and mix well. Place 1 cup of the mixture into the 2 quarts of water, and then apply to floor with a sponge mop. Rinsing will not be necessary. **Keep out of reach of children.**

INSTALLING CARPETING OVER SQUEAKY FLOOR
Be sure and nail down all squeaky floor areas with deck screws through the subfloor and into the joists.

THE SECRET TO SCREWING SCREWS
If you want to make screws go in easier, just push the screws into a bar of soap before trying to screw them in. They will also never come loose if you place a drop or two of clear nail polish in the hole before you finish tightening it up. Another trick to keeping a screw tight is to wind a few strands of steel wool around the threads of the screw before screwing it in.

STOP SCRATCHING ME
The easiest method of stopping furniture from scratching wood floors is to place a few layers of masking tape on the bottoms of the legs or the bottom of rocking chair rockers. Place at least 2-3 layers so that the tape cannot be seen.

PINE BOARDS DON'T LOOK LIKE THE OLD ONES
If the new area gets sunlight it will gradually darken and look like the old flooring.

NEVER ON JOISTS

It is best to never lay a finish floor on joists. When you do this, you lose strength and the looks of the floor. Use a subfloor, which can be either planking or plywood.

POSITION IS EVERYTHING

Knots reduce the strength and do not look too good. If you have to use them, try placing the area with the knot positioned at the top of the joist.

WHAT DIRECTION FOR SUBFLOORING

Board flooring works best when installed diagonally. This will make your home more rigid and you can nail a finish floor on top of it in either direction.

STRIP!

The secrets of sanding a wood floor:

- ❖ Before you start, be sure and check for any protruding nail heads. If you find some, use a hammer and nail set and set them below the surface.
- ❖ The first pass with a power sander should be with coarse paper holding the sander at a 45^0 angle to the direction of the boards.
- ❖ The second pass should be with a medium-grade paper at the same 45^0 angles.
- ❖ The third and final pass should be with fine sandpaper and with the grain of the wood to remove any scratches from the floor.
- ❖ If you sand by hand, always sand with the grain of the wood, especially when you use coarse sandpaper.

SCRATCH, SCRATCH

If you get a small scratch on your wood floor, just use some shoe polish that matches the color. Use a soft cloth, dip it in the polish and buff the area. This will blend in the area and it will never be noticed.

THERE MUST BE A MOUSE UNDER THE FLOOR

If you have squeaky floorboards, purchase some powdered graphite in a squeeze tube and force the powder between the two floorboards. You can use a putty knife if necessary. The squeaks can be temporarily quieted using liquid soap, just pour some between the floorboards and the squeaks will be gone. You can also temporarily stop the squeak by sprinkling talcum power in the area and then walking over the area forcing the powder in the cracks. The oil from the powder will lubricate the boards and quiet them. Works great on stairs as well.

DEEPER SCRATCH, OUCH!

If there is a deep scratch, you will need to use superfine steel wool and dip it in paste wax. Rub the area and make sure you stay with the grain of the wood. The steel wool should even out the scratched surface and the wax will polish it. Buff with a clean soft cloth.

DANGER, WOOD GOUGE

You will need to fill the gouge to make it even with the rest of the floor. First, rub the area with superfine steel wool and make sure that it is smooth.

Using clear nail polish, place several layers over the area and allow it to dry thoroughly between coats. You may need several coats but the wood will shine through and you will not notice the gouge.

WOOD STOVES

GENERAL INFORMATION:
When using a wood stove, be sure and only burn seasoned wood that has been split and covered for at least 7-8 months. If the wood is too green, it will burn cooler and cause a buildup of creosote.

CAN I USE THE ASHES ON MY PLANTS?
Wood ashes can be used as fertilizer to help neutralize the acidity in the soil. However, never use coal ashes or you will kill your plants.

CAN TREATED WOOD BE BURNED IN A WOOD STOVE?
Treated wood should not be burned in a wood stove or you risk dangerous gasses and ashes.

WROUGHT IRON

PROTECT MY IRON
Liquid wax will protect wrought iron and help to retard rusting. Never use liquid wax on the wrought iron fireplace accessories since it may catch fire.

A RUSTY PROBLEM
Remove the rust stains with kerosene and a fine grade of steel wool. If it does not come off easily, try and allow it to remain on for a while to loosen the rust.

VACUUM CLEANER

SMELLS DUSTY IN HERE
Try placing a small piece of cotton inside the bag with a few drops of vanilla on it and remember never over fill the bag or you may hurt the motor. Change the filter regularly unless you have a machine with a filtered bag.

SNEAK-A-PEEK
Always check the floor for objects that may get into the vacuum cleaner fan and cause a problem. If you do hear a strange sound, turn the machine off immediately and clean out the foreign object.

GRANDPA'S VACUUM CLEANER PROBLEM SOLVERS

MOTOR WILL NOT TURN ON
1. Power is off at outlet – first check wall outlet to be sure you have power there. Look for a frayed or damaged cord.
2. Motor hums and will not run – You will have to take the cleaner apart and see if the fans are jammed – Remove any foreign object.
3. Switch to motor cord broken – Upright vacuums all have a handle cord, that is connected to the on/off switch that may be bad.

MOTOR RUNS BUT NO SUCTION
1. There is most likely an obstruction in the air passage – Clean out the hose or check and see if the bag is full. There may also be a leak in the hose or housing.
2. Fan loose or obstructed – Disassemble vacuum and clean out the fan or the shaft controlling the fans may not be rotating.
3. Motor binding – Poor lubrication, worn brushes, a binding rotor or a dirt commutator. It may also be a shorted wire in the field.

VACUUM CLEANER IS BLOWING FUSES
1. Circuit overload – Check and see if there are too many appliances on the same circuit.
2. Short circuit in power cord or plug – Replace cord or plug.

3. Short circuits in switch to motor cord – Fix, repair or replace cord.

VACUUM CLEANER IS TOO NOISY
1. Power brush noisy – Brush may be hitting the bottom plate and needs to be adjusted.
2. Fans blades loose or broken – Tighten or replace fan blades.

VACUUM CLEANER IS SHOCKING YOU
1. Power cord frayed – Best to replace it.
2. Leakage current problem – If you are getting a shock from a metal part take the machine to an authorized dealer.

GLUB, GLUB, BETTER BUY A NEW ONE
Unless the vacuum is made for water pickup, never pick up any liquid or moisture with a standard vacuum cleaner or it will rust the insides and ruin the machine.

COMB OUT THE BRUSHES
Use a common comb to comb out the debris and hair from the brushes regularly to increase the efficiency of the vacuum cleaner. The machine will not pick up efficiently if the brushes are dirty. Hair will also work its way to the ends of the roller and get around the end bearings causing the brush to slow down and place a load on the motor.

MISCELLANEOUS

BRONZE WOOL INSTEAD OF STEEL WOOL
If rusting is a concern when working on a project, try using bronze wool, which is available at most hardware or marine supply houses. Bronze wool will not rust so the small slivers that end up sticking to your project will not have a rust problem.

COLA WORKS GREAT TOO

If you're having a problem with a rusty nut or bolt, try placing a few drops of ammonia or hydrogen peroxide on it for 30 minutes.

HOW DOES ELECTRIC AIR CLEANERS WORK?

The newer electric air cleaners draw the air over a series of electrically charged metal plates that attract dust and pollutants. The plates must be removed periodically and cleaned. Another type is the porous silicon plate, which traps the particles like a magnet. This type of unit utilizes a blower motor to pass the air over the filters, which need to be washed.

SNOW SLIDE

If you want the snow to slide off your snow shovel with ease, all you have to do is save your empty butter wrappers and wipe the shovel off before using it.

HOW TO GET A RUN IN YOUR PANTYHOSE

Whenever you are using sandpaper to finish a wood surface, try placing an old nylon stocking over your hand and running it over the surface, the slightest rough spot will be found.

I'm your man, grandma!

FINDING A REAL STUD

If you don't have a stud finder, try using a compass, holding it level with the floor and at a right angle to the wall. Then slowly move the compass along the surface of the wall, when the needle moves that's where you will find a stud. Another method is to locate studs using an electric shaver. Just run it along the wall and when the tone of the razor changes, you found the stud.

OUCH
Use a split piece of old garden hose to cover the blades of a saw when storing it to be safe.

DO WINDSHIELD DEICERS REALLY WORK?
Most windshield deicers are made from alcohol and are overpriced products. They do, however, work fairly well depending on the thickness of the ice. If the ice is very thick it will take quite a while for the ice to melt.

Never place hot water on your windshield it may cause the glass to expand from the heat and then contract when it cools, cracking the windshield. Most deicers are similar to antifreeze. You can place a solution of homemade deicer in your window washer unit; just mix 1 part of any commercial antifreeze with 9 parts of 50/50 mixture of alcohol and water.

HANDY RULER
Remember a dollar bill is 6 inches long and almost 3-inches wide.

AND A LONNNNG EXTENSION CORD
If your pipes freeze and do not burst: try using a hair dryer to defrost them.

TRY TO KEEP IT TOGETHER
Lightweight materials that need to be glued together are easily held in place with spring clothespins.

TILL YOUR OLD AND GRAY
If you "weather" wood before applying stain, the stain will last years longer.

DON'T CRACK-UP & SAVE YOUR FINGERS

To prevent plaster walls from cracking when driving a nail in for a picture hanger, try placing a small piece of tape over the spot before hammering in the nail. If you are using small nails, like brads, try holding the nail with a small plastic comb to save the fingers.

OPENING A PLASTER CRACK

When you need to repair a thin crack in plaster, try using a can opener tip to widen the crack to 1/8th inch. Blow out the dust and any old paint that you loosened with a hair dryer. Dampen the crack with a sponge then fill it with patching plaster.

BUBBLE, BUBBLE, TOIL AND TROUBLE

Varnish never needs stirring. Stirring only creates air bubbles, which may ruin a smooth finish.

KEROSENE KILLS RUST

Kerosene is a fire hazard!

If you brush a small amount of kerosene on a rusted screw then wait 10 minutes before removing, it will come out easily. You can also dampen a rag with white vinegar and wrap the rag around the rusted screw and wait at least an hour before trying to remove it.

ODE DE CEDAR CHEST

If you would like the original cedar odor from an old cedar chest, try rubbing the inner surface lightly with fine sandpaper.

STOP SPLITTING WOOD

If you want to avoid splitting wood when driving a finish nail in near the end of the plank, just flatten the chisel end of the nail with a few hammer blows before hammering it in. The nail will tear through the wood instead of splitting it.

I WONDER WHERE THE IVORY YELLOW WENT?

If your piano keys are getting yellow, just dip ¾ of a lemon in salt and rub on the keys to whiten them up.

GET THE STINK OUT OF GASOLINE

To deodorize gasoline, just add 20 drops of sassafras oil to every gallon or solvent. Heat is then transferred to the substrate.

CHAPTER 18

LAUNDRY ROOM

DRYER

GENERAL INFORMATION:

The dryer is run by the timer, which is run in a pre-determined pattern sending an electrical signal to each dryer component at a specified time and for the correct amount of time. The dryer has knobs or buttons on the control panel that allows you to set the way dry certain types of clothing. The dryer has a switch that turns the dryer off when the door is opened, if this is not operational, the dryer should not be used.

The dryer motor drives a belt that is attached to one side of the drum and turns the drum. A fan blade is attached to the other side and will draw warm air through the drum pushing it out the exhaust vent. If the motor does not reach its proper operating temperature it should not turn on. The dryer also has a heating element, which consists of a burner and a thermostat that is controlled by the timer.

GAS DRY IS NOT HEATING UP

There are any number of things that can stop a gas dryer from heating up such as a bad glow bar igniter, thermal fuse on some models, thermostats, motor heat switch, timer, selector switch and sensor. Best to call a repairman.

WHAT'S THAT GRATING NOISE

If you hear a grating noise it is usually something stuck in the gaskets or around the drum or rollers.

POOR DRYER DIED

When dryer will not run it is usually an electrical problem, a clogged vent tube or a broken belt. These three things can easily be checked and repaired.

I'M GROWING A BEARD

If the dryer takes too long to dry clothes, the problem is usually that the vent is restricted or clogged. Move the dryer away from the wall and check the vent. Another reason is that the blower has excessive lint buildup.

DRYER ON, CIRCUIT BREAKER OFF

The circuit breaker is probably bad, not the dryer. Replace the circuit breaker first and if that does not work, it is probably in the dryer.

OUCH, OUCH

If the white vinyl tubing is getting hot and dust and lint collect easily, you have an older dryer. Most building codes in the United Stated now require metal aluminum tubing for clothes dryers. Lint will not collect as easily in a metal vent.

VENTS ARE PROBLEMS

Many birds tend to nest in vents, especially dryer vents. It is best to cover these vents with a netting to prevent the problem. Special plastic bird netting is available through a garden supply house or from InterNet, Inc. at (800) 328-8456.

MY DRYER IS NOT ON THE LEVEL

If your dryer is not leveled properly, you will wear out a number of the
parts, prematurely.

DRYER SHUTS OFF WHEN IT FEELS LIKE IT

If the dryer all of a sudden shuts down it is probably the split coils that are on top of the burner. If you tap the coils and it starts that will answer your question.

IT'S NOT MY CAR TIRES

If you hear a knocking and smell rubber burning, it is probably the drum rollers supporting the drum. These will wear out and may need to be replaced or lubricated.

SOUNDS LIKE A PIG'S IN THERE

If you hear squealing, it is probably bad drum gliders or rollers. WD-40 will sometimes help, however, if the bearings show through, it would be best to just replace them.

BELT ALERT, CALL GRANDPA

It is not too hard to replace the belt, just lift the lid and unscrew the front to get to the drum. Remove the drum with the belt on it and replace.

GRANDPA'S DRYER TIPS

- ❖ Always clean the filter between loads.
- ❖ Replace damaged filters immediately.
- ❖ Metal vent tubing is much better than plastic.
- ❖ Be sure and clean out any lint in the motor compartment.
- ❖ Check the belt every 8 months.

GRANDPA'S DRYER SHEET TIPS

FLYING INSECTS

If you place an anti-static dryer sheet in your pocket and allow it to stick out a little, it will keep the bees, yellow jackets and mosquitoes away from you.

BED BUGS

Place 4 anti-static dryer sheets between the mattress pad and the mattress to get rid of bed bugs then place duct tap (sticky-side out) around the legs and bed rails.

ANTS & UNCLES

Ants will not come near any area that has an anti-static dryer sheet.

MOUSE REPELLANT

Place a dryer sheet anywhere you have a mouse problem and they will run the other way.

ELIMINATE BOOK ODORS

Place a dryer sheet in any books that you do not use very often to eliminate the musty odor.

A LITTLE PIECE WILL DO YA

To save on money, try tearing a dryer sheet in half. Half a sheet will work just as well as the whole sheet.

NO STATIC SCREENS

Wipe your TV or computer screen with an anti-static sheet to eliminate static electricity.

NO SOAP SCUM

Clean the shower doors with a dryer sheet to remove the soap scum.

FRESH CLOSET

Hang a dryer sheet in the closet to keep the air fresh and clean. You can also place a sheet in the dresser drawers.

VACUUM CLEANER AIR

To keep the air smelling good while you vacuum, just place an anti-static sheet in the bag.

NO TANGLES

To prevent thread from tangling, just run a threaded needle through an anti-static sheet.

SUITCASE SMELLS

Place a dryer sheet in all your suitcases to get rid of any musty odors.

IMPORTANT NEWS YOU CAN USE

Dryer sheets have caused many dryers to either burn out the heating unit <u>or cause a fire</u> by blocking the filter. Even though you clean out the lint filter every time you use the dryer, there is a buildup of residue from the dryer sheet that sticks to the mesh and cannot be seen. The coating is invisible to the naked eye.

Try running water through the mesh filter and if the water will not go through easily it may be partially or completely blocked and you will see the problem for yourself. Use an old toothbrush every 3 months to clean the screen and you will see the difference. This will lower your electric bill, make the dryer more efficient and protect your property.

UNDER THE SEAT
To keep the car smelling fresh, just place an anti-static dryer sheet under one of the seats.

BAKED-ON FOODS
To clean baked-on foods after using a pan, just place a dryer sheet in the pan and add water. Allow the sheet to remain overnight and you should be able to just sponge it clean the next day. The soapy agent in the sheet will loosen the dried on foods.

BASKET BOTTOMS
Place a dryer sheet in the bottom of all the waste cans and garbage cans to eliminate the odors.

HAIR REMOVER
If you rub a dryer sheet over the furniture, it will remove cat and dog hair.

A BLIND TRICK
Wipe the Venetian blinds with an anti-static dryer sheet and the dust will not adhere to it.

VERY TACKY

Sawdust can be removed using a dryer sheet. The sawdust will adhere to the sheet like a magnet and do the same job as tack cloth.

SMELLY UNDERWARE TRICK

Place a dryer sheet on the bottom of the hamper and you will not have a smelly experience when you open it.

FEET SMELL?

Try placing a dryer sheet in shoes or sneakers overnight to eliminate the odor.

SUPER SOFT FABRIC SOFTENER

The following ingredients will be needed:

1	Tablespoon of unflavored gelatin
1 ¾	Cup of boiling water

Place the gelatin in the boiling water until it is fully dissolved. Add the softener to the final rinse after the washing cycle is completed.

MAKING YOUR OWN DRYER FABRIC SOFTENER

The following ingredients will be needed:

¾	Cup of baking soda (fresh)
1	Tablespoon of cornstarch
1	Tablespoon of arrowroot powder
2	Drops of essential rose oil (optional)

Place all the ingredients into a small bowl and mix well. Place a small amount in a small cloth bag that can be well secured with a drawstring or tied and place it into the dryer with the load. Be sure the bag is well sealed or it becomes a bit messy.

IRONING

✓ BEATS IRONING
If you want your sheer curtains to come out of the washing machine "wrinkle-free," just dissolve a package of unflavored gelatin in a cup of boiling water and add it to the final rinse. The protein has a relaxing, or softening effect on the fabric.

WASHING MACHINE

GENERAL INFORMATION:
The standard washing machine consists of a tub with holes for water to enter and an inner tub to hold the water with an agitator at the center that rotates both clockwise and counter-clockwise. This forces the clothes from the top to the bottom and back again. This motion will allow the detergent and water to reach all areas of the clothing.

The motors are on most models reversing so that they can run clockwise and counter-clockwise. The motor operates through a clutch or a type of transmission to spin the tub at speeds that vary from 400-800 rpm's. The pump removes the water by centrifugal force.

BOUND-UP WATER FAUCETS
Faucets that supply water to the washing machine should be closed and opened once a month to avoid bind-up.

I'M GETTING DIZZY
If the washer is wobbling, the washer is no longer level and needs leveling.

WHAT DETERGENT IS BEST?
If you have a front-load washer you should be using a low suds detergent. Top loaders are a little more forgiving when you add too much detergent.

LIQUID LAUNDRY DETERGENT

The following ingredients will be needed:

1	Cup of soap flakes (grated)
¾	Cup of washing soda
¾	Cup of borax
4	Tablespoons of glycerin
4	Cups of very warm tap water

Place all the ingredients in a large bottle and mix well. Be careful not to mix too rapidly or it will result in too many suds. Add ¾-3/4 of a cup to your tub in warm water and then use a cold, water rinse. This makes about 24 ounces and can be reduced or increased as desired.

TOP LOADER OR FRONT LOADER????????

Front loaders are more efficient than top loaders, even though they are a little more expensive to purchase. You will save money through using less detergent and water.

MACHINE ATE MY CLOTHING

When a piece of clothing comes out torn, it means that you have overloaded the washer. If you have a top loader, only place clothes to the top of the agitator and place them loosely. Front loaders can be filled up but loosely.

MY MACHINE IS RUNNING AWAY

Can I let an unbalanced load finish running? No! Be sure and balance a load or you will damage some of the delicate components.

WHY AM I INSIDE OUT?

Some clothes need to be turned inside out or they will receive abrasive damage. This protects the more delicate clothes.

I NEED A NEW RUBBER HOSE

All rubber hoses should be replaced every 4-5 years.

IT REALLY HITS THE SPOT

If you are going to wash a load of greasy clothes, try adding a bottle of cola to the load. It will really improve the cleaning action of most detergents. Colas contain a weak acid that will help to dissolve the grease. Cola can also be used to clean the rings off toilets.

DO DRY BLEACHES WORK BETTER THAN LIQUID BLEACHES?

There is a misconception that bleaches remove stains. Bleaches do not remove stains they only mask the stain so that you will not see it. This process is known as oxidation and utilizes one of two types of bleach.

The dry bleach is composed of sodium perborate, which is converted to hydrogen peroxide, which continues to break down liberating oxygen gas, which then oxidizes the clothing. Liquid bleach contains the chemical sodium hypochlorite, which cause the release of chlorine gas that oxidizes the clothing, thus bleaching the stain out. The more powerful of the two bleaching agents is the liquid bleach.

MAKING YOUR OWN WASHING MACHINE FABRIC SOFTENER

The following ingredients will be needed:

1 **Cup of white vinegar**
2 **Cups of baking soda (fresh)**
3 **Cups of cold tap water**

Place all the ingredients in a small bucket and mix well. Store in small plastic or glass sealed jars. Before using be sure and shake well. Add ¾ cup of the softener to the final rinse for the best results. Keep out of reach of children.

A LITTLE PREVENTION

Water faucets

They feed your washer and should be turned on and off at least once a month, especially if the water you are using is hard water. If you don't do this, they may bind up when you do want to close them off and they may also leak. Replace the washers in the hose ends every 2 years.

The best hoses are the braided high-pressure hoses for trouble-free operation. Also, be sure and clean the screens every 6 months.

Belts

Should be checked regularly and replaced before they break. Be sure and change the settings on push button machines at least every 10 loads. Just press all the buttons in and out once.

The Tub

Should be cleaned once a year if you use the washer heavily. Fill the tub with hot water then prepare a solution of ¾ cup of TSP, ¾ cup of household bleach and 2 quarts of water. Pour the solution into the washer and run the washer through the rinse and wash cycles.

SOFT WATER VS HARD WATER

Soft Water
- Will save up to 50% of the cost of soap and detergents.
- Saves on energy.
- Reduces deposits on appliances and showerheads.
- Reduces cleaning times.
- Eliminates rings around the bathtub and toilet.
- Clothing will last longer.
- Saves money on the purchase of abrasives and cleaning supplies.

Hard Water
- Leaves mineral deposits everywhere that can only be cleaned off with an acid such as vinegar or phosphoric acid (4%) or most cola's.

USE YOUR TOOTHBRUSH

If you really want a clean filter in your washing machine, use an old toothbrush to remove any lint buildup. Then soak the filter in white vinegar for 12 hours before rinsing with warm water.

NATURAL SOFTENER

If you run out of softener sheets, just use 1 cup of white vinegar during the rinse cycle.

BOIL THE SOCKS

If your white socks are grimy and you can't get them clean, try boiling them in water with a slice of lemon.

GRANDPA SOLVES WASHING MACHINE PROBLEMS

TUB NOT FILLING WITH WATER
1. No power at wall outlet – Replace fuse or check circuit breaker
2. Water inlet hose kinked – Reposition the hose or replace it.
3. Inlet valve screens clogged – Clean valve or replace it.
4. Power cord is defective – Test cord and replace.
5. Timer or selective switch faulty – Replace if defective.

WATER WILL NOT SHUT OFF
1. The air hose on water level switch has fallen off – Reattach
2. Inlet valve defective – Replace any defective part.

WATER IS AT THE WRONG TEMPERATURE
1. Faucets are probably connected wrong – Check hoses.
2. Inlet valve screen clogged or defective solenoid – Clean screen or replace solenoid.

TUB FILLS NORMALLY BUT MOTOR WILL NOT START
1. Lid safety switch out of adjustment or defective – adjust or replace.
2. Overload tripped or defective – Reduce wash load in tub and wait 15 minutes for it to reset. If it doesn't reset it needs to be replaced.
3. If the motor hums, the motor is faulty – Replace the motor or possibly the drain plug is jammed and needs to be un-jammed.

WASHING MACHINE IS AGITATING BUT WILL NOT SPIN
1. Machine is not balanced or is overloaded – re-distribute wash load, if this does not work reduce water in tub.
2. Lid safety switch out of adjustment – Adjust or replace.
3. Drive belt slipping or loose or broken – Tighten or replace.
4. Timer may be defective and needs replacement.

MY MACHINE IS EATING MY CLOTHES
Possibly too much bleach is being used or the agitator van is broken. The basket surface may also be too rough.

I'M NOT GETTING AGITATED
If the motor is running and the agitator will not turn, the belt is probably broken and you will need to replace it. If you are able to do this yourself, the belt should be replaced every 2-3 years if the machine is used 2-3 times a week.

MY CLOTHES ARE SWIMMING
Usually if the water will not leave the washer, there is probably a small piece of clothing or a sock stuck in the pump or the hoses that are connected to the pump.

NOT A JOB FOR GRANDPA
If you have an oil leak, it is probably the transmission, which is one of the most difficult things to fix. Call a repairman or if it is an old machine, buy a new one.

CHAPTER 19

GRANDMA'S SEWING ROOM

GENERAL INFORMATION:

The following is information regarding the needs to set up a sewing room in your home:

1. **The Hanging Area** – This will require about 70 inches off the floor to hang full-length garments.
2. **Mirrors** – You will need a full-length mirror to see a person's head as well as their feet. Preferably one mirror and two side mirrors at 45^0 angles.
3. **Fitting Room** – This may just be a fitting area that is elevated in front of the mirrors.
4. **Work Area** – There are three basic areas for cutting fabric, sewing and pressing. You should be able to move freely between areas for the most efficiency.
5. **Electricity** – Try and use electrical outlets instead of extension cords. Power strips and surge protectors are recommended.
6. **Cutting Surface Size** – The table should be 30 inches wide and 60 inches long and should be easy to reach from all sides.
7. **Ventilation** – Remember dry cleaned fabrics and even new fabric may contain chemical residues, which release fumes when heated. Also dust and lint can become a problem. Be sure that you have a good ventilation system.
8. **Stools** – Be sure and purchase a stool that is adjustable.
9. **Machine Height** – The height of the machine should be 25-29 inches high. The depth of the sewing table should be about 20 inches high.
10. **Pressing Surface** – Use an adjustable ironing board. If the height is fixed that you will be ironing on, be sure that it is a comfortable height that will not hurt your back.

SEWING MACHINE

MACHINE STOPPED WHILE SEWING

The machine may have been run at a low speed for a prolonged period of time. The machine has shut off to prevent the motor from overheating. Turn off the power and wait about 20 minutes and the machine should work fine.

NEEDLE NOT MOVING
The upper thread may have run out, the presser foot is in the up position, the bobbin winder shaft was left in the winding position or the buttonhole lever was not lowered when the machine was placed in the buttonhole mode.

MACHINE WILL NOT RUN
The presser foot may not be the right one and the needle is hitting the foot or the needle has come loose and is in the hook of machine.

UPPER THREAD KEEPS BREAKING
Any one of the following may be the problem:
- ❖ It may be threaded wrong.
- ❖ The needle has been inserted incorrectly
- ❖ The thread has a bad knot in it
- ❖ The thread tension is too tight
- ❖ The needle may be bent or blunt
- ❖ The needle and thread may not match
- ❖ You are stitching too fast
- ❖ Thread take-up level has not been threaded

BOBBIN IS BREAKING TOO EASILY
Bobbin may not be fully inserted into bobbin case or has been incorrectly threaded. The bobbin has not been wound evenly or there may be lint in the bobbin case.

MACHINE IS SKIPPING STITCHES
Any one of the following may be the problem:
- ❖ The thread tension may be too tight
- ❖ The needle is bent or blunt
- ❖ The needle is the wrong size
- ❖ The needle and thread do not match
- ❖ The thread take-up lever has not been threaded
- ❖ Light pressure on pressure foot
- ❖ The needle is set incorrectly

STITCHES NOT FORMING PROPERLY

The thread may not be pulled into the thread sensor guide or the bobbin case has been threaded wrong. The spool cap may also be the wrong size for thread spool.

MAKING IRREGULAR STITCHES

Any of the following may be the problem:

- ❖ The needle may be the wrong size
- ❖ The threading may have been done incorrectly
- ❖ Loose upper thread tension
- ❖ You are pulling the fabric
- ❖ Light pressure on pressure foot
- ❖ You may have a loose pressure foot
- ❖ Bobbin wound unevenly

MY FABRIC IS PUCKERING UP, SHOULD I KISS IT?

The stitch length may be too long for the fabric or the fabric is too sheer or soft. The problem can also be caused, by using two different kinds of thread or if the tension is incorrect.

THREAD IS BUNCHING UP

The upper and lower threads are not drawn back under the pressure foot or the feed dog is down and needs to be raised.

NEEDLE KEEPS BREAKING

Any of the following may be the problem:

- ❖ Using a thin needle for sewing a heavy weight fabric
- ❖ The needle may not have been full inserted into the needle bar
- ❖ The needle clamp screw is loose
- ❖ Using the wrong pressure foot
- ❖ Pressure foot too loose
- ❖ You are pulling on the fabric as you sew

LOUD NOISE IS HEARD

Dust has probably accumulated in the feed dog.

KNOCKING NOISE & JAM

There is lint in hook or the thread is caught in the shuffle.

MACHINE NOT FEEDING ITSELF
Any of the following may be the problem:
- ❖ The stitch length may have been set to zero
- ❖ The presser foot pressure is probably too low
- ❖ The feed dogs are lowered
- ❖ The threads may be knotted under the fabric

TROUBLE THREADING THE NEEDLE
The needle is probably not in its highest position.
Turn the handwheel until needle reaches its highest position.

NEEDLE THREADER WILL NOT RETURN HOME
The needle threader has been designed not to turn in order to protect it if the needle is not up. The needle just needs to be properly inserted.

Put the needle in right!

NEEDLE THREADER NOT RETURNED AND MACHINE STOPPED
The sewing machine may have been accidentally started while threading hook was still in the needle eye. Slightly turn the handle clockwise and remove the threader.

STATIC ELECTRICITY
If a pin or needle will not penetrate an article, try rubbing it in your hair before trying it again.

HOPE YOU DON'T HAVE A MAGNETIC PERSONALITY
Never place a magnet near a computerized sewing machine. Some machines may have a problem.

DENTAL FLOSS THAT MACHINE
Clean out the tension discs with dental floss. Just tie several knots in a length of dental floss and slowly run it through the discs.

CHAPTER 20

BEDROOM

BEDDING

FIBERS USED IN SHEETS

There are a number of different fibers used in the manufacture of sheets. The following are a few of the more popular ones:

- ❖ **Egyptian Cotton** – This is special cotton that has been grown in Egypt and feels softer than other cottons. It also will generate less lint and is stronger.
- ❖ **Pima Cotton** – This used to be called American-Egyptian and is high quality cotton developed from Egyptian cotton and is grown only in the southwestern United States. It is very strong and exceptionally soft and firm.
- ❖ **Modal** – This is a category of manufactured fibers that are known for their strength. The fabric does retain its shape very well.
- ❖ **Lyocell** – Manufactured fabric produced from trees. It is very strong and absorbent. It is soft and strong when wet and is similar to silk or suede. It has wrinkle-resistant qualities and can easily be draped.
- ❖ **Polyester** – The most common type is polyethylene terphalate (PET). This is a strong synthetic fiber that will resist shrinking, mildew, stretching, abrasion and wrinkling. It will wash easily and dries very fast.

THE HIGHER, THE BETTER

Thread count is the number of horizontal and vertical threads in one square inch of fabric. The thread counts can range from 80-700. Most stores sell bedding from 180-320. The higher the thread count, the softer the fabric will feel. However, the quality of the fabric is just as important as the thread count. Cotton sheets with a thread count of 180-200 are a good buy and will hold up well.

HOW SOFT I AM...................

I've got soft feather

Down is the soft inner plumage of waterfowl such as ducks and geese. It contains many light, fluffy filaments that extend in all directions, without a feathers quill shaft. Has the ability to spring back to its original shape, which is known as lofting. One of the more important aspects of down over synthetics is that it has the ability to let moisture such as perspiration escape in a process known as wicking. It is also more comfortable in varying temperatures and climates than other materials.

DOOR

GETTING SPOOKY IN HERE

If the bedroom door won't stay shut when closed and opens when pushed even though it shuts tight, the frame may a little too wide for the door. You can fix the problem by unscrewing the strike plate and placing a thin piece of cardboard behind the plate, which will move it just enough to allow the door to remain solid and not open when pushed.

MATTRESSES

GENERAL INFORMATION:

Mattresses do need special care if you want to keep them in good condition. Try and give the mattresses an occasional airing out in front of an open window on their side without the bedding. The fresh air will pass through and ventilate the mattress, freshening them. You should also sprinkle some carpet deodorizer on the mattress and allow it to remain for 15 minutes before vacuuming it off.

MATTRESS REPLACEMENT

The average mattress will last 8-10 years, however, this will depend on the quality of the mattress purchased and how much use it gets.

TURNING OVER

A new mattress should be turned every two weeks for the first four months and turned every two months after that. First turn the mattress head to foot then end over end. Do not use the handles to turn the mattress; they are only to be used for positioning the mattress.

BEST OF THE BEST

This is an individual choice and the person that is going to sleep on it, should be the person choosing it. If you sleep with a person, both people should be comfortable.

NEW MATTRESS, NEW BOXSPRING

All mattress designers make their mattresses and box springs to fit each other and provide a certain level of support. It is not recommended to place a new mattress on an old box spring.

POPULAR SIZES

The most popular mattress is the queen-size. However, there are many factors that should determine the size of the mattress such as medical problems, physical length and overweight.

FRAMING YOUR MATTRESS

The bed frame should allow the mattress to be able to breathe on all sides. Never place an all-natural mattress on a piece of wood. Slats or air holes are required.

A GOOD FOUNDATION IS A MUST

A standard foundation is a wooden boxed foundation that is covered with fabric. It has no springs and is the firmest and the most inexpensive (usually 7-inches thick). Commonly used with latex mattresses.

BOX SPRINGS

Box springs are more than 7-inches thick and are usually used with innerspring mattresses.

MY MATTRESS IS VENTILATED

You normally only find ventilation holes on synthetic mattresses. All-natural mattresses will breathe all over and ventilation holes are not necessary.

DROP IT OFF A CLIFF?

The best way to dispose of a mattress is to call the Salvation Army.

Call the Salvation Army!

FIRMNESS IS IMPORTANT

The number of coils in an innerspring mattress determines the firmness. If the innerspring is firm it has 364, extra firm has 510 and super firm has 780. In a latex mattress, it has an ILD rating. Medium is 25, firm is 31 and extra firm is rated at 35.

GRANDPA KNOWS MATTRESS CARE

❖ You need to cover both the mattress and the box springs with fitted, padded dust covers. If possible use one that will not allow dust mites to penetrate. Best to use the type that is quilted on both sides.

❖ Occasionally, air out the mattresses by removing all bedding and turning the mattress on its side, allowing the air to flow through. This type of ventilation will freshen the mattress.

❖ If the mattress has been soiled, it is best to use a special fabric cleaner, which can be purchased at most of the better mattress stores.

❖ Powder the mattress with a thin layer of baking soda and allow it to remain for 15 minutes before vacuuming it off.

PILLOWS

WOOL-FILLED PILLOWS

Wool pillows are excellent. They maintain their springy resilience and will absorb moisture from the head.

KAPOK BODY PILLOWS

You will get a molded form pillow for good support. Kapok is a natural seed fiber from the rainforest.

BUCKWHEAT, NOT THE OLD KID STAR

They can help to alleviate a stiff neck by providing proper support of your neck and head. The pillow will mold and conform to your head and neck. It also allows air to circulate better.

CAN YOU WASH A DOWN PILLOW

Best not to do it at home. Take the pillow to a laundry and use a front load commercial washing machine with regular detergent (never use a machine with an agitator). If the pillow is very old it may not be safe to wash it. It will take about 3 hours to dry two pillows in a commercial dryer on medium heat. Never place more than two pillows in a commercial dryer to avoid a fire.

CHAPTER 21

GRANDPA'S WORKBENCH

ADHESIVES

GENERAL INFORMATION:
If you want the best joint possible, it should be affixed with a combination adhesive and screws, nails or other type of fastener.

Don't get stuck-up

Carpenter's Wood Glue

This is white, creamy glue sold in plastic bottles and used to adhere furniture, craft and woodworking projects. It will set up in about one hour and dries clear without staining. However, it is vulnerable to moisture. If you stain wood, be sure that carpenter's glue is not present or it will leave a light-colored streak.

WOOD GLUE, FLIP-TOP

Try replacing the top to your wood glue bottle with the flip-top cap from a bottle of dishwasher soap. The cap will close tightly and is very easy to pop open and then close. You won't have a tiny lid that is easily lost.

Cyanoacrylate (instant glue)

Does not have good flexibility but has excellent strength and will dry in a few seconds. Its resistance to heat and moisture is excellent but can bond to your skin instantly and is toxic and flammable. You can clean it up with acetone and it is best used on smooth surfaces such as glass, ceramics, plastics and metal.

Epoxy

The only adhesive that has strength stronger than the material it bonds. Will resist almost anything from moisture to solvents. Best used in warm temperatures and make sure that you read the manufacturers instructions before using. Mixing must be exact if you want the desired results.

Hot Glue Gun

The strength of the bond will depend on the surface it is used on. It dries in about one minute and has a fair resistance to heat and moisture. Use with caution since it will give a bad burn. Heat will loosen the bond and it is best used on smooth and porous surfaces such as metal, masonry, glass or fiberglass.

Latex Acrylic Panel Adhesive

The strength is very good with a drying time of about 24 hours. The resistance to heat and moisture is very good. It may irritate the skin and eyes and will clean up with soap and water as long as it is still wet. Best used on porous surfaces such as framing lumber, plywood paneling, wallboard, foam panels and masonry.

Resorcinol & Formaldehyde

Normally mixed just prior to use, however, they can still be used up to four hours afterwards. Must be used at temperatures over 70^0F. Used to bond veneers or to bond plastic laminates to wood for tabletops and counters. Both surfaces should be coated thinly and allowed to dry a little before bonding them. Use in a well, ventilated area.

Silicone Sealant

Has a very flexible bond and good strength with a drying time of about 24 hours. Its resistance to heat and moisture is very good. It will irritate the skin and eyes and will clean up with acetone. Best used on smooth and porous surfaces such as wood, porcelain, fiberglass, plastics and glass.

Superglue

These are great for a quick tight bond but they should not be used on clear glass since ultraviolet light will break down the bonding agent. If the material is porous or has a vertical surface, use gel superglue.

Water-based Contact Cement

It has good strength and will bond instantly, drying in about 30 minutes. Its resistance to heat and moisture is very good, however, it will irritate the eyes and skin. You can clean it up with soap and water as long as it is still wet. Used best, on porous surfaces such as plastic laminates, plywood, flooring and cloth.

White Glue

Will provide you with a moderate to rigid bond but has poor resistance to heat. It cleans up with soap and water and can be used on porous surfaces such as wood (indoors), paper and cloth.

GRANDPA'S ADHESIVE TIPS

HOLD ON TIGHT!

Too much adhesive may weaken the bond. The only exception to this rule is when you use epoxy. Make sure that you rough up the surface to be bonded before applying any adhesive. Use a thin coat in most instances and clamp securely. Be sure and remove any excess after clamping.

Remember, when you ruined the counter, Grandma Paulette

SUPERGLUE REMOVER

If you are going to use superglue, be sure and have a bottle of nail polish remover handy. Nail polish remover contains acetone and will neutralize the superglue.

PUTT, PUTT

Carpenter's putty is an essential to have around if you're doing any wood repairs. It comes in different colors making it easier to patch different woods.

CLEANING OFF FLOOR ADHESIVE

Dried floor adhesive can be difficult to remove from your tools unless you place them into the freezer overnight. Remove them in the morning and just chip off the adhesive wearing goggles.

CLAMPS

GRANDPA'S FAVORITE HELPERS

C-Clamps

These are "C" shaped with an adjustable screw on one end and are great for holding objects on a work surface. They come in many different sizes and are inexpensive.

Spring Clamps

These have plastic tips and will protect the material. They are very strong and can be used in many different ways to secure objects.

Miter Clamps

These are mainly used to hold 45^0 angles together that need to be glued or nailed. They are commonly used to hold picture frames together.

CLEAR FINISHES

GRANDPA KNOWS HOW TO PICK A CLEAR FINISH

Natural Resin varnishes

Very effective: in resisting scratches and scuffmarks. Spar varnish can be used outdoors. To apply use a varnish brush or cheesecloth pad. The varnish will dry in about 24 hours unless the weather is humid then allow about 36 hours.

Resin Oil

This finish will soak into the grain as well as hardening it and will resist scratches. It is usually applied by hand, rubbing in 2-3 coats and needs about 10 hours to dry.

Polyurethane Varnish

Good varnish that will be mar-resistant, durable and will remain clear. Best to use a natural bristle brush; roller or it can be sprayed on. Allow it to dry for 1-2 hours and leave about 12 hours between coats for the best results.

Two-Part Epoxy Varnish

Has very high resistance to scuff marks and mars and is excellent for flooring. Best applied with a brush with the first coat drying in about 3 hours and the second coat in about 6-7 hours.

Shellac

Will be easily damaged by water and be put on either clear or pigmented. Best to use small brush that has a chiseled tip. Always thin with alcohol or other recommended solvent. Will dry in about 2-3 hours.

Lacquer

This varnish is fast drying and is excellent for furniture. It is best sprayed on in numerous thin coats and be sure and allow the last coat to dry for at least 50-60 hours. After it has dried, rub the finish with a fine steel wool or use a hard wax.

FASTENERS & CONNECTORS

GENERAL INFORMATION:
Fasteners and connectors are now being made for almost any job. They can be used to secure wood-to-wood, concrete to any surface and brick. Most are approved by the Uniform Building Code requirements. Fasteners can save you money on labor, materials and time when used properly.

TYPES OF FASTENERS & CONNECTORS:

- ❖ **Drywall Clips** – Used for wallboard or paneling.
- ❖ **Masonry Connectors** – Used as foundation anchors, brick wall ties or floor jacks.
- ❖ **Nail Plates & Plate Straps** – These are used as mending plates or for light-duty wood-to-wood splices and fence brackets. They help to simplify fence construction and will then allow for easy disassembly if necessary.
- ❖ **Post Anchors** – Supports a post from the ground up and eliminates deep post-holes. Prevents wood rot and termite damage.
- ❖ **Safety Plates** – Used to prevent accidental nailing into utility wires or pipes when they pass through the framing.
- ❖ **Sawhorse Brackets** – These will make a 2 X 4 or 2 X 6 into a supportive frame in just one easy step.
- ❖ **Stud Shoe** – Reinforces a joist stud or rafter after it has been drilled or notched during construction.

GRANDPA'S BASIC ANCHOR TIPS

The following are a few of the more common anchors that you should have available in your toolbox:

- ❖ **Plastic Anchor** – These are good for lightweight jobs, such as picture hanging or curtain rods. You will need to drill a hole for these, called a pilot hole.

- ❖ **Molly Bolt** – This is an anchor/screw combination and must match the thickness of the wall. Best for medium or heavy jobs, especially heavy mirrors or large pictures. Best to drill a pilot hole for the best results.
- ❖ **Toggle Bolt** – These are usually used for very heavy jobs, such as hanging shelves or hanging a bicycle from the ceiling. The object must be attached to the toggle bolt before you attach it to the wall or ceiling. Best to drill a pilot hole.

MY LANDLORD WON'T LET ME PUT A NAIL IN THE WALL

When the landlord says that you can't put a nail in the wall to hang a picture, just use a sewing machine needle, which will hold up to 30 pounds.

HAND TOOLS

GENERAL INFORMATION:

When it comes to hand tools, the average person who is not in a construction trade or have a background in repairs will have a problem choosing the right hand tool for the job. Since it would take a whole book to provide in-depth information, we will only be able to assist you in choosing the right tool for the job.

GRANDPA KNOWS THE BEST TOOLS FOR THE JOB

CHISELING

- ❖ **Socket Chisels** – Should always be used with a mallet, never a hammer. Always used to cut wood.
- ❖ **Tang Chisels** – Made for working with the weight of the hand only.

BE A GOOD CHISLER

Always start your blade digging into the wood just slightly inside your guideline mark and never cut too deep. Chisel are best used to chip and shave away using the beveled edge going into the work so that it constantly directs the chisel out of the wood giving you better control. Always keep the cutting edge directed away from your body and hands.

CUTTING

- ❖ **Backsaw** – Used with a miter box to cut a straight line across a piece of wood. Has a steel backing, which is used to keep it aligned.
- ❖ **Combination Saw** – Cuts both across and with the grain.
- ❖ **Coping Saw** – Follows an irregular, delicate or intricate cut in wood. Has a thin, fine toothed, removable blade.
- ❖ **Crosscut Saw** – Used to make cuts across the grain with small offset teeth.
- ❖ **Hacksaw** – Used primarily to cut metals, plastic and electrical conduit.

SAFE SAW TEETH

If you want safe saw teeth, just place a plastic report cover spine over the blade.

HERE A TOOTH, THERE A TOOTH

If you are cutting thin metal with a hacksaw or saber saw, be sure and choose a metal-cutting blade that has at least 3 teeth contacting the edge of the piece you are working on. If the blade has too few teeth it will catch the edge and dull the blade or even damage the piece you are working on.

❖ **Keyhole Saw** – Narrow tip blade saw used for cutting openings in drywall or paneling. Also, used for curved cuts.
❖ **Rip Saw** – Used to cut with the grain with large teeth.

I'LL GET HURT IN A TOOLBOX

Never store saws in a toolbox. The teeth will easily be damaged unless you use a plastic tooth guard.

EASY DOES IT

If you put a small amount of kerosene on the saw blade it will act as a lubricant and will make your work easier.

CIRCULAR SAW TIPS

When you are going to do a job using a circular saw, be sure you use the proper blade for the job. You need different blades for hardwood and softwood. You also need to know if you will be cutting across the grain or with the grain, this involves either ripping or crosscutting. When you purchase the blade for the job, be sure and tell the clerk what kind of job you plan to do.

PROTECT ME, PLEASE!

Saw blades need to be protected by coating them with paste wax or a light grade of machine oil. Saw blades should be stored in a piece of garden hose, just insert the blade teeth end first.

WHOOOOA

Be sure and buy a model with a safety brake that will stop the blade from spinning when the trigger is released

DRILLS

SAVE THOSE BROCCOLI BANDS
Try using the thick rubber bands that hold broccoli together to store your drill bits and screws on the side of your drill. Just wrap the rubber band around the body of the drill and snug the attachments under the band.

FILES & RASPS

Files are normally used for shaping and can be found in many shapes. They can be round, half-round, flat, square and triangular. Single-cut files have teeth that run in one direction and double-cut files have teeth that run in opposing directions. Double-cut will cut more quicker, but will be courser.

PESKY WOOD SHAVINGS
Cleaning out wood shavings from files and rasps can be a real pain. However, grandpa just uses a piece of masking tape and covers the length of the tool, presses it firmly and pulls off all the shavings.

- ❖ Use files with an attachable handle.
- ❖ Be sure and secure your work with a clamp or vise and at elbow height for general filing. Lower for heavier filing jobs.
- ❖ Always keep files very clean using a file brush after every use.
- ❖ Files should be stored in a rack or protective sheaths to keep them from becoming dull.

Rasps are different files in that they have teeth that are formed individually and not connected to one another. Files will cut smoother than rasps, but when working with wood, the file will work much slower and tend to clog frequently.

HAMMER

Great idea!

TENNIS ANYONE?
Woodwork is easily damaged when using a metal hammer to tap wood joints. To avoid doing damage, just cut open tennis ball with an **"X"** slit enough to get it over the striking face of the hammer.

PRACTICE YOUR AIM
You should be using a 12oz. Or 16oz. Hammer for the best results. Grasp the hammer with one hand toward the end of the handle and swing from the elbow. Make sure that you hit the nail head on or the nail will bend.

THE RIGHT DIRECTION
If you want to keep a wood hammer handle from breaking when removing a stubborn nail, just lever the handle to the right or left side of the nail instead of straight back.

NAILING WITHOUT SPLITING WOOD
Grandpa has a few secrets when you are going to nail into a piece of wood and are concerned that the wood may split. Try drilling hole smaller than the nail for the nail to follow easily or rub a small amount of soap or wax on the nail before you try hammering it in.

POWER PLUS
To remove stubborn nails, just place a small block of wood under the hammerhead to get added leverage. Make sure that the block is big enough to distribute the pressure from the hammerhead.

CHECK OUT THE GRAIN
When purchasing a hammer, check out the grain on the bottom of the handle. The grain should be running in the same direction as the head, if it is running perpendicular to the head it is not as strong and is more likely to break or come loose.

PLANES

These are used for removing thin layers of wood, trimming and smoothing straight edges. They can also be used to add a groove.

- ❖ **Block Plane** – Usually about 6" long and used for small jobs that require smoothing and fitting.
- ❖ **Grooving Plane** – Capable of cutting a long slot.
- ❖ **Jack Plane** – This plane is usually around 15" long and used to smooth rough surfaces with a 2" blade.
- ❖ **Rabbit Plane** – Capable of cutting recessed grooves along and edge.
- ❖ **Scrub Plane** – This will provide a hand-hewn effect and will work faster for rough cuts.
- ❖ **Smooth Plane** – Smaller plane usually around 8" long with a 13/4 blade. Used to smooth small rough surfaces.
- ❖ **Trimming Plane** – This type of plane is used for more delicate work and is usually 3¾" in length and only has a single blade.

PLIERS

There are several types of pliers and they all have a specific job:

- ❖ **Fence Pliers** – Designed to pull and cut out staples from fences as well as having a hammer, head.
- ❖ **Locking Pliers** – Adjustable, vise-locking pliers that allow you to have both hands free.
- ❖ **Long-Nose Pliers** – Have a pointed nose that is used for reaching hard to get at spots.
- ❖ **Slip-Joint Pliers** – These are usually a tongue and groove design. These pliers give you the convenience of an adjustable joint, which can be opened to the specific size needed.
- ❖ **Solid-Joint Pliers** – This type is not adjustable and has a rivet or pin attached to the joint.
- ❖ **Standard Slip-Joint Pliers** – For general use around the home and has adjustable jaw and can cut wire.

SAVE THAT OLD INNERTUBE

Best to save any old inner tube, leather belt or gloves to use as a liner for your pliers when you need to protect the finish of a surface from the pliers' teeth.

SCREWDRIVERS

There are many types of screwdrivers for every type of job. However, the quality of the screwdriver is very important. The following will provide information on the good quality and the poor quality screwdriver.

Good Quality

- ❖ Look for quality metal, a good finish and the amount of grinding on the tip.
- ❖ Make sure that the handle is of good quality and the bar attachment goes all the way through.

Poor Quality

- ❖ If the end starts chipping away.
- ❖ The tip is not flared, which will make it fall out of the slot easier.
- ❖ Blade not being attached properly to the handle and work its way out easily.

Don't lose your grip!

MAKE SURE IT FITS

When you shop for a screwdriver, hold it in your hand, be sure that it fits and is comfortable. A secure grip is very important.

WRENCH

You should have two sizes of adjustable wrenches in your toolbox. Purchase a small and a medium one so that you will have one for every size nut and bolt.

LADDERS

BY THE NUMBERS
Most ladders have a Roman numeral on one of the side rails indicating the strength of the ladder, which is the weight that each rung can bear safely. Type III household-grade ladders are rated at 200 pounds, type II are commercial-grade and rated at 225 pounds and type I is industrial-grade and rated at 250 pounds. The type that grandpa recommends for home use is a type II.

SOLID FOOTING FOR A LADDER
To get a better footing for your ladder and avoid slippage, just place the feet of the ladder into a pair of old rubber boots.

MAGNETIC SREW HOLDER
Glue a strip of magnet to the top of your ladder to hold screws when you are working.

MEASURING

CAN'T FIND THE YARDSTICK?
If you always have trouble finding the yardstick, just keep a yard long piece of string in your pocket. A dollar bill is about 6-inches long.

POWER CORDS

Bent Prongs
They can usually be straightened, however, you should replace the plug if the prongs are loose.

Cracked Plug Housing
Replace, do not patch or tape.

Discolored Or Pitted Prongs
Possibly could be a short circuit so check the wiring housing or appliance and replace plug if there are no other signs of a problem.

Exposed Wire At Plug
Just rewire the plug.

Frayed Cable
Cut the cable above the fray and then replace the plug.

Nicked Cable
Be sure and bend the cable and look for cracks or cuts and replace if they are found.

No Ground Prong
If the ground prong is broken off or missing, the plug needs to be replaced.

Worn Out Insulation
The wires will eventually become exposed. Cut away the worn out cable and replace the plug. If you need a certain length you may need a new cable.

POWER TOOLS

CUTTING & DRILLING

Always choose the proper saw blade for the type of material you are going to cut. Also, be sure and support the board properly using sawhorses to support the board from both ends allowing room for the saw.

- ❖ **Band Saw** – Useful when more creative cuts are needed, such as curves and precision cuts.
- ❖ **Circular Saw** – One of the most common consisting of a replaceable blade and a blade guard, which is spring loaded to move out of the way when you are sawing. Always set the cutting depth 1/8th" more than the thickness of the board. You can avoid binding if you keep the sole plate flat on the surface of the wood.
- ❖ **Jig Saw** – Used to make curving lines or very detailed cuts. If you want to start a cut from the inside of a piece of wood, just drill a hole and insert the saw blade.
- ❖ **Radial Arm Saw** – Same as table saw, but capable of being

used on heavier stock.

- ❖ **Reciprocating Saw** – Use to cut openings in existing walls. Can rough cut green wood, metal, linoleum and plastic.
- ❖ **Table Saw** – Capable of crosscut rip, miter, groove and bevel. Can make moldings and sand stock.

GRANDPA'S CUTTING & DRILLING TIPS:

- ❖ If you are going to rip cut, use a rip guide or tack down a straightedge and use it as a cutting guide.

METAL DRILLING TIP
If you are going to drill into metal, be sure and squirt a drop or two of turpentine instead of oil on the bit and even into the hole to tool the bit.

- ❖ Try pre-drilling a "pilot hole" with a smaller drill bit when nailing into hardwood as well as screwing into all other types of wood, especially if you are working with wood that will split easily.
- ❖ Be sure and unplug power tools when making adjustments or changing accessories.
- ❖ If you keep your tool adjustment keys taped to the cord near the plug end, it will remind you to unplug the tool.
- ❖ Always be sure that your tools are properly grounded.

NO MORE DRILL CORDS
If you purchase the right drill, you can get plenty of power to do almost any job. Be sure and purchase one that is either an **18-volt or 24-volt model**.

These models will feature a torque control and eliminate the stripping of screws.

HEADS-UP

If you are going to drill above your head, be sure and place a Styrofoam cup on the drill bit (cut it if necessary, depending on the length of the bit). The debris will then fall into the cup instead of your eyes, hair or clothing.

WOODWORKING WIZARD

An **orbital sander** is an indispensable tool. The sanding pad rotates in small circles at thousands of revolutions every minute. It is more of a finishing tool. You can also use it to sand rough paint on exterior siding.

SAVING THE SANDPAPER SECRET

If you place duct tape on the back of the sandpaper before placing it on the sander, the sandpaper will last 5 times longer.

PNEUMATIC TOOLS

These tools contain air and are attached to an air compressor that runs them. A variety of tools are available and are easy to use. There are, however, a number of common mistakes people make and tricks they should know:

- ❖ A major problem is not reading the instructions that accompany a pneumatic tool.
- ❖ Not using the right length or gauge of extension cord. The longer, the extension cord the less power and lower efficiency of the tool.
- ❖ Always use an extension air hose rather than a cord for long distances.
- ❖ Use the correct pressure for the job.
- ❖ The oil must be changed every 250 hours.
- ❖ Be sure and locate the air compressor on a dry, clean, level area.
- ❖ Always keep the compressor properly lubricated.
- ❖ Always wear eye protection.

- ❖ Make sure that the pressure has been completely relived before changing tools.
- ❖ Never point the blowgun toward your eyes.
- ❖ Test safety relief valve regularly.
- ❖ Open the tank valve after every use.
- ❖ Make sure that there is a belt guard in place.

ATTACHMENTS INCLUDE:

Blow Gun	Nail Gun	Sandblaster
Air Stapler	Air Sander	Spray Gun
Caulking Gun	Air Ratchet Wrench	Air Hammer
Air Drill	Impact Wrench	

STORAGE TIP

DON'T GIVE THE BOOT THE BOOT
A good use for an old boot is to use it for storage around the workbench. Just turn the old boot upside down and screw it into the workbench. It will hold drills or other power tools. Remove the heel and sole before you nail it to the bench.

TOOL BELT

WORK LIKE A PRO
Buy a good quality tool belt since you will have it for many years and you will find that you cannot do without it. It will free up your hands and keep the tools you need for a specific job organized. It is actually safer to use one than not to use one since people may fall over one of your tools.

TOOLBOX

GENERAL INFORMATION:
Carrying heavy tools around can be very difficult, especially at grandpa's age.

You need to choose a box that will organize your tools and only carry what you really need.

Really big tools should just be carried separately and not be in too big a toolbox, making it heavy.

THE PROFESSIONAL MUDDLE

Professional workers normally purchase heavy metal boxes since they tend to throw them into the back of pickups and need something durable and strong. However, grandpa uses a lightweight, plastic box, which is perfect for the home handyman. Find a box with a removable tray and one that has compartments like sliding drawers so that you can store small items. Keep your larger tools in the bottom.

FISHING FOR A BOX

An old fishing tackle box make and excellent toolbox for the beginner. Most have locking lids on small plastic boxes making it easy to find what you are looking for without tearing the whole box apart. Even the new ones are inexpensive and great organizers.

WOOD

COMMON GRADES OF WOOD

Clear - This grade of wood is an excellent grade and has no knots.

Select/Select Structural - Very high quality wood and will be broken down into Numbers 1-3 or grades A-D. The lower grades will have more knots.

Number 2 Common - Has tight knots, but no major blemishes and is good for shelving.

Number 3 Common - May have some loose knots and may be blemished or have some damage.

Construction or Standard - Type of wood used for general framing. Has good strength.

Utility - An economy grade that is usually used for rough framing.

GRANDPA KNOWS HOW TO SELECT SOFT WOOD & HARDWOOD

Selecting Softwood

Cedar or Cypress

Wood is similar to redwood, but only the darker color wood is rot resistant. Weak and brittle but will resist warping and has a pleasant smell. It is commonly used for siding, paneling, rough trim, roof shingles and decks.

Fir

A very heavy, strong wood that will hold nails well. Has good resistance to warping and shrinkage, however, it is somewhat difficult to cut. Used for framing studs, posts and beams as well as flooring and sub-flooring.

Pine

From eastern, northern and western trees! Has a very light, soft, but weak resistance to warping and has a tendency to shrink. Very easy to cut! Used for paneling, trim molding, flooring and cabinets.

REAL NEAT PANELING TRICK

Next time you install paneling, paint a one-inch strip the same color as the paneling where the joints come together. If the joints ever separate, even a little, the area won't be very noticeable.

Redwood

Very durable and is resistant to rot and insects if you get the darker-colored heartwood variety. Light, soft and not as strong as fir or Southern pine, however, it does have the tendency to split and is easy to cut. Used for exterior posts, beams, fencing, decks, siding and paneling.

Southern Pine

Very hard wood, stiff and has excellent strength. Tends to hold nails well but has a tendency to crack, splinter, warp and cuts with ease. Used mainly for flooring and sub-flooring.

Spruce

Lightweight and soft, but is fairly strong, resistant to splitting and warping. Very easy to work with! Used mainly for framing, flooring, sub-flooring and trim (molding).

Treated Lumber

Several types can be treated especially fir and Southern pine. However, the green and brown color will fade in time making the wood a grayish color. Very resistant to rot and insects! Used commonly for bottom framing plates that rest on concrete. Also used on other framing that will come into contact with water, decks and some types of fencing.

SAVING DOUGH

Softwood comes from trees that grow faster and will be less expensive. If you are not using the wood for major structural components such as floor and ceiling joists, you might want to save the money and purchase the softwoods. You may only find a few varieties of softwood at most retailers.

Selecting Hardwood

Birch

Very hard and strong-grained: resistant to shrinking and warping. The color is similar to maple and is sometimes used as a cheap replacement. It is hard to cut but takes a great finish. Used for painted cabinets, paneling and furniture.

Mahogany

Durable hardwood that is fine-grained and resistant to shrinkage, warping and swelling. It finishes well and is easy to cut. Do not get quality mahogany confused with the cheaper grade called "lauan mahogany." Used for fine furniture, cabinets and veneers.

Maple

One of the hardest woods: pieces with wavy grain or with bird's eye are the best. The colors will range from reddish to brownish-white. The wood will finish well but is difficult to cut. Used for flooring, especially bowling alleys and basketball courts, butcher-block counters and molding.

Poplar

One of the softer hardwoods: has a fine grain with colors from white to yellowish-brown. It is easy to cut and easy to paint. Used for painted furniture, cabinets, trim, and used to replace more expensive hardwoods.

Red Oak

Hard, strong wood with a very pronounced straight grain! It resists warping but has the tendency to shrink if it not dried well. The color is reddish, cuts easily and finishes well. Used for flooring, cabinets, furniture, molding and stair rails.

Walnut

One of the better hardwoods! It is heavy, strong and has a straight grain. It resists shrinking, warping and is found in light to dark brown colors. Finishes well and cut fairly easily. Used for fine furniture, cabinets, paneling, inlays and veneers.

White Oak

Opened grain, hard and a strong wood but the grain is not as pronounced as red oak. It resists shrinking and warping and has a pretty golden color. Finishes well but is somewhat hard to cut. Preferred over red oak for flooring because it has less variation in color. Also used for molding, furniture, cabinets and stair railing.

Only the best for grandma!

BUY THE BEST

Try to purchase "real" hardwood products if you are after the best quality. Many wood products that advertise some of the hardwoods are only using the hardwood veneers. Hardwood flooring especially is the best flooring you can put in your home. Select hardwoods that only have minor defects on one side only or no defects at all.

CHAPTER 22

GRANDPA'S USES FOR VINEGAR

CLEANING USES

Remove Water Rings
Mix vinegar and olive oil in a one-to-one ratio and apply with a soft cloth using slight pressure in a circular motion.

Polish Leather Furniture
Boil 2 cups of linseed oil for 1-minute then allow it to cool before stirring in 1 cup of white vinegar. Apply with a soft cloth then allow it to stand for 1-2 minutes and then rub off gently.

Remove Carpet Stains
Only works well if the stain is fresh. Combine 1 part of white vinegar to 3 parts of water and allowed to remain on the stain for 3-4 minutes. Using a sponge, rub the area gently from the center out then dry with a clean soft cloth. Try an area that is out of the way to be sure that the carpet is colorfast.

GRANDPA'S SPECIAL GUIDELINES FOR CARPET STAIN REMOVAL
- ❖ Always use a spot remover in an inconspicuous location first.
- ❖ Scrape away any residues with a blunt knife before starting.
- ❖ Never use a hard-bristle brush on a stain, soft only.
- ❖ Blot up any liquid until the paper towel used is dry.
- ❖ Vacuum after all liquid is gone to remove any residues.
- ❖ Try cleaning the area with clear water before using a spot remover.
- ❖ Never over-wet the area.
- ❖ If you get fresh mud on the carpet, allow it to dry before vacuuming it off.
- ❖ Club soda works great on fresh stains. The active ingredient is carbonic acid that produces the carbonation. Sop up any liquid first!

Chewing Gum Remover
White vinegar is capable of dissolving and softening chewing gum from a number of fabrics and carpeting.

Decal Remover
Apply warm vinegar on a sponge and allow it to stand for a few minutes then wipe with a soft dry cloth.

Mildew Remover
For severe buildup of mildew, use white vinegar full strength. For all other mildew buildup, use a solution of vinegar and water.

Plastic Upholstery Cleaner
Combine vinegar and water one to one and wipe the furniture with a dampened soft cloth. Follow with a dry cloth to buff.

Metal Cleaner
Use a small amount of vinegar, baking soda or salt to prepare a paste and use the paste to clean bronze, copper or brass pots or utensils.

KEEP BRASS SHINNING

After you polish your brass, try coating it with a small amount of wood finishing oil like tung oil. The shine will last at least 3 times longer. To clean the oil off the brass just use a small amount of paint thinner.

Clean Aluminum Pot Stains
Black stains on aluminum pots can be removed by boiling white vinegar in the pot up to the area of the stain. For large pots boil the vinegar in a small pot and pour it on the stain.

Wash Windows
Mix one-part water to three-parts of white vinegar. Use a coffee filter or piece of newspaper to clean the window.

Grease Cutter
Place a capful of vinegar in the dishwasher to cut grease.

Crystal Clear Glassware
If you want your crystal to sparkle, just rinse them in a solution of: one part white vinegar to three parts warm water.

Remove Lime Residue
Coffee pots, teakettles and irons are notorious for hard water residue buildup. When they get really bad, fill them with white vinegar and run them through a cycle.

Drain Cleaner I
Boil 2 cups of vinegar and pour it down the drain a small amount at a time. Allow the vinegar to remain in the drain for about 5-10 minutes before pouring a pot of very hot water down the drain. The alternative is to use ¾ cup of baking soda poured into the drain followed by ¾ cup of warm vinegar, cover the drain and allow it to stand for 5-10 minutes before running cold water down the drain.

Drain Cleaner II
Drop 3-4 Alka-Seltzer® tablets down the drain, the pour a bottle of white vinegar down. After 3-5 minutes run hot water down.

Clean Shower Head
Remove the head and place it in a container that will allow you to cover the head with vinegar. Allow soaking overnight, rinse and replace.

Weed Killer
Pour white vinegar on weeds in sidewalk or driveway cracks and they will be killed.

Pet, Flea Killer
Add 1 teaspoon of cider vinegar to every quart of water. Fleas will not go near your pet.

Cement Remover
When you are working with concrete or cement, try cleaning your hands with vinegar, works great.

Ant Remover
If you are having a problem with ants, just wipe your counters off with a solution prepared from equal parts of vinegar and water. Crawling insects hate vinegar.

Remove Scorch Marks

If you rub a scorched mark with a clean soft cloth that has been lightly dampened with vinegar it may remove a scorch mark if it not too badly imbedded.

Brighten Clothes

If you add 1¾ cups of white vinegar to your rinse water it will brighten up the colors. If you are dying a fabric, add 1 cup of vinegar to the final rinse to set the color.

Remove Crayon Stains

Moisten a toothbrush with white vinegar and rub the area lightly until the crayon is removed.

Eliminate Deodorant Stains

Perspiration stains can be removed by rubbing the area with vinegar before laundering.

Ink Stain Remover

Vinegar will remove most ink stains if they are fresh.

Rust Remover

To remove rust, just moisten the fabric with white vinegar then rub the area lightly with salt. Place the garment in the sun to dry, then launder.

MEDICINAL USES FOR VINEGAR

Dandruff

Massage white vinegar into the scalp 3-4 times per week, then shampoo.

Nail Polish Saver

To make nail polish last longer, just soak the fingernails in a solution of 2 teaspoons of white vinegar and ¾ cup of warm water for 1-2 minutes before applying the polish.

Sunburn Reliever
Place a piece of cloth that has been lightly dampened with apple cider vinegar on the burn. Replace every 20-30 minutes.

Athletes Foot
Rinse your feet 3-4 times per day in apple cider vinegar.

Morning Sickness
When morning sickness occurs, just combine 1 teaspoon of apple cider vinegar in a glass of water and drink it.

Indigestion
To relieve indigestion, just place 2 teaspoons of apple cider vinegar into a glass of water and drink during a meal.

A BUNION SANDWICH
In a small bowl, soak 2 slices of white bread, 2 slices of red onion in 1 cup of vinegar for 24 hours. Place the bread on the corn (bunion) and place a slice of onion on top. Wrap with a bandage and allow it to remain overnight.

AROUND THE KITCHEN WITH VINEGAR

Storing Pimientos
If you want to store pimiento peppers after opening a can or jar, just place then into a very small bowl, cover them with vinegar and refrigerate. They will last for 2-3 weeks.

Keeping Ginger Fresh
Prepare a clean jar filled with balsamic vinegar and add the grated ginger, seal tight and refrigerate.

Flavor Enhancer
When preparing soup or tomato sauce, add one or two tablespoons of vinegar to the soup or sauce during the last 5 minutes of cooking time. This will really enhance their flavor.

Over-Salted Foods
Add 1 teaspoon of vinegar and 1 teaspoon of sugar then reheat the dish or sauce.

Mold Eliminator
Always remember to wipe down the outside of canning jars with vinegar to eliminate the possibility of mold growing.

Vegetable and Fruit Wash
Mix 2¾ tablespoons of vinegar in 1 gallon of water and use the mixture to wash the outsides of fruits and vegetables before peeling or slicing into them.

Stops Food Discoloring
If you add 1-2 teaspoons of vinegar to the water you are boiling potatoes in, they will not discolor for a longer period.

Great Mashed Potato Trick
Once you have mashed the potatoes and added the hot milk, try adding a teaspoon of vinegar and beat a little bit more. It will fluff them up and they will hold their shape.

Firm Gelatin
In warmer weather, gelatin tends to lose its shape. Just add 1 teaspoon of vinegar to the gelatin to keep it firm.

If humidity is high, don't make gelatin

BETTER WEAR DARK SHADES
If you would like the crust on your fresh baked bread to have a great sheen, just brush the top of the bread with vinegar about 5 minutes before the bread has finished baking. Remove the bread before brushing on the vinegar, as the oven can get very cramped.

ALL CRACKED UP OVER EGGS
To keep the whites where they belong when an egg cracks during boiling, just add some vinegar to the boiling water.

VINEGAR, RISING TO THE OCCASION

Next time you steam vegetables, try adding 2 teaspoons of vinegar to the boiling water. It will prevent unwanted odors and stabilize the color of the vegetables.

WELL PICKLE MY EGGS

Pickled eggs are found in every English pub and will be sitting in a big jar of malt vinegar and spices.

FISH MASSAGE

Before you try and scale a fish, give the fish a vinegar massage and the scales will come off easier as well as keeping your hands from becoming smelling fishy.

CHAPTER 23

GRANDPA'S USES FOR BAKING SODA

USES FOR BAKING SODA

WHAT IS BAKING SODA?

Baking soda is actually bicarbonate of soda, which is derived from the manufacture of common washing soda also, known as "sal soda." Baking soda is composed carbon and oxygen molecules, which combine to form carbon dioxide gas. If batter has a sufficient acidic nature then only baking soda is needed to produce carbon dioxide. If the batter does not have sufficient acid, then baking powder, which carries both acid and alkali, is needed. All baking soda in North America is mined from the mineral, Trona, which is found in Green River, Wyoming.

The large deposit was discovered in the 1930's. Trona is actually composed of sodium bicarbonate and sodium carbonate, a very close relative. The ore is mined from deep mines, crushed, rinsed, and heated to produce sodium carbonate. The sodium carbonate is then dissolved in water and carbon dioxide is forced through the solution releasing the sodium bicarbonate crystals, which is washed, then dried and packaged as baking soda.

When baking soda is added to a recipe, it has an immediate rising action with the release of the gas, which means that your oven must be preheated and your pans greased before you even combine the ingredients. Baking soda should be added to dry ingredients first and the wet ingredients just before placing the food into the oven. Baking soda will last for approximately 6 months if stored in an airtight container and in a cool, dry location.

If you are not sure of the activity level of baking soda, try placing ¾ teaspoon in about 2 teaspoons of white vinegar, if carbon dioxide bubbles appear it is still active. Sodium bicarbonate is produced in the human body to assist in maintaining the acidity (pH) level of the blood as well as being found in saliva. It will neutralize plaque acids, which might otherwise dissolve our teeth. Another action in the body is to neutralize stomach acid so that we don't get ulcer, as well as assisting in the breathing process by transporting carbon dioxide from the tissues to the lungs for disposal.

IN THE KITCHEN

FLUFFY OMELET
If you want the fluffiest omelet ever, just add ¾ teaspoon baking soda for every 3 eggs.

NICE SMELLING FISH
If you soak raw fish for about ¾ hour in 2 tablespoons of baking soda in 1-quart of water, you will not have a fishy taste. Make sure that you rinse well and pat dry before cooking.

MASHED POTATO MAGIC
To really fluff up those mashed potatoes the way grandma did, just add a pinch of baking soda to them while you are mashing.

HOW CLEAN I AM
Add a small amount of baking soda to the water that you clean the insides and outsides of chicken in. Rinse with clean cold water and there will be no residue to worry about.

POTATO PANCAKE INDIGESTION CURE
Be sure and add 1 teaspoon of baking soda to the batter next time you make potato pancakes. Some people cannot tolerate the pancakes and tend to get indigestion.

VEGGIE CLEANER
You can clean dirt and other residues off fruit and vegetables by sprinkling baking soda on a wet sponge and scrubbing them then rinse well with water.

LOWER COFFEE ACID CONTENT
If you wish to reduce the acid level in coffee, just add a pinch of baking soda to a cup of regular coffee. The taste will not be affected.

HOW CLEAR I AM
If you add just a pinch of baking soda to a pot of steeping tea, the tea will not be cloudy. This will work for iced tea as well.

MAKE DISHWASHER DETERGENT
You can make your own dishwashing detergent by mixing 2 tablespoons of baking soda with 2 tablespoons of borax.

CLEANING AWAY MINERAL DEPOSITS
To get rid of mineral deposits from teapots and coffee pots, just bring a solution of 1 cup of vinegar and 4 tablespoons of baking soda to a boil in them and allow it to simmer for a few minutes.

AVOID A SMELLY BOTTOM
If you sprinkle the bottom tray of your toaster with a teaspoon of baking soda, it will eliminate any burnt smell from drippings and crumbs.

BARBECUE GRILL CLEANER
You can easily de-grease the grill on the barbecue by applying a paste of baking soda and water with a wire brush. Allow the solution to remain for 15 minutes before wiping it clean. The fire will burn away any residue that remains before you add food to the grill.

OVERNIGHT GRILL CLEANER
Place the grill in a large plastic garbage can and cover it with an industrial strength detergent. Fill the garbage can with water and allow it to soak overnight. This will remove all the baked on grunge and dirt then just hose it off.

A SHINY BOTTOM
If you want your copper pots to look like new again, just sprinkle them with baking soda then pour white vinegar over them. Allow the pots to stand for 15 minutes before rinsing them. If you prefer you can use baking soda and ¾ a lemon to scrub them to a shiny finish. Rinse well and dry before use.

RUST REMOVER
If you prepare a paste composed of 1 tablespoon of baking soda and 1 teaspoon of water you will be able to remove rust from a metal chair or table leg. Wipe the paste on to the area then scrub lightly with a piece of aluminum foil. Clean up with paper towel.

IN THE BATHROOM

The first thing to remember is that germs love moisture. If you keep surfaces dry it will reduce the incidence of bacteria getting a foothold and causing odors and unhealthy conditions. Disinfectants will kill bacteria and almost all molds, but only for a short period of time. Therefore it is necessary to clean the surfaces that are more susceptible to contamination more frequently than most other area of your home.

BATHROOM DISINFECTANT CLEANER

The following ingredients will be needed:

1	Quart of very hot tap water
11/3	Cup of powdered household laundry detergent
11/3	Cup of pine oil (Pinesol™ will do fine)
1	Half-gallon plastic container

Place the water and detergent in the ¾ gallon plastic container and mix until the detergent is fully dissolved. Skim off any foam that develops, and then gradually add the Pinesol™ or pine oil as you continue stirring. To use the solution, add 1 part disinfectant to 1-part warm water. For toilets, use full strength. Store in well-sealed container and as with all chemicals store away from children.

SCUM AND MILDEW BUILDUP, ACTIVATE THE SALT

Shower curtains will develop a layer of mildew and scum, especially over the course of a year. Most curtains can be washed in the washing machine, which should do the job. However, you may wish to use the following formula or at least soak the curtains in the bathtub in a strong solution of salt water before you hang them up after they get out of the washing machine. The salt bath should only be needed about once a year.

SHOWER CURTAIN CLEANER

The following ingredients will be needed:

¾	Cup of soap flakes
¾	Cup of baking soda (fresh)
1	Cup of white vinegar
	Mineral oil

Place warm water in the washing machine and add 2 large towels and the shower curtains. Add the soap flakes and baking soda and run the wash cycle. Add the vinegar and a few drops of mineral oil to soften the curtains in the rinse water.

MAKING TILE CLEANER
The following mixture can be used with a brush or sponge:
Mix together:

¾	Cup baking soda
¾	Cup white vinegar
1	Cup household ammonia
2	Gallons of warm water

A SLIPPIN & A SLIDIN
Try sprinkling baking soda in the bathtub then place 2 sponges or washcloths on the bottom and let you feet clean the tub. Only for the very agile!

CLEAN UP YOUR POTTY
If you sprinkle ¾ box of baking soda in the toilet tank then allow it to remain over night it will clean the tank and the bowl.

BATHROOM FIXTURE CLEANER
The following ingredients will be needed:

¾	Cup of white vinegar
1	Cup of clear household ammonia
¾	Cup of baking soda (fresh)
1	Gallon of warm tap water

Place all the ingredients in a small bucket and mix well. Pour into a number of smaller jars for storage. Place a small amount into a spray bottle and use on fixtures and soap scum. Wipe clean with a warm soft cloth.

DETECTING SEWER GAS
The following ingredients will be needed:

2	Ounces of lead acetate
1	Pint of distilled water or rainwater

Place the ingredients into a container and mix well, then place a piece of unglazed white paper into the solution. Remove the paper immediately and allow it to dry. If the odor you smell is caused by a sewer gas leak, the paper will turn a dark color.

THERE'S A STRANGE SMELL COMING FROM THE BATHROOM
If you have a septic tank, you are probably familiar with a strange smell occasionally and know to have it pumped or to add special bacteria. However, if you are not on a septic tank and you smell a strange odor, it may be from "sewer gas," which contains methane. The odor is usually associated with sulfur and you should call you're gas company or a plumber as soon as possible. Plumbers have special gas detectors and can locate the problem and correct it.

INEXPENSIVE AIR FRESHENER
Mix equal parts of your favorite bath salts with equal parts of baking soda to prepare a room freshener.

GENERAL BATHROOM CLEANER
The following ingredients will be needed:

1	Pound of baking soda (fresh)
4	Tablespoons of liquid hand soap
1	Cup of warm tap water

Place all the ingredients in a spray bottle and shake to mix. This formula is not as harsh as the one with ammonia. It is also safer around children.

AROUND THE HOME

SPARKLING WINDOWS
To clean a dirty window, just use a wet sponge sprinkled with a small amount of baking soda. Rinse the window with a clean sponge and dry well.

WATER SPOTS FROM WOOD FLOORS

Water spots can be removed from wood floors by applying a baking soda solution on a damp washcloth. Don't allow the wood to get very wet and dry well afterwards.

INEXPENSIVE CARPET MAINTENANCE

Best to sprinkle baking soda mixture on your carpet monthly to keep the carpet deodorized. Just sprinkle it on and allow it to remain overnight. Use a brush to rub it into the carpet then vacuum it up the next morning. The deodorizer is prepared from:

¾	**Cup baking soda**
¾	**Cup cornstarch**
10	**Drops of your favorite essential oil**

ICE REMOVER

You won't need cat litter or rock salt, just use baking soda to de-ice the steps or walkway. It will provide traction and will melt away the ice. It is safe and will not harm the outside surfaces, shoes or any indoor surfaces if you track it inside. You can mix it with sand for even better traction.

REMOVE PLASTIC TABLECLOTH ODOR

Plastic tablecloths tend to have an odor all their own and it is not very appealing. To remove the odor, just soak the tablecloth in a solution of baking soda and water over night to remove the smell.

INEXPENSIVE TOILET BOWL CLEANER

The following ingredients will be needed:

1	**Cup of Castile soap (liquid)**
¾	**Cup of borax**
¾	**Cup of baking soda**

Place all the ingredients into a container and mix well. Add a small amount of very warm water if you have a problem blending the ingredients. Pour into toilet and scrub with a brush.

FIGHT STINKY SHOES

If you sprinkle baking soda in shoes that have an offensive smell and allow it to remain overnight, the smell will be gone by morning.

Just tap out the baking soda.

SOME LAUNDRY TIPS

WHY BUY FABRIC SOFTENERS?
You can save money by not buying fabric softeners and just add ¾ cup of baking soda to your rinse cycle.

HOW BRIGHT I AM............
You can boost the whitening power of your bleach and use less bleach. If you normally use 1 cup of liquid chlorine bleach, you will use only half that amount if you add ¾ cup of baking soda to top loaders and ¾ cup of baking soda to front loaders. In fact, the whites will get even whiter.

PERSPIRATION BEGONE
Just make a paste of baking soda and water and rub into the area before you wash the garment. If the stain is stubborn, just allow the paste to remain in place for 2-3 hours before washing.

IRON CLEANER

You can clean starch buildup from the bottom of an iron by rubbing it with a paste prepared from baking soda and water. Be sure that the iron is cool before doing the cleaning.

IRONING TIPS FROM GRANDMA

If you need to remove melted plastic or fabric residues, just heat the iron on low temperature until the foreign material softens and scrape it off with a piece of wood. Baking soda and water made into a paste will also work well. If a steam iron clogs from lint, just fill the iron and allow it to steam until it runs out.

REMOVING IRONING SCORCHES

The following ingredients will be needed:

¾	**Cup of hydrogen peroxide (3% solution)**
¾	**Cup of cool tap water**

Place the ingredients into a small bowl and mix then allow the scorched area of the garment to soak in the solution for about 10 minutes. Rinse the garment in cold water. Works better with natural fibers than it does for synthetics.

FLOSS AWAY

An old dentists trick to remove more plaque is to dampen a piece of dental floss in baking soda before using it.

A CLEAN TOOTHBRUSH IS A HEALTHY BRUSH

If you place your toothbrush in a solution of baking soda and warm water overnight, the bristles will be sparkling clean.

SPIT POLISH

To remove any marks and to get a better shine on a cleaner shoe, try using a paste of baking soda and water to clean the shoes. This will not damage leather shoes.

GRANDPA'S GROOMING TIPS

Read the labels!

UNDER ARM MAGIC
Sprinkle baking soda under your arms for a natural deodorant. You won't have to worry about some of the ingredients that are in the over-the-counter products.

HOMEMADE TOOTHPASTE
The following ingredients will be needed:

1	Tablespoons of bicarbonate of soda
1	Tablespoon of table salt
¾	Cup of cold tap water
3	Teaspoons of glycerin (vegetable source from pharmacy)

Place the bicarbonate of soda, salt, water and glycerin in a small bowl and mix until it is a thick paste. Add additional water if need. A few drops of peppermint oil can be added to improve the flavor. Store in a sealed container.

CHAPTER 24

GETTING OUT THE STAINS

GRANDPA'S RULES FOR STAIN REMOVAL

- Never rub too hard to remove a stain since this will cause damage to the fabric, which can never be repaired.
- Never wash any fabric before attempting to remove the stain, Washing in a detergent may actually set the stain and make it impossible to remove later.
- Stains on washable fabrics should be treated as soon as possible.
- Remember; fresh stains will come out more easily than old ones.
- Non-washable items that normally go to the cleaners should be taken to the cleaners as soon as possible. Identify the stain for the dry cleaner. If you know what the stain is be sure and tell them.

MILDEW AWAY
Just moisten the mildew area with salt and lemon juice and allow it to sit in the sunlight to bleach out the stain.

POURING SALT ON AN OPEN SPILL
If you ever spill red wine on you're carpet, try pouring salt on the area as soon as possible and watch the wine being absorbed almost instantly, then wait until it dries, and vacuum it up. Salt tends to provide a special capillary action that will attract most liquids.

HELP! I CAN'T SEE MY STAIN
When trying to remove stains at home, make sure you do it on a clean, well-lighted work surface. Always use fresh clean rags or a towel.

STOP COLOR RUN-OFF WITH NEW CLOTHING
To eliminate the possibility of color run-off with new clothes, just presoak the garment in cool water with a small amount of white vinegar.

RUST REMOVAL
Rust stains can be removed by wetting the areas with lemon juice,

then sprinkle with a small amount of salt and allow to sit in direct sunlight for 30-45 minutes.

WELL, CLEAN MY CHROME
Automotive chrome cleaner will clean many kitchen appliances.

BACK-UP CHROME CLEANER
To shine chrome fixture, try rubbing them with newspaper while they are still damp. Baby oil and a soft cloth works well. Aluminum foil will also do the job.

YUK! MAKE SURE IT'S CHILLED
Bloodstains may be cleaned with cold club soda.

VINEGAR WILL WORK TOO!
A scorch can be removed by rubbing a raw onion on the scorched area and allowing the onion juice to soak in thoroughly for at least 2-3 hours before washing.

A WORD TO THE WISE
If you are going to use a commercial stain removal substance, be sure and follow directions carefully.

TESTING, ONE, TWO
Always test a stain remover on an area of the fabric that will not show to be sure of the colorfastness of the fabric. Allow the product to stand on the area for at least 3-5 minutes before rinsing off. If there are any changes in the fabric color, do not use.

HIDE THAT SPOT
When treating a spot, it should be placed face down on paper towel, then apply the stain remover to the underside of the garment, allowing the stain to be forced to the surface and not back through the fabric. The paper towel should be replaced a number of times if it is a tough stain to remove.

WHERE ART THOU COLOR
If you are going to use a bleach product, never use it on a colored garment. It is necessary to bleach the whole garment to avoid uneven color removal. If there is a change in color it will at least be uniform.

RESIDUES BEGONE

As soon as the stain is removed, launder immediately with your favorite laundry detergent. This will also remove the residues from the stain remover.

STAIN REMOVAL PRODUCTS

Prompt treatment is the key to stain removal, and it would be wise to have the supplies on hand at all times. The following is a list of some of the more common ingredients needed for most stain removal, however, more natural stain and general cleaning preparations are recommended.

BLEACHES	MISCELLANEOUS REMOVERS
Chlorine bleach	Ammonia
Fabric color remover	Rust stain remover
Non-chlorine, all fabric, bleach	White vinegar

DETERGENTS	SOLVENTS
Enzyme detergent	Dry cleaner spot remover
Enzyme presoaker	Nail polish remover
Liquid detergent	Rubbing alcohol
	Turpentine

SOAPS	SUPPLIES
Laundry detergent	Clean, white cloths
White bar soap	Paper towels

Any of the above products that cannot be found at the supermarket will be found at any drug store.

CAUTION

Some stain removal materials are flammable, while others are poison or toxic. Store them safely and use with care.

BEWARE! CHEMICAL ALERT

Keep stain removal supplies out of reach of children. They should be stored in closed containers with childproof lids and in a cool, dry location away from any food products.

LEMON TREE, VERY PRETTY..........

Lemon extract will remove black scuff, marks from shoes and luggage.

HARD ONE TO GET OUT
Stains from ballpoint pens can be removed with hair spray or milk.

READING THE WRITING
Read the labels on cleaning products and follow directions. Heed all label warnings and always try to store them in their original containers.

CONTAINER SMARTS
Empty and wash all containers immediately after using them. It is best to store stain removal supplies in glass or un-chipped porcelain containers. Solvents will ruin plastic containers. Rusty containers should never be used

> Be careful never allow chemicals near your face and especially your eyes. Wash any spilled chemicals off your hands as soon as possible. .

WEAR A GAS MASK
Use chemicals that give off vapors in a well, ventilated location, preferably outside. Try not to breathe the vapors.

POOOOF
Never use a solvent near an open fire or an electrical outlet.

YUM, YUM, FABRIC
Never add solvents directly into the washing machine. Always allow a solvent-treated fabric dry before washing or placing it into the dryer.

A WITCHES BREW
Never mix stain removal materials with each other, especially ammonia and chlorine bleach. If it's necessary to use both, make sure one is thoroughly rinsed out before adding the other.

RECIPES FOR SAFE CLEANING PRODUCTS

The following recipes are safe when mixed in the quantities indicated below. The mixing of other household chemicals may be dangerous.

- **All-Purpose Household Cleaner**
  Add 1 teaspoon of any liquid soap and 1 teaspoon of trisodium phosphate (TSP) to 1 quart of warm water.

  This is a very effective cleaner for many cleaning jobs including countertops and walls. However, try an area of the wall that will not show before using in case your walls are painted with a poor quality water-based flat paint.
- **Chlorine Bleach**
  Best to use hydrogen peroxide-based bleach.
- **Degreaser (engines, etc.)**
  Best to use a water-based cleaner that is well diluted instead of kerosene, turpentine, or a commercial engine degreaser. These are available in part stores and the label should read "nonflammable," "non-toxic," or "store at temperatures above freezing." These will be water-based products and will do the job.
- **Degreaser (kitchen, grill)**
  Add 2 tablespoons of TSP to 1 gallon of hot water or use a non-chlorinated scouring cleanser with a scouring or steel wool pad.
- **Fabric Softener**
  Fabrics produced from natural fibers do not need fabric softeners only synthetics.
- **Floor Cleaner**
  Vinyl floors use ¾ cup of white vinegar to 1 gallon of warm water.
  Wood, floors: may be damp moped with a mild liquid soap.

- **Furniture Polish**
  Mineral oil may be used, however, most wood surfaces may be cleaned with a damp cloth.
- **Oven Cleaner**
  Mix 2 tablespoons of baking soda or TSP in 1 gallon of warm water and scrub with a very fine steel wool pad (0000). Rubber gloves should be worn and the area rinsed well. For difficult baked-on areas, try scrubbing with a pumice stone.

> *If the above fails, try using an oven cleaner that states "no caustic fumes" on the label.*

- **Glass Cleaner**
  Use 2-3 cup spray bottle with ¾ teaspoon of liquid soap, 3 tablespoons of white vinegar and 2 cups of water. If the windows are very dirty, try using more liquid soap.
- **Laundry Detergent**
  Use laundry soap in place of the detergents. Washing soda may be used in place of a softener. An alternate would be to use detergents with no added bleaches or softeners. Bleach should be used in moderation when needed.
- **Mildew Remover**
  Scrub the area with baking soda or if very stubborn with TSP.
- **Scouring Powder**
  Baking soda will work well in most instances.
- **Toilet Bowl Cleaner**
  Use a non-chlorinated scouring powder and a stiff brush. To remove hard water deposits, pour white vinegar or a commercial citric acid-based toilet bowl cleaner into the toilet and allow it to sit for several hours or overnight before scrubbing.

> *NOTE: Washing soda and TSP are caustic and should be kept out of the reach of children.*

FABRIC ADVICE

Always get the stain out before washing

It is best to know the fiber content in clothing items. If sewn in labels are to be removed a note should be made as to which item it was removed from. Any durable press or polyester fabric such as Dacron holds soil very well and especially stains. A dry cleaning solvent will work the best. If the stain remains after the first treatment, try once more. If the fabric has been washed or has been placed in a dryer, the stain may never come out.

- Never use chlorine bleach on silk, wool, on Spandex.
- Never remove a stain from leather: take it to dry cleaners to send to an expert.

STAIN REMOVAL FROM WASHABLE FABRICS

A number of stains can be removed right in your washing machine. Laundry detergents that state that they contain enzymes will provide the best cleaning and stain removal. Enzyme presoak products provide extra cleaning and stain removal for fabrics that may have a more difficult stain. An enzyme detergent or enzyme presoak product should be able to remove the following common stains:

Blood	Gravy	Body soils	Egg
Fruits	Milk	Chocolate	Grass
Cream soups	Baby formula	Puddings	
	Vegetables		
Baby foods	Ice cream	Most, food soils	

I WONDER WHERE THE YELLOW WENT
Yellowed fabrics can be restored and even old unknown stains may be removed by first soaking in an enzyme presoak product (Proctor & Gamble has excellent ones) such as Biz and then laundering.

CAN'T PERFORM MAGIC
Remember, even the best enzyme detergent or enzyme presoak product is not capable of removing all types of stains.

A number of grease soils and highly colored stains may require special pretreatment before laundering. Since many stains require a variety of different soil removal treatments and techniques, it is important to identify a stain before trying to remove it. A number of stains may actually be set if the wrong method is used.

GRANDPA'S STAINS & THEIR REMOVAL METHODS

Beverage
Sponge the area with cold water or soak then sponge again. Launder with oxygen bleach and the hottest water that is safe for the fabric.

Blood
Soak the fabric in cold water as soon as possible. *Hydrogen Peroxide* If the stain persists, soak in warm water with a presoak product before laundering. Try club soda.

Candle Wax
The surface wax should be removed with a dull knife. The item should then be placed stain face down on paper towels and then sponge the remaining stain with dry cleaning solvent. Allow it to dry and then launder. If traces of color from the wax remain: try soaking it in Biz® or oxygen bleach before laundering again. If the color is still present, try laundering again using chlorine bleach, if the fabric is chlorine bleach safe.

Catsup\Tomato Products
Remove excess with a dull knife, then soak in cold water then launder using the hottest water the fabric will stand.

Chewing Gum/Adhesive Tape/Rubber Cement
First: apply ice to the stain to harden it. Remove excess stain material with a dull knife. Place the item face down on paper towels and sponge with a dry cleaning solvent.

Chocolate\Cocoa
Soak in cold water then launder with oxygen bleach using the hottest water the fabric will stand.

Coffee/Tea
Best to soak in Biz® or oxygen bleach; using the hottest water that is safe for the stained fabric then launder. If the stain persists, try laundering again using chlorine bleach if it is safe to do so.

Cosmetics
Dampen stain and rub gently with a white bar soap; then rinse well and launder.

Crayon

If there are only a few spots they can be treated the same as candle wax. If there are many items that are stained, first wash the items with hot water and laundry soap (e.g. Ivory Snow®) and 1 cup of baking soda. If the spots remain, have the clothes dry, cleaned.

Deodorants And Anti-Perspirants

Apply white vinegar, then rub and rinse. If; the stain remains, try saturating the area with rubbing alcohol, rinse then soak in Biz or an oxygen bleach and launder. If the stain remains wash in chlorine bleach if safe for fabric.

Dye Transfer

If; you have white fabrics that have picked up dye from a colored garment that "bled", try restoring the white by using a fabric color remover. Launder if any of the dye remains using chlorine bleach, if it is safe for the fabric.

Egg/Meat Juice

Remove excess with a dull knife then soak in cold water. Launder in oxygen bleach in very hot water.

Fabric Softeners

These stains usually result from accidental spills and can be removed by rubbing the area; with a piece of cloth moistened with bar soap then launder.

Formula

Soak in warm water then launder with oxygen bleach and the hottest water that is safe for the fabric.

Fruit\Fruit Juices

Soak in cold water before laundering.

Grass

The green area should be sponged with denatured alcohol before washing in very hot water and oxygen bleach.

Grease Stains

The stained area should be placed face down on paper towels. Dry cleaning solvent should be placed on the backside of the stain and then brushed from the center of the stain to the outer edges using a clean white cloth.

Moisten the stain with warm water and rub with bar soap or a mild liquid detergent, then rinse and launder.

Gum

Rub with ice and carefully remove the gum with a dull knife before laundering.

Ink Stains

For removal of ballpoint stains, place the stain face down on paper towels and sponge the back of the stain with dry cleaning solvent. If there is some ink left, try rubbing the area with a moistened bar soap, rinse and then launder. For any other type of ink stains, just try and remove the stain with a dampened cloth and bar soap, rinse and soak in Biz™ or oxygen bleach using very hot water. If the stain won't come out, try using chlorine bleach, if the fabric is safe. Some permanent ink may never be removed.

Ink, Felt Tip

Rub the area with Fantastic™ or Mr. Clean™, rinse and repeat if necessary. May be impossible to remove.

Iodine

Rinse the fabric from the underside with cool water, then soak in a solution of fabric color remover, rinse and then launder.

Lipstick

The stain should be placed face down on paper towels and then sponged with dry cleaning solvent replacing the paper towels frequently while the color is being removed. Moisten the stain with cool water and then rub with bar soap, rinse and launder.

Mildew

Fabric should be laundered using chlorine bleach if it is safe for the fabric. If not, try soaking it in oxygen bleach and then launder.

Milk

The fabric should be rinsed in cold water as soon as possible, and then washed in cold water using a liquid detergent.

Mustard

Moisten stain with cool water then rub with bar soap, rinse and launder using chlorine bleach, if it is safe for the fabric. If not, soak in Biz or an oxygen detergent using very hot water, then launder. It may take several treatments to remove all of the stain.

Nail Polish

The fabric stain should be placed face down on paper towels then sponge the back of the stain frequently and repeat until the stain disappears then launder. Never use nail polish remover on fabric, best to have them dry, cleaned.

Paint

Try to treat the stain while it is still wet. Latex, acrylic, and water, based paints cannot be removed once they have dried. While they are wet: rinse in warm water to flush the paint out then launder. Oil-based paints can be removed with solvent that is recommended on the paint can. If it does not give this information, try using turpentine; then rinse and rub with bar soap, then launder.

Perspiration

Moisten the stain and rub with bar soap. Be gentle as perspiration may weaken some fibers, especially silk. Most fabrics should be presoaked in Biz or an enzyme detergent and then laundered in hot water and chlorine bleach, if the fabric is safe.

Another method is to mix 4 tablespoons of salt to 1 quart of hot water and sponge on the fabric until the stain disappears.

Perfume (Same As Beverages)

Rust

Never use chlorine bleach on rust, apply a rust stain remover, rinse then launder. You can also use a fabric color remover and then launder or if the stain is really stubborn, try using 1 ounce of oxalic acid crystals (or straight warm rhubarb juice) dissolved in 1 gallon of water, mixed in a plastic container, then rinse and launder.

Scorch

Soak the fabric in a strong solution of Biz and oxygen bleach using very hot water if safe for the fabric, then launder. If the scorch remains, it will be necessary to repeat the procedure using chlorine bleach, if the fabric will take it.

Shoe Polish

Try applying a mixture of 1 part rubbing alcohol and 2 parts of water for colored fabrics and only the straight alcohol for whites.

Suede

Rain spots can be removed by lightly rubbing the area with an emery board. If there are grease spots, try using white vinegar or club soda then blot out the stain. Afterwards brush with a suede brush.

Tar

The area should be rubbed with kerosene until all the tar is dissolved, then wash as usual. Test a small area first to be sure it is color, fast.

Tobacco

Moisten the stain and rub with bar soap rinse and then launder. If the stain persists, try soaking it in Biz or an oxygen detergent, then launder. As a last resort use chlorine bleach if the fabric is safe.

Urine, Vomit, Mucous

Soak the fabric in Biz or an enzyme detergent: launder using chlorine bleach, if safe for the fabric. If not use oxygen bleach with detergent.

Wine/Soft Drinks

Soak the fabric with Biz or oxygen bleach using very hot water then launder. Use chlorine bleach if needed and if the fabric is safe.

GRANDPA'S NATURAL METHODS OF STAIN REMOVAL

TOTALLY THRIFTY

If you wish to use less detergent and save money, try using slivers of old soaps placed in a sock with the neck tied. Place the sock into the washer and you will use less detergent.

SETTING IT PERMANENTLY

To colorfast a possible problem garment: try soaking the colored garment in cold, salty water for 30 minutes before laundering.

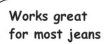

Works great for most jeans

DON'T GET STUNG

After washing a piece of clothing with a zipper that has given you problems, try rubbing beeswax on the zipper to resolve the problem and remove any grime that has accumulated.

BEGONE OLD SOAP

When washing clothes, to be sure that all the soap has been removed, try adding 1 cup of white vinegar to the rinse cycle. The vinegar will dissolve the alkalinity in detergents as well as giving the clothes a pleasant fragrance.

THE OLD BUBBLE MACHINE

Placing too much soap in the washing machine can cause problems. If this happens, just pour 2 tablespoons of white vinegar or a capful of fabric softener into the machine to neutralize some of the soap.

THE GREEN, GREEN, GRASS OF HOME

Grass stains will be easily removed with toothpaste, scrub in with a toothbrush before washing. Another method is to rub the stain with molasses and allow it to stand overnight, then wash with regular dish soap by itself. If all else fails, try methyl alcohol, but be sure the color is set, best to try an area that won't show first.

GREASELESS

Spic and Span placed in the washer is a great grease remover, 1/4 cup is all that is needed.

WRINKLE REMOVER
To avoid ironing many different types of clothes, just remove them from the dryer the second it stops and fold or hang up immediately.

CATCH THAT COLOR
Washing colored material for the first time may be risky unless you wash it in Epsom salts. One gallon of water to 1 teaspoon is all that is needed. The material will not run.

THE DISAPPEARING ACT
An excellent spot remover can be made using 2 parts of water to 1 part rubbing alcohol.

A DIRTY JOB
To remove difficult dirt, such as collars, mix 1/3 cup of water with 1/3 cup of liquid detergent and 1/3 cup of ammonia. Place the ingredients in a spray bottle. Rubbing shampoo into the area may also work.

LINT MAGNET
To keep corduroy garments from retaining lint, turn them inside out when washing.

HAIRBALLS
To avoid hairballs on acrylic sweaters, turn them inside out when washing them.

ONE OF THE TOUGHEST
Iodine stains can be removed using a mixture of baking soda and water. Allow it to remain on for about 30 minutes rub with mild action.

USE ONLY THE UNSALTED
Butter or margarine will remove tar from clothing, just rub until it's gone. The butter is easily removed with any type of spray and wash product.

INKA-KA-DINKA-DOO
Rubbing alcohol or hair spray may remove a number of ink pen stains.

BEWARE OF A TIGHT FIT
If you wash slipcovers, be sure and replace them when they are still damp. They will fit better and will not need to be ironed.

BLOWDRYING
If sweater cuffs are stretched, dip them in hot water and dry with a hairdryer.

A SPOT OF TEA, PERHAPS
Tea stains on tablecloths can be removed with glycerin, try leaving it sit overnight in the solution before washing.

INTO THE FREEZER
Candle wax on tablecloths can be removed by freezing with ice cubes.

YUK
Lace doilies should be hand washed in sour milk for the best results.

HOLD THE SHAVING CREAM
If you have a problem with small burrs on sweaters, try using a disposable razor to remove them.

EASY DOES IT
If you are washing a wool garment, be careful not to pull on it. Wool is very weak when wet. Lay the garment on a towel and roll it up and squeeze the excess water out.

NEUTRALIZER

If you have a difficult bloodstain try making a paste of meat tenderizer and cold water. Sponge on the area and allow it to stand for 20-30 minutes. Rinse in cold water, then wash. Hydrogen peroxide may also work.

BATHING STUFFED ANIMALS

To clean stuffed animals that cannot be placed in the washer, just place them in a cloth bag and add baking soda, then shake.

POWDER ME

White flour will clean white gloves, just rub.

A SLIPPERY SUBJECT

Lipstick stains will clean out of clothes by using Vaseline.

A REVIVAL

If you shrink a woolen garment: try soaking it in a hair cream rinse. This will usually make them easy to stretch back into the original size. Another method is to dissolve 1 ounce of Borax in 1 teaspoon of hot water then add it to 1 gallon of warm water. Place the garment in, stretch back to shape then rinse it in 1 gallon of warm water with 2 tablespoons of white vinegar added.

BE STINGY, BE SMART

When you are doing a small wash load tear the fabric-softening sheet in half for the same results.

A SOLID FACT

To make your own spray starch, purchase 1 bottle of liquid starch concentrate and mix one part of liquid starch to 1 part of water, use a spray bottle.

BUTTON, BUTTON, WHO'S GOT THE BUTTON

If you lose buttons regularly on children's clothing, try sewing them on with dental floss.

TRUE GRIT
If your iron is sticking, try running it over a piece of paper with sprinkled salt on it.

WELL, SEASONED CURTAINS
Water stained fabrics should be placed in salt water and soaked until the stain is gone.

BRING IN THE SUB
If you prefer not to use bleach, try substituting 3 tablespoons of hydrogen peroxide to the wash load.

SAVE THE BUTTONS
Always remove buttons before discarding a garment. They may come in handy at a later date.

ATTRACTIVE SALT
Cleaning silk flowers is easy if you place them in a plastic bag with 2 tablespoons of salt and shake vigorously while holding on to the stems. Salt tends to attract the dust.

IRONING SMARTS
When ironing, always iron the fabrics that require a cool temperature first as the iron heats up.

DEW TELL
Mildew on shower curtains can be removed with a mixture of ¾ cup bleach, ¾ cup powdered detergent, and 1 gallon of water. To prolong the life of shower curtains add 1 cup of white vinegar to the final rinse.

MAKING COLORS FAST
To prevent jeans from fading (if you want to) soak the jeans in 1/2 cup of white vinegar and 2 quarts of water for 1 hour before you wash them for the first time.

JEAN SMARTS
Blue jeans should only be washed in cold water then placed in a moderate heat dryer for only 10 minutes. Then they should be placed on a wooden hanger to continue drying.

DOLLAR SAVER
If you would like to save dollars on dry cleaning of wool blankets, try washing them in a mild dishwasher soap on a very gently cycle then air fluff to dry.

NO ONE WILL EVER KNOW
If you scorch a garment, try removing the scorch with cloth that has been dampened with vinegar. Only use a warm iron, not too hot. Cotton scorch marks tend to respond better to peroxide.

INSULATION
A sheet of aluminum foil placed underneath the ironing board cover will allow the heat to be retained for a longer period of time.

BUTTON, BUTTON....
Always remember to place a small amount of clear nail polish in the center of every button on a new garment. This seals the threads and they will last longer.

A SHOCKING SITUATION
A pipe, cleaner dipped in white vinegar should be used to clean the holes in the iron after it is completely cool. Make sure it is unplugged.

IF YOU'RE IN A SPOT
Glass cleaner sometimes makes an excellent spot remover if you need something in a hurry. Make sure the fabric is colorfast.

BRIGHTEN-UP
If you want to whiten your whites, try adding a cup of dishwasher detergent to the washer. Even whitens sweat socks.

ANY PENCIL WILL DO
A sticky zipper will respond to a rubbing with a lead pencil. Does an excellent job of lubricating it.

A TEMPORARY SOLUTION
If a button comes off, try reattaching it with the wire from a twist tie.

DON'T SUCK YOUR THUMB
If you use a thimble to sew or sort papers, try wetting your finger before you place the thimble on. This creates suction and holds the thimble on.

A SEALER
When you wash you sneakers, spray them with a spray starch to help them resist becoming soiled.

DIRTY BOTTOM
If the bottom of the iron gets dirty, just clean it with a steel wool soap pad. If you want to make it shiny again, just run a piece of waxed paper over it.

RUSTADE
Rust marks on clothing can be removed with lemon juice and a small amount of salt, easily rubbed in and then allowed to sit in the sun for 2 hours.

AND AWAY WE GO
To dry the insides of shoes or sneakers, try placing the blower end of the vacuum hose inside.

A TRIPPER-UPPER
If you have problems with your shoelaces becoming undone, just dampen them before tying them.

A WORD OF CAUTION

Silk clothing should be hand washed using cool water with Ivory liquid soap. When you rinse, try adding a small amount of lanolin to help preserve the material. Always drip dry, never place the garment in the dryer, and then iron using a soft piece of cloth over the garment.

SHAPE-UP, AND DON'T LOSE YOUR COLOR

Cold water should always be used in the rinse cycle to help the clothes retain their shape and color.

CHAPTER 25

GRANDPA KNOWS PAINTING

PAINTING (INTERIOR)

GENERAL INFORMATION:

There is more to painting than just buying a can of paint and painting a wall! There are different types of paints for different surfaces. You need to know the difference between oil-based, water-based, acrylics, primers, etc. and when they should be used. The equipment to paint with paints also varies depending on the project. However, the following are the bare minimum requirements for every painting project.

PROTECTING HANDS

If you rub an anti-static dryer sheet on your hands before your start painting or using glue, your hands will wash off easier.

CAULKING

Used to fill open crevices and cracks around doors and windows. Colored caulking is also available and makes for a great looking job.

BEAD A PROFESSIONAL LINE

Running a professional caulking bead is not as easy as the pros make it. You need to push the bead forward then pull it back. Be sure you are using the right caulking for the job and follow the manufacturers instructions. Practice making shallow beads before starting to use it on the job and use your finger or plastic spoon to shape the bead.

REACH FOR A SYRINGE

There are many places that an ordinary caulk gun can't reach and are hard to use. When you have this problem, just use a 20cc plastic syringe as a mini caulk gun.

TYPES OF CAULKING

Acrylic Latex
Easy to use indoor caulk and will last about 3-10 years.

Butyl Rubber
Very durable for outdoor use, however, it is difficult to clean up. The seal should last for about 10 years.

Siliconized Acrylic
Easy to apply and clean up and will last for 20-30 years.

Urethane Foam
Sold in aerosol cans with the foam expanding after release. Handy for filling hard to reach areas: best used around electrical outlets and new windows. Be sure and wear gloves when applying. Somewhat expensive!

- ❖ **Drop Cloths** – Plastic, to prevent spills from damaging areas. Purchase throwaway.
- ❖ **Masking Tape** – To protect non-painted areas and to hold down plastic drop cloths.

GRANDPA FOUND A NEW WAY TO MASK

A new product is now available for masking off windows instead of using masking tape. It is *acrylic latex* and is specially formulated to prime and seal wood trim around windows as well as masking off the glazing very quickly and efficiently. To use it, all you have to do is paint the thick, white paste onto the trim and lap it over the glass.

When the latex dries, if forms a clear, thin sheet that will adhere solidly to the wood. However, the latex will peel off the glass very easily and leave a clean, unpainted surface.

- ❖ **Paint Tray** – Disposable liners for trays.
- ❖ **Patching Compound** – Premixed or powder form for repairing cracks and holes.
- ❖ **Sandpaper** – You may need coarse, medium or fine grades.

LIFE EXTENSION
A piece of sandpaper will last longer and remain in position better if you dampen the backing slightly before you wrap it around a piece of wood.

CONVENIENCE GRANDPA STYLE
Keeping track of pieces of sandpaper is a real pain. However, grandpa keeps his sandpaper on a clipboard and hangs it on the wall for easy retrieval.

SANDING SMALL OBJECTS
If you need to sand a small object, try attaching the sandpaper to a flat surface and running the object that requires sanding over the paper.

GOOD USE FOR A POPSICLE STICK
Small, hard-to-get places can be sanded with the sandpaper wrapped around a Popsicle stick or an emery board.

BUY GOOD QUALITY HOSE
When you get through sanding an object, try placing a nylon stocking over your hand and running it over the sanded area to locate any rough spots.

❖ **Screwdrivers** – Both Phillips and standard for removing wall plates and door hardware. Can be used to open a can if you don't have a pint can opener.
❖ **5-Gallon Mixing Bucket** – Good for stirring paint from multiple cans.
❖ **Wall Cleaner & Sponges** – To clean up dusty areas, cooking grease spots, soot or cigarette damage.

EVALUATE THE PAINTS
Select a quality paint manufacturer. Inexpensive or poor quality paints will produce a mediocre job.

GRANDPA COMPARES INTERIOR PAINTS & PRIMERS

Acoustic
Used on acoustic ceilings and tiles and will not affect their sound-reducing qualities. Can be applied by spraying or using a special type of roller. The color choices are very limited, you don't need a primer and it will clean up easily with water.

Alcohol-based primer
This is the best primer for almost any surface with the ability to kill any almost any stain providing a slick surface. Needs to be thinned: will clean up well using denatured alcohol.

Alkyd
This best used for a rough surface and has excellent hiding power. Best not to apply the paint over unprimed drywall surface since it will cause the surface to become rough. It will dry slower than latex and the odor is somewhat strong causing it to be banned in some areas. To thin alkyd and for cleanup: best to use a solvent and be sure and coat unfinished surfaces with an alkyd primer.

Latex
This is the paint of choice for the majority of interior paint jobs. However, best not to sue it over unprimed wood, metal or wallpaper. The glossiness will vary from flat to high and will adhere to all surfaces with the exception of slick surfaces. It dries fast enough allowing you to apply two coats in one day; however, it is less durable than alkyd-based paints. Cleanup is easy with just soap and water. Be sure and prepare new surfaces with a latex or alkyd primer for the best results.

Latex primer
Best used to prepare patched areas and on new drywall. It is inexpensive and dries very fast. Very easy to clean up using soap and water!

Metal
Commonly used over primed or bare metal surfaces. Rusty metal primer can be used to cover rust areas. The self-primers will adhere to bare surfaces; however, preparation will depend on the type and condition of the metal surface.

Some can be thinned using only water, while others need solvent or mineral spirits. The primer will depend on the type of metal being covered.

Oil

These paints are rarely available anymore since they dry very slow and will give off flammable fumes. The paint will not stand up as well as alkyds. Cleans up well with mineral spirits, low odor thinner or turpentine.

Oil-based primer

One of the best all-purpose, oil-based primers, however, it dries slowly and will give off fumes. Cleans up with mineral spirits!

One-coat

Works well as long as the surface is sealed and of similar color. Be sure that there is not a lot of patchwork that may need to be covered. These are latex or alkyd paints with the addition of pigments, which will increase their hiding power, but makes them more expensive. Be careful thinning since it lessens the paint's ability to hide flaws. Will clean up easily with either water or solvent depending on whether its latex or alkyd.

Texture paint

Great at covering up imperfections and provide the look of stucco-finish plaster. Applying the paint is somewhat difficult and it is best to paint a section at a time, while keeping the desired effect consistent. Best not to thin since it defeats the purpose. Hard to stir and be sure and check the label for compatible primers.

DON'T BUY CHEAP STUFF

Purchase quality brushes. Inexpensive brushes will shed bristles and will take you twice as long to do the job.

PREPARE THE SURFACE FOR A GOOD JOB

Be sure and totally prep the room before starting with drop cloths and masking tape (if applicable). Different cleaning and prep methods need to be used depending on the type of paint you are going to use.

- ❖ Use blue painters tape around all edges, windowsills and outlets.
- ❖ Place a drop cloth on the floor and be sure and tape it to the baseboards or floor.

HELP! I'M CHOKING

Read the label on every can of paint you buy since the manufactures are always changing the paints. The drying times between coats may be different for different paint types. Be sure and read warning labels on paint cans. Chemicals are always changing. Paint fumes can be flammable. Don't smoke when painting and wear a respirator when working with solvent-based paints.

GRANDPA EVALUATES THE SURFACE

Rough vs. smooth surfaces will make a difference in the type of paint you choose. The following information will provide some valuable information regarding the type of different surfaces and how they need to be prepared:

Previously Painted Plaster

Start by washing the surface, rinse and dry then sand the surface lightly and remove any debris. Be sure and fill any cracks with spackling compound then sand and degloss before applying primer if necessary. Use polyvinyl acrylic primer if painting over a dark surface or if it had strong colors.

Previously Painted Wallboard

Make sure that the surface is free of any dirt or grime then rinse with water and dry. Apply flat latex primer if you are painting over dark, strong colors.

Previously Painted Wood

Start by washing the surface, rinse and dry then sand the surface lightly and remove any debris.

Wipe the surface down with a damp cloth and apply primer. The primer should be fast-drying oil-based or latex and only used on areas of bare wood.

Previously Varnished Wood

Start by washing the surface, rinse and dry then sand the surface lightly and remove any debris. Sand the surface to degloss then wipe with a damp cloth and apply primer. Use fast-drying oil-based or latex primer.

Unfinished Wallboard

Vacuum with soft brush furniture attachment and apply a flat latex primer.

Unfinished Wood

Be sure and sand the surface and wipe down with a damp cloth to remove any grime or dirt. You need to apply a primer that is fast, drying oil-based or a latex primer.

Unpainted Plaster

Sand the surface if necessary and dust with a vacuum using a soft brush. Apply polyvinyl acrylic primer.

PREVIEW THE PAINT COLOR

Preview the paint color on a computer at the store. To test a color to see if you will like it, test it on a natural gray card and allow it to fully dry for 24 hours. Glossy paints will brighten up a room and give the room a warm feeling. Study the colors in natural light as well as artificial light. Be careful, some store lighting is designed to tint colors to make them look better.

GRANDPA'S BASIC INTERIOR PAINTING TECHNIQUES

Slow strokes for a better job!

PAINTBRUSH

♦ Don't overload the brush! Only dip the brush to 1/3rd of the bristle length; then tap the bristles against the side of the can to remove the excess paint.

- Never dip the brush deep or you will overload the brush. Dragging the brush on the rim wears out the bristles.
- Cut in the edges using the narrow edge of the brush and press just hard enough to flex the bristles. Paint with long, slow strokes.
- Always paint from the dry area to the set area.
- Brush the wall corners using the wide edge of the brush.
- Paint all pen areas and be sure to cut in before the paint dries otherwise you will get lap marks.
- If you are going to paint large areas, apply the paint with 2-3 diagonal strokes. Hold the brush at a 45^0 angle and work the surface. Press only hard enough to flex the bristles. The paint should be distributed evenly with horizontal strokes.
- All the surfaces should be smoothed: by drawing the brush vertically from top to bottom of the painted area. Use light strokes and lift the brush away from the surface of each stroke. This method is best if you are using oil-based paints.

IS YOUR WALL BRISTLING

If you have ever had problems with the bristles coming out of the paintbrush and ending up on the wall, the problem is easy to solve. Just run a comb through the bristles on the paintbrush to get rid of all the stray hairs.

PAINT ROLLER

- Use a 5-gallon paint bucket with a paint screen, which will speed up painting of large areas. Load the paint roller right from the bucket and use a roller extension handle. Always keep the paint bucket on the floor and never on a ladder.
- Use a paint ray when painting small areas. Fill the paint tray reservoir then dip the roller fully into the reservoir. Lift the roller and roll it on the textured area of the tray, which will distribute the paint evenly on the roller nap. Make sure that the roller is not dripping when you lift it from the tray.
- Load the roller and make a sweep in the shape of a "W" that is about 4-inches long on the surface.

- On walls roll upward on the first stroke to avoid spilling paint. Best to use slow roller strokes, which will avoid splattering.
- For the second stroke, draw the roller straight down starting at the top of the first sweep. Move the roller to the beginning of the diagonal then roll it vertically and complete the uploading. If the roller begins to make noise, put more paint on it.
- Be sure and distribute the paint over the area using horizontal strokes. Smooth off the area by moving the roller in a vertical direction from top to bottom of the painted area. Then life the roller and return it to the top of the area after you make, each stroke.

PAINTING THE BOTTOM OF A DOOR
Use an old piece of carpet and place paint on it then work it back and forth under the door without removing the door.

A FLUFFER-UPPER
If you want to fluff up your paint roller, even it's soggy, just rinse it off and cut the handle off an inexpensive roller frame and be sure to leave enough stem to fit it into a drill. Attach the wet roller, chuck assembly into the drill and spin the roller inside of a big brown grocery bag until it's dry.

CEILINGS & WALLS
- Paint the wall and ceilings in small areas if you are looking for a smooth finish. After you roll a section, use a paintbrush and immediately cut in the edge before you continue on.
- If the rolled areas are left to dry before the edges are painted, visible marks will be left on the finished surface where you ended rolling out the paint.
- Always paint a ceiling first when painting a room.
- Plan the job so that you will always be facing the light. It will be easier to spot areas that you may have missed.
- If you are going to paint acoustical tiles, check with a professional where you purchase your paint before you start.
- Keep roller speed slow to avoid splattering.

- ♦ Mask off or remove drapes and any other window coverings.
- ♦ Pressurized power rollers and pads are great!
- ♦ Use a hand roller extension to make the job easier.

MY EXTERIOR IS PEELING

Surface was nor scraped and cleaned properly before painting. Sand, scrape, prime then repaint.

I'VE GOT A BLISTER

Moisture or solvent trapped under paint. Scrape, fill depression, sand, prime and repaint.

WRINKLE, WRINKLE, DRIP, DRIP

The paint was probably applied too thick and the surface will have to be sanded smooth and repainted.

FOUNDATION PEELING

You have alkali compounds on the foundation and will need to scrape, apply alkali neutralizer and repaint.

MY WOOD KNOTS ARE BLEEDING

Wood resin is seeping out. You will have to sand, apply stain killer and then repaint.

I DON'T LIKE ROLLER MARKS

They are probably from not using the proper roller cover or too a grade of paint. Quality rollers also make a big difference. Paint buildup on the ends of the roller may cause the problem. Make sure you spread the paint in a zigzag pattern, like an **"M"** or **"W."** Fill in the zigzag pattern with even, parallel strokes.

I'M GETTING KRINKLED

The paint is being applied too thickly and possibly the weather is too hot. You will need to remove the paint and sand the substrate if necessary. You may also be trying to use poor quality paint and are having trouble covering.

CRACKING & FLAKING IS NOT PRETTY

The splitting of dry paint is usually caused by poor quality paint, over-thinning the paint or poor surface preparation. Best to re-do the job after you scrape off and/or sand off the surface and do a better preparation job.

TOOTHPASTE & ASPRIN

If you want to quick fix a small hole in a white wall, just mix white toothpaste with a small amount of water or crush up a moistened crushed aspirin.

VINEGAR TO THE RESCUE
When you're paint, brushes harden, try softening them by soaking them in full strength white vinegar them cleaning with a comb.

LITTLE BOTTLE DOES THE TRICK
Empty nail polish bottles make excellent holders for touch-up paints.

BEAT THAT PAINT
Keep a small kitchen electric beater for use in your shop to mix paint with. Be sure and always mix it very slow or you will develop air bubbles.

TOPY TURVY
To reduce the amount of evaporation and seal the paint can better, try turning the can upside down with the lid secured for a few seconds then turn it right side up again. This will coat the inside of the top surface with a thin film and help to seal the lid better or just store the paint can upside down and it won't form a skin.

MIXING FLOUR AND PAINT...YUK
If you are painting old woodwork that has small holes that need patching, try filling the holes with flour and some of the paint, it will harden and will not be noticeable.

GETTING PICKY
Try using an ice pick to punch holes in the sides of the paint can so that any paint that does drip down the sides will go back in the can.

UP, UP, AND AWAY
Try placing a blown-up balloon, the size of the space in the can. It will reduce the air in the can and keep the paint fresher longer.

LOSE THE PORES
Using a hand moisturizer or creamy hand lotion when painting or doing other dirty chores will prevent dirt and paint from seeping into you're skin's pores, making personal cleanup easier. Thin rubber gloves work great and are disposable.

NO DRIPS
Next time you paint from paint can, be sure and have a wide rubber band available to place around the can lengthwise and use it to wipe your brush on. This will keep the drippings in the can and not dribbling down the outside of the can.

SMILE!
A method of cleaning dentures that works as well as the expensive spreads is to just soak them overnight in white vinegar.

A CLEAN RIM IS A HEALTHY RIM
If you place masking tape on the rim of your paint can before pouring the paint out, you can remove the tape later and the rim will be clean.

EYE PROTECTION
When painting ceilings, try wearing, a pair of old plastic goggles.

SUPER IDEA FROM PROFESSIONAL PAINTER
If you have lumps in your paint can, try cutting a piece of screen the size of the can and allowing it to settle to the bottom, it will carry the lumps to the bottom.

GRANDPA SAYS: GET IT RIGHT THE FIRST TIME!

Water, latex-based paints
The area to be painted must be pre-primed or painted over the previously painted water-based paint. This paint will clean up easily with soap and water and has store a partially used can of paint.

Latex, oil-based paints
Area should be primed before painting or painted over previously painted oil-based paint. Must use mineral spirits to clean up. Has longer drying time and odor.

Acrylics
Used mainly as a base or primer. If water-based latex won't adhere, use acrylic first. Problem surfaces that require primers are drywall and lathe and plaster walls.

Primers
Use primers on all non-porous materials.

OIL OR LATEX
Oil-based paints are usually preferred especially for a child' room since they will last longer and be easier to clean up. They are more expensive but well worth the extra money.

GRANDPA'S METHOD OF PAINTING OLD DRYWALL
If you want a smooth finish on old drywall, ceilings or walls it would be best to follow grandpa's method.

❖ First scrape off any of the old texture or loose paint using a 6-inch putty knife.

- ❖ Never try and remove old nails that show through: best to drive a new nail beside it, which will secure the existing nail in place. You can dimple the drywall with a hammer if necessary.
- ❖ Use a 6-inch drywall knife and fill the holes and dimples with drywall compound. Tape and repair all cracks and any open joints then allow the compound to fully dry.
- ❖ Apply a thin coat of drywall compound across the entire ceiling or wall surface using a 12-inch drywall knife then allow the area to dry fully.
- ❖ Lightly sand off the surface using 100-grit sandpaper then touch us any areas with drywall compound as needed. Allow the area to dry!
- ❖ Sand the surface with 120-grit sandpaper then using a roller with a ¾-inch nap, apply a quality latex paint and allow it to dry.
- ❖ Lightly sand the entire surface and touch up any bad areas that may still appear then cover them with drywall compound and allow it to dry.
- ❖ Complete the job by covering the surface with one or two coats of paint.

GOOD COLOR, BAD COLOR

Rooms should be painted with light or brighter colors. The darker the color the more the negative impact will be on the inhabitants. Dark colors may bring on negative emotions while bright or light colors have a positive effect. Children's rooms should always have bright colors; such as yellow, which is especially popular making the room appear sunny.

STABILIZING COLOR

If you add 7-10 drops of black paint to each quart of white paint, the paint will not yellow.

A CHILLY ROLLER SOLUTION

If you are going to use your roller and did not finish the job, just wrap the whole roller with the paint on it in a plastic bag sealed up well and place it into the refrigerator until the next day.

A LITTLE DAB WILL DO YA

Enamel or oil paint can easily be removed from your hands with paste floor wax then washing with soap and water.

BE A BLOW HARD

If you take a real deep breath and blow the air out into an open paint can just before you seal it really fast, the carbon dioxide from your breathe will prevent the paint from forming a skin and oxidizing.

A REAL GOOD TOPPER

To prevent a skin forming on top of the paint, try placing a piece of waxed paper the size of the opening on top of the paint.

HOW SOFT I AM

After you clean out a paintbrush, rub a few drops of vegetable oil into the bristles to keep them soft.

LAZY WAY OUT

If you don't feel like cleaning a roller: place it in a plastic bag and place in the freezer. This will keep it moist and usable for a few days.

CAN STILL GET TO THE KIDS

If you need to paint steps, try painting every other step, when those are dry go back and paint the rest. This will allow you continued access to the upstairs.

GREAT IDEA

When painting anything, make sure you dip a 3 X 5, index card into the paint to make it easier to match it at a later date if needed.

SMART PAINTING

If you are going to paint cabinet doors, try rubbing a small amount of Vaseline on the hinges, it will make removing the paint easier.

THE RIGHT ORDER

Paint windows and trim using a 1¾-inch tapered brush and do the crossbars first then the frames and end up with the sills.

SIZE MATTERS
If you are painting walls use a 3"-5" wide brush.

A REAL WINNER
If you are sure you will use up all the paint in a can, try punching a few holes near the rim you are removing the paint from. The paint that is wiped off the brush will go back into the can.

CEILING STAINS BEGONE
Water stains on a ceiling can be unsightly and can be eliminated most of the time by just blotting the area with a small amount of chlorine bleach. Older spots need a little more attention.

TENNIS ANYONE?
If you are going to paint a ceiling, try cutting a tennis ball in half and placing half on the brush to catch the drips.

CHOOSING THE RIGHT PAINT BRUSH

Paint brush bristles, are set in a base of solid resin to hold them together and will be either natural bristles (best is hog) or a synthetic fiber. The hest brushes have bristles that taper from a thick base to a narrow tip. The narrow tip gives the brush flexibility and is a sign of a quality brush.

The best brushes have longer bristles so that they will hold more paint.

Unfinished wood handles are best and will not slip out of your hand. If you are going to paint with an oil-based paint try and find a good hog-hair brush. Natural-bristle brushes should not be used for water-based (latex) paints since the bristles will absorb water and swell up. Use nylon or polyester bristle brushes with water-based paints.

ROLLER INFO
For semi-gloss and glossy finishes use a roller with less than a ¾ inch nap. When applying flat paints on a medium-smooth surface use a roller that is 3/8" to 1" thick.

PAINTING A POPCORN CEILING
If you have more than one room to do, it is best to rent an airless sprayer and get it over with. If you only have one room use a roller with a 1 ¾" nap and thin the paint with a pint of the appropriate thinner. The first coat does not have to cover, however, it will strengthen the popcorn material so that it will be easier to place the second coat on.

PREPARATION TIPS BEFORE PAINTING

- ❖ Be sure and thoroughly clean the surface.
- ❖ Repair any damage to the wall, such as nail holes or cracks with spackling then sand off and allow to fully dry.
- ❖ Always follow manufacturers instructions on the can.
- ❖ Mask off areas that may be a problem with masking tape.

GOOD ADVICE FROM A PRO
Remove one of the outlet plates in the room you are painting and place the paint type and number on a piece of masking tape on the back of the outlet cover. It would also be a good idea if you mentioned the amount of paint it took to do the room.

GOOD USE FOR OLD SOCKS

Save those old socks and place them over your shoes when you are painting to protect them.

TAKING CARE OF YOUR BRUSHES

- ❖ Clean the brush as soon as you finish the job.
- ❖ Always remove any loose bristles by tapping against a hard surface.
- ❖ Remove all excess paint.
- ❖ Wrap bristles in paper to store so that dust will not settle on them.
- ❖ Don't use paintbrushes for any other liquid chemical that it was not specifically made for.
- ❖ Always allow the brushes to dry fully between uses. Never use a wet brush.

BABY WIPE CONTAINER FOR BRUSHES

To keep the brushes in good shape between coats of finish, just store the brush in a pull-out baby wipe container that is full of the recommended solvent. The slit in the top will grip the handle and allow the bristles to hang suspended without them hitting the bottom and bending.

SOFTEN, HARD PAINT BRUSHES

The following ingredients will be needed:

¾	Gallon of cool tap water
1	Cup of baking soda (fresh)
¾	Cup of white vinegar

Place the ingredients into a medium pot and mix well, then place the brushes in and boil them until they become soft.

BRUSH WILL LAST LONGER

If you soak a new oil paintbrush in a solution of linseed oil for about 24 hours before you use it, the brush will last longer and be much easier to clean up. If you prefer you could just soak the brush in a small container of water with a capful of fabric softener in it.

TOOL & PAINT BRUSH CLEANER-UPPER

The following ingredients will be needed:

1 ¾	Cup of baking soda (fresh)
¾	Cup of white vinegar
3	Tablespoons of rubbing alcohol
1	Gallon of cool tap water

Place all the ingredients into a bucket and mix well. Works great on tools and paintbrushes. Store away from children.

COUGH, COUGH, HACK, HACK

When paint cans says; "adequate ventilation" it means just that. The number of people that end up in emergency rooms every year from breathing in paint fumes is probably in the hundreds. Vapor buildup indoors is a real problem if you can't get enough air moving in the room to keep the fumes down. Be sure and wear a "dual-cartridge" mask if you feel that there is not adequate ventilation.

PAINTING (EXTERIOR)

Exterior paints are usually more expensive than interior paints since they contain more resins and ingredients to make them last for a longer period of time. Most also contain more pigments giving them a more deeper and richer color. The exterior paints can be purchased in two varieties similar to interior paints: water-based or oil-based paints.

GRANDPA COMPARES EXTERIOR PAINTS & PRIMERS

Acrylic latex

The best quality latex paints will contain 100% acrylic resins since vinyl are not as durable. The latex will dry faster and is capable of covering almost any building material, which even includes masonry and primed metals.

Alkyd paint

The most common type of solvent-thinned paint! It contains almost all of the properties of oil-based paints, however, it will dry more rapidly and have excellent hiding ability. It has a thick consistency, which makes it somewhat difficult to apply, however, it will level smoother than latex.

Marine

Produced especially for boats, provides a durable finish on both wood and metal trim. It is very expensive and not appropriate for large areas. Its gooey consistency makes it somewhat difficult to work with.

Masonry

This type of paint includes latex, Portland cement, alkyd and rubber with some actually serving as their own primers. You need to seal masonry with a clear primer. Easy to apply paint!

Metal

The solvent or water-thinned types include priming ingredients that are rust-resisting helping to cover small bare spots. Be sure and prime all bare metal using rusty-metal primer to seal the rusty spots. You can use a brush, spray or roller to produce a broad range of finishes.

Oil

Oil paint takes about 12-48 hours to dry and has a strong odor as well as making cleanup somewhat difficult. It has excellent durability but the drying time sometimes causes problems with bugs and dust sticking to it as well as rain.

Porch & Deck

The most durable are alkyd and polyurethane types since they produce a hard, washable surface. However, some of the types are formulated for concrete surfaces and preparation methods will vary. The colors are also limited.

It is relatively easy to apply since you just pour it out on the floor and work it outward using a long-handled roller.

Primers

New wood or metal should be primed according to the paint manufacturers instructions to kill any stains or if you are going to apply latex paint over any existing solvent-based paint. The most effective is alcohol-based primer, however, solvent and latex types will work as well. Remember porous surfaces will soak up a lot of primer.

Stains

Both solvent and latex paints will provide transparent, semi-transparent or opaque finishes when used on natural wood siding and trim. Some of the stains may include a preservative and even offer a weathered look. They can be applied almost anyway that you are comfortable with such as spraying, rolling or using a brush.

Vinyl latex

This paint is easy to cleanup, has good durability and is fast drying. You can apply it over a damp surface and it is naturally mildew-proof but cannot be painted over a previous solvent-painted surface. Don't thin out latex and try and apply with one stroke using a brush or roller. Working it out too fast may cause thin spots.

MY HOUSE HAS SCALES

If the paint is cracking and it looks like the scales on the back of an alligator, it was probably caused by the application of a very hard coating, such as an alkyd enamel placed over a more flexible coating, such as latex primer. Remove the old paint and scrape the surface well then power wash the surface and sand it before painting again.

ROUGH SURFACE IS NOT GOOD

If the surface to be painted is rough and crinkly, the paint has formed a skin, which is caused by the paint being applied too thick or the paint was applied in too hot weather or cool, damp weather. It can also be caused, by painting over a contaminated surface. Scrape and sand the substrate to remove the wrinkled coating.

GRANDPA'S BASIC EXTERIOR PAINTING PREPARATION TIPS

SURFACE PREPARATION

♦ Be sure and tie, back any bushes and limbs that may get in the way. Cover all plants and work area with plastic sheets or tarps. Make sure you turn off the air conditioner and any exhaust fans in the paint areas. Best to cover and seal the air conditioner unit and tape it down.

♦ All shutters should be removed as well as the hardware. Close all storm windows if they are still on or remove them. Make any repairs to the siding and trim that is necessary and be sure to fill any rotted or insect damaged areas with wood filler.

♦ This is the best time to re-glaze the windows in any area that needs it. Carefully remove any old putty with a putty knife or small chisel being careful not to break the window.

♦ Starting at the top of the wall, scrape any loose paint or debris from the siding and trim.

♦ Use a power sander to remove any paint particles and to smooth out any wood-filled areas. Be careful not to damage the siding since the sander cuts through pint very quickly. Make sure that the sander you use is not too powerful or it will leave swirl marks. Speed should be around 10,000 rpm.

♦ Use a brush or stiff broom to wash the siding and all the trim with a solution of TSP (trisodium phosphate) or even better a phosphate-free cleaner. If you have a pressure washer use it or rent one for a really clean job.

♦ Be sure and rinse the entire house with a garden hose until the water runs clear. If you used TSP then rinse the house twice to be sure that all the solution has been cleaned off.

♦ Allow the siding to dry thoroughly for about 2 days before painting.

PAINTING EXTERIOR WALLS

♦ Be sure and wait until the surface is completely dry and that there is no rain in the forecast.

♦ Always apply primer to any bare siding and make sure you allow the primer to dry thoroughly.

♦ You can use a brush, roller or sprayer, whichever you prefer.

- If there are any masonry surfaces, they must be primed for the best results, especially if water stains are present or if glossy paint is to be top coated.

- Remember, cedar and redwood contain resins that will bleed through water-based paints. Be sure and use oil-based paint and primers on wood.

- Always paint the roof trim and soffits before the walls if they are going to be painted a different color. This will prevent any trim paint from dripping on the freshly painted walls.

- Use a corner roller or trim brush to paint the inside corners and around the trim.

- If you have clapboard or shingle siding, be sure and cut in the lip (bottom edge) of the siding before you paint the face.

- Whether you use a brush or a roller, always start at the top of the wall. Work as far as you can reach to your left and pull the roller or brush toward you. Finish the stroke right in front of you and repeat until the block of siding you can reach is painted then use the same method on the right side.

- If using a brush, start each stroke to the right by feathering the brush. Feathering means placing the surface of the brush against the siding gradually, instead of abruptly. This will eliminate a definite start line and will make it easier to blend the next block of strokes into the present block.

- Next blend the two strokes together in front of you and work quickly. It is critical to blend the new stroke into the completed stroke while the paint is still wet to avoid overlap marks. Never stop painting in the middle of a section. Paint into the corner of the house so that the paint color is consistent.

MY SKIN IS GETTING WRINKLED?

Oil-based paints are hard to remove from your skin! Most people tend to use kerosene, mineral spirits or paint thinner to remove the paint, however, these products are hazardous to the skin, cause irritation and can be absorbed into the body. Grandpa recommends using vegetable oil to remove oil-based paints safely without damaging the skin.

MY WAX IS BLEEDING

Wax bleed areas look similar to mildew areas but wax bleed area will bead water and mildew areas will not. These areas come from waxy substances in the reconstituted wood products used to make hardboard siding. They can be cause by failing to apply a proper primer to hardboard before applying the topcoat.

HOW BROWN I AM..............

Brown discolorations on the paint surface is usually due to the migration of tannins from the substrate through the paint film and usually comes from poor priming or not sealing the surface properly.

NOT HOLDING A GLOSSY LOOK

The loss of luster in a topcoat can be caused by direct sunlight, which degrades the binder and the pigment of paint. This causes the paint to "chalk" and lose its gloss.

It is often caused by, using an interior paint outdoors or a paint of lower quality. Poor surface preparation can also cause this problem.

I'M TOO IMMATURE TO BE PAINTED

Masonry must be cured for a full year before being painted if you use vinyl acrylic latex paint. The lime in the masonry must have a chance to react with carbon dioxide from the air or it will attack the paint. At least allow the masonry to cure for 30-60 days before painting. If this is not possible then apply a high quality latex sever weather primer followed by a premium latex house paint.

GRANDPA'S PAINT-SPRAYING TIPS

Paint-sprayer is usually best for a large surface area. The following are tips when using a sprayer to get a smoother, better appearing job.

❖ Make sure you always strain the paint before you place the paint in an airless paint sprayer. Occasionally, even new paint may contain material that will clog the sprayer filter.

- ❖ Be sure and keep the sprayer in motion to avoid a buildup. You should always start the gun moving before pressing the trigger and be sure and release the trigger before stopping the gun at the end of a stroke.
- ❖ If you are using an oil-based paint, be sure and clean out the sprayer with Martini Paint Solvent. Wipe out the canister first with a rag and then wash it good with solvent.
- ❖ Use lacquer thinner to clean the tip after using a water-based paint.
- ❖ Remember tips only last for 35-40 gallons and should be replaced after that.

I'M PEELING

This is caused by poor adhesion, seeping moisture through un-caulked joints, worn-out caulk or leaks in the roof or walls. You need to identify where the moisture is coming from and correct the problem before re-painting.

REDDISH-BROWN STAINS THROUGH THE NAIL HEADS

Non-galvanized nails were used and they are rusting or if you used galvanized nails, they have been subjected to sanding or excessive weathering. If you use non-galvanized, they must be countersunk. Try filling the hole with a high quality, water-based all- acrylic or siliconized acrylic caulk.

NOW I'M FLAKING OFF

This usually appears as hairline cracks, then flakes or chips away. It is often caused by, using a poor quality paint that has poor adhesion and flexibility. Also caused by over-thinning and spreading the paint too thin. This usually means cleaning off the old paint and re-painting the whole area.

I'M BLISTERING

This results from localized loss of adhesion and lifting of the paint away from the underlying surface. It can be caused by, applying oil-based or alkyd paint over a damp surface. It can also be caused by moisture seeping into the home through the exterior walls. Scrape or sand the area and prime it with a quality latex or oil primer then re-paint.

I'M FADING AWAY; HELP ME!

This can be caused by excessive lightening of the paint or paint on a southern exposure to the sun. Usually caused by using poor quality paint or interior paint outside. If the paint is going to be exposed to a southern exposure, be sure and purchase a paint that has a UV protectant in it.

CHEAPSKATE!

The paint easily accumulates dirt and dust particles, which is usually caused by using poor quality paint as well as air pollution. Clean off the dirt with a scrub brush and mild detergent solution.

BEWARE OF BAD SURFACES

Most paint failures; are caused by painting on hot, moist surfaces. Keep an eye on the sun and paint the shady side first then as the sun moves away from each side, go ahead and paint it. Painting in the sun will almost always cause a problem.

MOISTURE VS OIL-BASED PAINTS

Moisture will affect an oil-based paint so be sure and wait until all the dew is gone before painting an area. The moisture from latex paints; will not be affected by the dew. If it rains, it would be best to wait at least 24 hours before using oil-based paints for the best results.

NAIL HEADS & LATEX PAINT

All exposed nail heads need to be touched up with a primer or they may rust and cause stains. This is more important when painting with a latex paint.

ALL MIXED UP??????

Even though the paint is thoroughly mixed by machine when you purchase it, it would be best if you check it again before starting to use it. Best to pour half into another can then mix both halves with a wooden stirrer until all the pigment is well blended. Double-check it by pouring it back and forth a few times.

PROTECT ME!
Your plants and shrubs need to be well protected from the paint. Be sure and cover them with a lightweight drop cloth.

NO SMELL PAINT
If you add 1 capful of vanilla extract to the paint can, it will reduce the odor considerably. The vanilla will not affect the consistency or color and will only affect the odor.

GRANDPA KNOWS HOW TO ESTIMATE EXTERIOR PAINT NEEDS

- ❖ First, determine the average height of the house. If the house has a flat roof, measure the distance from the foundation to the eaves. If the roof is pitched, add two feet.
- ❖ Next measure the distance around the house (around the foundation).
- ❖ Then multiply the average height by the distance around the foundation, which will equal the surface area.
- ❖ Divide the surface area by 500 (the average American gallon of paint covers 500 square feet). Your results will equal the number of gallons required for one coat on the house.
- ❖ For the trim, the average six to eight room house will require 1 gallon of paint.

HANG 'EM HIGH
After cleaning your brushes thoroughly and rinsing them well, be sure and hang them up to dry allowing all the excess water to fall out and the brush air dry.

GRANDPA'S SECRET
Since you may have to go back and do some touch-up or re-paint an area, it is best to save your brush. You can just save the brush without extensive clean-up if you are going to use the same paint by just wrapping the brush in plastic wrap and placing the brush in the refrigerator.

466

CHAPTER 26

GRANDPA'S FISHING SECRETS

GRANDPA'S FISHING BAITS THAT FISH WILL DIE FOR

Grandpa is an avid fisherman and found a number of formulas that when placed on his bait would attract fish. These secret formulas will solve anyone's problem of catching more fish than you will know what to do with. These formulas are secret; so don't tell anyone else!

The following formulas will be effective when you place a small amount of your bait or lure. The ingredients need to be purchased in a health food store, herbal shop or pharmacy. Some fishing supply houses in major cities may also carry most of the ingredients. **The ingredients should be kept away from children.**

SUPER OIL-BASED FORMULA #1
The following ingredients will be needed:

5	**Parts of oil of rhodium**
2	**Parts oil of cumin**
1	**Part tincture of musk**

Mix all the ingredients together in a small plastic, bowl then pour into a sealed bottle.

SUPER OIL-BASED FORMULA #2
The following ingredients will be needed:

2	Ounces of oil of rhodium
¾	Ounce of tincture of musk
1	Ounce of oil of cumin
¾	Ounce juice of loveage root
	Breadcrumbs
	Cotton balls

Place all the liquid ingredients in a small bowl and mix well. Shred the cotton balls and mix the pieces with the breadcrumbs and pour the oil over the mixture (mix by hand) producing a paste. Try using small pieces of the cotton tied on to your hook as bait. Fish will fight to get to your hook.

SUPER OIL-BASED FORMULA #3
The following ingredients will be needed:

1	Pound ground aniseed
1/3	Pound ground allspice
1/8	Ounce of oil of cloves

Place the aniseed and allspice in a medium bowl and mix them together. Sprinkle the oil of cloves over the mixture and mix thoroughly. Allow the mixture to ripen in a sealed jar for 3 days before being used. Only 1 drop is needed on bait to do the trick.

SUPER OIL-BASED FORMULA #4
The following ingredients will be needed:

1	Ounce gum benzoin
12	Ounces of virgin olive oil
30	Drops of oil of rhodium
3	Drops of patchouli
1 ¾	Ounces of lard oil

Place the gum benzoin and olive oil in a double boiler and heat on low for 2 hours. Remove from heat and allow it to stand for 1 week. Strain the mixture through a piece of cheesecloth then add the rhodium and patchouli with a small medicine dropper. Mix the solution then add the lard oil and mix thoroughly. Only a drop or two is needed, preferably on a meat bait or worm.

SUPER OIL-BASED FORMULA #5
The following ingredients will be needed:

¾	Ounce of oil of rhodium
1/8	Ounce of oil of spearmint
¾	Ounce oil of anise
1	Ounce of glycerin

Place all the ingredients in a small bowl and mix thoroughly. Store in a well-sealed jar. It only takes 1-2 drops on your bait to work.

SUPER OIL-BASED FORMULA #6
The following ingredients will be needed:

¾	Cup of cod liver oil
5	Drops of red oil-soluble food coloring

Place the ingredients into a small bowl and mix thoroughly. Store in a small sealed jar. The bait should be dipped into the mixture for the best results.

SUPER OIL-BASED FORMULA #7
The following ingredients will be needed:

1	Pint jar with lid
3-6	Ounces of dead worms (most any will do)
20	Drops of oil of rhodium

Place the worms in a jar with a loosely covered top (to allow air to enter) and place the jar far away from your house. A barn or garage will do fine. The worms will liquefy in about 10 days. Pour ¾ ounce of the liquid off (no need to measure too close) and add the rhodium to the liquid and mix. One drop of this is enough to drive fish wild.

SUPER OIL-BASED FORMULA #8
The following ingredients will be needed:

2	Ounces of cod liver oil
20	Drops of anise

Place the ingredients in a small bowl and mix well. Store in a small well-sealed jar. Dip the bait into the jar for one of the best trout formulas ever.

SUPER OIL-BASED FORMULA #9
The following ingredients will be needed:

| ¾ | Ounce of oil of rhodium |
| ¾ | Pint of virgin olive oil |

Place the ingredients in a small bowl and mix well. It will only take a drop or two on your bait to make the fish bite.

GRANDPA'S INSECT REPELLENT
The following ingredients will be needed:

3	Tablespoons of jewelweed (from health food store)
1	Quart apple cider vinegar
1	Teaspoon of eucalyptus oil
1	Teaspoon of pennyroyal oil
1	Teaspoon of orange oil or lemon oil
1	Teaspoon of citronella oil
1	Spray bottle

Place the jewelweed in a jar and crush up as best you can, then pour the vinegar over it. Allow it to steep for 3 days then strain the mixture through a piece of cheesecloth and add the oils. Mix the repellent well and try a small dab on your arm to be sure that you are not allergic to it. Spray the repellent on clothing or any exposed areas of the body that you prefer not to be bitten.

GRANDMA'S INSECT REPELLENT
The following ingredients will be needed:

| 5 | Teaspoons of lavender flower water |
| 1 | Drop of essential sandalwood oil |

3   **Drops of citronella oil**
3   **Drops of essential eucalyptus citiadora oil**

Place the lavender flower water in a small spray bottle, then add the essential oils and shake well to mix. Shake before using. Store in a cool, dry location and it should last for about 6 months.

CHAPTER 27

GRANDPA'S TIPS FOR EMERGENCIES

PORTABLE ELECTRIC GENERATORS

MY HOUSE JUST FIZZELED OUT!

To avoid a serious problem, never connect a portable electric generator directly to the house wiring. This can be a deadly mistake to you as well as the neighborhood. The problem is called "backfeeding" and the pole transformer can then "set up" or increase the backfeed to many thousands of volts and can even kill a utility lineman who is making repairs a long distance from your home. This can cause extensive damage to your home as well as the utility equipment in your entire area.

Grandpa's suggestion if you need to connect it to your home is to have a licensed electrician come to your home and install a transfer switch, which will transfer power from the utility pole to your generator power.

HELP! I'M GETTING LOADED

Never operate too many appliances that exceed the output rating of the generator. Overloading it will cause serious damage to appliances and electronics. Only use a portable generator when they are really needed and only to power essential equipment or appliances.

```
LIGHTNING STRIKE
If lightning ever strikes your home, evacuate the house
immediately even though everything looks fine. There can be
electrical problems developing in the walls that will turn into a fire.
Call the fire department immediately! Also, be sure and have your
electrician check out the electrical box before you use any
electricity.
```

THERE'S A FUNNY SMELL IN HERE OR IS THERE?

Portable generators use an internal combustion engine just like your car. The engine emits deadly Carbon monoxide gas and should never be placed in the house or in a closed garage. It should only be operated outdoors or in a well-ventilated area. Be sure that the exhaust is away from any vents that enter the home. Always place it under a tent or other type of canopy.

PLUG IT IN, PLUG IT IN

Be sure and plug any appliances into the generator using heavy-duty extension cords that are out door rated. Overloaded cords may place you at risk of fire or damage the appliance. Never run the cords under a rug.

GROUNDED AGAIN!

Be sure and check the manufacturers instruction booklet for the proper grounding information.

KA-BOOM

Never store fuel indoors and be sure they are in safety containers and ventilated. Remember, the vapors can travel along the ground and even be ignited by a pilot light from a hot water heater in the garage. They can even be ignited by the electric arc created by just turning on a light switch. Never try to refuel an electric generator while it is still running.

GET OUT THE ALOE

Keep kids away from the generator while it is running since many of the parts are hot enough to give them a serious burn.

ROOF RETROFITTING

GABLED ROOFS

During a hurricane, the end walls take a very bad beating and if not properly braced it can collapse. It is recommended that you install 2X4's the length of the roof, overlapping the ends of the 2X4's across two trusses. The gable end trusses are attached to the top of the gable end walls. The bottom of the truss needs to be securely nailed to the top of the wall and then braced to adjacent trusses. This will stop the wind from pushing or pulling the gable end at the critical points.

To secure the gable end wall, just fasten 8-foot long braces to the bottom chord of the gable truss and the adjacent trusses with 16d nails.

Be sure that the braces are perpendicular to the truss and spaced at a maximum of 4-feet on center. Also, be sure and tie back the gable truss with at least one 8-foot long brace along the ridge of the roof to several of the interior trusses.

SHINGLES

Normally, shingles are not designed to withstand hurricane force winds. To make the shingles more secure you will need to cement the shingle tabs to the underlying shingles. Place two spots of quick, setting asphalt cement about the size of a quarter under each tab with a putty knife or use a caulking gun. Press the tab onto the adhesive and be sure and cement all the tabs throughout the roof. Be careful not to bend them any farther than necessary when you apply the adhesive.

HURRICANE STRAPS

For added protection install metal hurricane straps to provide a measure of strength and safety for the roof to wall connection. The practice of toenailing the trusses or rafters is often is not sufficient to hold the roof in place in high winds.

SHUTTERS

Impact-resistant shutters should be placed over all windows and doors to protect them from wind-borne objects but they can also reduce damage from sudden pressure changes if a window or door is broken.

SECURING ENTRY DOORS

Be sure and install head and foot bolts on the inactive door if you have double-entry doors. The doors should have three hinges and a dead bolt security lock, which has a minimum one-inch bolt throw length.

The bolts should extend into the door header and through the threshold into the subfloor.

SECURITY

GRANDPA & GRANDMA'S SECURITY TIPS

❖ Never leave house keys in common locations such as under the doormat or under a rock near the front door. Put a key in a small container and bury it under a plant.

❖ When you leave home place the phone ringer on low tone so it can't be heard from the outside.

❖ Use automatic timers to turn TV's, lights and radios on at different times.

❖ Don't cancel your newspaper or mail delivery, have someone pick it up.

❖ Be sure that your door hinges are not on the outside.

❖ Place safety bars on all glass sliding doors.

❖ Cover your garage windows so that a thief cannot see if the cars are gone.

❖ Be sure that you have a secure deadbolt on all entry doors.

❖ Notify your alarm company that you will be gone for an extended period and provide an emergency number.

GRANDPA & GRANDMA'S FAMILY DISASTER PLAN

❖ Be sure and list any type of hazard that might affect the family in case of storm surge, mudslide, earthquake, flooding or wind.

❖ Locate a safe room in your home or the location of a community shelter.

❖ Determine escape routes from your home to a safe location as well as an alternate route.

❖ Be sure and have an out-of-state contact for all family members. Use just one contact.

❖ Make a plan for your pet if you have to evacuate.

❖ Make sure that all children know how to dial 911 and have

emergency numbers near the telephone.

- ❖ Check your insurance coverage and remember flood insurance is a separate policy.
- ❖ Stock non-perishable emergency supplies in your disaster supply kit and have it handy so that it can be moved easily.
- ❖ Be sure that you have a NOAA weather radio and replace the batteries every 6 months.
- ❖ Make sure you have a good first aid kit and have taken a CPR and first aid class.

GRANDPA & GRANDMA'S DISASTER KIT

- ❖ Water – at least 1 gallon per person for 3-6 days.
- ❖ Food – enough for 3-6 days. Non-perishable packaged or canned foods and a non-electric can opener. Snack foods, paper plates, utensils and cooking fuel and tools if applicable.
- ❖ Blankets & pillows.
- ❖ Candles

SAVE THOSE BIRTHDAY CANDLES

One birthday candle will supply enough light to allow you to see in a room. To keep it burning longer and improve the light, just place the candle into a jar of petroleum jelly so that only the tip is sticking out.

- ❖ Clothing, seasonal rain gear, sturdy shoes.
- ❖ First aid kit, prescription drugs, general medicine.
- ❖ Special items – for any elderly or infant needs.
- ❖ Toiletries, hygiene items, moisture wipes.
- ❖ Flashlight & batteries.
- ❖ Radio, battery operated with TV if possible and extra batteries.
- ❖ Cash in small bills.
- ❖ Keys to house and car.
- ❖ Toys, book and games.

- ❖ Important documents in a waterproof container. Checkbooks, social security card, birth certificates, etc.
- ❖ Tools – Keep a small set in your kit.
- ❖ Vehicle fuel tank filled.
- ❖ Pet care items and records. Carrier or cage & current picture. If you have to take your pet to a shelter, you will need to have a current shot record.
- ❖ Medications.

GRANDPA & GRANDMA'S LOCATION, LOCATION, LOCATION

- ❖ If ordered to evacuate, <u>never</u> hesitate or delay your departure and if possible leave before the order is given. Even a slight delay may result in much longer travel times, as congestion will worsen.
- ❖ Best to select a destination that is as close as possible to your home, preferably in the same county or minimize the distance you need to travel to reach the shelter. <u>Remember</u> hotels and motels will fill up fast.
- ❖ If you have to evacuate to another county or far distance, be prepared with extra gas and supplies for a long ride with the possibility of no available gas station.
- ❖ If you can stay with a friend or relative near your home it would be best if their location were safe.
- ❖ If going to a hotel or motel, make reservations as soon as possible.
- ❖ Use a shelter as the <u>last resort</u>, <u>not</u> your first choice.

GRANDPA'S TIPS TO STOP KITCHEN FIRES

- ❖ **Fire in a Pan** – Don't move the pan, turn off the burner and the fan in the range hood. Place an oven mitt on your hand or use a hot pad and slide a lid that is larger than the pan over the top to suffocate the fire.

❖ Be sure and slide it on, don't place it over the top. You can also pour baking soda on top of the fire to put it out.

❖ **Fire on Stove Top** – If the fire has spread to the stovetop, turn off the burner and fan in the hood and pour a generous amount of baking soda on the fire until it is out. A fire extinguisher is the first choice.

❖ **Fire in the Oven** – Turn off the oven and close the door. This will sometimes put out the fire, if not have a fire extinguisher handy and use it.

❖ **Fire in Electrical Outlet** – Put out the fire with a fire extinguisher then turn off the main power to the house and call fire department.

❖ **Fire in a Wall Switch** – Stand clear of the switch and turn it off with a long handled wooden spoon or broom handle. Shut off all power to the house and call an electrician before you restore power.

DIFFERENT TYPES OF FIRE EXTINGUISHERS

TYPE A ORDINARY COMBUSTIBLES
Used to fight fires in wood, paper, rubber and most plastics. Can be used near fireplaces, most living areas and bedrooms.

TYPE B   FLAMMABLE LIQUIDS
Contains dry chemicals that will smother a fire fueled by substances such as oil, grease, solvents, gasoline or kerosene. Can be used in the kitchen, workshop areas or garage.

TYPE C   ELECTRICAL EQUIPMENT
Contains dry chemicals that will smother electrical fires. Can be used in workshops and electrical panels.

GRANDPA'S WATER STORAGE FOR EMERGENCIES

Remember, in case of emergency, you can live without food for a period of time, but you cannot live without water.

❖ There are two types of water: commercial and tap. Bottled water is safer to store for drinking purposes and emergency storage, however, the bulk of your water supply will probably be tap water due to the cost.

❖ One gallon of water a day is considered the minimum supply for drinking and 1 gallon pre person per day for cooking, washing, etc. Two people will require about 56 gallons of water to survive for two weeks. Forget the daily showers.

❖ Choose your water containers carefully and pick ones that will not leach chemicals into the water. Glass is excellent and plastic is fine as long as both are thoroughly cleaned before being used. Camping jugs and empty soda bottles are fine. A 2-liter soda bottle holds about 2-quarts of water.

❖ If you are unsure of the quality of the water or need to use suspect water in an emergency, place 10 drops of liquid chlorine bleach into 1-gallon of water. Adjust the number of drops for smaller containers. Boiling the water is always preferred if you have the heat available.

❖ Emergency water sources may be from a waterbed, pond, pool or hot tub, but should always be purified before drinking. These sources may best be used for toilet flushing. The water in your hot-water heater or toilet tank (not the toilet) may be used for drinking after purification. If you suspect a water shortage, clean the bathtub until it is spotless and fill it with cold water.

❖ Stored water should be rotated at least every six months. The containers should be emptied and cleaned thoroughly before you refill them.

WHERE OH WHERE HAS THE WATER GONE?

❖ To produce food for one year.................................... 1 million gallons
❖ To grow one large potato....................................... 18 gallons
❖ To produce one pat of margarine............................ 85 gallons
❖ To produce one loaf of bread.................................56 gallons
❖ To manufacture one pint of whiskey....................... 110 gallons
❖ To produce one pound of flour................................ 350 gallons
❖ To produce one pound of beef................................ 4,850 gallons
❖ To grow one ear of corn.. 61 gallons
❖ To produce a lettuce dinner salad.......................... 6 gallons
❖ To grow one tomato.. 3 gallons
❖ To produce one cola soft drink............................... 10 gallons
❖ Taking a bath.. 30 gallons
❖ Watering the lawn.. 200 gallons
❖ Brushing your teeth.. 1 gallon
❖ Washing a car... 100 **gallons**

SAFE WATER DRINKING HOTLINE – (800) 426-4791 (ask for free booklet)

GREENPEACE INTERNATIONAL – (202) 462-1177

CHAPTER 28

GRANDMA'S HOUSEHOLD TIPS

OFF WITH THEIR SHOES

Approximately 75% of all dirt in the home is brought in on people's shoes. If you think about all the places you have been during the day and what you have stepped in, you start to realize that some of that dirt, grime, lawn chemicals, sand, bits of gum, feces, mud, soot and even rubber from car tires may be on the soles of your shoes. The thicker the soles and the type of special soles that are deep cut are perfect to carry all sorts of garbage into your home.

Many of the churches of the world and museums will not allow people to enter unless they remove their shoes or at least wear special disposable slippers or other type of shoe coverings to protect the carpeting and exhibits. In every oriental culture, shoes are not allowed in the house.

Grandma had a small cabinet near her front door as you entered with slippers she kept cleaned.

GRANDMA'S SHOE RULES FOR PEOPLE & PETS

- ❖ Use the mat outside the door to scuff your shoes.
- ❖ Put on a pair of slippers or go in your stocking feet.
- ❖ All company had the same rules, which were on a little plaque by the front door.
- ❖ There was a boot brush hanging by the back door, which is where any workers entered (including grandpa).
- ❖ In winter you had to brush the bottoms of your clothing to get off any salt and snow, which may damage the carpets or furniture.
- ❖ Use a lint roller on your pet when it comes in from the outside to remove any debris it picked up as well as fleas.

EASY TO CARE HOUSE PLANTS

I've got a green thumb

GRANDMA PICKS HOUSE PLANTS THAT ARE EASY TO CARE FOR

Philodendron
This is one of the easiest plants to care for and really hard to kill unless you never water it. There are over 300 varieties and the plant will thrive in air-conditioned spaces as well as dimly lit areas.

Cactus
It is a member of the succulent family of plants and stores water in case you forget to water it occasionally. There are many varieties, some of which have prickly spines and colorful flowers. It does need sun and dry soil to do well.

Spider Plant
Looks like a big spider and likes warm, dry air with lots of sunlight and water, however, it will put up with tougher conditions.

Dracaena
Available in a number of varieties, however, the most popular is similar to a palm. It can grow as high as 15 feet and it thrives in a variety of light conditions ranging from full sun to deep shade.

Aspidistra
This is a very rugged plant that has large glossy leaves and will thrive in a dark, forgotten corner, but likes a little sunlight occasionally. Found in the outdoor section of the nurseries, but well indoors.

NO DUST ARTIFICIAL PLANT
You will never have to dust an artificial plant if you spray the plant with hairspray about every 2 months. They will not attract dust and retain their vivid colors.

EGG WATER BOOSTER

After the water cools from boiling eggs use it to water your plants. The water contains growth-stimulating minerals. Crushed eggshells are good to on top of the soil.

SNOW FOR PLANTS

Try melting snow and allow it to come to room temperature before using it to water your plants. Snow contains trace minerals that the plant can use.

RAINDROPS KEEP FALLING...........................

It's a good idea to collect rainwater and water your plants with it. The plants will get a healthy boost and the leaves will sparkle.

TOGETHERNESS

If you place a number of plants next to each other or at least near each other, they will create a moist environment and be healthier.

POOR SICK PLANT

If you have a houseplant that appears to be sick, just place a clove of garlic in with the plant and cover the plant with a plastic bag. Be sure and keep the soil moist and don't seal up the bag. Also, keep the plant out of the sunlight.

FEED ME, FEED ME

Houseplants need to be fed regularly with fertilizer or they may become nutrient deficient. Just use a commercial plant food and follow directions.

HOME ODOR & CLEANING PROBLEMS

In The Kitchen

❖ Be sure and air out the house regularly by opening windows and doors if screened.

- ❖ Bowls of white vinegar, charcoal briquettes or coffee grounds placed around will absorb odors.
- ❖ Be sure and change furnace and air conditioner filters regularly.
- ❖ When vacuuming, place a few drops of eucalyptus oil in the bag.
- ❖ Rub a half of a lemon over a cutting board when done.
- ❖ Run the disposal every time you place food in and run plenty of water to wash it away.
- ❖ Grind up a few slices or ¾ a lemon in the disposal occasionally.
- ❖ Run hot water in your kitchen drains every day.
- ❖ Wash out all cans before placing them into the garbage or trash compactor.
- ❖ If you don't use the dishwasher everyday, place some baking soda on the bottom.
- ❖ Never buy a glass-top kitchen table since it scratches too easily. If you do buy glass, make sure it is colored to hide some of the damage.
- ❖ The cushions on kitchen chairs should be easily removed for fabric replacement.
- ❖ Have plastic covers for the chairs when the grandkids come over.
- ❖ Store all glassware upside down to prevent dust and critters from getting in.
- ❖ Be sure that you do not use liners for your cabinets; that has a bug deterrent in it.
- ❖ Never dry silver on a rubber mat since it causes the silver to become darker.
- ❖ Never wash crystal in hot water and then rinse with cold water or it may crack.
- ❖ If china has a gold trim, be sure and never wash it in very hot water since the gold may run.

In The Closet

- ❖ Place cedar shavings in an old stocking and hang it in the closet.
- ❖ Never place smelly clothes back in the closet. If you wear

them, wash them!

- ❖ Allow closet doors to remain open occasionally to let them air out.
- ❖ Place a few drops of your favorite fragrant essential oil on a cotton ball and place it into the closet.

In The Bathroom

- ❖ Every week, place a small handful of baking soda down the shower drain followed by some white vinegar. Wait 10 minutes and then flush with hot water.
- ❖ Unwrap fragrant soaps and leave them in a basket. This will make the bathroom smell better and will make the soap last twice as long by reducing the moisture in the bar.
- ❖ Keep a scented candle and matches in the toilet area.
- ❖ Never wallpaper a bathroom that gets easily steamed.
- ❖ Always paint using high-gloss finish paint since it cleans easily and repels soil.
- ❖ Avoid water getting on the floor by weighting down the bottom of the shower curtain.

TOYS·TOYS·TOYS

In The Kids Room

- ❖ Avoid toy boxes and trunks since toys always get jumbled and the one they want always end up on the bottom.
- ❖ Try and rotate toys every 6 months so that the child will not get tired of them.
- ❖ Be sure and lower the closet rods to the child's height.
- ❖ Mount a battery-operated light in the closet if there is no light and easily reached switch.
- ❖ Buy a bed with built-in storage drawers.
- ❖ Purchase children's furniture that sits on the floor and has no legs raising it up so that toys and dirt can get underneath.

❖ Never wallpaper a kid's room. Paint with washable paint.

❖ Be sure and only purchase washable art supplies.
❖ If you have vinyl flooring in the room, be sure and place a washable carpet over a large area.

In The Bedroom

❖ Place a used fabric-softener sheet between the mattress and box spring.
❖ Place fresh flowers in the bedroom.
❖ Place some lemon peels in a small porous cloth bag and place in drawers.
❖ Never allow food in kid's rooms.
❖ Do not allow pets to sleep in the bedroom or bed.
❖ Place a bar of fragrant soap in a drawer to keep it smelling great.
❖ Purchase quality linens with a thread count of at least two hundred per square inch and be sure that it is non-ironing.
❖ The mattress should be turned twice a year.

In The Pets Bed

❖ Brush some baking soda on the pet's coat between baths.
❖ Place a few drops of essential lavender oil in the pets bedding to get rid of fleas and make it smell nice.
❖ Place a thin layer of baking soda in the litter box before adding the litter.

In The Fireplace

❖ Make the wood smell fragrant by placing a log of sweet-smelling citrus or juniper on the fire.
❖ Before lighting, add a few peels of dried citrus, cinnamon sticks or pine cones among the logs before you light them.
❖ Use some dried fragrant herbs as part of your kindling.

I CAN HELP, DON'T THROW ME OUT
Don't dispose of all the ashes. A good fire needs a two-inches

carpet of ash under the grate. This will help the fire start faster and help to radiate heat into the room.

Miscellaneous Tips

❖ Hang an old stocking filled with charcoal briquettes in the garage or basement.
❖ Keep a few cinnamon sticks wrapped in cheesecloth in cupboards.
❖ Place a fabric-softener sheet in suitcases that are not used very often.
❖ After you finish a bottle of perfume, leave it open in a drawer that might have an odor.
❖ Place a charcoal briquette in a filing cabinet to keep the papers from becoming musty.

YUK, DIRTY ASHTRAY

With the exception of glass and crystal, you can spray furniture polish on the bottom of ashtrays and the residues of the ashes will not stick to the ashtray.

GRANDMA MAKES KITCHEN CLEAN-UP EASY

❖ To clean the microwave easily, just place a cup of water with 2 tablespoons of baking soda in it and run the microwave for a few minutes then just clean the fallout.
❖ Use a grout sealer on all grout.
❖ Avoid glass doors on all appliances since they are hard to clean.
❖ Never use flocked or grass-covered wallpaper in the kitchen since they absorb grease.
❖ The best kitchen floor for easy cleaning is a vinyl floor with a low-gloss finish.
❖ Have glasses with the kid's names on them.
❖ Place honey or cooking oil on a plate when stored in the cabinet.
❖ Clean the blender with a soap shake.
❖ Use aluminum liners in the oven.

PROTECT ME! COVER ME UP

Grandma always protected her wall-to-wall carpet and hated to wash it. Whenever the grandkids came over she always have an old, clean piece of carpeting that was rolled out for the kids to play on.

GUARD ME

Protect all fabrics with a Scotch-guard coating. Costs a little, but is worth every cent. Spills will not seep into the fabric before you are able to clean them up.

CHEAP WINES STAIN MORE

Best to serve only quality wines, especially red wines. The inexpensive wines will stain the fabrics and carpets more easily since they contain higher concentration of colorant.

NEW GLASS FOR CLEANER WINDOWS

Weather Shield Manufacturing is making a glass called Kleen-Shield that has the ability to repel dirt, bugs and even water spotting using polymer that is like Teflon.

NATURAL FABRICS

GRANDMA KNOWS FABRICS TO USE IN THE HOME

Cotton

Very strong and versatile fabric: that has excellent pilling resistance and good resistance to abrasion. If it blended with any synthetic it will stand up to soil better.

Leather

Not a fiber: but is very strong and resistant to abrasion. Dust and grime will cause it to crack eventually if it is not conditioned to stay supple.

Linen

This fabric is crisp and cool to the touch; however, it will stretch and wrinkle easily unless it is blended with other fabrics. It will resist moths and soil as well as being anti-static.

Silk

Strong, supple and drapes easily. It is easy to dye and will add luster when combined with other fabrics. It has poor abrasion resistance, spots easily and can be very difficult to clean.

Wool

Very resistant to abrasion, resilient and warm and is susceptible to moths and mildew. It is easy to keep up, especially when added to other fabrics.

SYNTHETIC FABRICS

Acetate

Inexpensive, sunfast; drapes well but wrinkles easily and will damage easily unless it is blended with a stronger fabric.

Acrylic

Has good wrinkle and abrasion resistance qualities as well as being soft and retaining its shape well. Tends to darken when exposed to sunlight, however, it will repel soil, cleans up easily and blends well with many fibers.

Nylon

Excellent fabric that is soil, abrasion and mildew resistant. Is it very versatile and can be produced in tweed to silky velvets. However, it does have a tendency to pill and fade over time but adds strength to any other fabric.

Olefin

Very resistant to soil, abrasion and sunlight, however, it does pill and is occasionally scratchy when touched.

Polyester

Relatively wrinkle-free and can handle sunlight well as being abrasion and water-based stain resistant. Sometimes feels a little stiff, absorbs grease stains but is stronger when cotton is added to it.

Rayon

Very silky and inexpensive fabric: with the look and feel of a natural with the advantages of a synthetic. It will drape well, resists moths but may easily be subject to abrasion, fades easily and wrinkles. Best to purchase it when it is combined with nylon, cotton or wool.

Vinyl

This is actually a fabric-backed plastic that will resist most stains, however, body oils and perspiration will cause it to harden. It tends to feel cold, which makes it a poor choice for a sofa covering but excellent for chair seats and benches. If there is an animal with claws around, never buy this type of fabric.

TO STAIN OR NOT TO STAIN

Spray on fabric protection will only make the fabric stain-resistant and not stainproof. They will make spills and dirt stay on the fabric for a period of time allowing them to be cleaned up before they soak into the fabric. The protectors are available in two types: *silicone*, which can resist water-based stains, such as wine, juice and milk and *fluorochemical*, which can resist both water-based as well as oil-based stains (mayonnaise, margarine, etc.).

WHY PAY WHEN ITS FREE

The majority of upholstery fabric manufacturers spray their goods before they sell the fabric. When you purchase a sofa and the salesperson sells you the *"extra protection"* such as Scotchguard™, it may already be on the fabric.

NO DUST PICTURE HANGING

To prevent crumbles and drywall dust when hammering a nail into the wall, just place a cross of tape over the spot and pound away.

NO SCRATCHES, MY LADY

Always glue small felt pads on the bottoms of all lamps, ashtrays, vases or other knick-knack that you place on a glass tabletop to avoid scratches.

CHAPTER 29

Great wallpaper
tips & secrets

WALLPAPER SECRETS

WALLPAPER SECRETS

GENERAL INFORMATION:

There are many different kinds of wallpaper and you need to know what kind you are dealing with to solve any problem associated with repairing or cleaning it. If you are not familiar with the type of paper you have, try and bring a small piece to someone at a local paint and wallpaper store to identify the type of paper. Wallpaper will be either: washable, non-washable or scrubbable. Wallpaper is easily damaged and best to know what you are doing if you try and repair it.

GRANDPA'S TIPS ON CHOOSING WALLPAPER

Burlap/Grass Cloth

May be used anywhere except in a hard use area where grease, moisture or dirt may come into contact with the paper. Use mixed vinyl adhesive with ¾ pint less water than the directions asks for. Apply two coats of the adhesive using a mohair paint roller cover for the best results. The cost is expensive for this type of paper.

Cloth-backed vinyl

This is one of the best papers for high traffic and high-humidity areas. Able to be stripped but is stiff and difficult to shape to the wall or high ceiling surfaces. If you purchase lightweight paper, it is best to use a wheat-paste adhesive and if the paper is heavy weight, use a vinyl adhesive.

Foil

Used mainly in kitchens, bathrooms and laundry areas since it is easy to clean. Best to get a professional to hang this paper unless grandpa has done it before. Be sure not to crease the paper when you are pasting and hanging it and be very careful around the electrical outlets and switches.

Flocked

Best not to use in high traffic or difficult to clean areas! Be sure and keep the adhesive from getting on the face of the paper.

If it does it must be removed immediately with clear water and just blot it dry, never rub it. If the flocking does mat, use a suede brush to gently go over the area.

Hand-screened paper

Used to achieve a very stylish effect, however, it is very expensive and usually made of paper that is easily damaged. Best to have a professional do the papering.

Paper-backed vinyl

Best used in high-traffic areas or locations that may have high moisture content. Can be stripped and the hand-printed vinyl must be trimmed. Be sure and use a lot of adhesive and do not stretch it when hanging it. If the seams do curl, paste them down with vinyl-to-vinyl adhesive and be sure and remove any excess adhesive immediately.

Solid paper

This is the lowest price wallpaper and can easily be damaged if scrubbed too hard. Best to only use it in low traffic areas and it is hard to strip. Should be hung with wheat-based adhesive. Work very carefully since the material will tear easily. Be sure and butt edges and roll all seams then clean immediately using a damp sponge.

Vinyl-coated paper

Can be used almost anywhere as long as it is not around too much moisture. It is more durable than solid paper and is usually hung one strip at a time. The excess adhesive needs to be cleaned immediately after each seam is rolled.

Wet-look vinyl

Best used in kitchens, laundry rooms and mudrooms, however, it may be best to apply a lining paper first since any surface imperfections will show through.

HIDE BEHIND THE DOOR
When you are going to wallpaper an entire room, it would be best

to start behind a door with the first piece. It should be a spot that is not noticeable when a person first walks into a room.

As you work your way around the room, you may have a mismatched pattern at the last corner. It won't be noticeable if you start at an inconspicuous location.

SAME LOT = NICE JOB

When you buy wallpaper; be sure and check the lot number on every roll. If there are different numbers, it is best not to purchase the paper or you may notice a difference in color from roll to roll.

GRANDPA'S WALLPAPER REMOVAL METHODS

Removing wallpaper with no coating, such as vinyl

Step One: Apply a commercial stripper, which are usually sold in concentrated form. Use the manufacturers guidelines and add the right amount of water. You may use a stripper with enzymes to break down the adhesive if you prefer. Use a sprayer or large sponge is using a liquid stripper or a roller for a gel.

Step Two: Remove the paper starting at the top using a putty knife or any broad knife and scrape gently. You must be careful or you will gouge the wall and that will mean another repair job.

Removing multiple layers of wallpaper that may have been painted over

Step One: First, use a scoring tool to score through the layer do that the stripper can get to the adhesive.

Step Two: Apply the stripper, allow it to remain for a short period then remove the paper with a putty knife or broad knife.

TAKE IT ALL OFF

As soon as the paper has been removed, you will need to remove the leftover adhesive residue.

Dilute the stripper and wash the walls then rinse with clean water. You may still have to sand some areas if the adhesive has dried and really hardened over the years.

Removing strippable wallpaper

> **Step One:** Just loosen the bottom of the wallpaper with a putty knife and gently pull the paper off from the loosened end. It should come off easily, if not you will have to use stripper.

> **Step Two:** The majority of strippable wallpaper will leave a paper or fabric mesh backing on the wall. This will need to be removed using a stripper solution and be sure you follow the directions for removing wallpaper that has no coating.

NO HAMMER & CHISEL NEEDED

One of the best methods of removing wallpaper is to rent a steamer, which work very well, especially on plaster walls. However, steamers should only be used in the winter months (too hot in summer). Remember, the water dripping from the steamer is as hot as boiling water. Be sure and protect yourself when using a steamer.

SMOOTHIE

When applying wallpaper, try using a paint roller instead of a sponge to smooth the paper out.

DON'T USE THE WRONG METHOD

Always test an inconspicuous area first (behind a door or a piece of furniture) before trying to clean wallpaper. Wallpaper should be vacuumed regularly to keep the dust off. Dust wallpaper downward from the ceiling with a vacuum or long-handled soft-bristled brush. You can also use a clean cloth tied around a broom handle. If cleaning flocked paper only use a vacuum soft-bristled brush.

HELP! I'M FALLING AWAY

If the wallpaper is loose, you will need to know the type of paper so that you can use the right paste to re-paste it. Check with the wallpaper store for the correct paste, especially for plastic-coated wallpapers. However, ordinary rubber cement will do the job on almost all papers.

MY WALLPAPER IS BUBBLING UP

You will need to cut across the blister (keeping within the pattern) with a very sharp single-edge razor or sharp X-acto knife then lift the edges and place glue inside and smooth down with a damp cloth or sponge.

NEED A CHANGE HERE

When wallpapering, be sure and change the water frequently since there is an adhesive buildup that will make the job more difficult.

BUY DOUGH OR PAY DOUGH

Commercial wallpaper cleaners, which look like a glob of dough, are available through most hardware and paint stores. However, it is still advisable to test an area first and then vacuum the area cleaned afterwards.

CLEANING WASHABLE WALLPAPER

These are paper with a plastic coating, which can be cleaned using minimal water on a clean cloth or sponge. Use the water very sparingly and never saturate the paper.

- **Grease Stain -**Hold several layers of white paper towels over the spot and press with a warm iron until the grease is absorbed.
- **Crayon Stain -**This means that you have to remove grease, wax and color. Try and first scrape off any excess with a dull butter knife then use a warm iron and the same method for grease stains. ***Best to buy washable crayons for kids.***

KEEPING GREASE IN ITS PLACE

If you have grease spots after removing old wallpaper, try applying a coat of clear varnish to the spots. The grease won't soak through to the new paper.

CLEANING SCRUBBABLE WALLPAPER

These papers are made from vinyl or special vinyl-impregnated paper and can be scrubbed with a foam cleaner or all-purpose detergent. Be sure and use a soft cloth or a sponge and rinse well.

Never use any abrasive cleaners or you will scratch the finish. These are good papers for kids rooms or rooms that will get a lot of use.

CLEANING FABRIC WALLPAPER

If they are vinyl-coated they will be easy to clean with a sponge dampened in soapy, water. If they are burlap or grass cloth, best to go by the manufacturers suggestions.

CLEANING VINYL WALLPAPER

Never use an abrasive cleaner, even a soft-scrub type. Also, never use any type of solvent cleaner or it will dissolve the ink. Use a mild dishwasher detergent and water for the best results.

I'M COMING APART AT THE SEAMS

If one or more of the seams are opening, just fill a plastic squeeze bottle with wallpaper paste. The spout should be small so that it will fit under the edge of the seam. Just one squirt and a little pressure on the area should solve the problem. Make sure you remove any excess with a damp cloth and smooth the area down with a roller.

PUSHPINS TO THE RESCUE

When you hang a sheet of wallpaper, especially the heavier or wider paper, try pushing several pushpins in to secure each strip near the ceiling while you are smoothing the paper downward. You can then remove the pins, cut away the excess paper and smooth it out.

GRANDPA'S KNOWS HOW TO REPAIR WALLPAPER

Re-pasting

Lift the loose wallpaper and dampen with water, then spread a thin wallpaper paste underneath and smooth down with a clean damp cloth. Use a paste that is recommended for that particular type of paper.

To Remove a Blister (bubble)

Cut across the blister with a very sharp single-edged razor blade or X-acto knife along a line in the pattern. Lift the edges carefully then spread a thin layer of wallpaper paste underneath and smooth down with a damp, clean cloth.

Repairing Tears or Holes

Use a piece of leftover paper and tear a small piece to fit over the hole. Don't cut a piece since irregular edges will not be seen as easily as a sharp edge. Place wallpaper paste on it and paste it down.

Always size the wall first

GRANDPA EXPLAINS THE PROPER METHOD OF HANGING WALLPAPER

1. Purchase pre-pasted and strippable paper. Watch out for difficult patterns that may be hard to match.
2. Make sure that you repair and holes or cracks and sand them if needed making sure that the areas are perfectly smooth.
3. Be sure that the surface to be covered is clean and dry.
4. Before applying the wallpaper, be sure and paint any areas that will come into contact with the surface being covered. These include ceiling areas, moldings, window and door frames.
5. Best to apply a primer/sizer but there are a number of benefits to this step. First, it allows you to slide the paper onto the wall and reposition it easier. Second, It will make the bond stronger between the paper and the wall. Third, it will make it much easier to remove the paper when you want to remove it.

6. Next take a measurement and measure the width of your paper strip then subtract ¾ inch. Near the top of the wall, you will need to measure the distance out from the corner and mark it with a pencil. Never use ink or it may bleed through the paper.

7. Drop a plumb line along the pencil mark (vertical line is needed from the top to the floor to hang the first strip). Tack a chalk-coated string at the pencil mark and tie a weight to the bottom of the string. When the weight stops moving, hold the bottom next to the wall and pull it away leaving a mark to go by. Remove the string now that you have made a plumb line.

8. Since wall and ceiling joints are rarely straight, make sure you drop a new plumb line whenever you turn a corner.

9. Cut the wallpaper in strips of paper 6 inches longer than the wall height, which will give you three inches of overhang at the top and the bottom of the wall. The extra paper will allow for the unevenness of walls and ceilings. Be sure and match the pattern of every strip with the previous strip.

10. If you cut several strips at a time, be sure and number the strips   as you cut them on the backside with a pencil. The strips must be hung in the right order so that the patterns will match up.

11. Wet the pre-pasted paper by rolling the paper from bottom to top keeping the pattern on the inside. Be sure and place the paper in the water tray gently and push it to get rid of the air bubbles. Allow the paper to remain in the water for the time recommended on the manufacturers instructions.

12. When you remove the paper from the water do it very slowly and make sure that the adhesive back is wet and that there are no dry spots.

13. You now have to "book" the paper. This is done: by simply folding the bottom of the paper to the middle (on the adhesive side) and then the top to the middle (looks like a book). Make sure that you do not crease the paper. The reason for this step is when the paper is placed into the water it expands unevenly and will spread at the seams if it is hung immediately. The booking step allows the paper to stabilize and the adhesive to become activated. The instructions from the manufacturer should tell you how long to keep the pieces booked.

14. To start hanging the first strip of paper, unbook the top half, remembering to leave the three inches on top and be sure and line the edge of the paper with the plumb line, sliding it gently into place. If you pull it into place, you may damage the paper.

15. Use a smoothing tool to smooth out the paper. Always, start from the center of the paper moving up and down then smooth out the sides. This should eliminate all the air bubbles.

16. Trim off the excess paper on the top and bottom with a straight edge and a sharp utility knife or single edge razor blade device. Clean off

the ceiling with a damp sponge from any adhesive that may have gotten there from the excess paper.

17. Now unfold the bottom half of the paper and smooth it out onto the wall. Make sure that it lines up with the plumb line.

18. Trim the corner and bottom excess paper and clean any surface such as the baseboards and floor where the adhesive might spread.

19. Use your damp sponge to wipe down the wallpaper making sure that there is no adhesive residue on the paper.

20. You need to remember to book each strip and hang the top of the next strip first, placing it as close to the first strip as possible. Always use both hands to slide the strips into their place, matching up the patterns as you go.

21. Continue doing exactly as you did for the previous pieces making sure you clean up the areas and paper before moving on.

22. After the paper has been on the wall for 15 minutes, lightly roll the seams using a seam roller. Never push down on the roller hard or you will squeeze the adhesive out and the seams will eventually loosen up.

BE A SCRAP COLLECTOR

Always save scraps of wallpaper in case you will need to repair and area at a later date. You may also want the scraps to paper an outlet or ?

BORDER BEWARE

If you are going to hang a border, be sure and allow the wallpaper to dry for 2 days before adding the border. Best to use a vinyl-over-vinyl adhesive instead of wetting the paper. Be sure and follow the directions to the letter and let the border sit for the recommended amount of time.

CHAPTER 30

MISCELLANEOUS TIPS

GRANDPA'S MISCELLANEOUS TIPS

HERE A PART, THERE A PART, EVERYWHERE A PART
When you take an item apart, which has numerous small parts, try laying the parts on a piece of double-sided tape. This will make them easy to locate and you won't lose any.

DOUBLE, DOUBLE, OUCH!
If you are going to use a double edge razor blade, be sure and place a cork on one edge.

COLORING TRICK
If you have patched a small hole in a colored wall and don't have any of the paint leftover, just use some watercolor paints to blend in the color with the color of the wall.

AFTER YOU READ THE MAGAZINE
If you want to protect your walls and need to remove a nail, just place an old magazine under the head of the hammer.

NO SLIDE PICTURES
If you place adhesive tape around the center of the picture wire it will keep the picture from moving around on the hanger.

SQUEEKY DOOR HINGES
Lubricate the hinge pins with petroleum jelly instead of a spray oil product. Petroleum jelly won't leak on the floor or carpet and will last longer.

LOOSENING UP THE JOINT
To loosen up old glue on wood joints, try applying vinegar on the joints. Just fill a small oilcan with white vinegar and apply it liberally to the joints.

STAPLE THE PAPER

Staple leftover wallpaper scraps to your attic wall. If you need to repair paper, the paper on the attic wall should be just as faded as the paper that is on the wall.

SAVE THOSE OLD PHONE CORDS

Old phone cords can be used to keep the wires neat so that they won't get tangled up. Just place the cords around the wires in back of your computer to keep them separated.

ANOTHER USE FOR GLASS CLEANER

To remove paint from glass, just spray the area with window cleaner, wait 5 minutes and then scrape off with a razor.

GLOSSARY

ACACIA
Gum: that is obtained from trees belonging to the mimosa family. Normally, found in Africa and Australia.

ACCELERATOR
Substance: that has the ability to speed up a reaction.

ACETIC ACID
Biting, colorless liquid, which tends to congeal in cool temperatures and smells like vinegar. Vinegar can be substituted for acetic acid in a number of formulas.

ACETONE
Inflammable liquid: that is colorless and has an odor similar to ether. May be sold as dimethyl ketone.

AGAR-AGAR
Gelatin-like substance: that is produced from certain varieties of seaweed.

ALCOHOL, ETHYL
Normally, made from the fermentation of grains. Colorless liquid: that is easily mixed with water or caustic soda and is flammable. Absolute ethyl alcohol; is produced by removing water through distillation.

ALCOHOL, DENATURED
Ethyl alcohol: that has been changed by the addition of other chemicals, making it unusable for human consumption and alcoholic beverages.

ALUM
A natural mineral, crystalline substance that is usually used for

pickling and as a fixative for dyes. Can be a natural astringent.

AMIDOL
Powder, that can be either white or gray and used for photographic developing solutions.

AMMONIA, HOUSEHOLD
Commercial, chemical: used in many manufacturing processes. The fumes may be irritating and may react with other household chemicals, such as hydrogen peroxide, etc. Care is recommended when mixing or using this product.

AMMONIUM CHLORIDE
White: soluble crystalline powder that is also known as sal ammoniac.

AMMONIUM SULFATE
Fertilizer: that is prepared by neutralizing ammonia water with sulfuric acid and then evaporating the liquid.

AMYL ACETATE
Oily liquid: that is colorless and flammable. May also be known as banana oil since it smells like bananas.

ANILINE
Colorless; oily liquid that is derived from benzene used in the manufacture of dyes and is highly, poisonous.

ARNICA, TINCTURE OF
An alcoholic solution derived from the flowers of the herb *Arnica Montana*.

ARSENATE OF LEAD
These are white crystals that are very poisonous and usually used in insecticides.

ASPIRIN
Aspirin is a mild acid and may be called for in many cleaning formulas

BAKING SODA
Known as bicarbonate of soda and is an effective cleaning agent and deodorizer.

BALSAM PERU
Aromatic: sticky resin that will vary from black to brown and is obtained from a tree grown in San Salvador.

BARIUM SULFATE
Poisonous, white substance that is used in photographic chemicals and in the production of imitation opals and may also may be called "Mountain Snow."

BEESWAX
Made from wax that honeybees secrete when they construct their comb. May be sold in either white or yellow colors. The natural color is yellow, which is bleached to produce the white beeswax.

BENZENE
Colorless liquid: that is usually produced by the fractional distillation of coal tar. Flammable and should not be inhaled.

BENZOL
Liquid: similar to benzene.

BERGAMOT OIL
Golden, colored oil: that mixes easily in alcohol and is produced from the fruit of a particular plant; Citrus Bergamia Risso ET Painteau.

BLUE VITRIOL
Poisonous substance: that may be called copper sulfate and is sold as blue crystals.

BLUING

Blue compound: that is usually sold in liquid form containing ultramarine blue, soluble Prussian blue or coal tar blue. Primarily used to whiten fabrics.

BORAX

Borax is usually mined in desert area and makes an excellent water softener and a common ingredient in many household-cleaning products. When prepared into a paste it has good abrasive qualities.

BORIC ACID

Colorless, white powder that is easily mixed with water or alcohol and produced by adding hydrochloric or sulfuric acid to a borax solution, then crystallizing it.

CALCIUM CARBONATE

Also, known as chalk. White powder: that is easily mixed with water or acid and usually obtained from limestone.

CALCIUM CHLORIDE

White: porous and granular substance that is produced by the dehydration of white hexahydrate of calcium: using a heat source.

CALENDULA

An herb: from the marigold family that has been used historically to treat nausea. Was used externally as a first-aid remedy and as a wash and cream. Also, used effectively as an ointment to treat inflamed areas of the skin.

CARBOLIC ACID

Poisonous caustic substance: that is a colorless crystal. Also, known as phenol and is produced from the distillation of coal tar. Sometimes sold as an oily liquid.

CARMINE
Pigment: that has a vivid crimson color and is produced from cochineal.

CARNAUBA WAX
A natural wax made from the leaves of the Brazilian palm tree. It is the hardest natural wax known to man.

CASEIN
A white milk protein substance that is produced by separating it from milk by a curdling process using rennet or and acid.

CASTILE SOAP
A very mild soap; manufactured with olive oil and used to produce a foaming base to a number of products. Normally, purchased in drug stores or health food markets.

CAUSTIC SODA
Also, called sodium hydroxide and sold in white chips, which can easily be mixed with water or alcohol. Produced by the electrolysis of a salt solution. When mixed with water will heat up and may cause a burn to exposed skin areas. Should always be stored in an airtight container.

CERESINE WAX
May also be called mineral wax and is sold in either yellow or white colors. The wax mixes easily in alcohol and is produced by purifying ozocerite with sulfuric acid, then filtering the solution through a charcoal filter.

CHAMOMILE
Herb, than can be purchased in liquid form and will repel a number of beetles and insects, especially when Tabasco is added to it.

CHLORAL HYDRATE
A white crystalline narcotic that used to be known as *"knock-out-drops."*

CHOLESTERIN

Odorless and tasteless crystalline alcohol: that is usually obtained from nerve tissue, egg yolk or bile.

CITRA SOLV

A citrus concentrate, that should be available at most markets or health food stores.

CITRIC ACID

Derived from citrus fruits and used as a pH modifier and regulator in many facial-care products. Citric acid is a safe product for many uses.

CITRONELLA OIL

Obtained from citronella grass. Used to keep flying insects away and to increase the effectiveness of ant formulas.

CLAY

A natural substance composed mainly from aluminum, silicon and oxygen. It has excellent absorbing qualities and used extensively in facemasks. Also, used in shampoos as a thickener.

COCHINEAL

A dye used to produce crimson and other shades of red. Produced from the dried bodies of female insects of the **Dactyopius coccus** species.

COLLODION

Viscous liquid that is produced by: dissolving pyroxylin in acetone or alcohol and ether.

COPPERAS

Poisonous green salt: that may be called green vitriol or sulfate of iron (ferrous sulfate). Copperas turns brow when exposed to the air.

CREAM OF TARTAR
White crystalline substance: which has a somewhat gritty acidic taste. It is produced from purifying the crude tartar obtained from the fermentation of grape juice.

DAMMAR
Resin: that is obtained from certain trees grown in Australia, New Zealand and the East Indies.

DEXTRINE
A white, odorless gummy powder that is produced from the decomposition of starch using acids, heat or enzymes.

DIATOMACEOUS EARTH
Derived from dead, sea creatures called diatoms. These remains contain high levels of a number of minerals and up to 88% silica. Sold in either brick or powder form.

DRAGON'S BLOOD
Dark red resinous substance: that is obtained from a number of tropical trees including the Malaysian palm.

DRIER
Substance: that is dissolved in a varnish or paint to speed up the drying.

ESSENTIAL OILS
Oils that are derived from a plant's fragrance and usually used as a base for perfumes. Usually extracted by steam distillation or by soaking the plant in alcohol or oil.

ETHYL ALCOHOL
Common alcohol found in alcoholic beverages, such as liquor, beer or wine. When recipes call for ethyl alcohol, just use any inexpensive vodka.

ESSENTIAL OILS
These are volatile oils derived from the stems, rinds of fruits, flowers or tree branches. The oil; is usually extracted by steam distillation, pressing or a solvent extraction process. Usually, soluble in alcohol!

EUCALYPTUS OIL
Colorless oil; with a strong pungent aroma, which is easily mixed with water and alcohol. Should never be ingested since it is somewhat toxic.

FORMALDEHYDE
A solution used to preserve organic tissue made by the oxidation of synthetic methanol. This is very toxic and should not come into contact with your skin.

FULLER'S EARTH CLAY
Natural clay: that is used in a number of cleaning formulas because of its ability to draw out stains from surfaces that are porous. Found in health food stores.

FUSEL OIL
A flammable: oily fluid that is heavy and has a disagreeable aroma. It consists of amyl alcohol and is found in liquors that have not been adequately distilled.

GELATIN
Produced by boiling animal by-products with water. Capable of absorbing many times its weight of liquid!

GLYCERIN
Produced from glycerol, which is natural-occurring fat in vegetables and animals. Should be easy to purchase in a drug store of health food market.

GUM ARABIC
Gum: that is obtained from certain plants of the mimosa family. It

is transparent, colorless and soluble in water.

GUM ELEMI
Pleasant smelling resin, which is obtained from certain tropical trees.

HYDROCHLORIC ACID
Colorless: yellowish liquid that is poisonous and corrosive in concentrated form. Also, known as muriatic acid. It is actually a solution of hydrogen chloride gas that has been mixed with water. It is not flammable but will produce irritating fumes.

HYDROGEN PEROXIDE
Dilute aqueous solution that is colorless and may be very toxic if taken internally without diluting it with water.

HYPO
The chemical name is sodium thiosulfate, which is a salt used in photographic chemical solutions. Sold in the form of a clear crystal or a white powder by photographic supply stores.

ISINGLASS
An almost pure form of gelatin produced from the air bladders of codfish, carp and other fish. Sometime thin sheets of mica used in curtains for old stagecoaches were called isinglass curtains.

ISOPROPYL ALCOHOL
Also, known as rubbing alcohol and included in a number of cleaning formulas. It is available from most pharmacies.

JEWELER'S ROUGE
May also be called **colocothar**, which is a reddish-brown iron oxide that is produced from heating ferrous sulfate, keeping the oxide as a residue.

KAOLIN
May also be called *Cornish clay* or aluminum silicate. It is soft

white clay that is usually sold as a powder.

KIESELGUHR

A porous: loose earthy mineral that is known chemically as a form of *diatomite*. It is normally used in formulas as an abrasive.

LAMPBLACK

A fine: black soot that is produced by condensing a substance that contains carbon, such as coal, pitch or oil.

LINSEED OIL

The oil is best if purchased from a health food store instead of a hardware store. The hardware store products contain petroleum-based material and may be somewhat volatile. The food grade linseed oil is a natural product that is safe.

LITHARGE

Usually sold a powder and is produced by allowing lead oxide to melt.

LYE

This is a very caustic chemical that will easily dissolve in water. The crystals will cause a skin burn and care should be taken when handling it. Lye is very toxic if swallowed and immediate medical attention is required. If lye is spilled on skin, flush the area with vinegar, then cold, water as soon as possible. Always work in a well-ventilated area and wear protective gear.

METOL

Used as a photographic developing agent and sold as a white crystalline powder.

MONTAN WAX

Hard, white wax produced through extraction of lignite from coal.

NEAT'S-FOOT OIL

Yellow oil: that can be mixed with alcohol or kerosene. Produced by boiling the shinbones and feet (no hoofs) of cattle. The oil is separated from the fat.

NEROLI, OIL OF
Yellowish oil produced from the distillation of orange flowers.

NITRIC ACID
Also, known as *aqua fortis*. Is corrosive and very poisonous liquid that is usually colorless and produced by the action of sulfuric acid on nitrates.

NUTGALLS
May also just be called "galls." They are actually round swellings that are produced on certain varieties of oak trees by insects such as the gall midge and the gallfly. They are about the size of hazelnuts and are either blue or green.

JUNGLE RAIN
Produced from citrus oils and peppermint soap.

OLEIC ACID
Produced from animal tallow or certain vegetables oils and is easily mixed with alcohol or organic solvents. The color may range from yellow to reddish/orange.

OLEIN
May also be called *glyceryl oleate*, which is a colorless liquid fat at room temperature. It is found in most animal and vegetable fats.

ORRIS ROOT
The rootstalks of a European iris plant!

OXALIC ACID
Colorless: crystalline substance that is poisonous and has no aroma.

PARAFFIN WAX
Sold in white blocks and is soluble in warm alcohol, turpentine and olive oil. Produced through the distillation of crude petroleum oil and is flammable.

PATCHOULI OIL
Oily perfume that is extracted from the leaves and branches of a plant *called Pogostemon patchouli*, which grows in Asia.

PEARLASH
May also be sold as potassium carbonate or purified potash. It is a white salt that will produce a strong alkaline solution when it is dissolved in water. Pearlash is mainly produced from potassium chloride and wood ashes but can be made from sugar beets and wood scourings.

PETROLATUM
May also be sold as Vaseline, which is white or yellowish in color. When in its pure form it will be odorless and tasteless.

PINE OIL
Oil: that is produced by steam distillation of pine, wood and usually sold as an oily, light amber liquid.

PITCH
Dark-colored: sticky residue that is produced from the distillation of coal, tar, petroleum and similar substances. Naturally it occurs as asphalt.

PLASTER OF PARIS
Also, known as calcium sulfate, which forms a paste when mixed with water. Usually sold as a white, powdery substance.

PRECIPITATED CHALK
Purified form of white calcium carbonate.

PUMICE POWDER

Abrasive powder that is produced from a porous rock found naturally in nature.

PYRETHRUM
Prepared from crushed pyrethrum chrysanthemum flowers.

RESIN
Transparent or translucent substance: that varies from yellow to brown and easily melted or softened by heat. Resins are derived from certain trees, plants, coal, lignite and asphalt beds.

SAL SODA
Also, known as sodium carbonate, washing soda or soda ash. It is a white strongly alkaline salt that is composed of crystals that are transparent.

SANDARAC
An aromatic resin: that is derived from fragrant wood of the sandarac tree, which grows in Africa.

SHELLAC
Natural resin: that is secreted by the insect Laccifer and deposited on certain trees in India. It is easily mixed with alcohol

SILICON DIOXIDE (SAND)
White: crystalline powder that is only soluble in hydrofluoric acid. May be produced from waterglass.

SOAP FLAKES
A very difficult product to locate anymore! Best to make your own by grating a bar of soap.

SPERMACETI
Waxy fatty solid, that is obtained from the head of a sperm whale.

STEARIC ACID
May also be known as stearine, which is a white, fatty, crystalline

substance that is obtained from hard fats such as tallow.

STEARIN
White crystalline solid found in many types of fats.

SULFURIC ACID
May also be known as *oil of vitriol*. A poisonous: corrosive acid.

TALC OR TALCUM
A soft mineral, that is somewhat greasy to the touch. Usually sold as a powder.

TALLOW
A solid fat: that is extracted from cattle or sheep. It is usually white or yellow depending on the level of purity.

TANNIC ACID
These are yellow crystals, which mix well with water, benzene and alcohol. They are produced by extraction of certain nutgalls and sometimes tree bark using water and alcohol. **Can be toxic if ingested or inhaled.**

TARTARIC ACID
White: crystalline powder that can easily be mixed with water or alcohol. Produced from maleic anhydride and hydrogen peroxide. Caution when using!

TEE TREE OIL
Essential oil, that is derived from the tee tree and can be used effectively to repel ants.

THYMOL
White, somewhat aromatic crystal: which has antiseptic qualities and is derived from fragrant oil of a plant known as thyme.

TRAGACANTH
Gum, which swells up when it is placed in water and is obtained

from *the Astralagus gumifer* herb mainly grown in Europe.

TRIPOLI
A relatively soft, crumbly mineral that is produced by the decomposition of siliceous limestone and usually sold in powdered form. Tripoli is not the same as tripolite (diatomaceous earth).

TRISODIUM PHOSPHATE (TSP)
Sold as a colorless crystal or white powder and mixes well with water and alcohol. Produced by precipitating calcium carbonate (chalk) from a solution of dicalcium phosphate and soda ash.

TURPENTINE OR OIL OF TURPENTINE
Clear: oily liquid that is colorless and produced by the steam distillation of turpentine gum from certain pine trees. Caution: may be very toxic if ingested.

VINEGAR
Produced by the fermentation of fruits and grains. Normally brown, however, can be further distilled to a white color. Balsamic vinegar is made from grapes.

WASHING SODA
Also called sodium carbonate. A mineral: that may also be called soda ash or sal soda. Excellent cleaner for greasy, petroleum product messes! Found in most laundry sections of the supermarket.

WHITING
A white: powdery mixture of chalk (or other source of calcium carbonate) that has been ground up. Used as filler in paints, whitewash and even putty. Liquid whiting is also known as liquid bluing. Used to clarify water and as a bleach.

WITCH HAZEL
Clear: astringent liquid that will mix well with water and alcohol.

APPENDIX A

COMMON NAMES OF CHEMICALS

The following listing will provide you with the chemical names of some of the more common chemicals used in the book. This may make it easier to locate them if they are asked for by both names.

COMMON NAME	CHEMICAL NAME
Alum	Potassium aluminum sulfate
Aqua fortis	Nitric acid
Baking soda	Sodium bicarbonate
Blue vitriol	Copper sulfate
Borax	Sodium tetraborate
Brimstone	Sulfur
Butter of alimony	Antimony trichloride
Carbolic acid	Phenol
Caustic potash	Potassium hydroxide
Chalk	Calcium carbonate
Chloride of lime	Calcium hypochlorite
Cinnabar	Mercury sulfide
Copperas	Ferrous sulfate
Cream of tartar	Potassium bitartrate
Epsom salts	Magnesium sulfate
Fluorspar	Calcium fluoride
Grain alcohol	Ethyl alcohol or ethanol
Green vitriol	Ferrous sulfate
Gypsum	Calcium sulfate
Hypo	Sodium thiosulfite
Kaolin	Aluminum silicate
Litharge	Lead monoxide
Lye	Sodium hydroxide or Potassium hydroxide

Magnesia	Magnesium oxide
Methylated spirits	Methyl alcohol or methanol
Minium	Red oxide of lead
Muriatic acid	Hydrochloric acid
Oil of vitriol	Sulfuric acid
Pearlash	Potassium carbonate
Plaster of Paris	Calcium sulfate
Plumbago	Graphite
Prussian blue	Ferric-ferrocyanide
Pyro	Pyrogallic acid
Quicklime	Calcium oxide
Red lead	Red oxide of lead
Rochelle salt	Potassium tartrate and Sodium tartrate
Sal ammoniac	Ammonium chloride
Sal soda	Crystalline sodium carbonate
Sal volatile	Ammonium sesquicarbonate
Salt	Sodium chloride
Saltpeter, Chile	Sodium nitrate
Saltpeter, nitre	Potassium nitrate
Slaked lime	Calcium hydroxide
Soda ash	Sodium carbonate
Spar, heavy	Barium oxide
Spirits of salt	Hydrochloric acid
Sugar of lead	Lead acetate
Tartar emetic	Antimony tartrate and Potassium tartrate
Verdigris	Copper acetate
Washing soda	Sodium carbonate
Waterglass	Sodium silicate
White copperas	Zinc sulfate
White lead	Basic lead carbonate
White vitriol	Zinc sulfate
Whiting	Calcium carbonate
Wood alcohol	Methyl alcohol or methanol
Zinc white	Zinc oxide

APPENDIX B

SOURCES OF INGREDIENTS

THE PRODUCTS NEEDED TO MAKE THE FORMULAS WILL BE FOUND AT THE FOLLOWING LOCATIONS:

INGREDIENT	SOURCE
Acetone	Drugstore/Chemical supply house
Alcohol	Drugstore/Hardware store
Alum (aluminum sulfate)	Drugstore/Supermarket
Aluminum oxide (alumia)	Chemical supply house
Aluminum powder	Paint store
Aluminum stearate	Chemical supply house
Ammonia	Supermarket/Chemical supply house
Ammonium carbonate	Substitute:double-acting baking powder
Ammonium hydroxide (ammonia water)	Chemical supply house/Supermarket
Ammonium nitrate (salt peter)	Chemical supply house/Pharmacy
Ammonium oleate (ammonia soap)	Supermarket
Ammonium sulfate	Garden supply house
Amyl acetate (banana oil)	Drugstore
Antimony sulfide	Plumbing supply store
Barium sulfide (black ash)	Chemical supply house
Beeswax	Hobby shop/Hardware store
Borax	Supermarket/Drugstore
Buckwheat hulls	Health food store
Calcium carbonate (chalk)	Chemical supply house
Calcium chloride	Chemical supply house
Calcium oxide (lime)	Chemical supply house
Camphor	Drugstore/Chemical supply house
Carbonic acid (seltzer)	Supermarket/Chemical supply house
Carbon tetrachloride (cleaning fluid)	Dry cleaner/Chemical supply house
Carnauba wax	Chemical supply house
Castile soap	Drugstore
Castor oil	Drugstore/Supermarket

Ceresin wax	Paint store/Hardware store
Chalk	Paint store/Hardware store
Charcoal	Chemical supply house
Chlorinated lime	Hardware store
Citric acid (vitamin C)	Health food store/Drug store
Clay	Health food store
Coconut oil	Health food store
Copper sulfate (bluestone)	Chemical supply house
Diatomaceous earth	Garden or swimming pools supply
Dyes	Hobby shop
Essential oils	Health food store
French chalk	Sewing center
Fuller's earth	Drugstore/Hardware store
Glucose (corn syrup)	Supermarket
Glycerin	Drugstore
Graphite	Drugstore
Gum Arabic (acacia)	Drugstore/Chemical supply house
Hydrated lime	Garden supply house/ Hardware store
Hydrochloric acid (muriatic acid)	Chemical supply house/ Pool supply
Hydrogen peroxide	Supermarket/Drugstore
Iodine	Drugstore
Ipecac	Drugstore
Isopropyl alcohol (rubbing alcohol)	Drug store
Jewelers' rouge	Chemical supply house/ Jewelry store
Kerosene, deodorized	Hardware store/Paint store
Lacquer	Paint store/Hardware store
Lanolin	Drug store
Lard	Supermarket
Lemon oil	Drugstore
Linseed oil	Hardware store/Paint store
Lye	Supermarket/Garden store
Magnesium carbonate	Chemical supply house
Magnesium hydroxide (milk of magnesia)	Drug store
Magnesium sulfate (Epson salt)	Supermarket/Drug store
Mineral oil	Drugstore
Mineral spirits	Paint store
Montana wax	Chemical supply house
Naphtha soap	Supermarket/Hardware store
Neat's-foot oil	Hardware store

Oil of Mirbane	Drug stores
Oleic acid	Chemical supply house
Orris root	Health food stores
Oxalic acid	Chemical supply house
Paraffin	Supermarket/Hobby shop
Peppermint oil	Health food store/Drugstore
Pigments	Paint store
Phenol (carbolic acid)	Drug store/ Chemical supply house
Plaster of Paris (calcium sulfate)	Hardware store
Portland cement	Building supply/ Hardware store
Potash	Chemical supply house
Potassium alum	Drugstore/Chemical supply house
Potassium carbonate (cream of tartar)	Supermarket
Potassium chlorate	Drug stores
Potassium chloride (potash)	Drug store/ Chemical supply house
Potassium hydroxide (caustic potash)	Chemical supply house
Potassium sorbate	Health food store
Pumice	Hardware store/Paint store
Shellac	Hardware store/Paint store
Silica gel	Hardware store/Hobby shop
Soap flakes	Supermarket
Sodium bicarbonate (baking soda)	Supermarket
Sodium borate (borax)	Supermarket
Sodium carbonate (washing soda)	Supermarket
Sodium citrate	Drugstore/ Chemical supply house
Sodium hydroxide (caustic soda)	Supermarket/ Photographic supply
Sodium hypochlorite	Chemical supply house
Sodium oxide (sand)	Hardware store
Sodium perborate	Drugstore
Sodium silicate (waterglass)	Drugstore/ Chemical supply house
Sodium sulfate (Glauber's salt)	Drug store
Sodium thiosulfate	Photographic supply
Stearic acid	Chemical supply house
Strontium chloride	Aquarium supply/Pet store
Sucrose (cane sugar)	Supermarket
Sulfuric acid (oil of vitriol)	Chemical supply house/ Automotive supply house

Talc (magnesium silicate)	Hardware store/ Chemical supply house
Tincture of benzoin	Drugstore
Tinctures	Health food stores
Tripoli (brown buffing compound)	Lapidary supply house
Trisodium phosphate	Hardware store/ Builders supply
Turpentine	Paint store/Hardware store
Vinegar (acetic acid)	Supermarket 3-5% solution
Washing soda	Supermarket
Waterglass (sodium silicate)	Drugstore/ Chemical supply house
Whiting	Paint store/Hardware store
Witch hazel	Drugstore
Zinc sulfate (white vitriol)	Chemical supply house

If chemicals cannot be located: try looking the chemical up in the O.P.D. Chemical Buyers Directory, Schnell Publishing. This volume should be available at the reference desk of most libraries.

APPENDIX C

<u>TABLES OF WEIGHTS AND MEASURES</u>

Apothecary Weights

5 Grams = 1 Drachm = 77 ¼ Grains
20 Grains   = 1 Scruple
3 Scruples = 1 Dram
8 Drams   = 1 Ounce
12 Ounces = 1 Pound

Apothecary Fluid Measures

60 Minims = 1 Fluid Dram
8 Drams   = 1 Fluid Ounce

Standard Weights

437 ¼ Grains = 1 Ounce
16 Drams   = 1 Ounce
16 Ounces   = 1 Pound
7000 Grains   = 1 Pound

Standard Liquid Measures

4 Gills   = 1 Pint
2 Pints   = 1 Quart
4 Quarts   = 1 Gallon
31 ¼ Gallons = 1 Barrel
2 Barrels   = 1 Hogshead

Small Amount Information

¼ Teaspoon   = ¼ Dram = 15 Drops
1 Teaspoon   = 1 Dram = 60 Drops
8 Teaspoons   = 1 Ounce

4 Teaspoons   = 1 Tablespoon
2 Tablespoons = 1 Ounce

Metric Conversions

$\frac{1}{4}$oz. = 7g.
$\frac{1}{4}$oz. = 15g.
1oz. = 30g.
2oz. = 55g.
1lb. = 455g.

English Weights & Measures

1 Pound = 16 Ounces = 256 Drachms = 7,000 Grains (Troy) = 453.60 Grams
1 Gallon = 8 Pints = 128 Ounces = 1,024 Drachms = 61,440 Minims

Miscellaneous

1 Drachm   = 4 Grams
8 Drachms = 1 Ounce
1 Drachm   = 1/8 Ounce = 15 Drops

APPENDIX D

APPLIANCE LIFE EXPECTANCIES IN YEARS

APPLIANCE	AVERAGE LIFE EXPECTANCY
Air Conditioner (room)	11
Calculator (electric)	7
Can Opener (electric)	7
Charcoal grill	6
Clock (electric)	8
Coffee maker (perc)	6
Dishwasher	11
Dryer (electric)	13
Dryer (gas)	14
Electric Blanket	8
Electric Fan	16
Fax Machine	8
Floor Polisher	11
Furnace (electric)	18
Furnace (gas)	16
Garbage Disposal	10
Hair Dryer	4
Hi-Fi System	6
Humidifier	8
Ice Cream Maker (electric)	9
Iron (electric)	9
Lawn Mower (gasoline)	8
Microwave Oven	11
Personal Computer	6
Popcorn Popper	5
Range (electric)	15
Range (gas)	15
Refrigerator	13
Security Alarm System	14
Shaver (electric)	4
Smoke Detector	10
Telephone Answering Machine	5
Television (color)	8
Television (B&W)	9
Toaster	8

Trash Compactor	10
Vacuum Cleaner	11
Washing Machine	12
Water Heater (electric)	12
Water Heater (gas)	10